CAPTAIN THUNDERBOLT

& HIS LADY

What the critics said

An Irresistible Temptation: The true story of Jane New and a colonial scandal

'Baxter has written a work that captures the reader . . . This is largely because of her skill as a narrative historian, her capacity to tell a good story. In fact, this book is an excellent example of how telling a good story can illuminate the past.'—Gregory Melleuish, *Australian Literary Review*

'A . . . compelling work of popular narrative history.'—*Courier Mail*

'[Told] with a fine eye for the complex motivations, both political and personal, [Baxter] paints a vivid picture of Jane New's world.'
—Dr Kirsten McKenzie, *Sydney Morning Herald*

'. . . [a] vivid social history.'—*Canberra Times*

Breaking the Bank: An extraordinary colonial robbery

'The precision of the writing, the controlled but graphic descriptions of people and events, engage sympathy and arouse anger. *Breaking the Bank* should be a contender for whatever Australian history prizes are going.'
—Peter Corris, *The Australian*

'Baxter's tale of this extraordinary robbery is . . . racy and packed with vivid descriptions and incidents that make for a compelling read and an incisive look into our brutal convict era.'—*Newcastle Herald*

Frederick Ward
'Faithful portrait', published by *Truth*,
21 February 1892

CAPTAIN THUNDERBOLT

& HIS LADY

The true story of bushrangers
Frederick Ward & Mary Ann Bugg

CAROL BAXTER

ALLEN&UNWIN

First published in 2011

Allen & Unwin
Sydney, Melbourne, Auckland, London

83 Alexander Street
Crows Nest NSW 2065
Australia
Phone:(61 2) 8425 0100
Fax:(61 2) 9906 2218
Email: info@allenandunwin.com
Web: www.allenandunwin.com

Cataloguing-in-Publication details are available
from the National Library of Australia
www.trove.nla.gov.au

ISBN 978 1 74237 287 7

Internal design by Lisa White
Map by Ian Faulkner
Set in 11/15 pt Minion by Midland Typesetters, Australia
Printed and bound in Australia by Griffin Press

10 9 8 7 6 5 4 3 2 1

CONTENTS

Mary Ann Bugg
Courtesy of Kent Mayo, McCrossin's Mill

Turning her adrift to join Thunderbolt again would be far worse for the country than if half a dozen of the most hardened ruffians on Cockatoo Island were granted permits for his gang.

Sydney Morning Herald, 11 May 1866

CAST OF CHARACTERS

Baker, Edmund/Edward	Husband of Mary Ann Bugg; an emancipated convict
Britten, Frederick	Mail-coach robber; Cockatoo Island escapee
Bryden, Hugh	Collarenebri magistrate
Bugg, Charlotte	Mary Ann's Aboriginal mother
Bugg, James	Mary Ann's convict father
Bugg, Mary Ann	Bushranger Frederick Ward's 'wife'
Burrows, John	Second 'husband' of Mary Ann Bugg
Cleary, Andrew	Police sergeant, Bourke
Cook, Thomas	Police magistrate, Port Stephens district
Cowper, Charles	Colonial Secretary and Premier of New South Wales
Dalton, Charles	Police constable, Tamworth
Dumaresq, Colonel Henry	Commissioner of the Australian Agricultural Company
Dunn, John	Bushranger; joined Ben Hall's gang in 1864
Ebsworth, James Edward	Assistant Commissioner of the Australian Agricultural Company
Finlay, Henry	Police constable, Stroud
Garbutt, Elizabeth	Owner of Cooyal inn; wife of John Garbutt
Garbutt, James	Fred Ward's nephew, the son of his sister Sarah Ann Ward; older brother of John
Garbutt, John	Fred Ward's nephew, the son of his sister Sarah Ann Ward; younger brother of James
Gardiner, Frank	Bushranger; ringleader of the Eugowra gold escort robbery in 1862
Garvin, Henry	Chief Constable of Maitland and later Sub-Inspector of Port Macquarie

Gilbert, John	Bushranger; member of Gardiner's gang at the time of the Eugowra gold escort robbery in 1862
Hall, Ben	Bushranger; member of Gardiner's gang at the time of the Eugowra gold escort robbery in 1862; later had a gang of his own
Hogan, Thomas	Alias 'The Bull'; member of Fred Ward's first bushranging gang in 1865
Jemmy the Whisperer	Member of Fred Ward's second bushranging gang in 1865; full name unknown
Kelly, Patrick	Member of Fred Ward's second bushranging gang in 1865
Kerrigan, Thomas	Senior Sergeant, Maitland
Lang, William	Senior Constable, Wallabadah
Mann, Captain Gother Kerr	Superintendent of Cockatoo Island
Martin, James	Premier and Attorney General of New South Wales
Mason, Thomas	Fred Ward's young accomplice in 1867
McIntosh	Member of Fred Ward's first bushranging gang in 1865; full name unknown
McNally, James	Third 'husband' of Mary Ann Bugg; an emancipated convict
Monckton, William	Fred Ward's young accomplice in 1868
Morgan, Dan	Bushranger
Mulhall, John	Policeman, Armidale district
Norris, Charles	Policeman, Barraba
Pearson, George William	Workmate of Fred Ward's at Cooyal
Shaw, Jacob	Police constable, north-western district
Thompson, John	Young member of Fred Ward's first bushranging gang in 1865
Walker, Alexander Binney	Police constable, Uralla
Ward, Frederick Wordsworth	Bushranger; 'husband' of Mary Ann Bugg

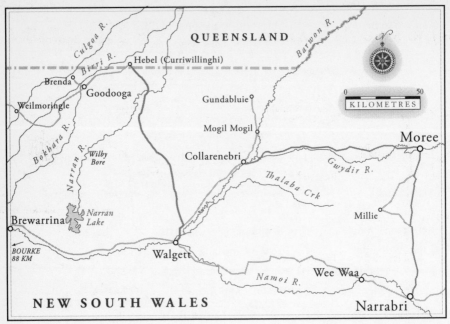

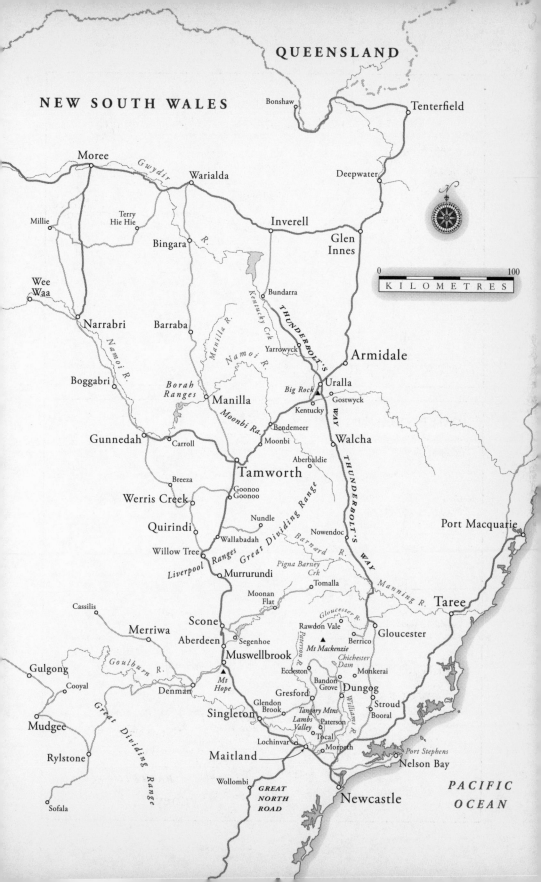

PROLOGUE

They know, as soon as they see her.

Skirts billowing, she hastens along the baked earth road—not the dainty mince of a parasoled young lady but a boyish stride, as if frustrated by the cumbersome layers of social constraint wrapped around her sturdy legs. Past humble cottages with children spilling out of doorways into gardens brilliant with colour. Past ramshackle inns with rum-swillers glued to wooden verandahs. Past church spires pointing triumphantly towards the heavens, each proclaiming that theirs alone is the true path to God's rewards, and woe betide any sinner who ignores His divine commands.

As she nears the town centre, her milky-brown countenance is a give-away—not that she is any darker than the average sun-baked settler's wife, but there is a look about her that hints at her Aboriginal heritage. Yet her broad, intelligent forehead reminds them that she is not simply an Aboriginal woman dressed to fit in, but one schooled to fit in—more educated, they all know, than most of the matrons ducking into shop doorways or the stockmen riding through town.

Her deep-set brown eyes flicker this way and that, then pause and focus on something: a moment of alert stillness as her mind seemingly gathers information. Then she glances away and her eyes flicker around again, all seeing, all knowing.

She slows her pace as she nears some gossiping women, dropping her gaze so they can see only her silky black hair confined in a demure bun—an appropriately obsequious pose. They don't realise that she is not submitting to their belief in their white superiority; rather she is hoping not to be recognised and preferring not to be snubbed, not that she really cares either way. More importantly, her dropped head hides her blank gaze as she listens to their conversations, as she tries to follow the various threads through the confusion of voices talking over each other. Any snippet could be useful.

She hasn't fooled them. They know who she is: Captain Thunderbolt's woman. She has so many nicknames: 'Thunderbolt's gin', 'Mrs Thunderbolt', 'Mrs Captain Ward', although she likes to call herself 'the Captain's Lady'. Few know her birth name, Mary Ann Bugg, although they all know her role. She is the notorious Frederick Ward's eyes and ears, the bushranger's right-hand man, his wily tracker, his commissariat, his lover and the mother of his children. And she is here in their town, which means Thunderbolt himself is nearby.

Not that he is likely to rob the town itself. He rarely does. He is craftier than that. Instead, he likes to know if the 'traps' are around, even in towns and villages with no police station of their own. The troopers might be passing through while carrying out their duties, and the last thing Thunderbolt wants is an unexpected encounter with a policeman escorting a minor felon or searching for lost sheep.

They notice her slightly cocked nose, a sign of her impetuosity, and her large mouth and chin that warn of her boldness. And bold she undoubtedly is, to ride with a bushranger, to parade through their town as if entitled to be there.

Sometimes she tries to fool them by pretending to be a boy, stuffing her hair under a cabbage-tree hat and clothing her five-foot, two-and-a-half-inch frame in shirt and trousers. But they know who she is, they know what she signifies—and they are afraid.

PART 1

LUST

Thy father is a chieftain!
Why that's the very thing!
Within my native country
I too have been a king . . .
The bush is now my empire,
The knife my sceptre keen;
Come with me to the desert wild,
And be my dusky queen.

William Aytoun, 'The Convict and His Loubra'

1

The Natives of New-Holland may appear to some to be the most wretched people upon Earth, but in reality they are far more happier than we Europeans . . .

James Cook, *Journals*

Looking back, it wasn't hard to pinpoint the moment. Yet each choice he had made, each path he had taken, had not led inexorably there—or thereafter. Most choices had merely nudged him in a certain direction. Most had involved little thought: a shrug, a wink, a coin flip, a triumphant swig of rum, or barely any conscious awareness of making a choice at all. And, with a similar unconscious unawareness, any of those choices could have been different, in which case he wouldn't have found himself in that particular place at that particular time—and history's spotlight probably wouldn't have turned on him.

When he did find himself there, his choice to engage rather than walk away somehow changed everything. Yet, while his choice might also have been unconscious, it was certainly not unaware. Indeed, it was driven by awareness. Romantics have a name for it—'love'—but it was more visceral than that. Lust.

She wasn't everything he could have imagined or everything he might have wished. How could she have been? She was an educated, intelligent, beautiful part-Aboriginal woman—and there weren't many of those around at the time. So he couldn't have dreamt her into his life. Instead she just appeared and everything changed.

The consequences were not immediate. They took time to unfold. And they weren't simply a product of the mawkish boy-meets-girl moment, even though this was pivotal to the events that followed. Rather they were largely a product of the past—of both their pasts.

So this was her story almost as much as his. And hers began first, not simply because she was older, but because her mother's ancestors had marched to the drumbeat of the Australian seasons for tens of thousands of years before his had even realised that a dragon-less expanse lay beyond the end of their maps. When they did realise, they wanted it for themselves.

'Be fruitful and multiply, and fill the earth and subdue it; and have dominion over every living thing that moves upon the earth,' decreed the God of the white people who appeared from the sea like ghosts upon a billowing cloud. They chopped down trees and cleared the undergrowth, pitching row after row of tents, catching fish and animals to eat, planting crops, disturbing sacred sites, and treating the land and everything on it as if it were exclusively their own, an economic resource to be exploited. They failed to ask permission from the Eora, the Aboriginal custodians of the land around the Sydney Harbour foreshores, and they failed to show respect.

When the Eora tried to assert their rights, the white people acted as if the Eora were trespassing and should find somewhere else to live. Many looked at the Eora with contempt, dismissing them as 'heathen savages', as if they were ants to be squashed under boots. Some greeted them with smiles and invited them to learn the white ways, explaining that education, particularly in Christianity and work skills, would bring them knowledge and happiness. Instead the Eora found themselves relegated to the lowest level of a hierarchical society, a level that their Aboriginality itself would never let them rise above. Gradually they drifted back to their own people, preferring to be valued for who they were, rather than condemned for what they were. And so the foundations were laid for the racial conflict that would devastate many lives in the years to follow, including that of a certain young girl and her family.

The white people continued to swarm from their immense ships, spreading out in every direction throughout the whole territory of the Eora and beyond. One who would climb from a boat and gaze around with mismatched eyes, one hazel, one grey, was a 24-year-old English convict with the unprepossessing name of James Bugg.

'A name? If the party had a voice, what mortal would be a Bugg by choice?' cried British humourist and poet, Thomas Hood. Yet, oddly enough, James Bugg's surname was not an allusion to the creepy-crawlies infesting his homeland but to its fey folk, its hobgoblins and bugbears and bogies—including the malevolent characters recently brought to life again in the Brothers Grimm's deliciously eerie fairytales. Inadvertently, the colonial authorities had foisted upon him a more prosaic surname. The ponderous wheels of bureaucracy had proved incapable of reversing to correct a clerk's mis-transcription, forcing him to grudgingly answer to 'James Brigg' throughout his years of convict servitude. He tossed off that government-ordained coil as soon as he could, wrapping his daughter in his own fey threads: a Bugg by choice indeed. Yet, considering the circumstances of Mary Ann's birth, she might have carried no surname at all—nor even a 'Christian' name.

Despite his surprisingly whimsical surname, James Bugg's world had always been as pedestrian as his surname sounded: full of sheep, in fact—those bleating, blundering creatures that provided warm clothes for winter and mutton chops for dinner. For at least a millennium, flocks had munched on the fattening pastures around James Bugg's birthplace of Little Horkesley in County Essex, England, the town name itself meaning 'farmland for herds'. Shepherding put supper on his table during his young adulthood, perhaps only a scanty repast considering his nocturnal adventures. The latter would prove his undoing.

In the summer of 1825, Bugg and a confederate slipped into a property at nearby Great Horkesley and stole two lambs, a wether sheep and two pigs. 'The men are notorious characters and have been long suspected of plundering the neighbouring flocks,' reported an Essex newspaper. 'Death recorded,' announced the judge without, fortunately, donning the dreaded black cap. The resulting reprieve to transportation for life gave James a berth on the convict ship *Sesostris*, which sailed across the turquoise waters of Sydney Harbour in March 1826. A year later he was assigned to New South Wales' largest business enterprise, the publicly listed Australian Agricultural Company.

A million pounds of capital; a million acres of pasture lands. These were unimaginable sums to a man like James Bugg, who had previously earned around £25 per year and whose chances of ever leasing land—let alone owning it—were slim indeed. However the 'A.A.Co.' or 'the Company', as it came to be known, was the vision of gentlemen whose minds reflected the seemingly limitless horizons of the Australian landscape, envisaging green pastures for the taking, a cheap convict labour force to watch over flocks that would increase exponentially through breeding, a caravan of wagons carrying fleece to be shipped to England's Midland mills, and a steady stream of gold sovereigns cascading into grasping hands.

Early in 1827, James Bugg stepped off another boat at Carrington, the Company's newly established headquarters on the northern shore of Port Stephens. There he found shelter in the bark-clad pole huts constructed some months previously with the assistance of local Worimi tribesmen. Two Worimi had guided the Company's Chief Agent Robert Dawson and his men overland to Port Stephens and had begun helping them construct the workers' huts, a task everyone soon realised would take weeks to complete. Suddenly, the Worimi men dropped their tools and disappeared into the bush, returning soon afterwards with a dozen companions—not an attack force, as it turned out, but a labour force. The men were each given a hatchet and cheerfully set to work, making notches high in the trees and stripping off large sheets of bark, then wrapping these around themselves and striding down the hill with only their bare legs showing, as if the trees themselves had decided to go walkabout.

The Chief Agent was determined that the Company would develop a cordial working relationship with the local tribes, and his honesty and openness provided a harmonious beginning. 'They are a naturally harmless people, desiring to seek rather than shun the society of white persons as soon as they saw a disposition to treat them with humanity,' Dawson wrote in his diary. 'I had no hesitation in trusting myself alone with them. The assistance which I derived from them, whether as guides or labourers, exceeded anything I can describe.' Considering that some of the convict cedar-cutters who had ventured into the area a decade previously had treated the Aboriginal inhabitants with horrifying cruelty—theft, rape, murder—the new trespassers had been greeted with a surprisingly welcoming and helpful attitude. But the Worimi would learn in the years to follow that future Company officials did not always share Dawson's benevolent attitude.

Initially James Bugg was assigned to shepherd a flock not far from Carrington, close enough for his skills to be easily assessed before he was sent to one of the sheep stations being established away from head-quarters. Two years later he was promoted to the role of overseer, one of only three convict overseers out of sixteen employed by the Company in 1832. He assumed responsibility for the Berrico outstation on the Gloucester River, part of the Company's Gloucester station on its northern-most perimeter. As an overseer, he received an allowance of £20 per year over and above his rations, a sum that Chief Agent Dawson's succes-sor would say was lavish and unnecessary—that convict overseers like Bugg would be just as thankful to receive £12 or £15 in addition to their rations. Not that those living so far from the settled districts had much to spend their money upon, whatever sum they received, except to drink or gamble it away.

There among the rolling grass-covered dales of the Gloucester River district, James would remain as overseer, responsible for three shepherds, a hut-keeper and five hundred or so sheep. Their closest neighbours were many miles away—their closest *white* neighbours that is, as dozens of Aboriginal people lived in the surrounding bush. At time's, when rumours spread of Aboriginal attacks in other districts, the Berrico shepherds were eerily aware of their isolation, knowing they had no protection in the event of any trouble, except for a few flintlock muskets tucked in the corner of Bugg's hut.

The naked young woman stepped out of the bush and began walking towards the shepherds, smiling a tentative greeting. Unthreateningly female, she was an ambassador for her people who clustered nearby, a human symbol of peace and friendship. She tried to ignore the flutters in her belly as she edged closer, propelled by her awareness of the importance of her role. Tentatively she offered herself to the shepherds' leader.

Her sexuality was intended as a bridge between the two cultures, like the nobleman's daughter of another culture whose marriage furthers her family's or country's ambitions, or the 'mail order bride' of a future era who humbly offers herself in marriage in order to send funds home to her struggling family. The young woman's offer was a gracious invitation to join her Aboriginal family, to become part of her kinship network, with its consequent rewards and obligations—most importantly reciprocal generosity. It was part of a tradition understood by all the people of her vast land, that kinship meant friendship, and everyone else was the enemy.

The shepherds watching her approach had little comprehension of her cultural traditions—or interest in learning about them. Naturally, the overseer was delighted to accept the offer, failing to appreciate that personally she was bestowing upon him a precious gift, and culturally the equivalent of a dynastic marriage. Instead, he and his men perceived her overture as just another sign of her inferior culture, that the Aboriginal people cared so little for their women that they would prostitute them for some flour and tobacco.

The shepherds were incapable of understanding that their own society's tradition of 'selling' a woman's virginity in return for a wedding ring and financial support was no less political or economic in its essence. Rather they saw any breach of their own marital traditions as a 'sin'. Rarely the man's sin, of course—only the woman's and anyone else who profited. So they accepted the young woman's offer while they judged and condemned, and they dismissed any gentle suggestion of kinship obligations—the simple morality of her egalitarian people that dictated that those who were blessed must support those who were not.

This fundamental morality had largely been lost in their own Christian tradition, a belief system ruled by the blessed and their vicar brothers who sermonised that God had intentionally rewarded them, and that those less blessed must uncomplainingly accept their lot in life; that if they did so they would be rewarded in the afterlife—'the meek shall inherit the earth'. It was the blessed who sat on the Board of the Australian Agricultural Company and placed golden pins on maps to mark out huge tracts of territory they could profit from. They were driven by a self-justificatory belief in the unspoken principle (later called 'terra nullius') that the Aboriginal people had no sovereignty because they claimed no recognisable title to their land or even laboured to improve it, and that the land could therefore be claimed by a more 'worthy' and industrious nation and parcelled out to those who would appropriately value and use it. Because they knew that the meek would never inherit the earth.

Nor were the convict shepherds fooled. Their uncaring society had forced them to develop their own morality, individualistic rather than kinship-oriented, expedient by necessity more than intention: whatever it took to survive.

As the Company's flocks grew larger and spread further across the land in search of fresh pasture, more and more Aboriginal women offered themselves to the shepherds. They were rarely turned away. And if none of the women offered themselves, well, coercion worked nearly as effectively. Ropes were not hard to find.

From their bushland homes the Aboriginal people watched to see how successful their female ambassadors would be, initially hopeful, then puzzled and confused, and eventually angry. Kin who failed to meet their kinship obligations could no longer be considered kin, would no longer be deemed friends.

James Bugg's young woman was around twenty years of age when he welcomed her into his overseer's hut. He called her Charlotte, and late in the winter of 1833 she fell pregnant.

Charlotte wanted her baby. There was no need for the toxic herbs her people had long known were effective abortifacients, used when food supplies were scarce or pregnancies too close together. There was no need for the simpler technique of pressing strong hands on a rounded belly, or the safest of all—for the mother, at least—a hand held firmly over mouth and nose as the newborn drew its first breath. On 8 May 1834 her baby was born at Berrico, a daughter who would be christened Mary Ann.

Did Charlotte initially call her baby 'Moorinna', as some would later claim? This melodious name was remarkably similar to the rare 'Marina' that Mary Ann would bestow upon one of her own daughters. Moorinna was the name Charlotte's people used for Merope, the smallest star in the Pleiades, a constellation that rose at dawn in the late autumn months when Mary Ann was born.

In another mythology, Merope had her own namesake: the adoptive mother of Oedipus, King of Thebes. Oedipus' unsuccessful quest to escape his destiny was immortalised by Socrates in his play *Oedipus Rex*, the Greek tragedy that raises the timeless question of character versus destiny, of the balance between fate and free will in determining a person's path through life. The same question would be asked of the little girl born in the Berrico backwoods who would ultimately become the most notorious Aboriginal woman in nineteenth-century Australia.

2

Plenty water before white man came, plenty pish [fish], plenty kangaroo, plenty possum, plenty everything; now all gone. Poor fellow now, black fellow!

Aboriginal man quoted in Alexander Harris, *Settlers and Convicts*, 1847

Nearly a dozen Williams River tribesmen drifted out of the Berrico bush and ambled up to James Bugg on Friday 8 May 1835, asking for flour and other foodstuffs—including tobacco, of course, beloved by most bushmen whatever their origins. James handed them some corn to roast and the craved tobacco, and the tribesmen seemed happy enough, in no particular hurry, lingering around the outstation for a few hours while the shepherds continued their work, chatting companionably about going to a great corroboree in the neighbourhood later that day. The Berrico shepherds recognised some faces from previous visits and even knew some of their names: Kotera-Jackey was wearing a distinctive white linen shirt that day, and Cromie was always easily identifiable because his right hand turned backwards.

Charlotte wandered around the hut carrying out her usual duties: washing and cleaning, and preparing the bushman's staple fare of mutton, damper and tea for every meal, with the judicious addition of yams and berries foraged from the bush. Mary Ann napped for some of the time, tired by the energy expended in crawling around and pulling herself up. She had celebrated her first birthday just the previous day, a toothy grin beaming from a light-brown countenance.

Around 3 pm James settled into a chair outside his hut and contentedly viewed his domain. The afternoon's shadows were already lengthening as autumn's briskness surrendered to winter's chill. He glanced idly towards the tribesmen still lounging around the outstation and noticed, without really thinking about it, that one of them had left his friends milling near the shepherds' hut and was walking towards him.

Suddenly, a flash of movement. A waddy slammed against his thighs. He fell off the chair onto the ground, waves of pain buffeting him. As his shocked eyes gazed up at his attacker, he saw the face of a tribesman who had earlier been near the shepherds' hut. The man must have sneaked up on him while his attention was diverted.

Another flicker of movement; another raised waddy. The tribesman he had noticed walking towards him had hurtled across the clearing and swung his own waddy. The man bashed James on the head and body, again and again, but James didn't notice the repeated blows. The first had knocked him senseless.

Henry Curtis, James Smith and the two other Berrico workers were in their hut when they heard strange noises from the direction of Bugg's. A moment later, a tribesman loitering nearby shouted something like 'Coolie' and slammed shut their door.

A primitive survival instinct kicked in. The shepherds threw themselves at the door, bursting it open before their attackers had time to fasten it. Smith looked over towards Bugg's hut. Two tribesmen were pounding at the overseer with their waddies—a ghastly noise: whack . . . whack. Bugg wasn't curled in a ball with his hands encircling his head; he was sprawled like a rag doll, clearly unconscious, maybe even dead.

The shepherds hesitated, uncertain what to do. They should go to Bugg's aid, but that meant crossing the open distance between the two huts. What if the blacks had already broken into Bugg's hut and armed themselves with the guns? As they wavered, they saw Bugg's woman step out of his hut carrying a musket.

Charlotte left Mary Ann inside as she slipped through the doorway, gripping the musket with both hands. She turned towards James. Blood streaked his pale countenance and matted his dark brown hair, pooling on the ground around him. Two men leant over him, rage scoring their black faces. They raised their waddies again, three feet long, solid and menacing. Wood slammed against bone with another sicken-ing crunch.

Senseless? Probably dead. And so might she and Mary Ann be if she didn't do something. She raised the musket and wedged the butt into the crook of her shoulder, as James had taught her to do—just in case. She sighted along the barrel at the two men raising their waddies again.

The tribesmen bludgeoning Bugg hadn't noticed the impending threat. Others paused as they saw his woman position one hand under the musket barrel to support it, curling the forefinger of her other hand around the trigger. Would she actually shoot at them?

The sudden explosion was shocking in its intensity. As the echo whipped back, it was a chilling reminder of a threat more deadly than a spear. The attackers fled.

The sight of Bugg's woman resisting the marauders spurred Smith and Curtis into action. They raced over to Bugg's hut and grabbed the other guns, joining her outside. Another two blasts breached the afternoon's stillness. More tribesmen bolted for the bushes, out of gunshot range. The Berrico men continued to stand there menacingly with their muskets raised, swinging the barrels in gentle arcs as they watched for further threatening movements.

Some of the tribesmen hadn't joined their companions' flight to safety. Taking advantage of the Berrico workers' distraction, they crept around to the back of the men's hut and broke a slat, knowing that most of the food and supplies were stored there. They began tugging at the wood.

The sharp crack had alerted one of the workers. He shouted an alarm. Smith and Curtis rushed back to the men's hut. They lifted their muskets again and aimed at the men standing only a few feet away. The would-be thieves backed off and scurried into the bush.

Stalemate. The shepherds had single-shot muskets, but no means of calling for assistance. They were also outnumbered nearly three to one. What if the attackers decided to call in reinforcements? What if they realised—as other black warriors had soon learnt—that the muskets had a critical weakness: that the best time to attack was after they had been fired, when the shooters paused to reload? The Berrico men con-tinued their vigil as the sun sank towards the horizon and day yielded to a ruddy sunset.

The Aboriginals began calling out, taunting them, daring them. Their English was good—as the shepherds already knew from the previous hours spent in their company.

'The soldiers will be sent after you,' Smith shouted at them.

'We don't care about the soldiers,' the Aboriginals yelled back defiantly. 'Plenty more blacks in the bush and we'll kill all the white men.'

Night-time's ebony cloak wrapped itself around the outstation, concealing the attackers in its secretive folds.

Blacks have attacked the Berrico outstation, declared the note handed to the Company's Commissioner, Colonel Henry Dumaresq, at Carrington late on the evening of 11 May 1835. The note reported that the attackers had severely beaten the overseer and nearly killed him, and had plundered the station, stealing a sheep and eating it. They had lingered at the station in the aftermath, threatening to kill the inhabitants. The shepherds were terrified.

Soon afterwards, the commander of Carrington's military detachment headed out on the long journey to Berrico, accompanied by three soldiers and two government constables. His orders were to capture the offenders, if possible, and to reassure the shepherds and other settlers in the district.

'Unless protection be promptly afforded,' Dumaresq would later write to the Company's British Governor, 'it is hardly to be expected that individuals like the convict shepherds who are so little interested in the property confided in their care should remain exposed to attacks from Hostile Tribes of Blacks for the purpose of defending such property.'

Naturally the Commissioner did not want his convict workers to use such a pretext to abandon their stations—and the Company's capital.

Back at Berrico, James, Charlotte, little Mary Ann and the four Berrico workers were no longer alone. Their numbers and spirits had been bolstered by the arrival of some men from nearby Riddlesdale station. Riddlesdale was not a Company station; rather it was the head station of the young Robert Ramsay Mackenzie, later a Scottish baronet and

Queensland politician. But employment allegiances were unimportant in these isolated frontier districts.

The Berrico shepherds remained at their huts, too scared to take their sheep out to pasture, exhausted by living in a state of heightened tension. They inhabited an alien territory, a hostile land where everything was threatening. They could die of thirst one day or drown the next, or starve if their supplies ran out or if they became lost in the bush, or suffer an agonising death from a snake or spider bite. Death normally lurked in every shadow, but now it had stepped out and shown its face. The tribesmen had turned on them without warning—men they thought they had befriended; men they regularly fed and supported. And the attackers were still out there . . . watching, waiting, no longer just a threat to the shepherds, but to Charlotte and Mary Ann as well, now that Charlotte had shown her allegiance.

Carrington's military detachment covered 67 miles in just over twenty-four hours. They travelled in the dark for the last few hours, tension increasing, alert to every noise and disturbance in the bush around them, eerily aware of being watched. When they eventually reached Berrico around 10 pm on Tuesday 12 May, four days after the attack, all was quiet. The tribesmen were gone.

With the troops' arrival, the Riddlesdale men departed the following day. An Aboriginal constable, Nillimo, travelled with them, under orders to observe the ranges as he passed, in an attempt to find traces of the tribesmen's encampment. Nillimo was employed by the Company as a district constable of sorts, praised by his superiors as being more useful to the Company than all the other constables put together, a terror to white and black alike. If anyone could find the marauders, it was the clever and tenacious Nillimo.

With the district seemingly quiet again, the military detachment headed south on the long journey back to Carrington. Their departure left Mary Ann, her family and all the other shepherds and workers alone once more in the isolated Gloucester district, without any military protection.

As Overseer David Campbell and his men drove their drays into Riddlesdale station that Wednesday afternoon after leaving Berrico, a large party of Aboriginals appeared from the bush. The Riddlesdale men abandoned the drays and hurried towards a hut, while Campbell and Nillimo eyed the visitors warily.

One of the tribesmen approached Nillimo and spoke to him for a moment, then returned to his companions. Some slipped back into the bush, while others lingered until after sundown, when they too disappeared.

As the Riddlesdale men maintained their guard, Nillimo headed out to find the Aboriginal camp. He returned a short time later, telling Campbell that the men had gone; however, before leaving they had asked if he would go to the Manning River with them. When he asked why, they answered ominously: 'To kill all the white men and their master.'

John Ross was concerned. He had told the watchman stationed at the Whattonbakh outstation, three-and-a-half miles from the Riddlesdale head station, to come to Riddlesdale on the evening of Thursday 14 May, but the man had not turned up. Nor did he appear on the Friday morning. Ross ordered one of the station hands to assist him and they headed towards the outstation to investigate.

The lingering smell of smoke was the first sign of trouble; the blackened wreckage of the men's huts the next. Where were the watchman and the overseer and the three shepherds who lived there? The sheep folds had been moved to a new location—one of the watchman's daily chores, to allow the sheep fresh pasturage at night—but they were empty. Where were the sheep?

Ross returned to Riddlesdale for assistance and his larger party headed back to Whattonbakh to search for the missing men and sheep. They found the sheep—all except three—but of the five men . . . nothing.

Commissioner Dumaresq's doorknocker pounded again on the evening of 16 May. Police Magistrate Thomas Cook was standing on the stoop, holding an express letter from Gloucester with news of the latest outrage. They discussed their options and agreed that the military detachment should retrace its footsteps, despite having only just arrived back in Carrington. At Booral, south of Stroud, the detachment would be joined by some of the Company's officers, including James Edward Ebsworth, the Commissioner's assistant.

After the troops departed, Dumaresq and the Police Magistrate penned some letters to be carried to Sydney by the steamer stoking its engines for the return journey. Dumaresq advised the New South Wales Governor that 'Mr Mackenzie's station in that neighbourhood has been attacked, that the sheep were driven away, five men murdered, and the huts destroyed by fire.' He requested that rewards be offered for the apprehension of the Berrico attackers, and that a small force of mounted police be sent to the district to help maintain the peace. Otherwise, he explained, a spirit of hostility would prevail and the feeling of alarm would become the pretext for acts of reciprocal violence and other irregularities.

The Police Magistrate wrote to his counterpart in Maitland begging that a detachment of mounted police be sent to the Gloucester River district. He also wrote to Riddlesdale's owner, Robert Ramsay Mackenzie, reporting that his men had been murdered.

Mackenzie immediately dashed off a letter to the Governor—not to mourn the loss of his men or to beg the government's assistance in protecting the others working in the district, but to protect his livelihood. He wanted five more convicts instantly. 'I must plead the urgency of the case, as should they not be replaced immediately I shall suffer seriously in loss of property.'

Never named in the correspondence and barely mourned, the five dead shepherds were just numbers in an accounting ledger, a business setback in the same way that livestock deaths were—an inconvenience like the droughts and floods and fires that threatened profitability. The dead shepherds were no more valued as fellow humans than their Aboriginal attackers.

The Carrington troops were still many miles to the south when a large number of Aboriginal men descended on Riddlesdale station early on Sunday 17 May. The inhabitants were instantly on the alert, muskets in hand. The tribesmen waited at a distance, however, and did not appear threatening.

Nillimo went over to speak to them. They told him that the 'old Buck Blacks' had murdered the Whattonbakh men and that they had found one man's remains. When Nillimo relayed the news, Overseer Campbell asked the tribesmen to bring the body to Riddlesdale, and offered horses to assist them.

The men returned at sunset with the body and additional news. They had found the remains of another two bodies, although they could not transport them because of damage from animals and the recent storm. The final two shepherds, they said, had been eaten by the men who murdered them.

Overseer Campbell gave the helpful tribesmen some flour, and a few took it back to their camp to make cakes. The others divided, with some heading towards the men's hut.

The station hands immediately retreated to another hut. Rumours had been spreading that the blacks intended to murder all the whites that Sunday night and the Riddlesdale men were too scared to trust any of them.

As darkness fell, the tribesmen continued to mill around the station, many of them carrying timbers. One stood by the door of the men's hut and tried to close it. A station hand forced it open again and the men rushed from the hut, only to be momentarily blinded when the tribesmen extinguished all the lights and ran off to their own camp.

As Overseer Campbell's eyes adjusted, he saw that some of the tribesmen had obtained other lights and were spreading around the camp, apparently intending to advance on the huts from all angles. His men had little ammunition and no motivation to stay, so they decided to retreat to James Bugg's station. Harnessing the drays, they headed towards the track that would take them back to Berrico.

Taunts from the darkness followed them. Then small clubs began to rain down on them. Huddled in the drays, they waited tensely for the spears that would surely follow.

The Carrington troops had just reached Gloucester when Riddlesdale's Overseer Campbell rode in with news of the latest attack. Fortunately, he was able to report that his men had reached Berrico without any further trouble.

The troops immediately headed back to Berrico, where Assistant Commissioner Ebsworth questioned James Bugg and the other men. James had recovered enough by then to provide an affidavit, as did Campbell himself. After hearing their accounts Ebsworth wrote that most of Campbell's statements were borne out, although he felt that the men's alarm had magnified some of the circumstances. In particular, he had received no confirmation that the Whattonbakh killers had actually eaten any of the shepherds.

Leaving a constable at Berrico to help protect James Bugg, his family and the other workers, the troops travelled on to Riddlesdale. The station was now safe: the tribesmen had not attacked after the Riddlesdale men had left, perhaps having simply enjoyed terrifying the station hands, a moment of one-upmanship in a world that had left them with little power.

On Tuesday 19 May, the remains of the three dead shepherds were interred at Riddlesdale. Prayers were said for the souls of all five, among them convict transportee Laurence Kennedy, who had sailed into Sydney less than four months previously. Nillimo and some blacktrackers then joined Ebsworth and the troops as they headed into the ranges after the Whattonbakh killers.

Nillimo had already tried to find the Berrico attackers. He had tracked them towards the Williams River, stopping at the fireplace where the men had obviously cooked and eaten the stolen sheep, but had lost their tracks soon afterwards. The trail left by the Whattonbakh killers was still there, however. The posse followed it to an encampment in the middle of the ranges and reportedly came within a short distance of the tribesmen, but the area proved impassable to the strangers. Finding it 'impracticable' to apprehend the murderers, they were forced to return Riddlesdale.

When Ebsworth later wrote his lengthy report to the Police Magistrate, he disclosed some alarming news received from Nillimo. The attacks had reportedly been instigated by a white man who was residing with the local tribes, a man known to Nillimo. Through this white man's initiative, the Aboriginals inhabiting the Upper Williams River district and those from the headwaters of the Manning River had joined forces and devised a plan for killing the whites at the distant stations. A small party was to attack James Bugg's Berrico station, another small party Whattonbakh, and the main body the principal station at Riddlesdale. The tribesmen who had descended on Riddlesdale as Overseer Campbell's drays returned from Berrico on 13 May had in fact been the main attack force. They had intended to kill the white men and 'do worse' to the women—who were themselves

Aboriginal—and had also planned to steal all the flour, sugar and blankets; however, the arrival of Campbell and his armed men had deterred them. Such organisation, Ebsworth added, was enough to convince him that there had indeed been white involvement, as he had never previously heard of tribes joining forces in such a way.

Ebsworth had also learnt from Nillimo that the unarmed Whattonbakh men had been away from the huts at their respective duties when they were killed: the three shepherds while watching their flocks, the overseer on his way to visit one of the shepherds, and the watchman near the sheep fold.

For whatever reason, James Bugg's decision to keep his men at Berrico on the day of the attack rather than sending them out with their sheep almost certainly saved their lives as well as those of Charlotte and her infant daughter Mary Ann.

Commissioner Dumaresq wanted revenge. When informed that the requested detachment from Maitland was at Stroud awaiting instructions, he took the liberty of offering a suggestion. While he knew that the inaccessible nature of the killers' refuge had prevented the troops capturing them, some of their identities were well known. 'The party of Mounted Police,' he advised the police magistrate, 'should be directed to persevere in the pursuit of the parties known to have participated in the murder of Mr Mackenzie's shepherds until they succeed in taking or killing them.'

Dumaresq lacked the same benevolent attitudes held by the Company's first chief agent, Robert Dawson. He saw the Aboriginal people as 'savages' and believed that 'like all other savages' they responded only to the might of the law, and would cease their depredations only when its powerful arm was raised against them. He would declare in his report to the New South Wales Governor Richard Bourke: 'An act of aggression such as the one in question must be avenged!'

Meanwhile, the troops left behind in the Gloucester district continued to protect the inhabitants and investigate the attacks. Two weeks after the Whattonbakh massacre, the constable stationed at James Bugg's station received word that one of the murderers, a man named Charley, was camped about eight miles from Berrico. Guided by the resourceful Nillimo and accompanied by a Berrico shepherd, the constable ambushed the Aboriginal camp in the early hours of the morning.

Charley later described one of the murders. He and his two companions had attacked the man they knew as Fred—the overseer Alfred Simmons. As Charley raised his waddy to strike, Fred pleaded: 'Don't kill me! I am a budjeree [good] fellow. I am always kind to blacks.' Ignoring the plea, Charley thumped Fred on the head and wounded him, and Russian Paddy hit him on the back of his head and knocked him down. Then Black Boy came over to them and said, 'Three mess-mates make him die directly.' And they did.

'Why?' was the question everyone kept asking. Charley said that a white fellow lived with the blacks in the bush, a man they called Garregumme because he had been speared in one of their affrays over an Aboriginal woman. Garregumme had told them to go and kill the whites, and to bring their shoes and tobacco to him. Now Garregumme was wearing the shoes taken from the Whattonbakh overseer.

On 1 June Charley guided the troops to the Whattonbakh murder sites. The body was gone from the first site—previously carried to Riddlesdale by the helpful tribesmen—but a man's remains lay at the second. Two men had been killed at the third site, their bodies already interred at Riddlesdale, and Charley named some of their killers. Finally, he led them to the overseer's body. It was still there, part of it anyway, mainly bones. Neither of the remaining bodies had apparently been eaten, despite the initial gruesome claims.

As the troops escorted Charley south, two more Whattonbakh attackers—men who had supposedly helped carry away the plunder—were apprehended, although they would later be released.

But something else must have happened in the month after the Berrico attack, intimated in Dumaresq's report to his British superiors on 12 June, but not, seemingly, to the colonial authorities: 'Prompt measures were employed by the government,' Dumaresq wrote, 'and many of the parties engaged in these outrages have been captured or shot.'

3

I have heard again and again people say that they were nothing better than dogs, and that it was no more harm to shoot them than it would be to shoot a dog when he barked at you.

Reverend William Yate to the Select Committee on Aborigines, 1835

The news of the 'massacre at Mackenzie's' reached Sydney on 21 May 1835. Two days later the government announced a reward of £10 for each of the five Aboriginal men named in the reward notice: four involved in the attack against James Bugg's Berrico outstation, and the Whatton-bakh ringleader, Cobawn (Big) Paddy, who had been seen in the aftermath sporting a musket taken from the outstation.

James Bugg would later sign an affidavit that he had known the What-tonbakh ringleader for four years, that Cobawn Paddy was a regular visitor to Berrico, and was a friend of the tribesmen who attacked him. Riddlesdale owner Robert Mackenzie would also offer a £10 reward, saying that Cobawn Paddy had grown up at his station and knew the murdered men well, and was very familiar with the habits of stock-keepers and shepherds. Cobawn Paddy was a man to be feared.

As the days passed, more news flooded in from the northern districts. Police Magistrate Cook met with some of the 'more respectable' Upper Williams settlers on 29 May and heard tales of recent attacks on their stations, of sheep killed and huts plundered—even a man injured. One settler recounted how the Aboriginal men had amused themselves by throwing boomerangs at the lambs and breaking their legs. 'In short,' Cook wrote to the Governor, 'the blacks seem so daring that the shepherds are terrified out of their wits and can hardly be persuaded to follow their flocks.'

Garregumme the white ringleader was apprehended, but rumours circulated that he was not acting alone. Four bushrangers were reportedly directing the black warriors, each taking a party under his command and marking out territories and suggesting attack strategies, then keeping out of sight while they followed his plan. It was a terrifying combination: daring warriors led by white outlaws who had only death to face, whether in battle or on the scaffold.

Fear gripped the district, not only at James Bugg's Berrico outstation and at Riddlesdale, but all the way from the Manning River to the Hunter Valley. If friendly Aboriginals could attack and kill, how could any be trusted? The familiar was no longer comforting. Home was a battlefield, and the few guns scattered among the locals were no match for Aboriginals engaging in guerilla-style warfare. The warriors could launch a volley of spears from behind bushes or lay a torch against the dry wood of their huts while they slept. What could they do to resist such a seemingly implacable enemy?

Police Magistrate Cook told the settlers that he had devised a plan. If each settler would provide four of their most trusty servants and take charge of them, they could raise a formidable body. He in his official role as Police Magistrate would accompany the squad to the black's camp after dark and take them by surprise, and if possible capture the ringleaders.

'No!' replied the nervous settlers. 'We shall wait a little to see what His Excellency the Governor will do for us.'

The conservative *Sydney Herald* delighted in adding fuel to the flames of settler discontent when reporting on Aboriginal incursions. The settlers had been forced to purchase arms and ammunition in Maitland to defend themselves because of the Police Magistrate's inactivity, the paper announced. Protection offered by the mounted police? Not likely, the paper trumpeted. Moreover, the military were reluctant to fire on the 'enemy' in case they were dragged to the courts and tried for murder! The government should send a special force to the Upper Williams River with orders to severely punish the aggressors.

And if the fire wasn't already blazing, the *Herald* would gleefully light it. Cannibalism! 'Two of Mackenzie's men were eaten, the remains being found with the flesh cut from the thighs and other fleshy parts.' Of course, the newspaper added, certain 'cockneys' at Government House would not believe such reports, would declare that it *must* be the eaglehawks, that the blacks were not cannibals because it is contrary to human nature. 'People certainly do not eat each other in Cheapside or the Strand,' the *Herald* added sardonically, 'but we refer these respectable gossips to the evidence of any gentleman who has lived on the northern frontier, and if the cockney prejudice be not too strong, they will be soon convinced.'

Harangues from the press, pleas from the settlers: Governor Richard Bourke was forced to act. The government's attitude towards the Aboriginal people was largely one of head-in-the-sand benevolence, a tug-of-war between paternal concern, the type of concern that had recently driven Britain to abolish slavery, and a desire for the colony to help finance itself by exploiting its one seemingly unlimited resource, land—to sell, to farm, and to graze sheep and cattle upon. Bourke himself regularly condemned outrages against Aboriginal natives, declaring that both the black and white communities were protected by the same laws of the country. His predecessor had advised that the government could not fund military parties to protect those spreading out in search of good pasture. His successor added that pastoralists must realise they were running the same risks as if they ventured into wolf-infested terrain, the only difference being that the government would encourage them to kill the wolves, whereas all it could presently do was raise a voice in the name of humanity and justice—a voice in favour of the poor savage creatures whose own voice was too feeble to be heard at such a distance.

Although the feeble voices continued to be ignored, the government certainly heard the waddy blows. On Tuesday 9 June, Governor Bourke ordered Major Croker and the Light Company of the 17th regiment—four subalterns and upwards of fifty rank and file—to board the *William IV* steamer for Port Stephens. They were under instructions to protect the northern districts and to capture or otherwise punish the offenders.

'We trust that Major Croker is armed with full instructions to levy war against the enemy in a vigorous manner,' urged the vengeful *Herald*.

'What?' exclaimed the outraged editor of the *Hobart Town Courier*. 'The only alternative is to send a body of armed men against a comparatively defenceless people, the created lords and natives of the soil?—soil, too, which you are daily selling by piecemeal and by auction and most unjustly (in our opinion) applying the proceeds, not to protect, teach or support these outraged blacks but to bring out from England shiploads of wretched half-principled paupers.'

What else are we to do? *The Australian* countered: we either restrain them by the terror of example, or withdraw from that part of the country. Of course, few would recommend withdrawing, it opined, and anyway the natives do not suffer by our occupation of the soil. The depasturing of our cattle creates no scarcity of opossums or goannas, their stuff of life, and if it interferes with their comfort, they can remove without inconvenience. And while some claim that their anger is aroused by white men taking their gins away from them, those well acquainted with them know that they value the 'fairest jewel of their tribe' lower than their boomerangs and nulla nullas . . .

'"Hath not a savage eyes? Hath not he hands, organs, dimensions, senses, affections, passions? Fed with the same food, hurt with the same weapons, subject to the same diseases, healed by the same sun, warmed and cooled by the same winter and summer as *a white man is*?"' quoted a lone voice from Maitland, denouncing *The Australian* for such a heartless dismissal. 'We hanged a black the other day for committing an outrage against an English female. Are not the blacks then justified in spearing a white who, as the phrase goes, "craummers their gins"?'

Why such an uprising at this time, pondered *The Colonist*, advising that such outrages generally occurred as a consequence of sufferings inflicted on the native blacks by ticket-of-leavers and free men who lived in the distant unpoliced parts of the colony. A Vagrant Act was the solution, the editor advised, allowing the authorities to seize and punish such persons and in so doing protect both the black and white communities.

Hmmm, said the *Sydney Gazette*. It was true that Aboriginal attacks usually followed aggressions upon the natives themselves. Moreover, the previous Company Commissioner's actions in hunting sheep-stealers and murderers had likely been unlawful. But what about the future? Reports suggested that free men had joined the convict-led tribesmen and that a group of absconded soldiers was heading for the Hunter district. Disciplined and resolute, the soldiers' arms and confidence would render any conflict all the more dangerous. The frightening prospect left them little choice: 'We hope that the powers invested in the hands of the military officer will enable him to teach the convicts and aborigines that the day of retribution, when it arrives, is terrible and bloody.'

As for those living in the bush, their proffered solution was simple: shoot all the blacks. 'In all our opinions', said one man, 'it is the readiest way of quieting the countryside, for the idea of carrying on a warfare or taking these cannibals prisoner is all nonsense.'

On 22 August 1835, the self-confessed Whattonbakh killer stood inside the sandstone walls of Sydney's Supreme Court, facing Chief Justice Francis Forbes and a military jury on the charge of killing Overseer Alfred Simmons. With acclaimed linguist Reverend Lancelot Threlkeld by his side, Charley defended himself by testifying that his people carried a ball-shaped charm called a *Mura-mai*, a charm made of agate quartz and other stones that ensured longevity and protection from evil to the possessor, but meant death to any woman who dared look at it. Simmons had obtained Charley's *Mura-mai*, pulled it to pieces and shown it to his gin, a breach of tribal rules that meant death for them both. Charley and his friends were ordered by their elders to enforce the penalty. They were determined to kill Fred first and the woman afterwards.

True? Perhaps. Issues regarding white men and Aboriginal women were generally the catalyst for frontier violence. But Charley's explanation did not account for the earlier attack on James Bugg and the Berrico men, or the other planned attacks in the district, or the stated desire to kill 'all the white men'. More likely this was simply the last straw, the teetering domino that had been given one shove too many. Behind their decision to attack Berrico and Riddlesdale and Whattonbakh lay years of frustration and despair, of gun-toting horsemen who rode into Aboriginal territory and commandeered the most fertile land for their flocks and herds, destroying waterholes or blocking access to them, even poisoning the water in some instances so the black nuisance would permanently disappear, slaughtering kangaroos and other native animals, and caring nothing that they were depriving Aboriginals of the meat and water, the wild fruits and seeds and grasses that were essential for their survival. The pastoralists' intention was simply to open up grazing land for their livestock—the flocks of sheep and herds of cattle that grew larger and larger. But the animals ate the grass and trampled the other plants, upsetting the bush's delicate life cycle in a territory that the Aboriginal people had carefully managed for 50,000 years.

Despite the European belief that the Aboriginals had not fenced it or farmed it or laboured over it and therefore had no legal dominion over it, the land was distinctly their own. They had, in fact, shaped their territory to suit their purposes by firing the grass behind them, which shrank the forests and increased the area of grassland, clearing the ground for easy walking and for kangaroos and other edible animals to forage. Coastal peoples had often built fish traps, while others had constructed wildlife traps and sometimes even permanent dwellings to return to—not that managing their land gave them any greater or lesser right to a 'legal' title over it.

Additionally, every feature of their landscape had a story, a narrative that served as a mnemonic—and these tales were akin to a surveyor's pegs and ropes. Some marked out their borders, warning against crossing into an enemy's territory. Some served as milestones along the well-trodden paths of their terrain. Each tale not only explained how the features of their physical landscape came to exist, but provided rules to follow, like the tale of the taboo waterhole that was their ancestors' way of protecting them from drinking unhealthy water. Their lore was also their law, and was to be remembered and lived by and communicated to the next generation by song and story. To be forced to leave their territory was akin to casting them adrift on an endless sea, with no map or instructions as to how they should survive. Leaving their land also forced them to encroach on someone else's territory—perhaps kin who were struggling to feed themselves, or enemies who believed they were sorcerers and were driven to resist them, perhaps even to kill them.

They had tried to explain to the white people, they had sent their women as ambassadors, but no one seemed to understand—or care.

Because, on the other side of the frontier, the whites had their own interests and problems. Many had been expelled from their homeland because of criminal behaviour and, while some were bad by nature, most were victims of the failings of their own 'civilised' society, and were often brutalised by punishment until only the primordial instinct to survive kept them going. Banished to the opposite end of the earth, they were left alone in the wilderness, unmonitored and unreformed, incapable of feeling much empathy in general, let alone any interest in understanding an alien and seemingly inferior culture. Driven only by the desire to have their primary needs met—sustenance, shelter and sex—they were willing to do whatever it took to achieve that end.

Next there were the small settlers who saw hard work as the pathway to heaven, who envisaged themselves as the pioneers of civilisation, making the deserts 'blossom as the rose' and opening the way for villages and industry. To these settlers, the Aboriginal people were 'noble savages' when they remained a distant curiosity, but pests when they threatened dreams and livelihoods. As for the large graziers, the bastions of the mighty British Empire, they were investing for the nation's long-term well-being—and their own pocket-books, naturally—but they rarely chose to look down to see the plight of those they trampled upon.

Yet it was seemingly another group of whites who unleashed the tribesmen's desire for revenge in May 1835: the brutalised and vengeful runaway convicts who cajoled the Aboriginals into forming a resistance movement against the whites, into uniting and attacking before their world was destroyed altogether. When the irritating black flies that buzzed around the frontier district suddenly transformed into deadly wasps, the whites decided that the time had come to swat them.

This clash between two vastly different cultures—the two cultures that would push and pull at Mary Ann Bugg throughout her life—had produced a raging torrent of self-interest and misunderstanding and fear. It swept Charley along until finally depositing him on the altar of white justice, where he was sentenced to hang by the neck until he was dead.

When Governor Bourke received word that Charley was to be executed two days later, he immediately rescinded the order. What was the point of carrying out the law's retribution in Sydney? Although he deemed the punishment appropriate—an eye for an eye—he felt it would have little impact as a deterrent since Charley's fellow troublemakers were unlikely to ever learn of his fate. Instead, he decreed that Charley was to be executed closer to home at Dungog on a gallows constructed by the Colonial Architect and hauled to the desired location.

The convoy departed Sydney early in September 1835: the Under-Sheriff who was responsible for conducting the execution, the Major of Brigades and seven subordinates to guard the prisoner, and Reverend Threlkeld as translator and spiritual mentor. Threlkeld was impressed with his charge. The Congregational minister had considerable experience with Aboriginal people, having ministered to scores while running a mission in the Lake Macquarie district. He had mastered one local language and attempted to understand their culture. 'Charley's conduct displayed a greater degree of thoughtfulness and penitence than is generally attributed to the capabilities of the Aborigines of New South Wales,' he would later write to the Governor.

When they reached Dungog, Charley and his attendants were joined by the troops stationed at the Allyn River. It was an intimidating force, a visually striking example—the red-coated might of the British Empire, a lone black native, and the grim wooden symbol of 'civilised' justice.

Was the community's desire for vengeance sated? One black man for five whites: one death to ease the widespread fear and anger in the Gloucester district, to defuse the tension? Newspaper records and official reports would suggest so—although merely by their silence. Local stories, however, suggest otherwise. An angry band of settlers creeping through the darkness up the slopes of Mount Mackenzie; a cliff-ledge encampment of sleeping men, women and children; the night's protective darkness lifted as dawn's weak light penetrated the shadows; the startling crack of gunfire, screams of terror, bodies tumbling off the cliff into the thickets below . . . then a deathly resonating silence.

Perhaps such a retaliatory massacre did indeed occur at Mount Mackenzie in the aftermath of the Whattonbakh killings, as folklore suggests. Maybe dozens of lives lost, or a handful—or perhaps none at all. This story, however, more likely reflects a historical distortion, a twist on the references to the 'massacre at Mackenzie's', as the murder of the five shepherds was alliteratively known. Soon after their deaths, their master Robert Mackenzie removed his squatterdom north to the New England district, so only nearby Mount Mackenzie continued to bear his name. As time passed and Mackenzie and his squatting run were forgotten, the shepherds' deaths were also forgotten, but the phrase 'massacre at Mount Mackenzie' surfaced. As this 4700-foot mountain was a place where only Aboriginal people might have been living—and even they tried to keep to the warmer valleys in winter—only Aboriginal people were likely to have been massacred there. Over time, the phrase 'the massacre at Mackenzie's' appears to have been folklorically transplanted from Mackenzie's squatting run onto his mountain namesake, and as a consequence, the white massacre was transformed—in folk memory at least—into a black massacre.

Such a historical distortion by no means suggests that the local Aboriginal people escaped retribution. A month after the shepherds' deaths, Commissioner Dumaresq reported that 'many' of the attackers had already been captured or shot, when only three had actually been apprehended by that time. The Commissioner's choice of the word 'many'—which sits much higher on the numerical stepladder than its counterpart 'some'— communicates a sense of ominous magnitude.

A decade earlier at Bathurst, the murders of seven Europeans led to the retaliatory murders of dozens of Aboriginal people—deaths commemorated in the folkloric tale of the Bells Falls massacre, which bears a startling resemblance to the Mount Mackenzie massacre story and to many others throughout the continent. Three years after the Whattonbakh killings, cattle thefts at Myall Creek led to the retaliatory murders of another twenty-eight Aboriginal people. Considering Commissioner Dumaresq's demand for revenge, the Police Magistrate's offer to lead a posse, the newspapers' clamour for a bloody and terrible retribution, the settlers' desire to shoot all the blacks, and the powerlessness of the government in Sydney to prevent frontier violence, the question of whether retaliatory deaths were likely or even possible almost answers itself. The demand for retribution rang out not just from the terrified shepherds, but from the highest echelons of society, those who set the moral benchmarks.

Whatever the number and wherever these deaths occurred, the forbidding Mount Mackenzie became the focal point for memories of death and despair, a towering symbol of injustice, an indomitable reminder of the destruction of lives and lifestyle. The literal was transformed into myth and metaphor, overlaying a new cultural meaning onto this feature of the physical landscape.

But not for Mary Ann herself. She was long gone by then.

4

A mind once stretched by a new idea never regains its original
dimensions.

Anonymous

Young Mary Ann must have sensed the fear that invaded her home
during her early childhood, although it would be many years before
she understood the reasons. While the tension gradually eased and life
returned to a semblance of normality, it was clear to her parents that they
had to think carefully about their children's future.

This very issue first surfaced in Company circles in the spring of
1837, apparently after the Company's Gloucester superintendent, Edward
Robins, visited Berrico. Mary Ann and her baby brother, John, were difficult not to notice: two young children gambolling in the grass, their
mixed heritage evident in their features and colouring. Whether Robins
broached the subject or James did so himself, a simple message was passed
on to Commissioner Dumaresq: 'Bugg wishes his children to be brought
up so as to insure the abandonment of their savage life.' For the second
time in Mary Ann's short life, the attention of the Company's Commissioner and ultimately of the New South Wales Governor himself was to be
drawn towards the Bugg family.

Dumaresq wrote back advising that the children would need to be
separated from their mother. James and Charlotte gave their consent.
Dumaresq would later write approvingly that Bugg's woman had always
behaved in a faithful and exemplary manner and, like Bugg himself,
desired to elevate her children above the 'barbarism' of her tribe.

But where should they be sent? Dumaresq asked James if he would prefer the Church Missionary Society's Wellington Valley mission or the government's Port Phillip Native Institution near Melbourne. Not surprisingly, the Buggs opted for Wellington Valley, only 200 miles west of Berrico. James offered to provide £20 for each of his children to assist with their education—an astonishing sum that was both a testament to his love and to the opportunities afforded hard-working convicts in the colony. But all was not well with the Wellington Valley mission, plagued by internal squabbling, the alleged kidnapping of children from Aboriginal families, and reports of illicit relationships between staff and Aboriginal women. The Church Missionary Society suggested the Orphan School instead.

'Why not the Port Phillip Native Institution?' grumbled the Colonial Secretary after receiving Dumaresq's subsequent request. ''Tis preferable to the Orphan School Institution. Sir Richard Bourke objected some time previously to receiving children into the latter under agreements to pay money. But I do not see why they should not be educated at the school which is doubtless established by the Company at Port Stephens.'

No such school had been established at Port Stephens and, after this was pointed out, the Colonial Secretary agreed on 5 February 1838—John Bugg's second birthday—that the Bugg children could be sent to the Orphan School until the Native Institution at Port Phillip was in a 'sufficient state' to receive them. Before any further decisions could be made, however, Commissioner Dumaresq died suddenly of a stroke. In the ensuing Company upheaval, the education of the Bugg children was forgotten.

New South Wales was between governors when approval was granted for the Bugg children's education; Sir Richard Bourke had just left the colony and Sir George Gipps was soon to arrive. The peppery new Governor was not only the Crown's representative, but a walking embodiment of Britain's ideal man, an ambassador representing the human pinnacle of Britain's civilised state: earnestly moral, devoted to wife and the institution of marriage, pious, staunchly evangelical, a man of unflinching principles and little mirth. He was therefore not one to ignore Reverend Threlkeld's report, a few months after his arrival, that some Company servants had taken Aboriginal women from Newcastle to the Liverpool Plains against their wishes, and that these women had been murdered by the local tribes shortly afterwards.

A few weeks later, in June 1838, news reached Government House that convict and ex-convict stockmen and shepherds had massacred twenty-eight Aboriginal men, women and children at Myall Creek. The horrified Governor, who was already under pressure from the Colonial Office on the issue of frontier tension, was determined to set an example, to deter colonists from thinking they could eliminate frontier problems by exterminating the Aboriginal population. Despite vociferous protests from the public, he achieved his aim. In December 1838 seven white bodies hung from the gallows in Sydney.

Aware that much of the tension was caused by white liaisons with Aboriginal women, Gipps tried to deal with that problem as well. He could do little to control the behaviour of settlers or their convict servants; however, he could try to deal with Company infractions. The Australian Agricultural Company had signed a Charter that specifically disallowed liaisons between assigned servants and Aboriginal women. The need for convict labour was a noose around the Company's profit-seeking neck. It was time to tighten it.

James Ebsworth, the Company's interim commissioner, opened the letter from the Colonial Secretary's Office on 7 July 1838. Alarm swept through him as he re-read the bald words: 'The attention of the Governor having been drawn to the alleged fact of black or Aboriginal women frequently living and also travelling about the country with assigned servants of the Company, I am directed to inform you that, if the fact be well authenticated, His Excellency will be under the necessity of withdrawing the whole of the men in the district of the Company's possessions where it occurs.'

The Company had three districts, each employing around two hundred assigned convict servants. If the government could find proof that one such servant was living with an Aboriginal woman, all two hundred in that district might be withdrawn. If one such alliance was found in each of the Company's three districts, all six hundred convict servants might be withdrawn. The Company would be ruined. And what was the undeniable proof? The children. There must be scores of them.

Ebsworth grabbed some paper and began writing. 'I have only this day had the honour to receive your letter of the 20th June,' he began, his alarm leading him to misread the actual date, the 28th. He advised the Governor that the Company tried to prevent such improper intercourse, and that he had recently instructed the superintendents and would continue to remind them—no doubt forcibly after receiving this threatening letter—that any assigned convicts who breached the regulations must be reported to the police. He begged the Governor not to inflict such a costly penalty on the Company, and tactfully mentioned that no specific cases had been listed, intimating that the Governor was responding to rumour rather than report. And with every finger mentally crossed, Ebsworth waited to hear back from the Governor, desperately hoping that the behaviour of their sex-starved convicts was not about to destroy the Company under his interim guardianship.

Reverend William Macquarie Cowper was not intending to create problems for the Bugg family, or for the Company for that matter. The cleric had been asked by the Bishop of Australia to provide information about the habits, capacities, wants and dispositions of his district's Aborigines for the Legislative Council's Committee on the Aborigines Question. On 28 September 1838, he sat in the rectory of St John's Church of England at Stroud, and looked out its French windows towards the bushland beyond. Australia's first colonial-born Anglican clergyman inked his nib.

Aboriginal numbers have rapidly declined in the past decade, he wrote, most likely because of the immoral practices of the Europeans who have infected the natives with diseases. This combined with the recent measles epidemic, the rejection by black men of unfaithful wives, and the tendency of the blacks to kill newborn half-caste children, had contributed to their decline. He added that their habits were usually indolent, although they were not as aggressive or hostile as generally represented; rather they sensed when they had been wronged and, not surprisingly, reacted by taking revenge. They were no less capable of learning; indeed he knew of several who had become very able servants, stockmen, shepherds and sailors. Nor were they insensible to kindness or incapable of gratitude or affection. To illustrate this observation, he recounted a story that had struck him forcibly when he first heard it. A Company overseer at Gloucester named Bugg had been attacked by a group of Aboriginals, but had been saved by the black woman he had taken to live with him. She had seized the musket from the corner of the hut and fired at the attackers.

Two weeks later the Committee's report was ordered to be printed, with Cowper's letter included among the Minutes of Evidence. Thereafter anyone reading the evidence of the Legislative Council's Committee could see a specific example of a liaison between an Australian Agricultural Company employee and an Aboriginal woman.

James Bugg's name had no doubt been mentioned when the problem of Aboriginal liaisons was discussed behind the government's closed doors: the Colonial Secretary's offsider, T.C. Harington, who had approved his children's admission to the Orphan School a few months previously, was also responsible for writing the threatening letter to the Company in June 1838. Yet James' situation was different to most of the other Company workers. Officially he was no longer an 'assigned servant', having received his ticket-of-leave four years before. This colonial version of a parole pass allowed him to reside and work as he chose, so long as he remained within the stated district and attended the necessary musters. James had initially planned to leave the Company—as most convicts did—requesting Goulburn as his future residence, yet at some point between submitting his application and receiving the crisp piece of paper, he had changed his mind. He chose Berrico and Charlotte and little Mary Ann, grateful also for the hefty pay rise from an appreciative Company.

As a ticket-of-leave holder, James owned his own labour, so the government could neither withdraw his services from the Company, nor hold the Company to ransom because of his personal relationships. But the government could unofficially suggest that the Company terminate his services if they wanted to make sure that their assigned servants had no example to follow. Even worse for James, the government could revoke his ticket-of-leave and assign him wherever they wanted, forcing him to abandon Charlotte and the children. Having an Aboriginal family was not a breach of the ticket-of-leave regulations as such, but a pretext wouldn't be hard to find, accompanied by a quiet word in the local magistrate's ear. A ticket-of-leave provided only a fragile liberty.

Most likely, as the year unfolded and as Charlotte fell pregnant with their third child, James had no idea that discussions about Company convicts and their relationships with Aboriginal women were being conducted not only in Sydney's Government House but also back in London, among the worried countenances of the gentlemen sitting around the Australian Agricultural Company's board table. The Company's British Governor refused to meekly submit to Governor Gipps' threat. His angry letter to the Secretary of State for the Colonies declared that the threat was driven by 'animus', by jealousy of the Company's favoured status. He complained about the lack of police protection in outlying districts and also about the quality of the convicts assigned to the Company, saying that many were the most depraved characters from the Iron Gangs, difficult to control by anyone, Company superintendent or free settler alike. He reminded Lord Glenelg that if the New South Wales Governor carried out his unreasonable threat, the result would be disastrous for the Company. Which was also a subtle threat in itself—unhappy shareholders meant unhappy voters in a country where the franchise had recently been extended.

A carefully phrased reply from the Colonial Office advised that the New South Wales Governor most assuredly had no intention of withdrawing convicts without proof that a Company officer had neglected his duty. As it turned out, the Company was soon to face more serious labour problems. Regulations were being implemented that would phase out the assignment of convicts, and the year 1840 saw the cessation of convict transportation to New South Wales altogether.

For a moment, just a fraction of a moment, the future of the Company had rested in the hands of the Aboriginal women whose world had been trampled by the Company's livestock and greed. Naturally, however, no one was going to let the fate of such a large capital investment—or even a small one—rest in the hands of some ill-treated Aboriginal women and their misbegotten offspring. Capital had a power of its own, smoothing pathways and nudging away hurdles—or kicking them aside. Thereafter it was business as usual.

The Company's assigned convicts, warned against keeping 'gins' in their huts, deposited them in Aboriginal camps and visited them there. James Bugg and his family were left alone until eventually the Assistant Commissioner was reminded that nothing had yet been done about the education of Bugg's children.

'The Female Orphan Institution should not be like a Boarding School for Young Ladies who have some prospects in life, but like a House of Industry,'

Reverend Samuel Marsden had grumbled some years earlier. It wasn't the educational regime itself that offended Reverend Marsden, but rather its appearance. The building looked like a Georgian mansion, a gentleman's country house, elegant and sophisticated in its Palladian design, tranquil in its setting but with a commanding air of wealth and authority. A suitable building to house orphans?

Society's benevolence was never intended as a social stepping stone: the girls received enough religious instruction to deflate any social pretensions. A bell awakened them at 5 am, or an hour later in the cold winter months—not out of kindness, of course, but practicality: it cost more in lighting and heating when it was dark. A bell at 7 am signalled morning devotions, which included prayers, psalm reading, extracts from Bloomfield's *Family Prayer Guide*, and hymn singing. Washing, dressing and breakfast between 8 and 9 am, then the formal schoolwork began: instruction in Mrs Trimmer's *Scriptural Catechism*, reading from the New Testament, and the basics of spelling, writing and arithmetic. Exercise from noon until 1 pm, dinner and free time until 2 pm, then three hours of needlework training in which the girls learnt how to make clothes, sheets and mattresses. Supper at 6 pm, evening devotions at dusk, including a New Testament reading, then bed.

Benevolence, well-intentioned though it was, had a price. The Orphan School factory aimed to produce perfect workers, or mothers who would themselves produce ideal workers: pious, honest, well-trained and hard-working, obsequiously polite and respectful to the point of being invisible, compliant—unlike their noisy, defiant convict parents—an example to their peers of the advantages of honesty and industry.

Most of the girls were not orphans in the true sense. Some had destitute parents. Some had been abandoned by one parent through death or desertion, leaving the other parent unable to cope. The Orphan School served as their lifeline. Mary Ann, however, was different, not simply because of her Aboriginal heritage but because of her family's circumstances. This may explain why her name was not recorded in the Female Orphan School admission register, or that of her brother in the Male Orphan School register. No admission entry presumably meant no admission—unless separate long-forgotten registers covered children like the Buggs.

The Company's Assistant Commissioner had not confirmed that it was still acceptable to send the Bugg children to the Orphan School when the matter was raised again in February 1839, a year after receiving permission to send them there. He merely wrote to the Colonial Secretary saying that the children had been baptised the previous day and were on their way to Sydney with their father, and that Bugg would dispose of them as the authorities directed.

Somewhere, tucked into James' boots or in one of his pockets, was the money he had agreed to provide for their education. Forty pounds, a huge sum, most of his annual income no doubt—a hefty investment in his children's future, with more to come if required. Perhaps this prompted the government to enrol them elsewhere—in a day school with bed and board organised separately perhaps, or in the home of a cleric who supplemented his income by taking in some students. Somewhere in Sydney, according to later reports.

Silky black head lowered, fingers clenched around a slate pencil, Mary Ann painstakingly copied the letters onto her slate, beginning the process of learning how to read and write that would engross her for the next five years. No doubt in the early years she cried for her family, for her carefree world among the sheep and lambs, for those endless days when she had little perception of who she was—or what she was, for that matter. She discovered soon enough upon her arrival in Sydney. Sideways looks. Sneers and taunts. She felt the contempt behind words such as 'savage' and 'godless heathen', through the tone of voice and looks that accompanied their delivery.

Other words came to mean something strangely personal as well—'dog', 'ape', 'monkey'—as if the speakers saw something different to the human figure reflected back at her when she walked past a window, the figure that seemed much the same as all the other girls. Not identical of course, but none of them were identical. Some had black hair like her own; some brown like the ageless trees around Berrico, or flaxen like the dead grass in summer; some with a burnished redness that shimmered in the firelight. Different coloured eyes, different shaped bodies, different heights, so why was she the only one marked out for such derision when her skin colour was little darker than many of the other children's?

Because she was a 'half-caste'—another strange word regularly tossed at her, as if she were only half a person, as if there were a line drawn across her middle that split her in two like a half-full glass of milk, or a line from top to bottom that made one side of her appear different to the other. But which was the 'half' and which was the 'caste'; which was good and which was bad, because half was clearly bad? Or was the good and bad all stirred together like her milky-brown skin colour, not light like her father or dark like her mother, but a creamy mix of both. Perhaps there was no good in her at all, because everyone knew that 'half-castes' were doubly damned, the spawn not only of native blacks but of Britain's convict refuse.

The regular church services and endless Bible readings and prayers didn't help her understand. If God loved everyone equally, if God said they were to love everyone equally, then why didn't the people who made her go to church and who read aloud from the Bible treat her as God said they should? To those people, it didn't seem to matter how well she did at school or at sewing or cooking, or what she was like as a person. It didn't matter who *she* thought she was, only what *they* thought she was. Her skin colour seemed like a veil that enveloped her, preventing them seeing the real person beneath.

Gradually she learnt that white was considered clean and pure, that black was dirty and evil. Her father's people were Christian and civilised, blessed by God, and they were graciously bestowing civilisation and the Christian faith on the 'wild savages' who had inhabited the land before them. Christian missionaries were travelling all over the world bringing 'enlightenment' to all the heathens, not just in Australia but also across the water in New Zealand. Wild savages the Maori were as well, yet the voices that spoke of them were not as sneering, not as contemptuous. It was . . . enlightening.

She tried not to let them treat her like she was just the scrapings from their boots. Resilient, fiery and passionate, she learnt how to stand up for herself, with adults as well as other children. She learnt how to slough off the jeers, to find the weaknesses of those who were nasty and to send a sharp jab back at them. School taught her far more than reading and writing, far more than the domestic skills she needed to find suitable work as a servant. It also taught her how to be cruel as others were cruel to her, and to revel in their discomfiture.

5

We have always trusted full in the pure and noble instincts of women, who, unlike our more calculating sex, act best when they act on the impulses of the moment.

Sydney Morning Herald, 2 November 1863

The tinkle of a sheep's bell carrying on a light breeze; the angry barks of warning from the outstation's dogs: Mary Ann had returned home to Berrico after five years in Sydney. Another three siblings now breathed the crisp Berrico air, and an additional three would follow at regular intervals. All would marry and have families of their own, except for her eldest and youngest brothers—but that was much later, of course.

Her father was walking taller somehow, no longer under His Majesty's stern thumb or Her Majesty's equally resolute fingernail. The precious piece of paper declaring him to be a free man—so long as he remained on colonial shores—would later be replaced with an extended conditional pardon, one that allowed him to travel anywhere in the world except Great Britain and Ireland. He had no interest, however, in deserting his family or settling abroad.

Nor was he content with having an Aboriginal 'gin' hidden in his hut. He wanted a wife—in the eyes of God and Man. In 1841 he applied for permission to marry Charlotte, a request passed on to Bishop Broughton for approval, but the conservative prelate believed that one of his Church's primary roles was to uphold the social structure, and his letter of response remarked upon the 'spiritual illegality' of unions between white men and black women. Broughton knew his Bible well: 'Do not be unequally yoked together with unbelievers', and time's wisdom was showing that baptised and unbaptised Aboriginal people alike were mostly unbelievers. 'When the Lord your God brings you into the land which you go to possess . . . you shall conquer them and utterly destroy them,' instructed Deuteronomy, 'nor shall you make marriages with them.' Permission refused.

However, the Bishop did grant permission for their children—those offspring of an 'illicit union'—to be baptised, although he recommended shunting them off to the Orphan School or the Port Phillip Native Institution afterwards. Not surprisingly, James decided that the Church of England had no need for any more souls, not his own family's at any rate. He delayed baptising his younger children until a Wesleyan minister passed through, one who agreed to marry him in addition to baptising the children. But that was much later as well.

From the noisy bustle of Sydney to the calm solitude of the Berrico downs, Mary Ann's world had changed again. Yet still she was being schooled—by Charlotte this time. Mary Ann shared the women's duties with her mother and her sister Eliza, born soon after she went to Sydney. Charlotte showed them how to dig up highly nutritious yams and to gather edible fruits, seeds and berries. She also taught Mary Ann how to read the landscape like her Sydney teachers had taught her to read books, to hear the bush noises and interpret them, to track animals and catch and kill them, and to find water—the most essential survival skill of them all. Consciously or not, Charlotte imbued her daughter with a sense of her Aboriginal heritage and an understanding of the cultural and physical landscape around her.

Was there any other child like Mary Ann in New South Wales at that time, a child who had received the best of both worlds? She was beloved by both parents, a couple who had expressly shown their own love and commitment to each other: James by choosing to marry, and Charlotte by lifting a gun in his defence. She had received a town education, despite her country origins, and had developed a love of reading, and of knowledge in general, that was a far cry from the sporadic and soon-forgotten schooling received by the few Aboriginal or mixed-race children who received any education at all. Yet she had also received a 'country' education, spending much of her youth on a sheep station, while also acquiring the bush knowledge and life skills of her Aboriginal forebears.

Even her brother John, educated as he also was, wouldn't have learnt the ways of both worlds. Mixed-race boys who were accepted by their European fathers were taught their father's ways, missing out on the Aboriginal rites of passage—the critical bonding time when Aboriginal boys learnt men's business and passed from childhood to manhood.

As a result of her upbringing, Mary Ann was a chameleon, a woman who could adapt to both cultures and environments whenever circumstances demanded. Not only could she survive in both, she could thrive in both. In later years, this would save her life.

'Wilt thou take Edmund Baker to be thy lawful wedded husband?'

He stood beside her in the chilliness of St John's Church at Stroud as the weak winter sunshine struggled to warm them. He was only a smidgin taller, but much older—nearly forty to her just-turned fourteen. Hazel eyes gazed at her from a ruddy pock-pitted complexion, the tattoos of a woman and a mermaid hidden by his shirt sleeves.

Baker had lived in the district since before she was born, a convict transported on the *Lady Harewood* in 1831, a country man like her father who was snatched up by a pastoralist when his skills were announced: 'a shepherd who ploughs, reaps and mills'. The pickpockets who roamed London's streets, their ears accustomed to the eternal roar of England's Babylon, rarely had any useful skills and could find the solitude of the Australian bush strangely oppressing, indeed madness-inducing. But not a country-born man like Baker. Transported for poaching rabbits, he was listed as Edward Baker in the convict records (a slip of a clerk's pen again—or was Edward his real name, rather than Edmund?). Assigned to Major Sullivan of the Williams River, he was among the many shepherds who had ventured out warily to mind his flock during the troubles of 1835; however, he had chosen to remain in the district after receiving his ticket-of-leave a few months later, and again after his sentence had expired. Whether he was Mary Ann's choice as a husband, or whether her parents urged him upon her, she stood before the altar on 1 June 1848 and announced: 'I do.'

'Gold!'

The specks glittering in the shallow mountain streams had long been noticed by the local Aboriginals who splashed through them, but were known to have little practical value, being inedible and unusable, too soft for crafting tools. Yet the looks of astonished delight and wonder, hope and lust in the faces of the settlers who spotted the tiny specks in the streams near Bathurst revealed that, to them at least, this 'gold' was seemingly more precious even than water to a parched traveller.

In May 1851 they came: from Bathurst itself and its neighbouring farms and squatting runs, from towns near and far, eventually from all over the world—a plague of red or blue-shirted locusts that travelled inexorably west towards 'the diggins'. The roads became as busy as if a huge army had just marched past and its baggage was lagging behind. Musket-bearing men sat atop drays loaded with stores and mining cradles. Foot soldiers strode after them, their California hats shadowing determined countenances, their dusty new boots chafing tired feet, the word 'gold!' echoing in every weary footstep as they tried to ignore the laughing jackasses mocking them from nearby eucalypts. First, to Ophir, north-east of Orange, arrogantly named by the self-proclaimed gold discoverer, Edward Hargraves, after the source of King Solomon's wealth. Then late in June across the ranges east to the Turon River, to the ford on the road between Bathurst and Mudgee where the town of Sofala sprang up overnight.

And Mary Ann was there to see it all.

She was already living in the vicinity when the excited words 'Turon River' and 'Bigger and better!' started to spread. She saw the miners swarming over the ridges and down the mountain glen, setting up their tents among the swamp oaks lining the Turon's banks, lighting the fires that sent bluish streams into the sky, smoke signals that gave hope to exhausted travellers that they were nearly there. She heard the initial sounds of gravel swishing around the handful of metal cradles, then as bodies continued to throng over the ridges, the noise increased until it was an incessant roar from dawn to dusk, as if a mighty cataract was plunging from a cliff ledge nearby. The sound eased off as darkness fell, to be replaced by the crackle of fires and the spitting of mutton chops sizzling on frying pans, punctuated by laughter and chatter and the occasional drunken shout. Then the sounds eased until dawn, when it began all over again.

Perhaps Mary Ann staked out her own claim in those early days at the Turon, although this seems unlikely as she would have struggled to bend and lift, bend and lift: on 17 July 1851, two days after local squatter W.H. Suttor drove his cart into Bathurst carrying a rock bearing a hundred weight of gold, she gave birth to her eldest son, James, in a rain-lashed hut near the Turon. The child's father? A shepherd named John Burrows.

Burrows was probably one of the many steerage passengers who had arrived in New South Wales unannounced, a Lancastrian from Liverpool, England, according to later reports. When their son was born, he was possibly shepherding for Suttor, one of the two squatters who ran sheep along the Turon's banks in that vicinity. The massive gold-bearing rock had been sitting unnoticed in the middle of Suttor's popular sheepwalk, serving as a backrest for unwitting shepherds until someone noticed a yellow glint and drew a tomahawk from his belt. No doubt, in the aftermath, Burrows himself left no stone unturned—or uncleaved—as his sheep grazed nearby, if he didn't toss away his metaphorical crook and start digging himself.

It was the establishment's greatest fear that gold fever would lead workers everywhere to down tools and head to the diggings, abandoning wives and children to starve in their absence. They also feared that labour shortages would lead to astronomical price rises, that riots at the diggings would draw most of the state's military and police forces towards the district, and worse, that the forces of law and order might be unable to control the violence, that towns and villages across the country would be left unprotected and at the mercy of thieves and highwaymen—that anarchy would reign over New South Wales, all because of that simple four-letter word, 'gold'.

Still the diggers came. By October 1851, a horde of 12,000 miners had descended on Sofala and the Turon, but they were not alone. Others had realised that certain fortunes were to be made at the diggings by supplying goods and services for the miners. Tents listed their callings: blacksmiths, carpenters, surgeons, lemonade sellers, as well as a 'Hair Cutter and Tooth Drawer' and 'Jones' Circus'. However, the Burrows were not among the Sofala residents at that time, if they ever had been. When their son was baptised at Kelso's Holy Trinity Church of England that same month, John was still listed as a shepherd at the Turon River.

John and Mary Ann left the Turon within the following two years, heading north-east to James Walker's Loowee sheep station near Rylstone. There Mary Ann gave birth to her second son, John, in October 1853, and had him baptised early in 1854 at St John's Church of England in Mudgee. In 1855 she fell pregnant again, giving birth to a daughter Mary Jane in March 1856. The father? An Irish Catholic ex-convict named James McNally.

McNally was also around Mary Ann's height, but he was twenty years older, an 'indifferent' Irish tailor from Cork who, with two others, was sentenced to seven years' transportation for assaulting and robbing a man. Arriving in New South Wales on board the *Backwell* in September 1835, he was assigned to a settler in the Paterson district north of Maitland and remained in the area after receiving his ticket-of-leave. He was probably among the thousands lured to the Bathurst district by the gold rush, eventually settling to farm at Cooyal, north-east of Mudgee. He and Mary Ann had a further two children in the years that followed—Patrick Christopher in December 1857, and Ellen in March 1860.

Then one day early in 1861, Mary Ann fell pregnant again. The father? Another man entirely.

Four partners in thirteen years. Was Mary Ann the victim of serial abandonment by her white partners, like so many other Aboriginal and mixed-race women? Firstly her husband Edmund Baker, then shepherd John Burrows, then farmer James McNally.

A Stroud magistrate who knew her family would later ask what had happened to her husband. 'Dead,' she would tell him. 'At Mudgee.'

And now?

Married again, she would reply airily, 'by a Wesleyan minister'.

In truth, this was nothing more than a convenient fiction. At that critical moment in her future life, it was essential to suggest that she had abided by at least some of society's mores, for much of her behaviour was of a more questionable nature.

The infant James Burrows, for example, was not her first child. Her husband Edward Baker apparently fathered her eldest child, a daughter named Helena born around 1849. He then disappears from colonial records. Perhaps he died within a year or two of their marriage and was buried in the bush, as so many were at that time—although almost certainly not at

Mudgee, as there is no evidence to suggest he ever lived there. More likely, he was still alive. But who broke up the marriage?

Mary Ann's actions both then and later suggest that she effected most, if not all, of the separations. Flaws in Baker's character or behaviour might initially have undermined her marriage. Or maybe Mary Ann was tugged away by the demands of her own character, lonely, bored and frustrated by a marriage of obedience to an illiterate man old enough to be her father. Yet for a young mother to walk out of her marriage, to defy the rules drummed into her during her years attending school and church, to break a sacred union blessed by God—a union that her father had tried so hard to make with her mother—would require either remarkable courage or social defiance, traits that Mary Ann would later amply display.

Within a year or two of her marriage she encountered young John Burrows, only twenty-two years to her sixteen when she fell pregnant with his son. They presumably met while the Bakers were residing near Stroud, then ran away—before or after Mary Ann fell pregnant—travelling west to the Bathurst district where John found work as a shepherd.

A different part of the world, but the same lonely existence among the bleating sheep. Mary Ann seems to have left John Burrows of her own volition, as few men who abandoned their wives took responsibility for their children like Burrows did. She seems to have abandoned James McNally as well, as he also took responsibility for their older two children in the aftermath, having them baptised in Mudgee's Catholic Church a few years later.

Her fourth partner? At Cooyal her eyes alighted upon young Frederick Ward, a stockman and horse-breaker working at a nearby property—a flash, talkative fellow, and a tall man, compared with her previous partners at least: a colonial Adonis.

Mary Ann's decision to leave James McNally for the wiry young horse-breaker—and in particular her pregnancy to that horse-breaker—would lead to more than just the birth of a daughter. The circumstances surrounding her daughter's delivery would play a pivotal role in the birth of a legend, that of the gentleman bushranger Captain Thunderbolt.

PART 2

VICE

The children born in this colony from European parents
are very robust, comely and well-made . . . They are remarkably
quick of apprehension, learn anything with uncommon
rapidity, and greatly improve in good manners,
promising to become a fine race of people.

G. Paterson, *The History of New South Wales*

6

'The natives' [white colonial-born] know little about old England and care less. They generally suppose that it is the head-quarters of a large convict population, judging from the number of those gentry whom it annually casts forth.

J.P. Townsend, *Rambles and Observations*

James Nicholson was puzzled. A clerk for distillers John and William Nicholson of Woodbridge Street, Clerkenwell, London, he had been working in their counting house on the bleak winter's evening of 16 February 1814 when he noticed Thomas Dodman lurking at the top of the cellar stairs. Not that Dodman's presence itself was a problem: the 37-year-old was a servant and had a right to be there. It was the way Dodman stared back that aroused his suspicions. He left the counting house and hastened towards the servant, noticing as he neared that Dodman's offsider, 26-year-old Michael Ward, was nowhere to be seen.

'Where's Ward?' he demanded.

'Down in the cellar,' the strangely furtive servant admitted, continuing to hover near the cellar door as Nicholson clumped down the stairs.

In the gloomy cellar, Nicholson spotted Ward and headed towards him, asking what he was doing. The usually ruddy-complexioned servant seemed agitated. He offered trifling excuses to explain his presence and skittered around the cellar as if trying to avoid the clerk. Nicholson dogged his heels, following him back up the stairs and through the distillery until Ward was forced to take a sharp turn. A splash teased the air.

'What are you hiding?' Nicholson demanded, as he reached out to grab Ward by the collar. The glum servant reluctantly pulled a bladder of rectified spirits from his breeches and handed it over. Nicholson kept his grip on Ward, while shouting to another clerk to collar Dodman, who had foolishly followed them into the distillery; then he sent for the distillery owner and the police.

A quick change-over left the owner in charge of the docile Michael Ward and James Nicholson, his less tractable companion. Dodman immediately begged to be allowed a visit to the 'necessary'. James Nicholson told him not to move. Dodman seemed to stand still as ordered; however, unseen by his captors, he slipped his hand inside his waistcoat pocket and began slowly pulling it out again.

'He's drawn a knife!' James Nicholson yelled, glimpsing the flash of the blade. He seized Dodman's arm and the two men began to fight for control of the knife. The distillery owner released his grip on Ward and leapt into the fray. As his body collided with Dodman's, they all heard a clatter on the floor nearby. Dodman had deliberately tossed the knife away.

The three men wrestled while Michael Ward stood by watching, making no attempt to flee. Outnumbered, Dodman was thrown onto his back, but he refused to accept defeat. With a mighty heave he pushed the other men aside and scrambled to his feet. Instead of taking to his heels, however, he threw himself down again, this time onto his belly.

The astonished Nicholsons pulled Dodman up again and frisked him. They soon discovered the bladder of spirits stashed in his pants. Dodman had thrown himself onto his belly in an attempt to burst it. And the knife? It wasn't intended to threaten or wound his captors, as they had initially thought. Rather, it was his first abortive attempt at destroying the incriminating evidence.

They tied Dodman's hands, but still he refused to submit. He pretended to faint, slumping onto his back. When a police officer arrived soon afterwards, the Nicholsons showed him the fainted felon. 'I'll soon bring him back,' the officer assured them, and gave Dodman a thump on the head. Then he handcuffed the thieves and hustled them to the nearby police office.

'How did you come to do it?' the officer later asked Dodman.

'We are two rogues together,' was the simple response.

Would-be rogues more likely. The pair lacked the calculated insouciance of professional thieves, their giveaway agitation a sign of inexperience and guilty consciences. Yet whatever drove them to steal from their employers, the consequences were devastating: at their Old Bailey trial on 20 April 1814, they were ordered to the gallows. To a society that placed a high value on possessions—indeed, that judged a person's worth by the value of their possessions—Ward and Dodman's lives were worth less than a couple of gallons of grog.

Fortunately a reprieve to life transportation banished the two felons to Antipodean exile, sailing on the convict transport *Indefatigable* later that year. Michael's bride, Sophia Jane Elizabeth Ann Ward, applied to join him, arriving in Sydney with her daughter Sophia in June 1815, two months after her husband. By that time Ward—who was perhaps using the name Michael as an alias, as he later called himself Handley Thompson Ward—had been forwarded to the Windsor district, 30 miles north-west of Sydney, for assignment to a settler. Sophia immediately wrote to the Governor requesting that her husband be granted a ticket-of-leave so he could support his needy family.

Governor Lachlan Macquarie believed in the civilising influence of marriage and family life, and abhorred the colonial trend of illicit cohabitation. He knew that a married woman left on her own might soon find a 'protector' in a colony populated by four lustful Adams to every Eve. His Scottish frugality also saw the disadvantage of extra burdens on the government purse, particularly when he had grand plans for Sydney's development. He scrawled his hasty approval. Accordingly, after serving only fifteen months of his life sentence, Michael Ward was effectively paroled. There on the banks of the mighty Hawkesbury River, he and Sophia were reunited, spending the next few decades tilling its rich alluvial flood plains.

A 'currency lad' was their son Fred Ward, one of the growing breed of colonial-born males who bore the nickname with pride. A military paymaster had first used the terms 'currency' and 'sterling' to distinguish colonial-born from British-born; the circulating 'colonial currency' of Spanish dollars, Dutch guilders, ducats, promissory notes and anything else that found its way ashore had a lesser value than the imperial 'pound sterling', and the nicknames soon slipped into the common vernacular. Haughty British settlers tried to use the term 'currency' disparagingly, determined to remind such colonial-born parvenus that their very birthplace meant they were second-rate and lacked their superiors' 'sterling' qualities. The colonials gradually turned the tables on them, puffing up with pride and delighting in the irritation it caused.

Frederick Wordsworth Ward—to use his full name, one that even a hoity-toity British matron would coo over with pride—was the youngest of ten children born to Michael and Sophia Ward in the two decades after they were reunited. Most grew up on the family's two-acre block in Wilberforce, north of Windsor. Michael rented nearby farming land, although he was seemingly a reluctant agriculturalist: in 1828 he applied to have his ticket-of-leave district transferred to Sydney. If his request had been granted, Fred would have grown up as a town lad, probably apprenticed to a trade rather than being tossed into a saddle before he could even walk. How different his life might have been—those bred in Sydney rarely became rangers of the bush.

Fred himself was born in 1835, around the time the Wards left what was little more than a flourishing village and moved a few miles south across the Hawkesbury River to Windsor. There they settled in a brick or stone house in Macquarie Street, the main thoroughfare of the pretty market town, with its well-built houses and vivid gardens, its churches and amply supplied shops. The town itself sat on a sandstone cliff high above the Hawkesbury, undaunted by the majesty of the Blue Mountains in the distance.

A 'gloomy grandeur' was Reverend Thomas Atkins' dismissive appraisal of Windsor when he resided there soon after the Ward's relocation. As for the town's 1200 souls: 'Ignorance, immoral practices and irreligion prevailed,' he would later rage in his memoir. 'Indeed, "the grace of God, which bringeth salvation to all men" had not taught them that "denying ungodliness and worldly lusts, they should live soberly, righteously and godly in this present world".'

Irreligion? In the Ward household, absolutely. Only one baptised child, whose spiritual salvation was not considered necessary until she was ten and probably ill.

Immoral practices? A plague upon thy house indeed. Second daughter Sarah Ann already had two bairns clutching at her skirts by the time she decided to tie the knot. As for ignorance—well, what could the gentry expect when many of their brethren, including clergymen, rejected the idea of national education for fear that the masses would forget their place in society and question both the social hierarchy and the tenets of religion— even the power of the church itself?

While Michael Ward had little interest in religion, he saw the value of schooling for his burgeoning family. He financed his elder children's education at the Church of England school at Wilberforce, and probably paid for Fred to attend the local Windsor school after the family's relocation there. Michael's willingness to fund his children's education perhaps reflects middle-class origins, a background suggested by his family's use of middle names, a trend rarely followed by the lower orders at that time. Honouring their youngest son with the middle name 'Wordsworth' not only suggested a middle-class love of poetry, but reflected hope for the future: that the shadow of greatness—an educated greatness—might fall over their infant son. It was not to be. Like some of his elder siblings, this horse-loving youngster resisted drinking too deeply from that worthy trough. Fred later reported that he could read only; like so many rural menfolk he was barely literate.

The Wards were not alone in having little interest in Reverend Atkins' sober and godly existence. Most Windsor residents were too busy trying to make money and have fun. While the fettered prisoners mending the roads provided a sober reminder of the consequences of sin, their military guardians were a boon to the town's social life. The sight of the uniformed officers mounted on their spirited chargers sent many a young maiden into a swoon, and the lads into wide-eyed hero worship—not necessarily aimed at the riders. 'A jolly lot of fellows,' the military men were called by the 'sterling' townsfolk, who welcomed them at pubs and picnics, dinners and dances. They tossed coins alongside them and shouted for their favourites at cockfights and dog-fights and boxing matches. They played cricket together and eagerly awaited the horse-races. Indeed, the sport of kings was a particular favourite among the officers as well as the locals.

The Windsor meet was one of the biggest events in the Hawkesbury social calendar, not just a series of horse-races but a county fair. Gentlemen from Sydney and distant parts of the colony swept into town in their handsome equipages, settlers bundled family members into carts, locals strolled to the racetrack. Most brought food with them, but had no need to carry grog: the local publicans were happy to oblige. Men huddled at booths betting on games of chance or the races themselves. Musicians struck up a jaunty tune. Lads and lasses flirted on the dancing platform. And those who 'drank not wisely but too well' were shackled to a huge chain outside the racetrack and spent the next few hours howling their indignation.

The pot for the races was only small. Men hunched over horses' necks and thundered down the racetrack for the glory of winning, while wide-eyed boys watched and admired and dreamed, young Fred Ward among them.

Meanwhile, over all the fun and frivolity, the massive belltower of St Matthew's frowned. It saw the results of wages lost drinking and gambling, of beaten wives and starving children, of desires that exceeded limited incomes. But its peals of warning were rarely heeded.

While the 'sterling' townsfolk enjoyed the military presence, the emancipists and their native-born offspring weathered their contempt. To the gentry and military officers, to the government officials and free settlers, an indelible 'broad arrow' emblazoned the emancipists' foreheads, while their offspring bore a sins-of-the-father tattoo. And nobody was allowed to forget it.

Earlier governors like Lachlan Macquarie had tried to foster a different attitude, arguing that emancipists—the time-expired or pardoned convicts—had paid their dues to society and should be treated according to their own merits. Land was one of his rewards. The land taken away from the Aboriginals was given to those he considered worthy, freed convicts among them, although the powerful and wealthy were the main beneficiaries.

The gentry disagreed with Macquarie's treatment of the emancipists. Once a convict, always a convict, they proclaimed. Their anger at Macquarie's attitude fed the dark clouds amassing on his horizon, and their views found support from Commissioner John Thomas Bigge, who had been despatched to the colony to determine if transportation was still effective as a punishment and deterrent. The resulting storm of dissatisfaction washed away liberal attitudes as well as many of the old regulations, those affecting land alienation among them. By the mid-1820s, land grants were restricted to those with capital, mainly wealthy free settlers who strutted their superiority over the emancipists and colonial-born. Those with land aplenty were allowed to grab more, while those without were dismissed empty-handed. Grants were abolished altogether in 1831, and thereafter Crown land was sold at a price only the financially well endowed could afford, with the resulting funds used to finance assisted immigration rather than rural development. The rights of the colonial-born to a foothold on their own land were ignored. In a society where landholding size was increasingly a measure of social worth, Fred and his siblings, like most of the white native-born, had no more value than the Aboriginal people their society had displaced.

Resentment grew. Resentment at the establishment, who saw them as members of a 'criminal class', the offspring of Cain, a stigmatised race not only bred to crime but trained to crime and unworthy of receiving the government's largesse. Resentment at the wealthy farmers who gobbled up their small farms when environmental forces wreaked havoc on crops and pocket-books. Resentment at the wealthy squatters who paid next to nothing for domains that stretched across increasingly larger areas of countryside, and at the immigrants whose own demand for land made them competitors, even enemies. And resentment at everyone who failed to recognise that those born and bred to the land—those who felt one with the Australian landscape—had a better chance of successfully living off the land than strangers transplanted onto alien soil.

A few travellers who discarded the blinkers of prejudice saw that most of the native-born had not been bred to vice, that they were generally loyal and honest, sober and industrious, the worthy offspring of emancipist parents who had themselves settled down to a lawful existence in this new land of opportunity. They realised that New South Wales was not the hotbed of crime that a country populated by the 'criminal class' should have been—if such a class truly existed. But, of course, the powers-that-be saw only what they wanted to see, particularly those who wanted a two-class rural system, with a landed aristocracy supported by a labouring class: a little England on Antipodean soil.

Like most marginalised groups, the rural native-born grew closer together, developing their own values and codes of behaviour, a shared world view, a loyalty and clannishness that led them to support each other— the iconic Australian 'mateship'. They refused to grovel to authority, as expected of the 'lower orders', and despised those who so demeaned themselves; indeed, they distrusted and felt alienated from authority altogether, like their convict parents before them. They scorned British arrogance and the notion that the British Empire was God's gift to mankind, and felt few ties to the Crown. They rejected British class distinctions, where birth and wealth were the stepping stones to power and prestige; rather they had an egalitarian attitude, an instinctual democratic viewpoint, believing that everyone should be allowed a 'fair go'—everyone who wasn't a newcomer or outsider, that is. They valued physical prowess rather than educational or cultural achievements, and were quietly courageous with a strength of will that led them to 'soldier on' despite the hardships and injustices they faced. And they made sure that the 'tall poppies'—anyone who tried to overstep their mark, or to lord it over the rest of them—were soon chopped down to size.

The establishment was appalled at the colonial-born's refusal to bow down before their superior Britishness, and scorned them all the more. Others who saw the injustice in the treatment meted out to them pondered what the outcome might be. Would the colonial-born eventually rise up in rebellion, seeking to chop off these oppressive hands?

And if they did so, what might be the trigger?

7

His whole ambition seemed to be what he was—an oracle upon all subjects
connected with his own peculiar occupation and the most fearless rider in
the district, one who had never yet failed to 'head [the animals]' or refused
to follow them down anything short of a precipice.

Quoted in Russel Ward, *Australian Legend*

The boat was late.

Unbeknown to young Fred Ward, waiting patiently in Morpeth
early in 1847, his employer's vessel had run aground in the choppy mouth of
the Hunter River at Newcastle. Thomas George Wilson, Esq., co-owner and
soon to be resident manager of the Aberbaldie station east of Tamworth,
had begun the long journey from Sydney with his family. Accompanying
them was fifteen-year-old schoolboy Frederick Milford, the son of Samuel
Milford, Esq., Master-in-Equity of the New South Wales Supreme Court
and co-owner of Aberbaldie. Over the next few months, Fred Ward would
come to know Milford Junior very well indeed.

Milford Senior had long aspired to join the squattocracy. On Britain's
social ladder, gentlemen with landed estates perched proudly on the golden
rungs allotted to the gentry, and a similar ladder scaled the more modest
heights of New South Wales society. While elegant Sydney mansions and
quaint country estates were socially advantageous, pastoral properties
provided the greatest source of wealth—a double advantage for successful
barristers and government administrators who sought lucrative profits as
well as social esteem. For those profiting from less noble pursuits—from

that dirty little word 'trade'—investing in pastoral estates served as a form of colonial money laundering.

Squatting runs were easily acquired in New South Wales. Ten pounds was all the squatters had to pay the government for their annual licensing fee, for their right to hold thousands of acres—tens of thousands in many instances. An insignificant fee indeed, yet it was considerably more than the 'nothing' they had paid a decade previously: hence the appellation 'squatters'. Of course, the purchase price demanded by a current licence-holder might be thousands of pounds if stock was included, and if the land was ideal and the economy booming, although the New South Wales depression of the early 1840s had deflated land and livestock prices.

Gentlemen squatters with vast pastoral estates enjoyed the topmost rungs of the social ladder, members of the colonial nobility—albeit by perception (principally their own) rather than title. While most remained on their perches enjoying the view—especially down their noses at the colonial riffraff—some used their rungs as launch pads to spring across to a new ladder: politics. Cattle and sheep provided the income that allowed unpaid politicians to support themselves while they enjoyed the power and prestige of politics. Not surprisingly, these squatter–politicians kept their own interests firmly in mind when it came to making new laws regarding domestic affairs. These laws even regulated the private employment of rural lads like Fred Ward, who continued to wait in Morpeth until his employers arrived three days later.

Fred was the 'generally useful hand' employed by the Aberbaldie agents to accompany the cavalcade from Morpeth to Aberbaldie, and to remain at the station in the aftermath. A skilled horseman, he knew the route well and came highly recommended. Presumably the agents mentioned that the new station hand was only eleven years of age—if Fred had told them his true age. Milford Junior would later write that Fred Ward was 'around twelve' when he worked at Aberbaldie. Eleven . . . twelve . . . thirteen: the moon waxed and waned no differently for youth than adult, yet the physical and emotional changes during the same timeframe were extraordinary. Moreover, while twelve-year-old boys were considered suitable candidates for apprenticeships and other trainee positions—neophytes lapping up a master's wisdom—their duties carried little responsibility. Employing a boy aged 'around twelve' as the only guard and guide for a trap-driving city gentleman, his pregnant wife and infant son, and their nurse and school-boy companion as they travelled 240 miles in territory that could still suffer bushranger incursions was a different matter entirely. Clearly the Aberbaldie agents thought Fred a lad of exceptional maturity indeed—knowledgeable beyond his years, capable, trustworthy and reliable.

These skills were not learnt in the schoolroom. Fred's father had finally given up his agricultural pursuits in the mid-1840s, moving his family to the thriving town of West Maitland, west of Newcastle, where he found work with businessman Jacob Gorrick. Presumably he served in one of Gorrick's stores, as he would later be described as a 'dealer', suggesting that he eventually established his own business.

Most of Fred's elder brothers, however, had little interest in town pursuits. They had long worked in the pastoral industry and regularly took the younger boys droving with them. Stockmen like the Ward brothers sometimes built up herds of their own by accepting wages in livestock, and supplementing their income by some judicious cattle duffing. Under-standably, these were among the vanguard that pushed the frontier inland, as they sought suitable grazing land beyond the nineteen settled counties and the easy reach of the law. Not that they were the only rural dwellers to dabble in stock theft. Struggling landholders occasionally supplemented their diet by butchering a sheep or cow belonging to a prosperous neigh-bour, while wealthy pastoralists themselves turned a blind eye to their own stockmen's depredations. Livestock thefts were largely shrugged away by the rural community—so long as they remained small-scale. They were considered more a nuisance than a crime.

While Fred's brothers were not among the stockmen-turned-squatters whose livestock roamed the frontier lands, they were men well versed in bush law. As they hunkered around night-time camp fires, warming hands over crackling blazes and bellies with swigs of rum, they recounted tales of their own adventures, or those heard beside other dancing flames, unwit-tingly communicating to the enthralled lads the wisdom and values of the bush. The rural status quo was among the many lessons in bush law that Fred received during his stockman training—an apprenticeship that began the moment he was first lifted into a saddle, and ended when he was taken into the Aberbaldie owners' employ at the age of eleven, if not before.

•

The three-day delay while Fred's employer's boat lay aground at the mouth of the Hunter River was little hardship, considering the weather conditions. Pelting rain, gale-force winds: a bleak existence for those on board, as well as anyone taking to the roads. Eventually the river bed loosened its grip and the boat sailed on to Morpeth, where the Aberbaldie party disembarked and rested for the night.

The cavalcade set off the following day, Wilson and family in a large trap pulled by two horses while Master Milford and Fred Ward trotted behind on their own horses. Although Aberbaldie lay 130 miles due north of Morpeth, Fred directed them to the Great North Road, which arched west around the almost impassable mountains (now known as the Barrington Tops), adding another hundred miles to their bone-jolting journey.

First to Maitland, then along the main road towards Patricks Plains (now Singleton), where they would sleep the second night. As the two young horsemen followed the trap, Fred pointed out places of interest, even explaining to Master Milford that the Hunter River, a salty estuary at Morpeth, was the same freshwater stream that gurgled over a pebble-bed at Patricks Plains. He was a chatty lad, a font of local knowledge, and Milford would later be able to recollect many of his tales.

The next day they travelled on to Muswellbrook, where they were greeted with an unexpected invitation to stay at Segenhoe station, some seven miles distant. So they did—for six weeks. For Fred's employers, the visit was both business and pleasure, as the large Segenhoe station was managed by two Scottish overseers, who had themselves purchased Aberbaldie's neighbouring Walcha station. For Master Milford, it was all pleasure as he joined the large party of residents and guests at their picnics and dances and leisurely rides into Scone and Aberdeen. Well, almost all pleasure: the dangers of the Australian bush were ever-present, as he realised one day when he lost his way during a long country ramble and noticed four dingoes eyeing him as if they had just agreed upon their dinner menu.

As for Fred, he was relegated to the stables. While the Aberbaldie party enjoyed Segenhoe's hospitality, he helped pay the price. He looked after his party's four horses and assisted the Segenhoe station hands with their own duties, all the while watching and listening and exploring, adding to the encyclopaedia of rural knowledge that his young brain already contained.

When the Aberbaldie party eventually left Segenhoe, he knew as much as anyone needed to know about the station itself and the nearby terrain.

From Segenhoe they headed north to Murrurundi, with Fred continuing to educate and entertain his young companion. He pointed east towards a mountain crowned with a drift of smoke, as if an invisible Aboriginal tribe was keeping the camp fires constantly burning, and mentioned that it was called the Burning Mountain. Aboriginal eyes had seen a seated woman in the mountain's barren escarpments, the Stone Woman of Wingen: a distraught wife who had cried tears of fire after her warrior husband failed to return from battle, tears that transformed her into stone and set the mountain alight. Geologists, as intrigued as young Milford, had identified the smoke's source as a layer of perpetually burning coal inside the mountain itself. The 5000-year-old smoke signal was nature's beacon for those travelling in the bush.

The stories continued as they rode north from Murrurundi the following day, passing Doughboy Hollow, a gully between two hills. Fred led Milford over to a thicket of gums and pointed to some gashes in the stringybark. 'Bullet holes,' he reported with relish. As they rode off again, keeping within sight of the lumbering trap, Fred recounted the tale of the day when the trees received their distinctive scars. 'A notorious bushranger who went under the name of "the Jewboy" had collected nearly a score of government men [convicts] to form a daring gang which had committed various robberies and murders and other atrocities for some weeks,' he began.

In the eerie quietness of the bush, the stillness broken by sudden rustles in nearby shrubs and discordant cries of invisible birds, Fred had his young companion's wide-eyed attention. It was the type of tale that delighted adventurous youths, particularly those who bucked at society's apron strings.

'They had been camping at Doughboy Hollow for some days,' Fred continued, 'when Mr Denny Day, the police magistrate of Maitland, got news as to their whereabouts and followed them with some dozen mounted policemen. Leaving their horses and taking advantage of the trees, they came close to the bushrangers.'

The young bush bard knew when to pause for a moment, to drop his voice, to stretch out the tension. 'They shot the leader, the Jewboy, and two others while the remainder made a fierce resistance but at last they all laid down their arms and were taken to Maitland and tried at the next assizes and were all hanged.'

Young Milford would always remember Fred's tale of 'the Jewboy'—the bushranger Edward Davis, who had been executed only a few years previously. Yet by the time Milford eventually recounted the tale in his own memoirs, it wasn't the story itself that intrigued him, but the irony.

Horseback rides from Sydney to the beaches and races, the 240-mile journey from Morpeth to Aberbaldie: young Milford was becoming quite arrogant about his prowess on a horse. Until, soon after their arrival at Aberbaldie, he tried to ride one of the station's stock-horses.

Fred and his fellow stockmen enjoyed wiping the smirks off the faces of Hyde Park promenaders. The gentlemen's sons were ideal targets, especially those who thought themselves superior simply because they were 'pure merinos'—the latest nickname for the British-born gentry, one that was also implicitly insulting to the colonial-born. Rural lads like Fred could ride the spirited stock-horses so confidently that they made it look easy—too easy, as Milford would soon discover. The rapid spins and sudden darts in the opposite direction proved an unsettling reminder of the contents of his last meal. With new eyes of respect, Milford watched Fred and the other Aberbaldie stockmen after he stood on shaky legs beside one of the station's nimble stock-horses.

Fred remained at Aberbaldie for some time after the trip north. A pretty station, park-like in appearance, it ran thousands of sheep—not that colonial lads like Fred would deign to work with sheep. Shepherds huddled on the lowest rung of the rural occupational ladder, their menial duties considered suitable only for the 'government men'. Stockmen enjoyed a higher status, horse-breakers even higher again, their skills in the saddle embodying all that was considered masculine in the bush.

Some stockmen remained on a station for years, however most regularly moved on; the colonial-born equivalent of going walkabout was driven by a restlessness that led them to seek new environments and adventures. Most stockmen spent time droving, and even at the age of eleven—or likely twelve by this time—Fred was experienced and responsible enough to take young Milford droving. They were ordered to ride 120 miles to a station near Barraba and collect some cattle, then drive them back to Aberbaldie. Except, in this instance, collecting the cattle didn't mean counting them out of the stockyard. They had to muster them first.

An early breakfast, hot and filling, then Fred and the other stockmen picked up their stockwhips and punched on their hats, gripped with a suppressed eagerness like a British youth on his inaugural fox-hunt. Calling the cattle dogs, they mounted their well-rested stock-horses and headed out, splitting into parties of two or three as they rode into the mountains, scouring the ranges and gullies until they spotted a beast. Bullocks three or four years old and wild as mountain stags, cows defiantly protecting their calves, young bulls who glared at the intruders while ominously pawing the ground. A voice hollered, a whip cracked: the startled beast bounded towards his usual camping place with the determination of a frightened toddler seeking the folds of his mother's skirts. Fred darted off in pursuit, skilfully flicking his whip so the thong-tip snapped the flesh on the 'wrong' side, forcing the beast to bolt in a new direction. He plunged down the scrubby mountainside after his prey, knees gripping the saddle, reins held almost vertical, a challenging, exhilarating descent.

More and more cattle hurtled from the bushes and joined the unhappy herd on the plains, cows frantically lowing for their lost calves and calves for their mothers, bulls bellowing their fury. As the sun's rays weakened, Fred and the other stockmen retreated to the plains and began driving the beasts towards the makeshift cattle yard. The noise grew louder as hundreds of reluctant hooves began to pound the soil, a deep-seated rumble as if the earth itself was protesting against the assault. Horses and dogs continued to prance around the perimeter, momentarily darting away in pursuit of a determined escapee before urging it back into the fold. Eventually the stockmen closed the gates and slipped from their exhausted horses. Man and mount would rest for a day, then return to the mountains to flush out more cattle.

It was a world where men were not judged by their birthplace or pedigree or title, by their wealth or the name of their school or tailor. Indeed, such measures of worth seemed absurd in the bush, where triumph—indeed survival—rested upon physical prowess and courage. It was a world as different as any young Milford could have imagined, one that would seem almost dream-like during his later medical studies back in England, and his years lecturing at the University of Sydney's Medical School and serving as Senior Surgeon at both St Vincent's and Prince Alfred Hospitals. It was a time bound up with memories of a particular young yet eminently capable bushman, although their paths parted during that Barraba cattle muster. Instead of returning with the cattle, Fred Ward left Aberbaldie's employ to seek work elsewhere.

Perhaps Fred found work at the Tareela station near Barraba in the aftermath, or possibly his employment there as a stockman and horse-breaker occurred in later years as he roamed through the Hunter River, Liverpool Plains and New England districts. His parents continued to reside in West Maitland and welcomed home their roving sons whenever their dusty boots strode up the path.

Sometimes Fred's older brothers settled at their parents' home for a while, variously advertising the services of Young Bassano and Honest Tom, a couple of 'entire horses' the family kept for breeding. The Wards had stud-farm aspirations; however, the sons of rural-dwelling emancipists often found it difficult to achieve business success. Most lacked the necessary capital or affluent friends, and the banks' attitudes naturally mirrored those of the gentry. The sins of their father continued to haunt these Australian sons.

Life meandered along for the Ward family in the decade after they settled in West Maitland. Fred's eldest sister Sophia died around the time of their relocation, and the gravediggers were again employed for brothers Edward and George, in 1851 and 1854 respectively. George was working for Charles Reynolds of the famed Tocal cattle and horse station on the Paterson River, north of Maitland, when he and Tocal's superintendent, Henry Lowcock, attempted to drive cattle across a West Maitland ford. The mob took the wrong track. George rode around to head them off, but his horse stepped into a hole and fell, hurling him into the deep, swiftly flowing water. Lowcock, who couldn't swim, had the sense to throw out his stockwhip lash, but George said he was all right and foolishly didn't grab hold of it. His inquest jury was so concerned at the many recent deaths there that it recommended employing a constable to stop people crossing when the river was 'in fresh'.

No one was to blame for George's unfortunate death, and relations between Tocal and the Wards seemingly remained cordial. Fred himself worked there as a stockman and horse-breaker for a year, and his brother William for eight or nine months after Fred left. Soon afterwards, William went into partnership with Michael Blake, growing wheat and grazing cattle at Lambs Valley, a secluded property some twelve miles north-west of Tocal.

Then late in 1855 or early in 1856, the brothers' 21-year-old nephew, John Garbutt, made contact again with his West Maitland relations.

Life would meander along for the Ward family no longer.

John Garbutt was only a month shy of his fifth birthday when he saw his father drown. It wasn't the first drama in his young life. His father, John Garbutt Senior, had a drinking problem, which perhaps explains why his mother, Fred Ward's elder sister Sarah Ann, ran off with another man in 1836 or 1837. Sarah was around twenty-one at that time and already had three children: James, born in 1833, the product of a previous relationship, although he too would carry the surname Garbutt thereafter; John himself, born in 1834, and Maria in 1836. Garbutt Senior refused to allow Sarah custody of their two children, but he didn't fight for Sarah herself after her new partner paid him off with a horse. Young Maria was in the care of a nurse and John in the boat with his father when Garbutt Senior drowned in August 1839.

'What is to be done with Garbutt's property and children?' asked the Coroner, his reference to the children seemingly almost an afterthought.

Young John was eventually taken in by John Crowder, a farmer and pastoralist who lived at Lochinvar just a few miles west of Maitland. He remained with Crowder until 1849, before making his way north to what is now Queensland. In 1853 he accepted work at a Darling Downs property adjacent to that of James Snowden Calvert, who had accompanied the renowned explorer, Ludwig Leichhardt, on his first expedition into the interior.

Two years later, John fled south. The authorities had issued a warrant for his arrest for horse-stealing.

•

Fred was in trouble as well.

'I know nothing,' the twenty-year-old chimed when brought before the Muswellbrook Bench on 3 December 1855, on charges of cattle-stealing.

Fred was a drover at the time, having been employed by Augustus Frederick Anderson to help drive a mob of cattle south to the markets. At Murrurundi their mob mingled with another. At Muswellbrook, Anderson sold two bullocks and handed over the requested receipts. Soon afterwards, the purchasers gave the required butchering notice to the Chief Constable, who pulled out his Inspector of Cattle eyeglass and discovered that the bullocks' brands failed to match those listed in Anderson's receipts.

'I was only employed by Anderson to drive the herd down the country,' Fred declared to the Bench when he and Anderson were prosecuted by the rightful owners.

Fred's defence would ultimately prove successful—but only because he wasn't present when the cattle were sold. Perhaps his claimed ignorance was true; more likely he had turned a blind eye to Anderson's activities. Such was the way of the bush.

This close shave with the law should have taught Fred a salutary lesson. It did, although not quite the lesson the authorities intended.

8

The infectiousness of crime is like that of the plague.

Napoleon Bonaparte

Constable Richard Keating of the Wollombi police prided himself on the watchful eye he kept over neighbourhood activities, so he wasn't about to let a large mob of horses pass through unchallenged on Tuesday 22 April 1856. 'Chief Constable' was a title he aspired to, although his recent application had proven unsuccessful. Still, another opportunity might arise in the future if he continued to monitor his district to the satisfaction of both the Police Magistrate and the local community.

The forty or so horses, some with foals ambling beside them, were heading south along the road to Wiseman's Ferry, driven by three stockmen. Drawing near, Keating recognised Fred Ward, although the other faces, one white and one black, were unfamiliar. He called out a greeting to Fred and the two chatted for a moment, then the young drover hopped down and began to inspect Keating's mount. Ward was known for his ability to spot good horseflesh, so it was pleasing when he remarked approvingly, 'I can tell your horse is fast by the halter under his feet.'

Keating himself cast a quick look over the mob, noticing in particular two heavy grey mares and a black mare, as well as the chestnut pony ridden by the Aboriginal man. He moved closer and examined the brands of the grey mares, jotting 'WZ' in his notebook. Then he farewelled the men and they continued their journey south.

•

Thomas Sleath, innkeeper of the Traveller's Rest on the Wollombi Road, was an enterprising man. In an attempt to drum up business, he had advertised two months previously that travellers could use his paddocks for free. What else were they to do in the middle of nowhere while their live-stock rested if they didn't purchase a drink or two from his inn, or even a full night's accommodation?

Sleath had learnt to ask few questions, but to notice everything—like the two drovers and their Aboriginal servant who left a large mob of horses in his paddock after dark one April evening. He also noticed that they drove the mob away before dawn the following morning yet, curiously, left a chestnut mare behind. One of the drovers returned for the mare two weeks later. His name, Sleath would later discover, was Frederick Ward.

'I have nothing to do with the horses,' replied the curly-headed drover when Wiseman's Ferry licensee, Edward Walmsley, asked if his horses were for sale. 'The other man is the Master,' he added, pointing to his light-haired companion.

The three drovers had just arrived from the north and were about to swim their horses across the crisp waters of the Hawkesbury River. The droving master waited patiently while Walmsley picked out four horses, then he took charge of the £14 payment and handed back a receipt. The ferryman helped the drovers swim the remainder of the horses across the river, then watched them take the road to Windsor.

Walmsley would never see the master again, although he did see the curly-headed drover who had disclaimed all responsibility for the horses—and learn that his name was Frederick Ward.

Constable William Granger had a good memory, a useful attribute for any police officer, particularly when that memory included advertisements for future stock sales. Admittedly, wanting to purchase a new horse had sharpened his memory in this instance. He had read Martyn & Schroder's advertisements in the *Sydney Morning Herald* advising that they had received instructions from Mr Ross to sell forty draught mares from the Clarence, and that the sale would take place on 30 April at Windsor. Personal interest led him to ask some questions when he saw three men, one an Aboriginal man, driving a mob of horses through Pitt Town towards Windsor.

The drovers approached him first. The light-haired young man asked if the constable knew where they could find a paddock. Granger provided directions, then started questioning the curly-haired drover—Frederick Ward, as he would later discover.

'Are the horses to be sold at Windsor?'

'Yes. They come from the Clarence.'

'Are they Ross's?'

Ward agreed that they were, adding that he himself had nothing to do with the horses.

'They don't seem like the horses advertised.'

'The draught horses are behind,' interjected the light-haired drover, 'and will be sold on Saturday week.'

Granger continued inspecting the mob, noticing the WZ brand on several of the horses. He asked Ward if the broker was of good standing.

'The master is,' Ward said, pointing towards his light-haired companion.

'I heard it is Ross,' Granger said, and Ward declared that he was correct, that his companion was indeed Mr Ross himself.

Windsor auctioneer George Seymour had received a message. A man at Mrs Eagan's public house wished to discuss business with him.

Seymour walked over to Mrs Eagan's soon afterwards and found three men sitting on the verandah, one an Aboriginal servant. Frederick Ward was among them, a man he had known for some years, although it wasn't Ward who stood up when he stepped onto the verandah. The other white man invited him into the parlour, leaving his own companions on the verandah out of earshot.

'My name is Mr William Ross,' the man told Seymour as they sat down. 'I am the nephew of Mr Robert Scott Ross, the candidate for the Cumberland Borough. I have a number of horses I want sold by auction. They are in Mr Tebbutt's paddock, and you can advertise them and sell them any day you think proper.'

Seymour questioned him about the horses. Ross said that they were his own, that he had bought most of them and had thirty-seven available for auction, foals included. Ross continued talking about the horses, discussing a few in particular, like a proud father boasting of his progeny's achieve-ments. His air of assurance and knowledge of the horses inspired confidence in the auctioneer, who steered the conversation around to the all-important issue of terms and dates. Ross agreed to his terms and the men decided that the sale would take place five days hence, on 30 April.

As they continued talking, Ross mentioned that he had another mob of horses on its way south. 'I employed Mr Martyn, the Sydney auctioneer, to sell them for me,' he told the Windsor auctioneer, 'which I am now sorry for, as I would sooner that you should sell them all.' He added that these horses were running late, which would prevent him attending Seymour's auction. 'I have to go to Sydney to Mr Martyn's to countermand the other sale,' Ross explained, 'but you are to make the most of the sale and keep the money until I return.'

'A bay mare and foal,' Mr Seymour called out to the expectant crowd watching the horses parade in front of them on 30 April.

'John Wood £19.15s' his assistant scrawled in the ledger after Seymour slammed down his gavel. The auction was going well: £15 for the first lot, a mare and foal, £9.5s for a dark bay mare, and now the highest price of all for this sturdy bay mare and foal, the first of many carrying the WZ brand. The quality was good and the buyers keen, knowing that every horse was to be sold without reserve. Horseflesh interest was heightened as the Hawkesbury races were scheduled for the following week. Prizes as tempting as a 150-sovereign purse were drawing out keen race-goers, although there appeared nothing suitable for the races among this mob.

The sale continued: thirty-seven horses in all. Most purchasers bought just the one horse, although carrier John Wood kept raising his hand. He was always in need of strong draught horses and he paid more than £72 for the seven horses he purchased. Cattle dealer Joseph Windred also paid £11.10s for a filly and roan branded CR and a pony branded WZ. Seymour even bought a couple himself, making the most of his opportunity as an auctioneer to spot a good bargain. He knew that Mr Ross would be happy with the day's takings: over £215.

Then the rumours began.

Joseph Windred was one of the first to hear the gossip. The horses were not Mr Ross's horses, someone told him a couple of days after the auction. They were stolen. And the supremely confident Mr Ross was not the would-be politician's nephew, but a horse-thief named John Garbutt. Windred hurried over to the auctioneer's and reported the rumours.

Seymour was concerned yet pragmatic. Selling stolen livestock was an occupational hazard for auctioneers, so they generally added a hidden insurance premium to their charges. However, it was frustrating that he had been fooled enough by the young whippersnapper to dip his fingers into his own pocket. But all was not lost, he told Windred. They still had a chance to recover their money. He had handed over the proceeds not long before, and Ross had mentioned that he was heading back to Sydney.

The two men hurried outside. Seymour scanned his surroundings, ignoring the women clutching their baskets and the children scampering around them, the lounging agricultural workers in their Jim Crow hats, and the white-haired, cane-toting gentlemen. He was looking for a slender, tallish, respectably dressed young man with fair hair . . . There, he pointed, that's him.

The name rang a bell. Constable Granger pulled out the back issues of the *Police Gazette*, and skimmed through the pages. He discovered that a Moreton Bay warrant had been issued for John Garbutt's arrest a year previously, for horse-stealing as it turned out. The rumours might indeed be true.

Granger reported the situation to Chief Constable William Hobbs, who ordered him to follow Mr Ross and apprehend him. Another importunate purchaser had joined Windred at the police station: the carrier John Wood. The two men between them had purchased one-quarter of the auctioned horses. Not surprisingly, they insisted on joining the hunt.

As the posse set off along the Windsor Road towards Parramatta, twenty miles distant, Chief Constable Hobbs asked Seymour for a list of the horse's brands. He sent the details to Sydney to be published in the next issue of the *Police Gazette*.

Joseph Windred's frustration was increasing. The other horses were too slow. John Wood might invest heavily in horseflesh, but carriers rarely needed swift horses. And the constable's mount? A nag, like many of the police horses. They were pursuing a horse-thief who would certainly be riding a fast horse, yet to keep pace with the constable he had to rein in his horse—and his temper.

No longer, Windred decided. He turned to his companions and announced he was pushing on ahead, that he was determined to catch the thief and recover his money. With a sharp kick to his horse's flanks, he sped off.

Near Kellyville, around halfway between Windsor and Parramatta, Windred spotted another horseman, a man who seemed to resemble the light-haired Mr Ross. He urged his horse forward. Upon reaching the man's side he called out, 'Good morning! Is your name not Mr Ross?'

Blue eyes looked at him enquiringly as the man said, 'Yes.'

Windred reached over and grabbed the horseman's reins with one hand, pulling out a pistol with the other. 'You're my prisoner!' he announced, pointing the gun at Ross.

'What for?' was the indignant reply.

'Because the horses you sold in Windsor were stolen.'

Ross said nothing for a moment, his silence an admission of guilt in itself. Then he asked, 'Who claimed them?'

It wasn't quite the response Windred expected. 'I cannot tell you,' he replied. He added that some constables were behind him, and that Ross must return with him to Windsor. Keeping his pistol aimed at the young miscreant, he tugged on the reins and wheeled both horses, urging them into a loose canter.

Ross remained silent for a short time as they followed the gently undulating road leading back to Windsor, past farmers sowing their wheat fields for the spring crop, past cattle resting in their paddocks. Then he asked: 'How many horses did you buy, and what did you pay for them?'

'Three,' said Windred, 'but not at a heavy price.'

Ross reached into his pocket, pulled out a wad of notes, and offered them to his companion. 'I'll give you £150 if you let me go.'

Windred looked at the notes and back at his prisoner. 'No, I cannot,' he said firmly. 'There are two constables very closely behind.'

They continued west, their horses' hooves crunching the copper leaves scattered on the roadway from the trees and shrubs bordering their route.

Noble gums soared above them, their gnarled arms stretching into the distance as if to shield the tree stumps littering the terrain like beheaded mushrooms, victims of the scythe of British progress.

'I can go no further,' Ross suddenly cried out, slowing his mount near a fenced paddock. He tossed some bank notes at Windred and slid to the ground.

'If you run, I'll shoot,' threatened his captor.

'Well, shoot away,' Ross challenged, and bolted through the fence into the bush.

Windred scrambled from his horse and grabbed the fluttering notes, stuffing them into his pockets and glancing around to make sure he hadn't missed any. Then he looked up at the fence. Ross had picked his location well: the fence was too high for his horse to jump. He broke off the top rail and remounted, then jumped the fence and raced after the escapee. But the cunning horse-thief had delayed him for just long enough.

Darkness had fallen by the time Constable Granger reached the Parramatta terminus of the Sydney–Parramatta railway. The state's first railway line had opened only seven months previously and already most travellers chose the cheaper, faster journey—despite the rattling and shaking, the soot and the noise. Some of the old folk preferred the old ways, but Granger realised that a young fellow like Ross would almost certainly choose to return to Sydney by train. If he stuck to his previous plans.

Constable Granger had learnt of Ross's capture and subsequent escape when he encountered the crestfallen Joseph Windred riding back to Windsor with Ross's horse in tow. The advantage of surprise having been lost to them, both Windred and Wood decided to give up the chase and return to Windsor. Duty dictated that Constable Granger push on towards Parramatta, to the railway station in particular—just in case.

As he rode through Parramatta, he peered at every trousered figure: the horsemen trotting past him, the drinkers lounging in pub doorways. Despite the flickering orbs sitting atop lamp-posts and the glow from windows and open doorways, the darkness made identification difficult. The odds of finding the young horse-thief were slim indeed.

•

Auctioneer Charles Martyn was confused. Why was Mr Ross at Parramatta station boarding the train to Sydney? The horse owner was supposed to be up at Windsor, preparing for the next day's auction.

Ross had arrived at the auction house a few days previously to report that the draught horses had not yet arrived in Windsor, and that the auction would have to be delayed until Saturday 3 May. Accordingly, Martyn had inserted advertisements in the *Sydney Morning Herald* announcing the new date. Another advertisement would be published in the following day's issue. Was there further delay?

Martyn was a busy man, one of the partners in Martyn & Schroder, the thriving Pitt Street auctioneers. They had many distinguished clients, among them Charles Reynolds of Tocal, whose CR brand was becoming synonymous with quality; indeed, they had advertised just a few weeks previously that Reynolds' stud was now considered the best in New South Wales. But there were other more dubious characters in the industry, and he was starting to wonder about this latest client, Mr Ross. So when he saw the familiar face of Windsor's Constable Granger, he decided to have a little chat.

A lamp! He needed a lamp! It was too dark to identify Mr Ross without one.

As the train's demonic shriek filled the air—an insistent demand to the boarding, a wrenching farewell to the departing—Constable Granger grabbed a lamp and sprinted over to one of the first-class carriages. Pulling open the door, he climbed into the carriage and swung the lamp in front of each face. He knew he would recognise the audacious drover who had asked for directions to a Windsor paddock—if he saw him.

Another first-class carriage. Another milky blur of faces.

Then he spotted the young horse-thief.

9

Alas! How difficult it is not to betray one's guilt by one's looks.

Ovid

William Zuill looked over his Bellevue property on the Paterson River, north of Maitland, and couldn't see his large grey mare—not where she usually ran, or anywhere else on the property. She was one of his best horses, worth more than £100—more than a year's wages for most of his workers. Zuill spread the word that he was seeking information, and someone reported having seen a moustachioed man and his Aboriginal servant driving away the grey mare, along with some other horses.

Other horses? On Saturday 3 May, the alarmed owner and his men searched the entire property, discovering that nearly all the heavy mares were gone, including another grey also worth over £100. He didn't know how many were gone or when they had disappeared, but he had no doubt whatsoever that they had been stolen.

A couple of days later, he walked into Maitland's police office and reported the theft. Had anyone found his horses? Chief Constable Henry Garvin had just received the latest *Police Gazette* and he flipped through the pages to the relevant section. It contained welcome news.

Tocal's superintendent, Henry Lowcock, was used to receiving visitors from the neighbouring Bellevue property, but this latest visitor brought news both unexpected and unwelcome. William Zuill advised that horses with the brands HL and CR had recently been sold at Windsor, along with others branded with his own WZ. Did he know anything about them?

Lowcock knew that neither he nor his master Charles Reynolds had authorised Martyn & Schroder—or anyone else for that matter—to sell any of their livestock. They must have been robbed as well.

A few days later, he and Zuill headed down to Windsor to recover their stolen horses, and to determine who had been audacious enough to steal such a large and valuable mob in a single drove.

'Who has been to claim the horses?'

Mr Ross was in Constable Granger's charge on 2 May, en route from the railway station to the Parramatta lock-up, when he inquired again about the horses' claimants. He didn't explain why he was so keen to learn their identities.

Mr Ross—who was indeed Fred Ward's nephew John Garbutt—was not to know that the horses hadn't yet been claimed, that they hadn't even been reported missing because their owners were only just realising they'd been robbed.

Granger had quickly searched the horse-thief after taking him into custody at the railway station, and had discovered a parcel of notes amounting to £183, plus ten shillings in silver. With the £51 Garbutt had thrown at Windred, it was enough cash to support a family for some years—a most profitable villainy indeed.

A thorough search at the Parramatta lock-up turned up a note-of-hand signed 'F.B. Bennett' for the sum of £126. Francis Bowden Bennett was a familiar name to the Windsor constable, a horse and cattle dealer from Richmond. What else had 'Mr Ross' been up to?

It wasn't 'Mr Ross', as it turned out, but 'George Flemming'. And not horses, in this instance, but seventy-five head of cattle stolen the previous February from James Walker's Baradean station on the Liverpool Plains. The theft was discovered when Francis Bowden Bennett attempted to sell the cattle a couple of weeks later and the purchaser recognised Walker's brand. Bennett immediately flourished George Flemming's receipt, claiming to have purchased the cattle from a respectable-look-ing 20-to-25-year-old stranger at the inn belonging to his brother-in-law William Eaton.

In the aftermath, Flemming could not be traced, and the general consen-sus was that 'George Flemming' must be an alias. His true identity had remained a mystery until the receipt was found in John Garbutt's pocket. Initially Garbutt denied being Flemming but later, after Bennett officially identified him, Garbutt confessed to the cattle theft. He added snidely, 'The less Bennett and Eaton say about the cattle the better, as they know just as much as I do.'

The Windsor magistrate agreed. 'It is impossible to believe that Garbutt's statement is not the truth,' he wrote to the Attorney General, after weighing the various statements against the receipts. 'There are so many who appear to be concerned in the felony charges against Garbutt that it is difficult to believe they are not connected with many others in a systematic course of horse and cattle stealing.'

Yet even the magistrate was unaware of the full extent of John Garbutt's villainy. As 'William Neil', he had employed East Maitland auctioneer Alexander Dodds to sell twenty-eight horses on 1 April, horses that later proved to belong to a Castlereagh River pastoralist, William Wilson. As 'George Den' of New England, he had commissioned William George of Paterson to auction ten dray horses and twenty saddle mares and geldings on 12 April, most stolen from Hunter River properties. Who knows what else he and his accomplices had managed to steal, or had intended to steal, before the law caught up with him at Parramatta station.

Meanwhile, Constable Granger attempted to question his prisoner on 3 May while their carriage rattled from Parramatta to Windsor. All Garbutt would say about the horses auctioned at Windsor was: 'I bought them from a person named Anderson for £3.10s a head. Anderson told me that he bought them out of the sale yard at Maitland, but I believe they were "shook", that Anderson picked them up anywhere he could.'

'John Garbutt?'

The name didn't ring a bell, nor the face when Henry Lowcock and William Zuill were taken to the Windsor lock-up to identify him. 'I do not know the prisoner,' was Zuill's response. 'He is a stranger to me.'

'I never saw him before, that I'm aware of,' was Lowcock's equally certain response, and that of his master, Charles Reynolds. But when they heard the name 'Frederick Ward', their reactions were quite different.

'I have known Frederick Ward for some years,' Reynolds would later testify. 'He was employed by me for a year as a stockman and horse-breaker.' Reynolds added that Ward had remained in contact in the years since. In fact, he had visited Tocal only recently, in February or March, and had offered his assistance in mustering some cattle, remaining at the station for a couple of weeks.

The realisation struck them all. This prime judge of horseflesh had volunteered to work at the state's pre-eminent horse stud just a few weeks before some of its most valuable horses were stolen, seemingly by his nephew.

'Arrest Fred Ward!' Windsor's Chief Constable ordered his counterpart in Maitland.

'I know nothing about it!' said Fred, looking innocently up at Maitland's Chief Constable Henry Garvin, who had just announced that he was taking him into custody for stealing horses from Zuill and others.

Naturally Garvin hadn't expected Fred to instantly confess. He advised the lad that he intended to question him further and cautioned him about his responses, explaining that the information could be used against him in a court of law. Then he asked: 'Did you cross Wiseman's Ferry with John Garbutt?'

Fred said that he hadn't.

'Do you know Garbutt?'

Fred admitted that he did. All of Maitland knew the answer to that question, so there was no point in lying.

Garvin searched him but found nothing of interest. He then took him to the Maitland lock-up and turned the key in the door.

John Garbutt had deliberately misdirected the police when he tried to blame 'Anderson' for the horse theft, perhaps alluding to the man indicted with Fred at Muswellbrook a few months previously—the man who had fled while on bail and been killed while resisting arrest. Garbutt's choice of a name proved unfortunate for two other drovers who had just arrived in

Maitland with a mob of cattle. They were immediately arrested and thrown into the Maitland lock-up with Fred. While they were later able to prove their innocence, Fred was not so lucky. He was committed to stand trial at the next Maitland Quarter Sessions and, in the interim, was refused bail and despatched to Maitland Gaol.

Back at Windsor, John Garbutt was committed to stand trial at Sydney's Supreme Court, the state's highest legal authority, the only court entitled to try cases punishable by death. Not that death was—any longer—the punishment for horse and cattle theft.

'Case of Wholesale Horse Stealing,' reported the awed *Sydney Morning Herald* correspondent who attended Garbutt's committal hearing. The story was picked up as far away as Tasmania, the island's newspapers astonished at such audacity, that anyone could steal so many horses in one drove. The press had no idea that it was merely the tip of the iceberg, that the once respectable young man—now looking rather wild with an 'exuberant' beard—had grand visions and was attempting on a large scale what so many others were practising on a small scale. Indeed, the *Herald* had recently lamented that horse theft was common in the bush because horses were so easy to steal and carry away. The stolen goods obligingly walked to their new home—or galloped.

John Garbutt's biggest mistake lay in his sense of direction. He had steered his stolen livestock towards places where either he or their brands were known. If he had sent them north to Queensland, his thievery might have eluded detection.

Garbutt wasn't immediately forwarded to Sydney's Darlinghurst Gaol to await trial. The police were hoping to indict him for the theft of James Walker's cattle—and anything else that might surface. Meanwhile Granger and the Chief Constable continued to question him, recognising that he was a talkative lad rather than the strong silent type. Eventually on 16 May, Garbutt admitted not only to stealing Walker's cattle, but also to his involvement in the theft of Zuill's and Reynolds' horses. And he informed on his accomplices as well.

'Frederick Ward and a man living in the last house on the right-hand side of the Paterson lane from the falls and a man I don't know, but Ward does, brought the horses to me near Joshua Rose's public house,' he told Chief Constable Hobbs, 'then Ward, myself and a black boy came on to Windsor with them.' He added that the Paterson lane man was the owner of the racing mare, Queen of Hearts.

As the police investigated Garbutt's claims they realised that he might well be telling the truth, but that it wasn't the whole truth. He had omitted one significant detail: Lambs Valley.

Michael Blake refused to be implicated in any villainy committed by the relatives of his business partner, William Ward. He told the police that brothers John and James Garbutt had driven a mob of horses to their Lambs Valley property in April and that the horses had remained there for around ten days, cared for by William Ward's servant and a 'black boy'. Fred Ward had arrived at Lambs Valley a few days beforehand and had left with the Garbutt brothers when they drove the horses away; however, the Aboriginal servant, who worked for the Wards' brother Joshua, had remained behind for a couple of days.

The police immediately focused their attention upon William and Joshua Ward and James Garbutt. William Ward was apprehended at Muswellbrook a couple of months later, driving a mob of his own fat cattle; however, he was fortunate enough to be given bail and the case against him eventually lapsed. While Lambs Valley was the perfect hideaway for stolen livestock, the authorities could not prove that he had known the horses were stolen.

Joshua Ward also slipped through the law's net. The involvement of his Aboriginal servant was not immediate proof of his complicity: he could have lent his servant to his brothers. The police tried to question him but discovered that he had gone a-droving.

James Garbutt was the first taken into custody—although, surprisingly, for complicity in 'William Neil's' crimes, rather than those of 'Mr Ross'. Witnesses stated that they had seen James at the East Maitland auction on 1 April, and that he had talked about 'Neil's' horses as if he knew them. James bounced between the court and the lock-up for some weeks while the police sought further evidence of his complicity. Eventually the court discharged him because of insufficient evidence. He would not leave the court with clean hands however, the magistrate advised darkly.

If James breathed a sigh of relief, he breathed too soon.

10

A jury consists of twelve persons chosen to decide who has the better lawyer.

Robert Frost

'Frederick Ward and James Garbutt,' the clerk of the Maitland Quarter Sessions called out through the rustling in the courtroom, as voices gradually quietened and eyes turned towards the speaker. 'You are indicted for having feloniously stolen, taken and driven away twenty horses, twenty mares and twenty geldings, the property of William Zuill, and five horses, five geldings and five mares, the property of Charles Reynolds, at Maitland on the 21st April. A second count charges you with "receiving the stolen horses knowing them to be stolen". How say you?'

Seventy-five horses stolen at Maitland on 21 April? The place was wrong, the date wrong, and the number of horses wrong. The prosecutor should have scuttled from the courtroom clutching the 'case dismissed' paperwork, his ears ringing from the judge's coruscating denunciation, yet at Fred and James' trial on 13 August 1856, their barrister did not challenge the error-ridden indictment.

All eyes turned to the two prisoners in the dock, who chimed 'Not guilty'. James Garbutt was the taller of the pair, the epitome of a colonial 'cornstalk' with his light hair and blue eyes. At nearly five feet ten inches, his slender frame would tower over most of the convicts, their growth stunted by inadequate food and sunshine. Two years older than Fred, he was wiry and capable, a turner by trade, apprenticed during his youth to a Maitland tradesman. By his side, Fred was an inch or two smaller, although his thatch of curly brown hair made up some of the difference.

The robed and periwigged Justice Alfred Cheeke presided, quill and inkpot sitting next to the open notebook in front of him. While not renowned for his skills as a lawyer, the Quarter Sessions Chairman was a respected member of the legal community, a deeply honourable judge, a jurist who relied upon experience and common sense in reaching his judgements. He was patient in the courtroom and courteous outside of it, with a genial nature appreciated in his business and social dealings, and particularly on the turf. Wherein lay the problem. This lover of the sport of kings, this horse-breeder himself under the name A. Chaffe, was perhaps not the ideal judge for a case involving a gang of audacious horse-thieves.

'I wish to call your attention to the wholesale nature of the robbery that the evidence will prove to have been perpetrated,' the Crown Prosecutor began, addressing the twelve good men and true who sat in the jury box on the late winter's day. Many others had sat down before them, only to find themselves unceremoniously ejected from the courtroom when the prosecution or defence decided to challenge their presence.

'It would appear that other parties were involved in the matter, that another man of the name of Ward assisted in the care and disposal of the horses in question,' the Crown Prosecutor added pointedly, intimating that this was quite a family affair—as the community well knew. Many had read the newspaper reports about the case and about the notorious ringleader, John Garbutt, who had pleaded guilty in the Supreme Court two months previously and was sentenced to ten years' imprisonment.

The Crown Prosecutor finished outlining his case; then, one after another, the witnesses stepped into the witness box: Maitland's Chief Constable Garvin who had arrested Fred Ward, Paterson's Constable Hart who arrested James Garbutt, victims William Zuill and his son John of Bellevue, as well as Charles Reynolds and Henry Lowcock of Tocal, and Michael Blake of Lambs Valley. Each described their knowledge of the thefts or their encounters with the two prisoners who stood sullenly in the dock. Then Lambs Valley employee Walter McLeod took the stand.

'I was at Lambs Valley four or five months ago with William Ward,' the boy told the jury. 'I recollect some horses coming about three weeks after

I came. I was there about five weeks. The two Garbutts, Prisoner James one of them, fetched the horses, 34 or 36 in number. I was sent out to herd them. Mr Ward said he would break my neck or kill me if I didn't. I herded them for ten days.'

The prosecution asked if he had encountered Fred Ward at the time.

'He was there before the horses came. Four or five days before,' the boy advised. 'I don't know his business.'

And when the horses left?

'Prisoner Ward and John Garbutt took the horses away. John Garbutt gave me two shillings when he returned after the horses went away. Ward and John Garbutt returned about six days after they took the horses away. James Garbutt came two days after. They all remained for a bit at William Ward's.'

The prosecution asked about the horses themselves and the steadfast lad said he remembered them well, that he had described some of their brands to the police at the time, one being the letters WZ. He had later seen some among a mob of horses at West Maitland and had identified one in particular, a dappled grey mare owned by Mr Zuill. Just a week previously, he had seen four or five more at Mr Zuill's and Mr Reynolds' places and had recognised the brands and a few of the horses themselves. 'The bay mare had a foal, a little dark one,' he told the court, remembering its warm brown eyes and skittish jumps.

The parade of witnesses continued: Constable Richard Keating and the other men who had encountered Fred driving the horses towards Windsor, Constable Granger and, finally, auctioneer George Seymour. The accounts were compelling, the evidence damning—against Fred, at least.

'It is a circumstantial case,' Fred and James' defence attorney announced dismissively. The two prisoners had engaged the eminent Sydney barrister, Ratcliffe Pring. Arrogant and opinionated, the thirty-year-old was vain about his looks and skills—with good reason. A newspaper would later eulogise that as a defending barrister in criminal practice he had no superior in Australia, and that the number of bushrangers, murderers and horse-stealers his forensic skills had snatched from the law's clutches was equalled only by those he had successfully prosecuted. On 13 August 1856, he directed his energies and abilities towards prying Fred and James loose.

Facing the jury, Mr Pring began to account for the prosecution's evidence. The *Maitland Mercury*'s correspondent, who was sitting in the courtroom scribbling notes, later reported that the barrister addressed the jury at great length and with great ability. During his discourse, Pring reminded the jurymen that none of the witnesses had testified that James Garbutt was ever in possession of any of the horses.

Justice Cheeke was taking notes as well, in his almost incomprehensible scrawl. He jotted down this comment, along with Pring's pointed remarks about the discrepancies in many of the witnesses' testimonies.

Pring had just called the jury's attention to a fragile link in the prosecution's seemingly compelling chain of circumstantial evidence. Zuill himself had testified that he had last seen his grey mare at Bellevue on 20 April, while Constable Keating reported seeing Fred Ward and the horses near Wollombi on 22 April. Yet two of the Crown's key witnesses—the only witnesses to incriminate James Garbutt—had testified that the horses were held at Lambs Valley for a week or ten days. Moreover, neither witness was able to say exactly when the horses arrived at Lambs Valley or when they left, other than that it was in April—or perhaps May.

'The horses at Lambs Valley and the horses seen on the road to Wiseman's Ferry were not identical,' Mr Pring finally announced to the jury, summing up his argument that the prosecution had offered no evidence whatsoever to incriminate James Garbutt.

As for Fred Ward? 'There was nothing unusual in Ward's presence at Lambs Valley on a visit to his brother,' he reminded the jurors, 'seeing as he had finished his work at Mr Reynolds' twelve miles away. His occupation as a drover well accounted for his presence with the horses when he was seen on the road, and his acting as shown by the Crown's witnesses proves him to have acted in the capacity of a servant only.'

Pring was attempting to use Fred's 'I-know-nothing' defence—the claims made to the various witnesses as he travelled with the horses to Windsor—to demolish the charge that his client had knowingly been in possession of stolen goods. After a few additional comments, he warned the jury to think carefully about the evidence itself and the effects of their judgement on the lives of the two young men still standing in the dock. 'The evidence is anything but calculated to shut up the mind to the conviction that the prisoners were guilty—of either count!'

Mr Pring then informed the court that he had two defence witnesses to back up his claims. As the name 'William Ward' rang out, footsteps could be heard crossing the courtroom and stepping into the witness box.

Although five years older, William was Fred's closest surviving sibling, his childhood companion, two boys who tail-ended a large family and hero-worshipped their three much older brothers. Only Joshua now survived, but he had skedaddled, determined not to join Fred and the Garbutts in the dock. William alone was left to try to defend his younger brother, despite the risk to his own freedom. Indicted for the same crime but currently out on bail, he had to be careful he didn't hand the court his own head on a platter, either for the crime itself or for blatant perjury.

'The two Garbutts brought a mob of horses to my place in February or March,' William told the court, adding that he couldn't remember the actual date, but knew it was before he commenced ploughing at Lambs Valley on 10 March. Yes, Walter McLeod had herded the horses for a week; however, the horses carried the brand WM, not WZ, and did not include any heavy horses—not even the grey mare later identified by McLeod.

The Crown Prosecutor cross-examined him. Who owned the horses? Where had they come from? When exactly had they arrived at Lambs Valley—and left? Where had they been sold?

'William Wilson claimed those horses,' was all Fred's wary brother would say. He was stepping into dangerous territory.

A rumble in the courtroom reflected the spectators' mutters of acknowledgement: Wilson was a victim of John Garbutt's 'William Neil' alias, and his recent endeavours to recover all his stolen horses had kept his case alive in the local press. William Ward's attempt to assist his brother had reminded everyone of this other horse theft perpetrated on their very doorstep, a crime for which James Garbutt had been apprehended and only reluctantly discharged. Would the jury be able to ignore such incriminating testimony from a seeming gang member himself?

As William Ward left the witness box, Mr Pring called John Garbutt. A hum of interest stirred the courtroom. Chairs squeaked and fabric rustled as spectators turned to watch the ringleader shuffle towards the witness box, his shackled ankles preventing him from using this short-lived reprieve from incarceration to make his escape. He looked like his brother James, another tall, slender cornstalk with blue eyes and light hair, although—like Fred—his years in the saddle had darkened his complexion.

'I took a mob of horses and my brother was with them,' John told the court, having already pleaded guilty to some horse-stealing charges. 'It was in March. The horses remained at Lambs Valley for five or six days and were branded WM. We took them to Maitland. They were sold at Maitland.'

John was also alluding to Wilson's stolen horses, explaining away the horses' brands and their Lambs Valley sojourn as William Ward had done. But he too had just incriminated his brother James in the earlier crime. The heat of the unexpected spotlight was burning hotter and hotter.

Mr Pring asked about the other horses.

'I later drove a mob of horses to Windsor,' John admitted to the court. 'I employed Ward to drive them with a black boy I brought down from the country. The second lot of horses were branded Zuill and belonged to him. They were not at Lambs Valley.'

The Crown Prosecutor took over the questioning, asking for additional details about the horses sold at Maitland. 'My brother helped me with Wilson's mob to Lambs Valley from Lochinvar,' John reported, finally admitting that Wilson was the owner of the horses he took to the Maitland auction. 'I received Wilson's mob but I won't tell who stole them,' he added cagily.

Was his brother involved in the theft?

'I have been stock-keeper to several persons at the Darling Downs and I told James they were my horses. I also claimed the Windsor mob and I had them when I met Ward. The Windsor mob was never in Lambs Valley.'

The Crown Prosecutor eyed the shackled prisoner for a long moment before turning to the jury. 'It is with great regret that we should see, in a position to give evidence, such witnesses as have been produced for the defence,' he said disgustedly. 'The facts admitted by them merely prove the existence of a system of wholesale horse stealing in which several persons must have been engaged, and in which Lambs Valley served as the planting place.'

If Fred and James didn't realise that their defence witnesses had just nailed their hides to the gaol-house door, they were alone in the courtroom.

As the Crown Prosecutor returned to his seat, all eyes turned to Justice Cheeke, who began to sum up the evidence. He carefully compared the witnesses' statements, attempting to account for the obvious discrepancies. He pointed out that the evidence regarding Fred Ward—if believed— might serve to convict him on the second count, the 'receiving' rather than 'stealing' count, but that the case would first have to be considered with regard to James Garbutt, and would depend on the comparative credibility of the evidence. Then he left the jurymen to make up their own minds.

Ten minutes was all it took. While Mr Pring had expressed some valid concerns about the discrepancies in the witnesses' testimonies, the jury decided that the weight of the other evidence more than counterbalanced those concerns. They couldn't forget that the lad Walter McLeod had reported herding Zuill's and Reynolds' stolen horses at Lambs Valley for ten days and that, months later, he had accurately identified some of them, therefore his claim that the stolen horses had been at Lambs Valley must be true. Accordingly, his claim that he had seen James Garbutt arrive with the horses suggested Garbutt's complicity in the theft itself. And Lambs Valley partner, Michael Blake, had testified that he had seen James Garbutt arrive *and* leave with the horses. As for Fred Ward: he was seen at Lambs Valley with the horses, he left with the horses and he called his droving companion 'Mr Ross', well knowing that Ross was not his nephew's surname. His lies proved, if nothing else, that he knew his nephew was up to no good.

'Guilty of stealing the horses,' announced the jury foreman, after the judge asked for their verdict in the case against James Garbutt. As the courtroom's eyes turned to watch the reaction of the taller prisoner, the jury foreman announced Fred's verdict: 'Guilty of receiving the stolen horses knowing them to be stolen.'

Justice Cheeke gave them the usual judicial tongue-lashing, then sentenced both to ten years' servitude on the roads. Which didn't mean they would actually be sent to join a gang of chained convicts labouring on the New South Wales roads—this form of punishment had been abolished. Rather they were destined for the dreaded penal establishment on Cockatoo Island.

PART 3

DESPAIR

As one reads history . . . one is absolutely sickened,
not by the crimes that the wicked have committed,
but by the punishments that the good have inflicted.

Oscar Wilde

11

Let the punishment fit the crime.

Anonymous

The age-old conundrum: how to punish, deter, reform and profit—all at the same time. Draco's Ancient Greek code of justice had recommended a simple punishment for everything from laziness to homicide: death. Hence the term 'draconian' punishment—prisons were merely holding pens until the offender was sentenced. No need to worry about reformation. The Magna Carta in 1215 included imprisonment as a form of punishment, although physical punishments—beheading, branding, blinding, amputation, flogging and, of course, hanging—continued to dominate for the following few centuries. By the sixteenth century, prisons were privately run businesses that allowed inmates to pay for better-quality accommodation and food. Profitable indeed; reformative, never.

Crime increased over the next few centuries, mainly property crime caused by social dislocation but also by legislation—an increasing number of activities were being legislated as 'criminal'. The ruling classes had begun to fear the 'dangerous classes' crowding into the slums of Britain. Soon Britain's bulging gaols could no longer house all the nation's offenders. Since they could not execute all wrongdoers, exile became a safety valve: transportation to the American colonies and later to Australia. But there the problem reared its stubborn head again. What to do with local offenders? Exile them to Britain? Not likely!

Meanwhile, philosophers had turned their thoughts towards the causes of crime and the efficacy of punishment, and this awakening interest gradually led to changes in attitudes, and ultimately to the criminal laws themselves. By the mid-1800s the gallows were rarely used, and then mainly for homicidal crimes. Transportation was also becoming anathema, too closely associated with the recently abolished slavery. Prisons had become the focus of the penal system, and punishments needed to deter so as to keep down prisoner numbers, to reform the many 'hardened' criminals being released back into society, and to be profitable because it cost more to house prisoners for ten or fifteen years than to kill them.

Sir George Gipps had found the problem of penal incarceration sitting squarely on his desk soon after he stepped through the hallowed doorway of Government House in 1838. Britain wanted him to withdraw the recidivist prisoners from Norfolk Island and find another 'prison' to house these incorrigibles—men who had repeatedly defied the rule of law and mutinously resisted the lessons of punishment, paying the price for their obstinacy by enduring servitude at that *ne plus ultra* of penal punishment. Soon these desperate men would be back on Sydney's streets, off-loaded from makeshift transports and marched down George Street into the crumbling confines of Sydney Gaol.

Governor Gipps quickly found a solution. Banishment again. To another island surrounded by deep, shark-infested waters. No fresh water; lots of snakes. Not surprisingly, the rocky sandstone outcrop that he had in mind was uninhabited, holding little appeal for settlers. Situated at the entrance to Parramatta River, it was also under the Governor's eye as it lay just a few miles from Government House. Birds wheeled overhead and nested in the island's trees, principally the *biloela*, as the local Aboriginal people called them: the showy-crested, raucous cockatoos.

The first convict gangs arrived on Cockatoo Island the following year, building temporary barracks for themselves and their military overseers. Others soon followed, old lags from Norfolk Island, as well as the newly convicted, under orders to dig grain silos out of the solid rock and to hew the resulting sandstone into blocks for Sydney's construction sites. Soon Cockatoo Island was New South Wales' most important penal settlement, with a captive labour force that Governor Gipps realised would be suitable for large projects. Prisoners who earned their own keep? Ideal.

Governor Gipps had seemingly hit on the perfect solution, although his services as Governor had ended by the time the prisoners began constructing the dry dock and repair facility on Cockatoo Island's south-east corner. The dockyard was principally intended to service the Royal Navy ships that patrolled the world's oceans. The work would be harsh, thereby serving as a punishment and a deterrent, both to the criminals themselves when later released back into the community, and to the criminally inclined. The prisoners could also learn skills that would assist them in finding future employment.

Named after Gipps' successor, the Fitzroy Dock was nearing completion when Fred Ward and James Garbutt disembarked onto Cockatoo Island on 27 August 1856. There they were reunited with the architect of their misery, James' blackguard brother, John Garbutt.

Imprisonment on Cockatoo Island had not yet cowed John. Although he hadn't succeeded in keeping his minions out of gaol, the man with the bold visions had a new idea: he had information to trade for their freedom.

The news broke in a brief letter to the *Sydney Morning Herald* on 14 April 1857. A letter-writer signing himself 'Z' ventured that he might have news of the whereabouts of Ludwig Leichhardt, the internationally acclaimed explorer who had disappeared during his third expedition across Australia a decade previously, reportedly killed by Aboriginals.

The tantalising feeler elicited delighted responses. 'I shall not attempt to describe the emotions of my heart when I read in this morning's *Herald* that there was still a hope left for the existence of Leichhardt,' wrote Justitia. Lamenting that Leichhardt and his gallant band had perished in the Australian wilderness without any serious enquiry as to their fate, he asked in the name of humanity that his fellow well-wishers provide funds for a search party. He would begin the fund by donating £20.

Spurred by such a response, Z tossed out another morsel. 'There is a fair and beautiful country, directly in the track Leichhardt was pursuing, known only to a few besides its present possessor,' he wrote to the *Herald*. Runaway convicts and their Aboriginal wives and children populated the district, growing corn and grazing large herds of cattle along the banks of a wide unnamed river. When Leichhardt stumbled upon the camp, the residents feared he would report their existence to the authorities, so they took him into custody. He was treated with respect and spent his time teaching the children, although he complained to Z's informant when they last met in May 1855: 'I think it very hard to be detained here without fault. I am as secure from escape here as though I were locked up in Newgate.'

The *Herald*'s reporters discussed the startling revelation, recognising that such a community could indeed exist, that rumours of mixed tribes in inland districts had long circulated. Moreover, such a tribe would have good reason for keeping Leichhardt and his men in custody. But could the claim be true?

One reader used his sources to dig deeper, to discover what Sydney was clamouring to hear. Z's informant, he soon announced in a letter to the *Herald*, was a convict serving on Cockatoo Island with his brother and uncle, a man by the name of John Garbutt.

'Might I have the pleasure of knowing your name?' the man with the black moustache asked in his accented English. John Garbutt had spotted the French or German man during his first visit to the camp, a few hundred miles west of the Darling Downs, late in 1853. The man's white California hat, Scotch twill shirt, tweed trousers, waistcoat and topcoat stood out in the bush community. However, they had not spoken until this second visit, after Garbutt had agreed to act as a cattle dealer for the camp.

Garbutt introduced himself, then enquired politely about his companion's name, although he already knew the answer. 'My name is Dr Leichhardt,' the man said, looking around furtively as he did so. John asked him about his situation. Leichhardt described how his party had been overpowered by Aboriginals, adding: 'They did not bind me or ill-treat me but kept a strict watch over me. They cautioned me against going out of sight of the houses unless in the company of two or three of the camp's men. One or two of my men attempted to escape but the blacks tracked them for a day and a night and brought them back.'

As the two continued talking, Leichhardt asked plaintively, 'Has there been much talk of me in the settled parts?'

'I've not heard anything particular,' John reported unsympathetically, not bothering to mention the searches and the intense sorrow when the community realised he had disappeared.

Noticing John's indifference, Leichhardt eventually said, 'There is little doubt of your doing anything for me as you appear to have too much interest in the place.'

'I don't know what I might do for you some time or other, but at the present I won't interfere in the matter,' replied the self-interested opportunist.

John told the magistrate who questioned him at Cockatoo Island on 19 April 1857 that he had sold 1500 of the camp's cattle for £6000, and had visited the camp for the final time after the horse-stealing warrant was issued in March 1855. After staying a couple of months, he had travelled with one of the camp's men to Maitland to assess the market. The man agreed to bring a mob of horses and asked John to make arrangements to sell them. When the horses failed to appear, John stole some others—one of the crimes, he admitted, that ultimately led to his incarceration on Cockatoo Island.

Then came the demand. 'If the Government employs me to conduct a party, I should in the event of being successful, of which I am confident, expect a pardon for myself, my brother and my uncle.'

Which raised the obvious question: why should his brother and uncle be granted pardons as well?

Because, Garbutt explained, his brother and uncle—yes, Cockatoo Island inmates James Garbutt and Fred Ward—had also been to Leichhardt's camp and had seen the explorer for themselves.

The news spread quickly, picked up within days by the Brisbane, Melbourne and Tasmanian papers. Most reports were sceptical. 'No doubt the narrator of this romantic tale would be glad to exchange his present position for that of a guide to a searching party,' wrote the *Moreton Bay Courier*, 'trusting to ingenuity and chance for an opportunity of enlarging his freedom.'

Meanwhile, enterprising confidence men were collecting 'subscriptions' to fund a search party, targeting in particular Leichhardt's fellow German nationals.

An intimidating cast stared at the trio when Fred and the Garbutt brothers were ushered into Superintendent Ormsby's offices on Friday 1 May 1857. Familiar faces were among them, including the superintendent himself and the superintending engineer. The unfamiliar faces proved the most daunting, in particular a pair of steely eyes set in a harsh, frowning countenance. The New South Wales Governor, Sir William Denison, was taking John's claim very seriously indeed.

The questioning began. John was first. Who was he? What crime had he committed? Why was he taken to visit the settlement? When did he see Leichhardt? How had his brother and uncle also seen Leichhardt? John was soon forced to admit that James and Fred had not in fact visited the settlement, although he had long ago told them about his visits. The other questions he answered with a quiet confidence, a steady assurance.

The authorities soon realised that they didn't know enough about Leichhardt or the interior to unravel the web of deceit—if indeed it was a web of deceit. They would need the assistance of men who had known Leichhardt or were familiar with the districts he had travelled through. Governor Denison empowered a Board of Inquiry to investigate Garbutt's claims, and the Board gathered on Cockatoo Island on 8 May: Hovendon Hely, the leader of the first expedition in search of Leichhardt, John Stephen Ferriter of the Condamine, John Macarthur of the Darling Downs, and the Inspector General of Police, John McLerie. Despite John Garbutt's admission that his brother and uncle had not visited the inland settlement, all three were to face interrogation by the Board. John again was the first.

'We have a minute from the Governor to the effect that if we find your statement to be false, you will not be entitled to ask for any indulgences,' McLerie began. 'You must serve out your full sentence of ten years' imprisonment without remission.'

John knew that the remission system would reduce his ten-year sentence to only four or five years of actual servitude if he worked hard and behaved well. His next words could force him to endure another half-a-dozen years in the Cockatoo Island hellhole. But he didn't hesitate. 'I am perfectly willing to undergo any punishment if my statement is not found to be correct,' he boldly assured them.

Then the examination began, question after question, hour after hour: his own background, how he first came to visit the camp, the route taken and the terrain along the way, what the camp was like, what Leichhardt was like, what happened to Leichhardt's men. John admitted that he couldn't tell them anything about Leichhardt's men as he hadn't asked about them.

'I think you showed a great want of curiosity then,' declared those desperate to find answers regarding the beloved explorer's fate.

'I did not wish to enquire for I had no benefit to expect from it,' was the dismissive response.

The Board asked for details of the cattle sold: the brands, the purchasers, how much they paid and how he dealt with the money. The wily ne'er-do-well refused to incriminate others or himself, despite their repeated assurances that the information would not be used against anyone. By dinnertime, John was getting weary, but his interrogators knew that his exhaustion was their best chance of catching him out in a lie.

The interrogation recommenced after his half-hour midday break: question 447 . . . 448 . . . 449 . . . Sometimes his answers were sarcastic; sometimes he alluded to other criminal activity to justify his failures of observation. His exhaustion was showing by question 717 when he complained, 'I have had so much talking and so many questions, that I am bothered and not knowing what I am saying.' Eventually, after the 810th question, he quailed under the assault. 'I will not be cross-haggled any longer!' he exclaimed and refused to answer any more.

Fred was the third to face the Board. They asked him about his relationship with the Garbutt brothers, when he had last seen John Garbutt, and what John had mentioned about his activities in the bush.

'That is a question that I do not . . .'

Inspector McLerie interrupted him. 'You can do it with perfect freedom for no advantage will be taken of it. It will neither affect you nor Garbutt.'

Fred was not as untrusting as his crafty nephew. 'John Garbutt was not living in an honest way,' he admitted.

'How was he getting a living?'

'Among horses and cattle.'

'Did he say where he was getting horses and cattle?'

'In different parts of the colony.'

'Did you know that Garbutt was selling cattle he did not come by honestly?'

Fred remained silent.

The Board inquired if John had mentioned visiting the inland camp.

Fred said that he had. In fact, he himself had seen two of the camp's men in John's company at Maitland early in 1856.

They asked if John had money on the occasions Fred had seen him.

'Yes, he had a great deal of money.'

'How much?'

'I saw him with about £1500 in his possession—notes and gold.'

They asked if he had questioned John about the money, but Fred said that he hadn't.

'Did it not appear extraordinary that a man in his position should have so much as £1500?'

'No.'

'How did you come to know what money he had?'

'Him and me had a little dealings,' Fred admitted slyly.

Hovendon Hely would later describe Garbutt's claims as an 'impudent and ridiculous fabrication'. Nonetheless, considering the public's dissatisfaction with the previous search efforts, Hely suggested that the government send Garbutt out with another search party in order to disprove his statement. John Macarthur suggested similarly: Leichhardt's lingering ghost needed to be laid to rest.

The government eventually did fund a search expedition—although it dispensed with John Garbutt's magnanimous offer of assistance. In March 1858, explorer Augustus Charles Gregory led an expedition from the Darling Downs via Lake Blanch to Adelaide. While they found no trace of

Leichhardt's men except an 'L' cut into a tree, Gregory's description of the countryside renewed interest among the South Australians in the region north of Lake Torrens.

Meanwhile, as the ripples from John Garbutt's self-interest crossed the continent, the trio faded back into Cockatoo Island obscurity.

12

The miserable have no other medicine
But only hope.

William Shakespeare, *Measure for Measure*

Fred had been offered the post of wardsman. It was a promotion of sorts, easier than labouring on the works. While the penny-per-day gratuity was less than the threepence some could earn by exceeding their task-work quota, at least it paid for the luxuries of tea, sugar and tobacco. The duties weren't onerous: he and his fellow wardsman had to stay awake all night, parading up and down their ward making sure that all was well. Except that they were in charge of dozens of men who were attempting to sleep under difficult conditions, lying in coffin-like cavities one atop the other, many without mattresses as they had to pay for their own, constantly bitten by fleas and lice and other vermin, breathing in the fumes of stinking breaths and unwashed bodies and the effluvium of four or five open tubs that provided the only sanitary services during lock-up. A few small windows offered the only ventilation, except, of course, for the additional holes in the ceiling that provided an unwanted shower for those slumbering underneath. Tempers frayed, particularly in summer when the trapped heat left the prisoners gasping at the gratings for fresh air. The stench was intolerable—even to the sentries outside.

The sentries would not go into the wards at night. No free man would: it was too dangerous. Things happened in the dark. The prisoners were supposed to sleep from 8 pm when most of the lamps were doused, but many didn't—or couldn't. Gambling, smoking, ribald conversation, fighting, and the rustlings in the berths of 'Lady Godiva' and 'Long Sal'.

A penny a day? It was safer for the wardsmen to find a berth for the night and have a nap. Sometimes they were even bribed to do so. Sleeping was against the rules, so if they were caught . . .

Fred was, in October 1857. 'Neglect of duty by sleeping in the wards,' the Visiting Magistrate ruled, sentencing him to three days' imprisonment in the solitary confinement cells.

Gone were the days when Cockatoo Island inmates were flogged. Ideas about the treatment of prisoners had changed in preceding decades. Physical punishments intended to discipline and deter by maiming or destroying the body had been replaced with psychological punishments such as solitary confinement. These new 'enlightened' forms of discipline were intended to reform character by quarantining miscreants from healthy society, allowing them to reflect on their own misbehaviour and to be cured of their immoral ways so as to become more useful members of society. In reality, solitary confinement flogged the mind rather than the body, and eventually sent many sufferers mad.

A trapdoor under the prisoners' ward opened, allowing a fetid wash of air to escape from the well-like cavity underneath. Fred's new quarters had been bored out of the island's solid sandstone bedrock. A ladder dropped down to its rotten wooden floor and he grasped it and began climbing. One rung; another. Some of the cells required longer ladders, twenty feet down to the bottom; others hardly needed a ladder at all.

He passed a small grating that supplied fresh air. When he reached the bottom, he could barely swing his arms around. Six feet by four feet was the base, with a raised wooden platform as a bed. The guards withdrew the ladder, then placed a covering over the opening, like the lid of a hatbox. He was alone in the cramped cell, trapped within its narrow slimy walls, a prey to the vermin that delighted in the latest addition to their food supplies.

A spy-hole allowed his captors to lower his rations: the ubiquitous punishment diet of bread and water. One-and-a-half pounds of bread only—starvation rations. Otherwise, he had a candle and worthy books that he could barely read to help him endure three days of an existence as different from his years of droving and horse-breaking as it was possible to imagine.

On his release, the blaze of sunshine and the fresh salty air seemed almost surreal. Fred didn't break the rules again.

Month after endless month followed until, eventually, early in 1858, Fred and James decided that eighteen months on Cockatoo Island was long enough. James had good reason for thinking so. His barrister had justifiably argued that there was little evidence to convict him. While witnesses had reported seeing him arrive at Lambs Valley with John Garbutt and the horses, they failed to show that he actually stole the horses or was 'in possession' of the horses at any time, or that he knew the horses were stolen or would profit from the sale. Yet their horse-loving trial judge had sentenced James—and Fred for that matter—to an interminable ten years of servitude, the same sentence imposed by the New South Wales Supreme Court on John Garbutt, the ringleader of the much larger horse- and cattle-thieving operation.

Had James truly stolen the horses? When the Leichhardt Board of Inquiry questioned him about his crime, he grumbled: 'I never did steal the horses at all.'

'How came you to be apprehended on this charge?' the Inspector General of Police asked curiously.

'Through the malice and envy of my uncle.'

'Not the uncle who is here on Cockatoo Island?'

'No,' James agreed. He wasn't referring to Fred Ward but to Fred's older brother: William Ward's attempts to exonerate Fred had nailed James' coffin. And so had John Garbutt's defence statements, for that matter.

Fred's sister Esther and her husband made a timely visit to Cockatoo Island in March 1858 and, a month later, identical petitions in favour of Fred and James were despatched from Maitland to the Governor's office.

'We the undersigned inhabitants of Maitland and its vicinity do hereby testify that we were acquainted with Frederick Ward and, with the exception of the mentioned charge, we always considered him to be an honest and industrious young man,' claimed the twenty signatories to Fred's petition, among them a clergyman, surgeon, military officer and Parliamentarian. The clergyman, Rev. William Purves—who had some years previously married Mary Ann's parents—explained that he was not personally acquainted with Fred; however, the testimonies of others who had known the young man had motivated him to sign the petition. Another signatory referred to the influential support backing the petition and urged the Governor to consider it favourably.

Evidently the Maitland community—indeed all social classes within the Maitland community—believed that Fred was a good lad whose usually clear vision had been blurred by the rose-coloured glasses offered him by his swindling nephew. But the requested report from the Cockatoo Island superintendent mentioned Fred's three-day punishment in the cells. 'Application refused,' was the unequivocal response.

James Garbutt had maintained an untarnished record; however, his name was too similar to that of his notorious younger brother. Sir William Denison scrawled on James' paperwork: 'By Garbutt's own account of himself to me, he was engaged in purchasing stolen cattle; he was also at another time absconding from justice. In fact, he is or was an inveterate horse stealer and does not merit any indulgence.'

Yet John was the inveterate horse-stealer, the absconder from justice, not James. Unfortunately for James, his brother's infamy would continue to rebound on him in years to come.

The days and weeks and months passed, with James working in the carpenters' shop, John working as an engineer on the dry dock, and Fred presumably continuing as a wardsman. They all behaved well, knowing that their servitude clock was ticking down—a half-day remission for every full day worked, and an early release on a ticket-of-leave if they continued to behave well. They ignored the smouldering discontent among the recent arrivals—those sentenced since June 1858 who worked alongside them, undertaking the same tasks for the same hours, yet required by law to serve every single day of their sentence. They ignored the summer's searing heat, the smothering humidity, the irritating flies, the wretched atmosphere in the wards that left them looking more haggard in the mornings than after labouring on the works.

But there was one incident they simply could not ignore.

The drama began around half-past ten on a cloudy Sunday morning, 19 February 1860. Moderate breezes caressed the island from the south—a pleasant day for the most humid month in Sydney's calendar. The prisoners didn't work on Sundays. Instead they attended divine worship in the mess-shed, where services were conducted by the minister of whichever faith they had an allegiance to: Church of England, Roman Catholic, Presbyterian, Wesleyan. Naturally, it was difficult to generate a suitable atmosphere of reverence when the men also ate and relaxed in the house of God. Yet, despite the difficulties, the men were most attentive—indeed one of the most attentive and active congregations in Sydney, according to the Anglican minister. Each service was conducted separately, the order determined by whichever minister arrived on the island first. When he finished preaching, the men filed out and the next lot shuffled in.

As the prisoners idled in the barrack yard awaiting their turn that Sunday morning, two suddenly exploded. Their anger, for some reason, was focused on a free overseer named Horford. Convict transportee John Williams and his colonial-born friend, Richard Stone, began to pummel the overseer, knocking him to the ground and kicking him over and over.

The prisoners loved a fight: brawls and wagers were the most exciting events in their tedious existence. But to a few men standing nearby, this was no evenly matched tussle. This was a deadly assault. The overseer didn't stand a chance against two enraged prisoners, brawny after years of heavy manual labour.

Fred, the Garbutt brothers and two other prisoners waded in, grappling with Williams and Stone and pulling them off the overseer. Then they picked Horford up and assisted him until the guards arrived. Horford was lucky to survive, and months passed before he was back on duty. The attackers were sentenced to another two years' servitude working in irons. Fred and his nephews had their helpful actions noted. And their servitude clock continued to tick.

As winter approached, the escape attempts increased. Two men remained hidden on the island for two days before being caught. Another took to the water in a heavy shower of rain. Rumours spread that a mutiny was brewing, that the prisoners were planning to rush the ration boat—but nothing happened, probably due to the heavy police reinforcements that arrived on the island. One prisoner hid for some hours under the bellows in the blacksmiths' shop. Another remained missing for four days until apprehended by a police sentry as he crept towards the shoreline. Desperation led to drastic measures, with two men climbing through the 'seats' into the rainwater-flushed sewerage drains. John Garbutt was sent down to search the drains and discovered them there, driving them up before him.

Meanwhile, the Convict Board approved Fred and James' applications for a ticket-of-leave based on time served and hours worked. On a crisp winter's morning, just a few days after the drain-hiders were discovered, the pair stepped off Cockatoo Island's sandstone wharf into a boat that would ferry them back to Sydney. They knew that if they abided by the ticket-of-leave rules they need never return.

Surprisingly, John Garbutt was granted his own ticket-of-leave a month later: fortune continued to favour the ne'er-do-well.

A ticket-of-leave allowed a prisoner to work for himself so long as he remained within his chosen district. Naturally, the authorities preferred that felons who were granted such indulgences did not return to their old thieving grounds, so Windsor, Maitland and the Hunter district were out of the question.

What district did the trio ask for?

Mudgee, of all places.

13

A ticket-of-leave is the most tender kind of liberty.

Sydney Gazette, 18 August 1825

Why Mudgee? Why not Bathurst, the capital of the west? Indeed, why the west at all?

The gold rushes, perhaps. Recent gold discoveries near Mudgee were drawing miners to the district. Definitely not the sheep flocks—the woolly-coated bleaters were beneath their contempt—but possibly the cattle herds. Or maybe Mudgee was simply the closest western town to the northern districts they knew so well, just 100 miles across the Great Dividing Range from Muswellbrook. Cooyal, fifteen miles north-east of Mudgee, was even closer. Which was where John Garbutt ended up soon after arriving in Mudgee—and probably Fred as well.

Not surprisingly, the blue-eyed confidence man immediately landed on his feet. John Garbutt, aged twenty-six, caught the eye of 42-year-old widow Elizabeth Blackman, the eminently capable licensee of the Cooyal inn, heir to her husband's land and livestock, a woman of 'considerable means and independent circumstances'—meaning she was a great catch in the colonial marriage pool. Whatever made her fall for the smooth-talking trickster, let alone marry him only four months after he arrived in the district carrying a criminal's ticket-of-leave, is anyone's guess.

Her late husband's family were appalled. John was everything the Blackmans feared he would be. He was in the Mudgee courtroom so often, he may as well have camped there. An assault led to his first appearance only two

108

weeks after his wedding—and a fine of £5. A charge of inflicting damage on some working bullocks he had impounded led to another appearance, although the case was eventually settled out of court. A request for a liquor licence? The Licensing Board wisely demurred.

Then there were John's *own* charges, including those against his wife's ex-brother-in-law, Thomas Blackman, for stealing a steer from Cooyal. Money underpinned much of the acrimony, in the form of entitlements to land held by the Blackman family for decades. One witness told the court that John offered to withdraw the charges if Blackman resigned all claim to the property, while another said Elizabeth had tried to bribe him to 'lag' an innocent man. The jury eventually acquitted Blackman. When John responded by laying perjury charges against two of the defence witnesses, the Blackmans took their own revenge.

Was it at John Garbutt's Cooyal wedding in December 1860 that Fred first saw her? The intelligent brown eyes framed by the beautiful light-brown countenance, the black hair cascading down her back, the slightly cocked nose that suggested spiritedness, a defiance of convention.

Likely, he had already noticed her during his months in the Cooyal district. It is even possible that he first encountered her in the years before his conviction—if he ever travelled between Maitland and the New England district via Gloucester, or if she ventured into Maitland—although that window of opportunity was surprisingly small. Mary Ann had lived in Sydney until the mid-1840s, and out west from at least 1851 onwards, while Fred's work as a drover, stockman and horse-breaker largely kept him on the Tamworth side of the Great Dividing Range.

Whatever the circumstances of their first encounter, by February 1861 Mary Ann was pregnant.

James Garbutt hadn't managed quite as well for himself. Indeed, he was in a destitute condition, with his feet sticking out of his shoes, when Messrs Dickson and Burrows took pity on him early in 1861. They employed him to work as a light porter in their Mudgee shop, providing an income as well as bed and board, and were satisfied with his labours—until they discovered a stash of their unsold goods in his bedroom.

When his case came to trial at the Mudgee Quarter Sessions in July 1861, James was acquitted. Not because of reasonable doubt, as it turned out, but unreasonable behaviour by a jury member: 'I'm too drunk and too sleepy,' the juryman told the court when required to examine the stolen goods. 'I want a match to light my pipe,' he called out at another point in the proceedings. When the deliberations began, he steadfastly refused to accept James' guilt, and his obstinacy drew others to his side.

If James breathed a sigh of relief as he hastened from the courtroom, he breathed too soon. A month previously the Inspector General of Police had cancelled his ticket-of-leave, stating that even in the event of an acquittal he was to be returned to Cockatoo Island to complete his previous sentence. It was an object lesson that a ticket-of-leave provided only a tenuous liberty—that the rocky outcrop hundreds of miles away at the mouth of the Parramatta River was in fact no further away than the width of a pen stroke.

James wasn't the only Mudgee ticket-of-leaver whose freedom was cancelled in that letter from the Inspector General of Police. Some months previously, a couple of shepherds had been drinking at the Cooyal inn when sixty or seventy of their sheep disappeared, later to be found with John Garbutt's flock. John claimed to know nothing about the sheep, saying that he hadn't counted his flock for months. When his case came to trial at the same Mudgee Quarter Sessions, the prosecution's witnesses included the two men John had charged with perjury over Thomas Blackman's case. Who was telling the truth? The jury decided that John was guilty, although they added a strange proviso to their verdict: if one of the witnesses charged with perjury was found guilty, John should be pardoned. A perplexed letter-writer queried in the *Western Post*: 'Was this not evidence of reasonable doubt?'

Soon afterwards the Garbutt brothers—John with an additional five years added to his previous sentence, and James judged guilty of no crime at all—were transported back to the barbarous confines of Cockatoo Island.

•

What on earth possessed Fred? Unlike his Garbutt nephews, he had learnt the lesson intended by his Cockatoo Island servitude. He had no desire to return to gaol, particularly now that he had a family to support. He knew that the law's chains had wrapped themselves around the Garbutts again. He knew the ticket-of-leave rules: that he must not leave the Mudgee district without a pass, that he must attend the Mudgee courthouse on the specified day every quarter to be mustered. If he was found out of his district without a pass, or if he failed to attend the muster, his ticket-of-leave would be revoked.

So why did he decide to take the heavily pregnant Mary Ann back to her family at Monkerai near Dungog, where her father had settled to farm a few years previously? He wasn't taking her home to be enveloped in her mother's love and tender care during her first delivery: Charlotte had recently died at Monkerai and was buried in a garden grave, while Mary Ann had already given birth to half-a-dozen children. Maybe she simply wanted to go home to Monkerai to be with her grieving family. Or maybe she had no one to assist with her delivery, shunned by the district's women both for her Aboriginality and her 'morals'.

The easygoing morality of the early convict years was long gone. The immigrant ships had brought new ideas and ideals, Victorian values that would gradually permeate society. A woman's body was to be a temple, pure and clean, unadorned even with make-up's allurement; she was to be a saint in looks and deeds. Her greatest aspiration was to be a good wife and mother, to be 'respectable', faithful to her husband, untainted before marriage, and seemingly untouched in the aftermath, as if all her children were the products of virgin births. But Mary Ann? She wasn't a colonial Virgin Mary but Mary Magdalene, the Scarlet Woman, the feared Jezebel, the temptress whose sexual wiles might lure men away from wives and families.

The cloak of Victorian prudery had settled around the community, yet peeping from its folds was its sensual lining: prurience. Gossip thrived in small communities, and a beautiful part-Aboriginal woman who flitted openly from one man to another couldn't help but be noticed. Particularly by the menfolk.

Salacious eyes gazed at the Aboriginal women—eyes that would blink and look away if they encountered a settler's wife or daughter. The Aboriginal women were seen as fair game, as their menfolk were mere 'boys', emasculated by colonial contempt.

Salacious talk littered the white men's conversations as well, particularly at drunken carouses. They had all heard the stories: that Aboriginal people had different sexual mores, perhaps even different practices . . . It was titillating. It was enticing. Many a staunch church-goer loosened his moral belt when escaping the constraints of sober Christian society.

As for Mary Ann herself, she was an oddity, a paradox. She might look like a white woman—almost. She might speak like one, behave like one, read and write far better than most—yet clearly she was free with her sexual favours, as the paternity of her many children attested. She simply wasn't respectable. And she wasn't allowed to forget it, for those who fell from grace helped buff the halo of those who didn't. Naturally, those who wanted the shiniest haloes were the busiest gossips.

Mary Ann kept her head up, her dignity intact, but there were times when pride and dignity were not enough. Her mother's kinfolk might have walked into the bush to have their babies, treating childbirth as a private business. Their physical fitness usually ensured a successful outcome. However, Mary Ann had lived a European lifestyle, and knew that a private birth could come at a heavy price.

Perhaps Mary Ann demanded or pleaded, or perhaps Fred was the instigator, motivated by a deep concern for her well-being. Whatever the reason, nothing but love can account for Fred's decision to leave the Mudgee district while still on a ticket-of-leave, risking his own freedom for Mary Ann's benefit and that of his soon-to-be-born child.

Fred was working for Elizabeth Garbutt at Cooyal in mid-1861 when he decided, or agreed, to take Mary Ann back to Dungog. If Fred advised his employer of his plans she was evidently unable to talk him out of it, if she was even interested. Elizabeth was busy making her own plans. John Garbutt's perjury charges against the Blackman witnesses were due to be heard in October and, in the meantime, Elizabeth was travelling to Sydney to fight for his freedom—by whatever means necessary. Claims would later surface of an 'alleged extortion' at Cockatoo Island, that some officers had received £80 from Garbutt's wife without his knowledge.

Fred and Mary Ann decided that only a small party would undertake the journey. Mary Ann left her sons James and John Burrows at

Mudgee; aged ten and almost eight, they were old enough to shepherd with their father. Her eldest McNally children, Mary Jane and Patrick Christopher, remained at their father's Cooyal farm; he later baptised them in the Mudgee Catholic church while Mary Ann was at Dungog. Only the youngest, Ellen McNally, one-and-a-half years old, too young and demanding to be left with a working father, was among the little band of travellers who began the exhausting journey to Mary Ann's father's farm near Dungog. One hundred miles across the Great Dividing Range as the crow flies—although even the crow might baulk at flying over the lofty mountains in winter. The road journey was much longer, and perhaps that was the problem.

Fred couldn't stay away long. He was out of his district without a ticket-of-leave pass, in breach of the rules drummed into him. Having safely deposited his family at Monkerai, he turned around and galloped back to Mudgee, desperately trying to get back in time for his muster, increasingly desperate as the hours passed.

But he was too late.

'Frederick Ward, prisoner of the Crown, illegally at large.'

It was Fred's turn to make his presence felt in the Mudgee courts—albeit by his absence. After the Police Magistrate invoked his name on 13 September 1861, no voice piped up to say 'I am here'; no plea to explain why the wrath of the law should not descend upon him. The Bench ordered his return to Sydney, but he wasn't around to hear that his ticket-of-leave had just been revoked.

When he did appear, he compounded his problem by riding in on a 'stolen' horse.

'I didn't steal it,' Fred told Chief Constable Hardy when the copper announced to the exhausted rider on 19 September that he was taking him into custody for stealing Thomas Best's horse. 'I bought the horse off a man named Charles Williams, a digger at Cooyal.'

Hardy offered him the chance to prove it, asking to be shown the purchase receipt—well knowing, of course, what the response was likely to be.

'I lost it,' Fred admitted.

A ticket-of-leaver initially convicted of horse-stealing, who claimed to have lost his title to the horse he was riding? A receipt more precious than gold? Little wonder the authorities snorted with derision at the foolishness of the 'criminal class'.

Another Quarter Sessions court; another robed and bewigged judge; another charge of horse-stealing—or, if that failed, receiving. This time Fred knew exactly what to expect. He employed Mudgee attorney James Dudden Brodribb to defend him, to offer him any chance of evading his almost foregone fate.

'I don't know the prisoner Ward,' Thomas Best testified at Fred's trial on 3 October 1861, 'but the horse in the courtyard is my property.' He had purchased the stallion the previous January and had left it running with his mares at his Upper Meroo property, some twelve miles south of Mudgee. 'It wasn't easy to catch, but it had been ridden,' he admitted. 'I lost it from my run five months since and afterwards heard that it was running about Cooyal.'

Lost? Not 'stolen'? To the spectators, this was a noteworthy admission. When a horse ran loose on a property, it was often hard to determine whether escape or theft lay behind its disappearance—but why would anyone bother to steal a skittish and barely broken-in stallion from among a herd, when another 250,000 horses chomped at New South Wales' grass and hay? 'Lost' it almost certainly was. Yet if Best had 'afterwards heard' that it was running about Cooyal, why hadn't he bothered to go there and recover it?

The prosecutor asked what the horse was worth.

'I previously refused £20 but do not now think it worth £5,' said the angry owner.

That explained it. Fred Ward, a ticket-of-leave horse-thief, had been found with Best's exhausted and now nearly worthless mount. And so he had to pay.

Fred's barrister called his workmate George Pearson for the defence. 'I am well acquainted with the Cooyal diggings,' Pearson told the jury. 'I knew a man there named Charles Williams. He was digging at Cooyal and was there eight months ago.'

The jury waited; however, Pearson had nothing further to say. No declaration that he had seen Williams with the horse or had spoken to him about it, or had seen Fred purchase the horse or had seen Fred's receipt before he lost it. Pearson's defence was, unfortunately, no defence at all.

Fred, of course, was not allowed to testify. The law 'protected' him from incriminating himself. He had to rely on his barrister to speak for him, to convince the jury of his innocence.

The jury retired for only a few minutes. 'Not guilty,' they announced— but only to the 'stealing' charge. The judge sent Fred back to the lock-up to reflect upon his actions and to stew over his fate before his sentence was imposed.

A deliberate act of criminality, or an unfortunate borrowing choice?

Borrowing was common among Fred's equals, a reflection of the collectivist ethos of old and a primitive 'needs must' morality—a survival strategy in a society that offered them few favours. Borrowing was tolerated so long as the borrowed item was returned largely intact. But Best's horse hadn't been.

Perched on their own high horses, the squattocracy now demanded harsh punishments for any stock 'theft'. Crime must not be committed with impunity, they decreed. Stock thieves who eluded detection sent the wrong message to their criminally inclined cohorts, so those who were caught must pay the price to protect the broader community.

Such views echoed Britain's long-held attitude to property crime—the grounds for laws that had, until only recently, sentenced those found guilty of stealing a cow to death and those found guilty of killing a rabbit to a lengthy gaol sentence—if not transportation. That the rabbit might have been killed to feed an otherwise starving family was irrelevant in the eyes of the law: the 'needs must' morality prevailed only among those who had personally suffered the exigencies of need. While theft was no longer a capital offence in Britain or in Australia, injustice still prevailed—and rankled. The rural working classes were well aware of the hypocrisy underlying the squatters' demands: that many a squatter had built up his own herds by rustling cattle, and that some still turned a blind eye to the activities of their own stockmen. So what right had the squatters to demand harsh punishments for those who were merely following in their footsteps?

A 'finders, keepers' mentality also prevailed in the rural districts of New South Wales, particularly as 'ownership' was often difficult to determine in such a vast land. Why look a gift horse in the mouth—particularly a difficult-to-catch stallion that had just wandered into your territory? Or perhaps Charles Williams or someone else had indeed stolen the horse and clandestinely sold it to someone capable of managing its intractability.

Whatever the situation, Fred, languishing in the lock-up, must have been tormented by frustration, by the knowledge that the legal system's blinkers had prevented them from seeing the truth. If he had intentionally stolen a horse or knowingly received a stolen horse, why would he ride back to Mudgee—indeed, why would he *gallop* back to Mudgee—straight into the hands of the police?

'Surely it would suffice the ends of justice if Ward's ticket-of-leave is cancelled,' Mr Brodribb pleaded at Fred's sentencing hearing the following day, having addressed the court at some length in favour of mitigating his punishment.

'The fact of the prisoner being a ticket-of-leave man was rather a reason why he should be more severely punished,' Judge Cary retorted. 'He has not only shown himself ungrateful to his country, but he has done an injury to his fellow prisoners, for the more crime committed by ticket-of-leave men, the less inclined the Government to grant future tickets.'

Looking back at the penitent Fred Ward, Judge Cary decreed: 'You are to be employed on the public works of the colony for a period of three years, to commence after the expiration of your present sentence.'

Which meant another nine years on Cockatoo Island. For want of a speedier horse, Fred's freedom was lost—and this time there would be no parole.

As Fred remained in Mudgee Gaol waiting to be transported back to Cockatoo Island, the *Sydney Morning Herald*'s typesetters were laying out the issue of 9 October 1861. 'Frederick Ward was indicted for stealing a horse,' they began, giving no thought to the impact of their words on a heavily pregnant woman residing 140 miles north of Sydney. 'Sentence, three years' hard labour on the public roads.'

Mary Ann could read between their carefully typeset lines. Fred would not be coming back. Not for a very long time, if at all.

She gave birth to their daughter, Marina Emily, on 26 October 1861 at her father's Monkerai property. Minnie became the infant's nickname—just another tiny, fatherless child born to a mixed-race mother and white father. The father had not deliberately abandoned her, as many did, but whether he would return in nine years after his sentence expired was a different matter.

Deliberate or accidental, the effect was the same. Mary Ann was on her own for the first time since she was married at the age of fourteen. She would have to find some means of supporting herself and her two young daughters.

14

Men will do for liberty what they will not do for lashes.

Alexander Maconochie

They must have crossed paths unwittingly: Fred on his journey back to Cockatoo Island, John Garbutt on his departure. 'A very peculiar verdict,' the Attorney General had written regarding John's Mudgee conviction, before authorising the return of his ticket-of-leave. A year later, appeals for a pardon would prove successful as well, despite the Chief Justice's vehement disapproval. Only six years after masterminding an audacious horse-and-cattle stealing operation, John Garbutt was a free man.

Meanwhile James Garbutt, judged innocent of the Mudgee thefts, remained at Cockatoo Island on a cancelled ticket-of-leave. With no wealthy wife to fight his battles, James' only hope for the return of his ticket-of-leave lay in his own behaviour, so he had a strong motivation to abide by the rules. But his wound was doomed to fester for another four long years.

And Fred? Another nine years. Nine years! The words must have thrummed in his brain, echoing with each hoof beat on his journey from Mudgee to Darlinghurst Gaol, with each slap of the waves as he crossed the sparkling waters of Sydney Harbour to Cockatoo Island, a litany of desperation and despair.

Fred hadn't been gone long—only fifteen months—and the Cockatoo Island officials remembered him well, in particular his good behaviour. Within a few months, they recommended him for a promotion. While good conduct, a short sentence and no previous incarceration were the usual

118

grounds for a promotion, Fred's supporters included the island's superintendent, Captain Gother Kerr Mann.

Some months previously, Mann had written a report about Cockatoo Island and its prisoners, mentioning that the ticket-of-leave system often expected too much of the men. A petty offence that would cost a free man a small fine, for example, was enough to send a ticket-of-leave man back to gaol for an indefinite period. Mann himself authorised Fred's promotion, his return to a position of trust, assigning him to the role of constable of the cells.

Fred's duties involved monitoring the inmates locked in the solitary confinement cells under the prisoner's ward. Although he was not issued with their cell keys, he could communicate through the trapdoor opening, calling down to the men every so often and checking that all was right. If they needed medical attention, he would ask the prisoner gateman to alert the sentries, and the message would be passed on.

Fred had endured three days in the cells, so he knew what the inmates were suffering. Was it sympathy or a promised pecuniary benefit that led him to assist some of the men on the night of Monday 5 May 1862? Or something else entirely?

Quietly, while the ward prisoners were sleeping, Fred worked at the cell locks until, somehow, he was able to release two of them. He carefully lifted off the trapdoor lid and whispered to the men to climb up. The conspirators then sneaked through the ward to one of the windows and began tampering with the latch, trying to open it. But not quietly enough: some of the prisoners awoke. At the sounds of rustling and murmured voices, Fred and his companions slipped away, back towards the cells. Fred sealed the locks, leaving no evidence of tampering, no evidence that he had been conspiring to assist in their escape.

Well, that was the story an informant told the superintendent the following morning, a charge supported by other prisoners in the same ward.

Captain Mann told Fred that he was to sleep in the cells himself while they awaited the arrival of the visiting magistrate. Meanwhile, he ordered that the cell locks be replaced with new ones—which meant that the warden had even more keys dangling from his enormous keyring. That evening, when he was issuing blankets to the cell inmates, he mixed them all up.

Hours it took the guard and warders to sort them out, trying one key after another, attempting to keep to an order, but finding there were smaller rings of keys hanging from bigger rings and that each looked disconcertingly like the other, and that the keys kept clunking back together when they endeavoured to separate those they had already tested from those they hadn't. It became increasingly difficult, as they moved from one cell to the next, to remember which keys they had already tried and where they were in the sequence. As they ground their teeth and muttered increasingly louder curses, particularly at one cell lock that seemed stubbornly determined to defeat them, they gave up. They called the mechanics to knock off the lock so they could close the trapdoor. After all the delays, after all the cells were finally secured and the problem seemingly resolved, two cell inmates called up that they needed medical attention. And the warden realised that all the keys were mixed up again.

But did he think to make new arrangements for these important keys?

The troubles continued the following morning when they had to unlock the cells again. Eventually they called the mechanics to knock off all the cell locks, while Captain Mann authorised a warden to travel across to Sydney and purchase twelve new padlocks specifically for the use of the cells.

As for Fred, the visiting magistrate arrived the same day and heard the charges against him: 'Tampering with the prisoners in the cells with the view to assist them in attempting to effect their escape.' He remanded the case for a week, and eventually discharged it through lack of evidence. Without any physical signs of tampering he had only the prisoners' accusations to rely upon, accusations perhaps motivated by malice alone.

The damage was done. Fred was no longer considered quite as trustworthy.

The Cockatoo Island prisoners laboured together at the dockyard, in the kitchen, in the laundry, in the gardens, matching each other stroke by stroke, shovel by shovel, every minute of every hour of every working day. Yet there was a difference between the men, a stark difference reflected in their jacket colour and demeanour. Some laboured under the old prisoner regulations—the 'old Act'—while others laboured under the new.

Fred was once among those who had smirked at the 'new Act' men, complacent in the knowledge that he had been convicted before 1 July 1858 when the new regulations were implemented. In those seemingly halcyon days, he had two carrots dangling in front of him: a half-day sentence remission for every full day of labour, and the likelihood of a ticket-of-leave if he worked enough hours and behaved well. But with his latest conviction he was now a 'new Act' man: no carrots, only a large stick. Hard work and good behaviour would benefit him naught. He had to serve every single day of his sentence without any hope of a remission, yet ever present was the threat of punishment if he misbehaved.

The regulatory changes wouldn't have seemed so unjust had he been sent to a gaol housing only the 'new Act' men. However, the authorities had given little thought to the impact of the new Act on the prisoners themselves. They were too busy listening to the judges and police officials who warned that felons were not paying the price society imposed upon them for their criminality; that an individual found guilty of manslaughter rather than murder, or a murderer reprieved from the gallows, would be sentenced to fifteen years on Cockatoo Island yet receive a ticket-of-leave after only four years' servitude—or possibly less; that sending such dangerous criminals back into the community after so short an imprisonment served neither as an appropriate punishment nor as a deterrent to others, and put the community at greater risk.

Naturally, such an example sent a tremor of horror through the community and the Parliamentarians. The kneejerk reaction of the resulting change in regulations booted out more than just the reward system: it eliminated any motivation to work hard and behave well, particularly among men like Fred who were forced to work shoulder-to-shoulder with the 'old Act' men. Human nature thrives best when achievement is rewarded—to some extent at least; anger and despair are the only outcomes of a system driven by threats of punishment alone. The once industrious Cockatoo Island prisoner now worked no harder than necessary to keep himself out of trouble, while too many others directed their energies towards devising means of escape. Significantly, there had been no escape attempts from Cockatoo Island in the year before the 'new Act' was implemented.

If Cockatoo Island had merely been a prison, the ramifications of the new regulations would only have been personal. However, Cockatoo Island was a business, and Fred and the other prisoners were its labour force. No longer could the engineers entrust skilled work to the prisoners, or duties that required care and precision. As for coercing the men to undertake dangerous duties like diving operations, they hadn't a hope. Productivity decreased, quality deteriorated, costs increased—not a good outcome for any business, government-owned or otherwise.

The prisoners' frustration smouldered, a grumbling volcano that the prison authorities seemed determined to ignore. It had already erupted once—in January 1861 while Fred was away at Mudgee. An ensuing Parliamentary enquiry run by Henry Parkes had listed as its first recommendation that 'good conduct should be taken into account so as to encourage the prisoner to accomplish his own redemption by a reformed course of life'. How did the government respond? To a question in Parliament six months later, Premier Charles Cowper admitted that the report had not been adopted, although they had ordered it to be printed. The committee hadn't made any specific recommendations for carrying out prisoners' sentences anyway, he said, so Parliament had no concrete directions to follow.

Cowper's dismissive response was hardly surprising. As Colonial Secretary in 1858, he was largely responsible for the 'new Act's' regulations.

The government shelved the problem. Printing the committee's recommendations was seemingly solution enough, as if the printed word itself might magically solve any problems. Most Parliamentarians kept their gazes turned firmly away from Cockatoo Island and blocked their ears to the evidence of increasing discontent within the prison system.

But, eventually, the clamour became too loud.

Oliver Twist's entreaties were not being echoed by the Cockatoo Island inmates. Who would ask for more burnt or sour bread or more inedible meat? Even the authorities agreed that they could not feed such rations to the prisoners, particularly when the men received only two meals a day: breakfast and dinner (the midday meal). Bread and meat were the staples of their diet. Each man was issued a daily ration of half a pound of maize meal (which was made into hominy for breakfast), a loaf of bread, a pound of beef or mutton, two ounces of vegetables (when available), and some salt and sugar. Without their bread and meat, the prisoners would starve. And, most importantly, they would be of little use at their work stations.

The ration problems began a week before Christmas 1862. The contractor solved the problem by sending up biscuit—the hard, dry, teeth-breaking tablets that needed to be soaked to be edible. The problems escalated in the new year. More sour bread on 6 January. On the 7th, the prisoners' bread and its replacement biscuit were both rejected by the officers, and the bread again on the 8th. When the contractor refused to send further replacements, an officer was ferried to Sydney to purchase enough supplies to tide them over. That night the prisoners began to riot. Fred was among them.

Cockatoo Island's Chief Warden preferred sleeping in his bed than being called out to deal with any prisoner issue, let alone the most dreaded: a riot. The very word sparked a frisson of fear in all experienced gaol wardens. Uprisings were an ever-present threat, particularly on an unfenced island that was only a swim away from freedom. Desperate prisoners made deadly choices, a danger not only to themselves but to everyone in the vicinity—including the women and children who lived in the officers' houses on Cockatoo Island.

The prisoners usually behaved, much to the community's relief. Gun-wielding sentries and threats of harsh punishments controlled them—or so the community believed. The discerning, however, realised this was only part of the explanation. An unspoken agreement lay at the heart of gaol stability, a tacit acceptance to abide by the rules, harsh though they might be, so long as the rules or the rulers remained reasonable. But the guards' immediate fear reflected the fragility of the status quo. 'Riot!' was enough to instantly sweep away the Chief Warden's sleep-induced cobwebs.

The Chief Warden wasn't really surprised. Riots always had a trigger and this one was obvious. Summer: twelve hours locked in sun-baked, poorly ventilated wards, breathing the unbearable stench of the open tubs and the ubiquitous tobacco smoke, with bugs biting every square inch of exposed flesh. It was more surprising that the prisoners refrained from rioting. Yet the men put up with these conditions every summer, so why riot now, particularly when the weather wasn't at its extremes?

The ration problems, of course: although the men were not forced to eat the bad rations, they had endured a long wait for their dinner. Hot, tired and hungry: a volatile combination.

'We will break out!' one voice cried. 'We will strike work in the morning!' another bellowed, while their companions continued to hoot and jeer. Fred and his fellow prisoners had not taken kindly to the Chief Warden's remonstrances. The prisoners pushed and shoved to get to the tiny windows, thrusting their arms through the bars and gesticulating at the guards—even reaching for them.

The Officer of the Guards ordered his men to maintain a close watch, just in case the prisoners found a way to break out. Guns clutched firmly in their hands, the sentries marched up and down outside the wards, ignoring the catcalls and keeping clear of the flailing hands.

It was going to be a very long night indeed.

A surprisingly obedient line of prisoners filed out of the wards shortly after sunrise the following morning. The guards monitored the men carefully as they ambled towards the camp. At 6 am the wardens would muster the men and despatch them to their usual duties.

About 190 names—half the number that were imprisoned on Cockatoo Island during Fred's first incarceration—yet it still took some time to get through the muster roll. As Messrs Grimley and Byron read out each name, a prisoner stepped forward and fell into line. Or should have. On Friday 9 January 1863, many of the men from Ward 1 acknowledged their presence, then deliberately, defiantly, stepped out of line and huddled together.

Name after name; choice after choice. Fred had already made up his mind. He was a veteran of the old remission system and had nearly eight more years to endure on Cockatoo Island under the new system. He had received no visitors in the fourteen months since his return, and had no reason to expect any in the years to come, particularly not from Mary Ann who would struggle to afford the cost of a journey to Sydney. And he had never even met his young daughter—indeed who knew if he ever would? So what did he have to lose? When his own name was called, he too announced his presence, then stepped out of line.

'We refuse to go to work!' he and the other mutinous prisoners told the wardens. 'We are getting no indulgence in time. We could not be worse off than we already are!'

Prisoners dictating to the government the conditions under which they would work and the time they should serve? Not under his superintendence, Captain Mann announced to the thirty-six glowering faces when he reached the muster station. Mann reminded them that they had been sent to the island as a punishment, and that work was part of their punishment. If they refused to work they would, of course, face further punishment.

'However I am offering you a choice,' he added as an appeasement. 'If you choose to go to work now, you may do so.'

And he watched and waited.

Mann had some sympathy for the prisoners' plight. All of the island officials could see the differences in the prisoners' labour and behaviour since the introduction of the new Act, but his duty was to implement the government's rulings not question them—not in front of the prisoners, anyway. And he had to maintain his authority or the fragile equilibrium would instantly disappear. So he continued to watch and wait.

All thirty-six men stood their ground.

Nine o'clock: the mid-morning muster, the second of the day. Another two prisoners standing in the warm sun fell out and joined the strikers. Thirty-eight men now—one-fifth of the prisoners under his charge, and the day was only beginning. The last thing Captain Mann wanted was for the strikers' ranks to keep swelling, yet he had few options for dealing with intransigent prisoners. He couldn't flog them into submission, much as he might have wished. He couldn't throw them into the cells and leave them there until all recalcitrance was spent. He was permitted only to lock them in the cells and await the arrival of the visiting magistrate. Not that there were enough solitary confinement cells for all the strikers, anyway.

Meanwhile, he would appeal for more guards—just in case.

Captain Samuel North, the Water Police Magistrate, stepped off the boat at Cockatoo Island on the following Monday morning, ready to sentence the rebellious prisoners. He had visited the island on the Saturday and listened to the various testimonies, but had delayed the sentencing hearing for two days.

When the temporary courtroom was ready, the thirty-eight prisoners filed in, wary gun-toting guards surrounding them, alert for any signs of violence.

Captain North read out the first charge: 'Disobedience of orders in refusing to go out to work on 9 January.' Then he began to call out the names.

Fred stood among the rebels, waiting for his sentence to be passed. Four names were called first: the ringleaders. Captain North sentenced each of them to fourteen days' solitary confinement on bread and water. Another name; a sentence of ten days in the cells. Fred then heard his own name among the remaining thirty-three: 'Seven days in the cells on bread and water.'

This was twice as long as his previous stint, and another charge was pending.

'Making a disturbance after hours in No. 1 ward and persisting in it when desired to leave off—again on 9 January,' Captain North read. He then added: 'These prisoners having all been sentenced to various terms of solitary confinement for the previous offence, this trial is postponed until after their terms of imprisonment have expired.'

Thirty-eight prisoners; twelve solitary confinement cells. Naturally, 'solitary confinement' lost its impact when multiple prisoners were packed in the same cell. Instead, Fred and the other minor rebels were incarcerated in Ward 2, although not just for the seven days of their initial sentence. On their release they again refused to go back to work and were ordered to spend another twenty-eight days in the cells.

Bang! Bang! It sounded like someone was beating a tom-tom. Bang! Bang! Bang!

The island's free residents pulled pillows over their heads and tried to go back to sleep. Night after night they had been disturbed by the shouting and singing from Ward 2, the hoots and howls. Everyone was tired of it, including the other prisoners. Barely able to sleep, they had to labour on the works, whereas the rebels could lie in their beds, refusing to work, even refusing to hand over their bedding, saying that rolling up their bedding was 'work'.

Bang! Bang!

'Why are you making such a noise?' Captain Mann called out plaintively just before midnight on 27 January. He was standing outside the ward with the Chief Warder and a detachment of soldiers and policemen. 'Would it not be better to let the men who were out at work all day go to sleep?'

Bang! Bang!

'Give me the tin!' Mann shouted.

'We have nothing to give and would not give it if we had!' the defiant prisoners yelled back. Then they swore at the guards, using the opportunity to vent all their anger and frustration in a few choice epithets.

Captain Mann ordered the warder to open the gate. He and his men filed in. Again he demanded that the men hand over the drum. Again they said they had nothing of the kind. Sergeant Lane spotted a prisoner covering something underneath a hammock. It proved to be one of the large mess dishes. He lifted it, intending to carry it away. A prisoner grabbed hold of his coat to stop him.

'The best thing you can do is to go to bed,' Captain Mann exhorted them.

'We will not go to bed!' the men shouted. 'You are bloody wretches and dogs! You are all drunk and you come here to annoy us at this hour of the night!'

Captain Mann ordered the light to be trimmed and told the warder to take down the names of those standing in the passages. He praised one of the prisoners who was heading for his hammock, and suggested that the others follow suit. Instead, a prisoner named Stewart walked towards him.

'No force shall put me into bed or any of the other men,' Stewart proclaimed defiantly. 'We will remain up as long as we think proper.' Then he reached out and grabbed Sergeant Lane's revolver.

All semblance of order collapsed as the prisoners mobbed the troops. Shouting, scuffling, wrestling. Suddenly two distinctive cracks breached the clamour.

Stewart and another prisoner had been shot. Flesh wounds only, but it was enough for another forty-eight men to fall out the following day, demanding a thorough investigation.

•

Thirty-six days Fred had been locked up, stifling in an oven for twenty-four hours a day during the hottest month of the year, yet still he wasn't released on 15 February. The 'disturbance after hours' charge from 9 January had seemingly been forgotten, but he was among a group who continued in their refusal to work, and were sent back to the 'cells' for another seven days.

Otherwise he and his companions had seemingly quietened down, but this was mere illusion. Secretly they had been busy making plans during their endless days and nights locked in the ward: an iron hammock bar sawn through and pulled out, a flagstone pried up, the beginnings of a hole in the wall's masonry.

The military and police sentries had not seen or heard anything, nor could they convince any of the prisoners to talk. All they could do was relocate the men to Ward 1 and keep a closer watch.

By 25 February, Fred had been locked up for forty-six days. Many of his rebel companions were gone, swapped with others from Darlinghurst Gaol. Only five faced further charges of refusing to go back to work.

Without the strength of numbers, Fred's fight left him. When the visiting magistrate asked if he too would return to work, he agreed. All other charges against him were then dropped.

Fred was no longer among the favoured few. His infractions had relegated him to the labourers' ranks, and he joined the men trudging towards the works six days a week, labouring in the summer's heat or the winter's chill.

A notepad-holding visitor watched the prisoners and jotted down his thoughts about their air of dejection and filthy appearance. He walked up and down the wards and later wrote that the men were locked up at 5 pm like wild beasts, and that obscene language and scenes of iniquity were inevitably enacted there each night with impunity, scenes too gross for him to pollute the newspaper's pages by describing. He gazed into the solitary confinement cells and decided they were constructed with the sole purpose of torture in mind—'the mind revolts from such cruelty in the nineteenth century'. He glanced into the schoolroom and asked why so few prisoners were interested in gaining the education that would help their employment prospects after their release. 'Because the miserable pittance capable of being earned by overwork is lost to the prisoner who attends school,' he wrote despairingly. This was the very pittance that paid for their night-time meal and any additional luxuries like tea and tobacco.

He wondered no longer at the prisoners' air of dejection, at the faces so devoid of hope, and he asked himself if anyone forced to endure such conditions could possibly emerge from the prison system a better man, a reformed man.

15

If there were any pluck anywhere!

William Cobbett

Weary prisoners stood around the muster area, some bound by shackles, others bound by psychological chains. Their day's labour had finished and they would soon return to their yard for a wash and supper—if they had any leftovers, or money to purchase bread; their rations did not include an evening meal.

The rollcall began, a name followed by a muttered acknowledgement and a shuffle of feet as the prisoner stepped into line. Another name, another mutter: many times a day like a metronome ticking their life away. As the rollcall continued, the remaining prisoners waited, listening idly for their own names. Then all of a sudden there was silence.

For a moment they didn't notice—until the silence lengthened, intruding into their drifting thoughts, demanding their attention.

'Ward!' the voice called again.

The prisoners glanced up at the muster clerk, then around at each other, a spark of interest lighting their dull eyes as they searched for the wiry five-foot, eight-inch frame, the cropped brown hair.

'Ward?'

Still no one stepped forward.

The muster clerk finally looked down at his list again and snapped out the next name, and the next.

Smiles tugged at the prisoners' lips as they paused for a moment before announcing their own presence, taunting the muster clerk before ambling into line. Then, suddenly, there was silence again.

'Britten!' the muster clerk yelled.

Frederick Britten was a bolter. They already knew that. The 'flash, talk-ative rascal' had twice attempted to escape from police custody before being locked up in Darlinghurst Gaol, charged with being one of three men who had robbed the Bathurst mail on 5 November 1862. After his February 1863 trial, the judge sentenced him and an accomplice, George Willison, to fifteen years in gaol, the first to be spent in irons. Try bolting with irons binding your ankles was the message Britten received, loudly and clearly. He did try, twice in July, but didn't succeed. Evidently he hadn't stopped trying.

'Britten and Ward work in the same gang,' the grim muster clerk told Captain Mann soon afterwards, adding that he had questioned the foreman about the absconders. The pair had been employed at opposite ends of a short tramway, and had last been seen by the foreman about twenty minutes before the first bell rang. Clearly, they had slipped away at least half an hour before the muster, maybe more, and could already be long hidden. No one else had reported seeing them, and the prisoners, of course, claimed to know nothing about the escape—nothing at all.

Soon afterwards, a bell pealed. The sound carried across the water towards Balmain 450 yards to the south, towards the North Shore 330 yards to the north, towards the boats and barges gliding by. All over the island, the prisoners and workers, the officials and their wives and children paused for a moment and lifted their heads to listen. No one required an explanation. They hadn't heard its distinctive tones as frequently in recent months, but its insistent demand was always the same.

Prisoners are missing. Find them!

Captain Mann dashed off a couple of letters to the Balmain Police Station and the Water Police Station with descriptions of the two absconders, then continued barking out orders. The day sentries are to remain on duty. Two more police and two more military sentries are to be stationed around the island. A police and a military unit are to patrol the island throughout the night in case the men try to sneak across the island and into the water. Find them!

They all knew that the prisoners had picked an ideal time to escape. Sunset was an hour after the muster, darkness half an hour after that. September was ideal as well: the days getting warmer but not too hot, the nights not as cold. The men wouldn't need as much food for warmth, or water to stave off thirst. And the harbour's waters lapping the shore might seem almost inviting—to those who could swim, anyway.

Saturday 12 September 1863. Nothing. Despite the additional sentries and the two patrols, the fugitives hadn't been seen.

Captain Mann had delayed informing the New South Wales Governor, hoping his men would find the prisoners by morning, in which case his report would briefly mention their escape and subsequent recovery. He couldn't delay the task any longer. He sat at his desk and inked his nib. 'Yesterday evening, Friday, at the muster at ¼ to 5 pm the two prisoners named in the margin were absent,' he wrote, before recounting his unsuccessful attempts to find them.

Would the Governor understand that Cockatoo Island absconders were surprisingly difficult to find? The prison was not simply a brick box surrounded by a high fence. While admittedly an island, it was over 30 acres in size and populated by cunning prisoners who kept thinking up innovative places to hide. If only they were as innovative in undertaking their work! One absconder was found after an informant disclosed his hiding place: between the joists under an officer's new floorboards; his carpenter mates had nailed the floorboards over him. Other prisoners made a mast lug sail and concealed it behind a platform in a building under construction, awaiting the right moment to attempt an escape. One prisoner even hid in a solitary confinement cell. So many desperate characters; so many hiding places because of the size and complexity of the dockyard operations; so many opportunities for communicating with Sydney when vessels were being repaired in the dock. So unsuitable a place of punishment, and still considered only 'temporary' despite two decades of operations.

It wasn't surprising that they couldn't find the men. What was more surprising was that, until now, few Cockatoo Island absconders had actually reached the mainland. The last successful attempt had been opportunistic: two prisoners working until 11 pm pumping out the dock, a small dinghy left unsecured at the landing jetty with its mast and sail and paddles still on board—in a penal outpost! What prisoner would turn his back on such a gift? Fortunately, the escapees were caught within days, by luck more than anything else. One was spotted in Sydney by the very constable who had apprehended him in the first place.

Fred Ward was an inmate at the time of the almost-successful escape, and Captain Mann knew he would have learnt from the fugitives' mistakes. But the superintendent had also learnt from the lessons of the past, and the next move in this cat-and-mouse game was his.

Before signing his letter, Captain Mann advised: 'I do not intend to let the prisoners out on the Works today, and with your permission I propose to keep them in for a longer period if necessary.'

The prisoners were not surprised to learn they were to remain locked in their smelly, bug-ridden wards until the superintendent's pleasure. They all knew why Captain Mann was keeping them locked up: if Ward and Britten could hide for long enough, the superintendent would eventually be forced to cancel the extra night-time sentries and patrols, and the pair could slip away into the darkness. But to remain undetected, they needed a secure hiding place—one never used before, one no one would think to search—and enough food and water. The only food they could stockpile was the rock-hard biscuit issued when bread supplies were wanting, but to eat biscuit they generally needed water to soften it. They needed drinking water anyway if they were to survive for more than a day or two. Where might they get water? From their fellow prisoners, naturally.

Captain Mann's decision to sacrifice the labour of 170 men in return for recovering two was not an economic decision. Although Chief Engineer of an important government enterprise, he was first and foremost super-intending a prison and he knew that this gambit would choke off the fugitives' supplies. But what if they had indeed stockpiled ample rations—unlikely, but feasible—or if it rained enough for them to collect water? He tried to put himself in their shoes, to out-think the runaways. The last thing he wanted was to cancel the extra sentries and patrols just before thirst or starvation forced them to give themselves up.

On the other hand, the dock work couldn't be delayed forever, and the extra sentries and patrols were a cost someone had to bear. He also risked a riot if he kept the other prisoners locked up for too long.

He sat down to write another letter, this time to the officer commanding the island's military detachment. 'In the event of the Prisoners not being found today, it will be necessary to post and keep up the same sentries round the Island during tonight, and take the same precautions as were adopted last night.'

He would keep the extra sentries and patrols for another day or two. If luck went his way, he might starve out the runaways. Or one of the other prisoners might sidle up to an official and whisper some news.

Sunday 13 September 1863. The stars glared down from the clear night sky as the sentries patrolled the island. The air was so still that even the wavelets barely swooshed against the island's shore. The melancholy hoot of the night-birds warned of foolishness afoot, but no one was listening.

Did anyone notice the two figures creeping towards the shoreline opposite the North Shore, the dull thud as something metallic dropped to the ground, the soft mound that suddenly appeared by the water's edge, the strange eddy on the water's surface, the ensuing silence?

Monday 14 September 1863. A ruse, Captain Mann decided. As if the fugitives would stand at the water's edge barely a stone's throw from one of the sentries and file off Britten's irons. The noise alone would alert the sentries—if they hadn't managed to notice two men sneaking towards the shore on such a quiet, starlit night. And if the fugitives had filed off Britten's irons while in hiding—which was plausible considering the material at hand in the dockyard—why would they carry the irons with them? The clang of metal if they knocked or dropped them would also alert the sentries. The discovery had to be a bluff to trick him into calling off the search.

He pulled out some paper and began another letter to the Governor. 'The search is still being continued, there being no doubt that they are secreted on the Island: the irons of Britten and part of the clothing of both of them has been found. I think it advisable that the other prisoners should not go on the Works today as any provisions that the absentees may have had with them must be now nearly exhausted.'

He welcomed the additional eleven soldiers who stepped off the boat that day, and ordered another exhaustive search of the island. The discovery continued to niggle at him, however. Unless an ally had deposited the items, the runaways might have escaped the island after all. The irons and clothing were found on the shoreline, so surely if the pair had managed to reach the water unnoticed they would just slip in and swim away. But why were Britten's irons left at the water's edge and not where they had been hiding? Maybe they had carried them to use as a weapon in case they met resistance. Or maybe they had left them there deliberately. What better way of thumbing their noses at their superiors than by ostentatiously discarding the symbols of their servitude at their place of triumph.

The puzzled superintendent inked his nib again and addressed a letter to the Inspector General of Police in Sydney. 'The clothes of Britten have just been found at the water edge on the northern side of the island, which would indicate that he had effected his escape last night. I should therefore suggest that descriptions of Britten and Ward be at once telegraphed to Parramatta and the other stations on the Telegraph Line if not already done.'

He also despatched some constables in the guard boat to the North Shore, the shortest swim from the site of the discarded clothing. From there, the constables walked nearly two miles north-west to Hunter's Hill, calling at all the houses along the way and asking the residents if they had seen or heard anything. When they arrived back at Cockatoo Island later that day, they had little to tell the superintendent. 'We made enquiries in every direction but could get no tidings of them.'

They must still be on the island, Captain Mann decided, and again called in the search leaders. Find them!

Tuesday 15 September 1863. The worried look on the officer's face didn't augur well. Captain Mann heard the latest news with foreboding. Apparently the soldier on sentry duty nearest the discarded clothing on the Sunday night had once deserted his regiment while stationed at Cockatoo Island— and a friend of his, also a deserter from the same regiment, was currently a prisoner on the island.

'I now think that the prisoners must have made good their escape from the Island,' the superintendent wrote a short time later. 'Some very suspicious circumstances have come to my knowledge and lead me to fear that their escape was effected with the connivance of one of the Military Guards.'

The night of the 13th/14th was clear and starlit and the water so calm and smooth that it is difficult to understand how any person could have entered it without detection.'

Captain Mann realised that such a grave charge shouldn't be made lightly, nevertheless the consequences of such an infraction were so serious that he felt he couldn't withhold the information from the government. Military connivance would explain how the fugitives had evaded the sentries—and also, perhaps, why the exhaustive searches had proven unsuccessful.

'I propose continuing the sentries by night and day until all doubt is removed, but without confining the rest of the prisoners to the prison yard,' he concluded.

One soldier's neck for the chopping block.

Captain Mann had managed to shift the blame for one of the only successful Cockatoo Island escapes onto the military—justifiably or otherwise. Not that the press, at least initially, was calling for anyone's neck. Indeed, the news of the escape didn't break until Wednesday 16 September, five days after the pair absconded, and even then the *Sydney Morning Herald* inaccurately identified the escapees as Willison and Britten. As usual, the *Herald*'s report was then repeated by newspapers across the country. No doubt the delay in reporting their escape and the error in identifying Fred Ward helped the fugitives to evade detection.

The press might have been eager for more information, but little was available—no description of their hiding place, no explanation as to how they managed to escape from the island. Soon afterwards, a dramatic escape from Berrima Gaol grabbed the press's attention, and interest in Ward and Britten waned.

Concerns about prison escapes in general, however, elicited more press coverage. A letter-writer to the *Herald* asked why the number of gaol attempts was increasing, a much higher proportion than suffered in England. 'We have had experience enough in a system as nearly approaching to perfection as any human scheme probably can. The fault must lie with the agents we employ.'

A prison system nearly approaching perfection? The liberal *Empire* was aghast. The recent visitor to Cockatoo Island described the filthy and degraded prisoners whose faces were devoid of hope and compared them with the clean, hopeful faces of the Darlinghurst prisoners, labouring under a disciplined and sanitary system, with reformation as an objective. 'It is too much the fashion now-a-days to charge him who has any philanthropic feeling towards a prisoner with a sympathy with crime,' he rebuked the public. 'I boldly admit and glory in the sympathy—not with crime, but with the criminal, in so far as an earnest desire exists for the repression of crime and reformation of the criminal, together with the amelioration of the criminal code.'

The prison employees were not the problem; it was the system itself. When it drained every shred of humanity . . . every spark of hope . . . who could blame the prisoners for seeking their own redemption?

PART 4

LIBERTY

Reader, if male thou art,
Look to thy purse;
If female, to thy heart.
Much havoc has he made of both.

A highwayman's epitaph

16

For if your employment you'd like to be changing,
There's a fine opportunity now for bushranging.
Just steal a good race-horse; and travellers fleece,
And don't care a hang for the New Police
In their truly rural tooral looral right ridiculous uniforms gay.

Bell's Life in Sydney, 10 October 1863

Three issues a week required a lot of words. The *Maitland Mercury*'s editor was happy to fill his columns with information lifted from other newspapers, the daily Sydney papers in particular. Sometimes, he chose political reports, British as well as Australian; sometimes interesting snippets. This particular report from *The Empire* had the added advantage of providing a community service: here was something the public needed to know.

He copied the item into the *Mercury*'s issue of 19 September 1863: 'On the muster roll being called at Cockatoo Island on Sunday evening, two of the prisoners named Britten and Ward were found missing . . .'

Eyes in the Dungog district skimmed the column for further news. Ward was a common surname, so there might be two of them at the penal settlement. The eyes stopped and reread the final sentence. 'Ward was a Windsor resident and was under sentence for cattle-stealing.' Wrong—but near enough. Was it him?

Soon afterwards, there was a night-time knock on the Buggs' door.

•

Marina Emily Ward was almost two years old before she met her father. Mary Ann had not intended to be left stranded at Monkerai without a husband to support her, with a squawking infant and an eighteen-month-old whining for attention, and her older children living so far away at Mudgee. The strange hiatus forced upon a woman by her pregnancy generally lingered for some months after she gave birth, as if she had been stepping warily along a bridge over a precipitous gorge, but had not quite reached the other side. An experienced mother like Mary Ann had some idea of when she would finally step off, but Fred's forced abandonment had left her inching along with some uncertainty. What was she to do after her baby was weaned?

Three extra mouths were too much of a burden for her father. She would have to find work to support her own family, yet her options were limited. She could remain in the Dungog district and leave her little girls in the care of her sisters. Or she could beg her father for the funds to travel back to Mudgee—but who would care for her daughters while she earned an income? Dungog it would have to be. Fortunately her education and years as a wife and mother had provided all the skills she needed for the one field of employment open to her in an area like Dungog—the one socially acceptable field, that is: domestic service.

Monkerai lay fifteen miles from Dungog, a bumpy trip in Mary Ann's father's cart along what was little more than a horse track. Mary Ann stepped off into the world of domestic service, employed by a family living near Dungog for the next year or two. It was the first time she had worked for her living.

Her world was to change again, however, in the aftermath of that rat-a-tat on the wooden door.

Hunger was an occupational hazard for prisoners on the run. A side of cured bacon hanging from a ceiling hook was a tempting reminder of the pungent aroma of bacon fat sizzling in a frying pan. After their monotonous prison diet, it was simply too enticing to resist.

Ward and Britten had travelled nearly 250 miles north to the New England district in the six weeks since their escape from Cockatoo Island.

Their prison garb was long discarded, replaced with ordinary bushmen's attire which allowed them to travel incognito. But when they arrived at a shepherd's hut on the Gostwyck run near Uralla around 10 am on Saturday 24 October 1863, their blackened faces were a giveaway.

'Where is your husband?' the frightening figures demanded.

The shepherd's wife was alone when the two men dismounted from their bay mares. Her eyes were immediately drawn to the weapon one was cradling: a single-barrelled shotgun. She stammered that her husband wasn't home, that he was away—at the head station.

'We won't molest you,' the men reassured her. 'We are only after food and arms.'

They entered her home and began searching, a quick rummage through the tiny hut. Picking up a double-barrelled shotgun, they checked it over: no point stealing a gun that didn't work. They saw the flitch of bacon hanging from the ceiling and lifted it down. 'We want the gun and bacon,' they said, before adding nobly, 'but we won't rob the house as we merely rob the rich and not the poor.'

The men added some tea and sugar to their bounty—the luxuries of bush life—before asking directions to the main road and the telegraph line. The woman said it lay just a few miles thataway and pointed towards the west. Clearly the men must have ridden from the coast or from the south—Walcha or even the Gloucester district—otherwise they would have crossed the Great North Road's hardened surface at some point before reaching her hut.

'We will soon be heard of again,' one tossed back at her as they rode off towards the main road.

Passing a creek, Fred and his companion stopped to wash the soot from their faces, glad to be rid of the camouflage. Dirtying their faces seemed demeaning somehow, as if they lacked courage and confidence, as if they feared their victims. Maintaining the camouflage could also be dangerous in the event they encountered others—like young Mr Franey, who provided further directions towards the mail road.

As it turned out, ditching their disguise delayed the law's pursuit for only a short time. Soon afterwards, Franey heard about the Gostwyck robbery and realised that the robbers resembled the two men he had just directed towards the mailbags: the unguarded sacks that carried most of the northern district's banknotes, cheques and gold. He galloped north towards the police station at Armidale.

Galvin, the mailman, stood on the bank of the Namoi River at Bendemeer on 27 October 1863 assessing the damage. The violence of the previous night's storm was unprecedented in the district: thunder that cracked so loudly it seemed as if the heavens themselves were being blown apart; sheeting rain and hailstones; tempestuous winds that uprooted gigantic trees, levelled fences, unroofed houses, knocked down barns and swept away a newly erected footbridge. A torrent of water continued to surge down the river, carrying branches and fence posts, furniture and carcasses. Even a dray and part of a weatherboard house had been seen bobbing along.

Should he attempt to drive his mail coach across the ford? Too dangerous, he decided: he would have to ferry the mail across. He stowed his mailbags in the government boat and was rowed across the river, then he loaded the bags onto a packhorse and continued his journey to Armidale, a further 45 miles north-east along the Great North Road.

Around mid-morning Galvin was nearing Kentucky, some ten miles south of Uralla, when two horsemen rode towards him. He immediately recognised the men, despite their disguises: Sergeant Stephen Grainger of the Armidale police and Senior Constable William Reynolds of the Rocky River police.

'We're out after two men who stuck up a hut on the Gostwyck run,' Grainger reported, as he considered the mailman's situation. The up and down mails generally passed each other along this stretch of road around this hour of the morning, so it would be best if they escorted the mailman through the district.

The trio set off in an arrow formation, the alert mailman in the lead, the two policemen flanking him, protecting the mailbags from the rear. Their seasoned gazes swept across the surrounding countryside, passing over the grassy plains and focusing on the thickets of trees where one or two horsemen could lurk unnoticed.

The mailman saw him first: a man crossing the road half a mile ahead.

The man was near the top of a gentle rise, a perfect observation point for anyone wanting a clear view along the road north and south.

Sergeant Grainger called out to the mailman to keep back. The two troopers dug in their heels and raced to the top of the hill where the Big Rock squatted like a beacon, a tumble of massive granite boulders climbing atop each other as if some giants of a previous epoch had been building a cairn. No one was there: the man's disappearance was suspicious in itself.

Senior Constable Reynolds pulled out his revolver and rode slowly around one side of the lonely grey outcrop, his senses alert. A stillness hung over the rock formation, an eeriness, as if it knew more secrets than mere humans could imagine. He kept his horse on a tight rein as it took one delicate step forward, then another. One moment he blinked, the next he was looking into the twin barrels of a shotgun.

'Police! Stand!' cried the hopeful copper as he aimed at the curly-headed villain gripping the shotgun. The man paused for a fraction of a moment, but he didn't lower his gun or raise his hands in surrender. Instead he turned and fled.

Reynolds pulled the trigger. Birds squawked in terror and soared from the trees. The man seemed to trip over a rock or a log or his own skittering feet and sprawled onto the ground.

Had the man just tripped, or had he shot him? Reynolds hesitated, easing back on his trigger. A moment later, the man scrambled up and dashed away, using the curve of the outcrop's huge circumference to hide himself.

While Reynolds circled around one side of the Big Rock, Sergeant Grainger was circling around the other. The sergeant had risen quickly through the ranks since his admission to the new police force early the previous year, and he had the reflexes of one born to serve. A moment after he heard the gunshot blast, he saw a man racing around the rock towards him. The man's eyes widened and his shotgun began to rise.

Grainger may not have faced the wrong end of a gun before, but instinct kicked in even before he saw the muzzle flash. He threw himself forward across his horse's neck. The red-hot bullet passed through his coat, burning his hand slightly. He remained crouching over his horse's neck, trying to shrink into nothingness as he waited for the blast from the second barrel, the bullet that would plough through his body.

The moment drew out, interminably. Then the silence was broken by the pattering of running footsteps. Raising his head, he saw the shooter bolt across the road in the direction of the Green Swamp. Grainger aimed his own revolver and fired.

Police pistols were unforgiving—for the powers-that-be who failed to invest wisely in the force's weaponry. Poor craftsmanship, frequent misfiring—and the lack of pistol training didn't help. The troopers were taught how to ride in cavalry formation and to make a handsome salute, but not how to fire a gun.

Grainger missed.

He fired again—and again missed.

The bushranger darted behind a wide tree and began to shoot back. Bullets zinged across the road, from the tree-hugging villain on the west and the troopers on the east, whipping up dust and plucking at nearby trees, but never reaching their targets.

The troopers cursed their poorly trained horses, too scared by all the noise to 'stand fire'—to stand still while guns blasted around them, rather than follow their natural instinct to bolt. Even the slightest startle could affect the troopers' aim and these horses were barely under control, quivering and snorting and rolling their eyes in terror. At this rate their bullets had a better chance of hitting an unseen bystander than the ruffian they were aiming for.

With only a few bullets left, the troopers dismounted and took careful aim. One after the other, they sent a final volley of shots towards their tree-protected foe.

Seeing the troopers pause to reload their revolvers, Fred used the opportunity to flee. Britten had been waiting on the opposite side of the road when the two troopers galloped up to the Big Rock, and had evidently managed to slip away unnoticed. He had probably returned to their horses, which were grazing near the Green Swamp itself.

Fred darted from tree to tree in the same direction, ignoring the hot throb from the gunshot wound behind his left knee.

Their weapons reloaded, the troopers threw themselves back onto their horses and raced after the fleet-footed felon—straight into the swamp.

The rotting brown vegetation wrapped itself around them nearly up to their horses' girths, a dark, stinking, slimy putrescence. They dug in their spurs and urged their horses forward, but their valiant steeds had decided that enough was enough. They lifted their feet fastidiously, then put them down again, refusing to go any further. Kicks, harsh tugs on the reins, curses: nothing would make them budge.

The troopers looked up to see the bushranger heading towards another man, who was holding two horses. If they didn't escape from the bog soon, the pair would get away. They slid from their saddles and pulled their reins over the horses' heads, trying to lead them, to physically wrench them out of the swamp. One squelching step at a time they reached firmer ground.

Mounting again, they looked for the shooter. He had reached his partner and was throwing his leg over one of their horses. They saw him gaze back at them for a moment, then he and his partner urged their horses forward. Half-a-dozen paces, a dozen . . . then their own horses foundered.

The delighted troopers dug in their heels as the bogged bushrangers jumped down into the swamp and pulled off their horses' bridles—more precious than gold if they wanted to steal another horse. They saw the shooter's partner lift his own single-barrelled shotgun and turn towards them. A blast broke the swamp's gloomy stillness. The troopers instinctively cringed as they kept riding. Mud sucked at their horses' hooves as they tried to steer around the murkier depths and keep to the firmer tussocks. They were forced to travel little faster than a walk. Glancing up again they saw the bushrangers bolt into the dense scrub. Then their own horses foundered again.

Constable John Mulhall looked warily up at the Big Rock. The two men had just disappeared—seemingly into the rock formation itself.

Mulhall had been out searching for the Gostwyck robbers earlier that day and was only a short distance north of the Big Rock when he crossed paths with mailman Galvin, who told him of the encounter between the troopers and bushrangers. As the bushrangers were still at large and the mail unprotected, Mulhall had decided to escort it to Uralla. After they arrived safely, he left the mailman to continue his journey alone, and asked for the services of another trooper. They backtracked along the Great North Road trying to spot the bushrangers before the pair acquired more horses and fled the district.

A few miles into his journey, Mulhall had seen the two men near the Big Rock hill. Had the bushrangers doubled back? It would be a clever move— the last place the troopers would think to search. He and his companion increased their pace. As they neared the rock formation they could see that it contained man-size cavities. Maybe the men had indeed slipped inside.

Mulhall climbed down from his horse and approached the rock formation, revolver clutched firmly in his hand, looking around carefully as he did so. He couldn't see anyone, or hear anything. With the rock wall shielding his body, he stuck his head out for a moment and glanced into one of the cavities, a slim hall-like passage, then whipped it back again. No gunshot blast erupted. He leaned out again and looked more closely. Still he couldn't see anybody. Warily, he edged into the cavity. One step . . . two. He continued to creep forward, following the passage through the rock until he exited out the back. His eyes swept the nearby terrain. Nobody in the vicinity. Nobody within the rock formation itself. He climbed back inside and searched all the crevices. That's when he discovered the single-barrelled shotgun and bridle.

The down mail passed the Big Rock a short time later, carrying a large sum of money in cash and cheques and gold.

'I should not be surprised to hear more of these desperadoes further down the northern line before long,' wrote a Uralla correspondent. 'The affair either appears to be a great bungle on the part of the bushrangers in alarming the whole neighbourhood by robbing the hut of a gun and a flitch of bacon, or else it is only a feint for more desperate action in another quarter.' The correspondent advised the gold escort to be particularly vigilant. Memories were still fresh of the previous year's Eugowra gold escort robbery by Frank Gardiner and Ben Hall and their gang, the audacious hold-up that had nearly netted them £14,000 in gold. 'It should be remembered that one of the bushrangers at least is well acquainted with the Northern bush. I allude to Ben Hall who resided for some years in the district of Murrurundi.'

Had bold Ben Hall indeed left Bathurst and travelled hundreds of miles north-east to the New England district, the community asked? Rumours as outlandish as the Big Rock itself began spreading through the community, claims that the new bushranging duo was part of a gang of three . . . or maybe four . . . or even five. As it turned out, reports from Bathurst would soon prove that Hall's gang had not left the Bathurst district, that they had just committed their boldest act of all—kidnapping the assistant gold commissioner and holding him to ransom. So who was this new bushranging pair?

Head and Tickle were the incongruous surnames borne by two men who were sawing in the bush near Kentucky Station on the afternoon of the Big Rock encounter. A man limped towards them, complaining of an injury and showing them his wound. A bullet had entered the fleshy part at the back of his left knee and exited on the opposite side.

Head took charge of the man's double-barrelled shotgun while they dealt with his wound. Sawpit workers always carried basic medical supplies: a bottle of rum to splash on the wound and swig for the pain. He handed back the gun when the man was ready to leave, noticing that one barrel only was loaded. The man used the gun as a crutch as he limped off again, his wound having stiffened from resting it.

It was wretched weather to be out searching for bushrangers. The torrential rain had eased; however, lesser bursts continued and the river at Bendemeer remained impassable. The police reinforcements from Tamworth had to swim their horses across and ferry everything else over in the government boat before travelling on to Uralla.

They soon learnt that their fellow troopers were getting nowhere. Again and again the police would receive information that the bushrangers were in one place, only to be told upon their arrival that the pair had never been there at all—although, now that the troopers mentioned it, the residents had seen a couple of men looking rather like the bushrangers over at so-and-so's place.

One section of the community was deliberately misdirecting the police— and of course, helping to hide and feed the bushrangers and having a belly-thumping guffaw about the whole affair. Another section was lashing out at the police for their failure to catch the villains. Meanwhile, frightened Uralla residents were talking about forming a vigilante group. The community had read about the lawless Bathurst district where the bushrangers were confident enough to kidnap the assistant gold commissioner. The last thing they wanted was to be at the mercy of such villains in their own district.

News of sightings continued to surface. A shepherd reported that on the day after the Big Rock encounter, he had returned to his hut to find the bushrangers sheltering from the rain and feasting on his supper. Another local said he had encountered the wounded bushranger about twelve miles from Bendemeer; the man claimed to be one of the Cockatoo Island escapees, and mentioned that only one shotgun barrel was loaded because he was short of powder. A couple of weeks later a stockman reported that the two bushrangers attempted to rob him near the Big Rock, but found only a stockwhip. A week afterwards a youth stumbled across the two men lying on the ground with their eyes glued to the main road, as if waiting in ambush.

The sightings dwindled away, and eventually one newspaper correspondent lamented: 'It is a thousand pities that they slipped through the fingers of the police, for, if they had been caught, it would in all probability have nipped bushranging in the bud in this locality at least.'

And one of Australia's iconic folk legends would never have been forged.

17

We have education establishments for the population of our towns and villages; we have a University in Sydney for which we pay a sum fabulous in proportion to the results obtained from it; we look carefully to the religious and moral wants of our convicts . . . but what do we do as a State for the many thousands of honest families whose poverty has doomed to the life of misery they at present endure on squatting stations? How often does the schoolmaster, missionary or minister of religion visit their outstation huts? What do we provide for them except the policeman, the gaoler and the hangman? . . . The result is shown in the popular sympathy of the people for the bushranger. We are creating in our midst a very Frankenstein.

Sydney Morning Herald, 26 July 1864

How to become an outlaw hero? It was as if Fred was reading from a manual, a list of do's and don't's unwittingly absorbed after years of sitting around campfires and listening to tales of heroic outlaws and bold highwaymen, the 'gentleman robbers' of old.

He could already tick the foundation items on the list. A victim of injustice—absolutely. Any rural dweller would agree that being thrown into gaol merely for borrowing a horse to get to a government muster was completely unjust. A victim of oppression—undoubtedly. He had been forced to escape from Cockatoo Island because of the government's oppression, its refusal to grant reasonable indulgences for hard work, its deceit in failing to honour its promises to change the system.

What about the outlaw hero's code of behaviour?

1. Rob the rich and not the poor.
2. Be courteous to women.
3. Do not commit acts of unjustified violence.
4. Be brave and courageous.
5. Be generous.
6. Elude capture by trickery or deception.

Of course, robbing a shepherd's hut was not exactly robbing the 'rich'. Nor could the shepherd's wife be considered a colonial Sheriff of Nottingham, a representative of an unjust government that protected wealthy squatters and oppressed rural workers. But he had merely stolen food and an old gun, and hadn't impoverished the shepherds. He had also quoted Robin Hood's mantra so his victim would know he was a noble brigand, a righteous robber, indeed an heir to the most righteous of them all. His intentions had been honourable thereafter—the government mail—even if his plans had been thwarted. Yes, that deserved a tick.

And another tick for items two and three. He had been courteous to the woman, not holding a gun to her head, not even presenting his gun, but reassuring her from the start that he meant her no harm.

Brave and courageous? He was one of the notorious Cockatoo Island escapees, his daring proven by that singular deed alone.

Generous? Well, not yet. He would need to rectify that.

But he could also tick off item six. He had cleverly eluded the police despite a massive manhunt, a thunderbolt that struck from the blue then disappeared.

The cunning bandit had recognised the outlaw hero irony: that to be acceptably bad, he had to be appropriately good. But to become an outlaw hero in the first place required a community that needed such a hero.

Fred's escape from Cockatoo Island had forced the 'outlaw' status upon him, that of a man who inhabited the terrain, both physical and metaphorical, outside the law's boundaries. Yet despite being an outlaw, he was not socially ostracised, for rural dwellers kept opening their rickety gates. An unspoken pact existed: that the community would support him and his continued villainy so long as his actions did not breach their moral boundaries. Hence the ticks, those essential ticks.

But why would a largely law-abiding community support villainy? The tale of the archetypal outlaw hero, Robin Hood, tells of a community suffering injustice and oppression from its rulers, a community that believed it had no recourse to the law to end its suffering, so the outlaw and his villainy became the community's avenging force against their oppressors. Yet the outlaw himself was no revolutionary but a reformer, one whose agenda was to right wrongs rather than to overthrow rulers and usher in a new social order. Societies riddled with such tensions often gave birth to outlaw heroes, and New South Wales in the 1860s was one of them.

Near the bottom of the colonial social ladder, the grumble of 'us' versus 'them' had been growing louder. The colony's penal origins were impossible to ignore. The old convict versus 'guard' battlelines were evident in the community's distrust of authority and its police enforcers, while a chasm continued to separate once-convict from always-free. For the next generation, the ocean was essentially the divider: colonial-born versus anywhere else, because colonial-born suggested convict spawn, that many an Antipodean cradle bore the stain of the 'criminal classes'.

The usual haves/have-nots social divisions were also inevitable in this outpost of British civilisation, although the dividing line was no longer as distinct. The barrier to riches had seemed like an unbreachable wall to most of the labouring classes until the word 'gold' was shouted from its ramparts in 1851. Suddenly, the labouring classes' primary asset, their ability to labour, was the shovel that would allow them to tunnel underneath. Everyone thought about going to the goldfields, if only for a moment. Everyone wondered if their own hand—the gloved paw of the merchant, the ink-stained fingers of the clerk, the grimy fist of the labourer, the chapped palm of the washerwoman—might be blessed with the Midas touch. And with that thought, that momentary speculation, that 'why not me?' realisation sweeping through all ranks of the community, society inevitably changed. The wealth wall no longer seemed unbreachable, the social divisions no longer God-ordained.

Many went to the gold rushes; some succeeded, but most failed. Those who succeeded often did so by supplying the miners' needs, rather than mining the gold itself. Those who failed were left with the bitterness of soured hope. Those too afraid even to try had to live with the ensuing 'what if' wonderings. The whole fabric of society was rent by a psychological and social upheaval greater than anything previously experienced in New South Wales.

Naturally, most of the colonial elite had no wish to change the status quo. They wanted an unlimited supply of docile workers to exploit—labour strip-mining—and had no interest in investing in their workers or the workers' community. They wanted servile servants like those in Britain, employees whose cap-in-hand presence attested to their own superiority, and were particularly irritated when the colonial-born resisted such subservience. They wanted similar controls over their free labour force as they had enjoyed over their assigned convict servants, and the legislators had obliged by passing the Master and Servant Act. While employees could bring cases of breach of contract against their masters, the rulings were handed down by magistrates, themselves masters. Not surprisingly, the courts served as places of punishment more than justice, where insolence or refusal to work could be punished with loss of wages or even a gaol term.

Many of the colonial elite also resisted the broadening of access to education and voting rights. They claimed that the working classes would not 'appreciate' their place in society if they received an education, and were not worthy of a voice in their own governance. Of course, education was available primarily to town-dwelling fee payers, and largely inaccessible to those living in the bush. Political representation worked similarly: the rural workers who roamed from job to job rarely met the voting qualifications—the six-month residency clause, at the very least—to the gentry's relief. They viewed itinerant workers with suspicion, tending to equate itinerancy with vagrancy, unmindful that such a mobile workforce saved them the cost of paying annual wages.

So many social divisions existed in New South Wales in the mid 1800s and somehow one section of the community kept finding itself on the 'wrong' side: the emancipated convicts and their ill-educated bush-dwelling offspring—like Fred. So it wasn't surprising that these rural dwellers were the first to provide support when one of their own locked horns with the authorities, a support sometimes grounded in personal acquaintanceship or a broader 'clan' loyalty, but often simply a product of the 'us' versus 'them' mentality. The outlaw was being chased by the police, those who enforced 'their' laws, therefore the police's enemy—their enemy's enemy—must logically be their own friend.

Yet Fred's rural-dwelling supporters were not restricted to emancipists and their families. British and Irish immigrants dwelling in the rural districts were among them. Visions of tilling their own soil had enticed tens of thousands to New South Wales over the previous few decades, only to find that the government's high price for Crown land kept it out of their reach. Some continued to struggle on small acreages. Some grasped the hand seemingly offered by the new land laws—the 'selection' laws, legislated by a liberal government a few years after New South Wales was granted responsible government in 1856. However these laws were poorly thought out, intended more to appease the liberals' anger at the squatters' economic power than to supply rural workers with a viable foothold on the land. And so the ranks of the dissatisfied rural workers continued to grow.

Despite all of these problems, the rural community had no conscious awareness of its need for a voice, or even that political representation would offer a voice. The food provided to the bushrangers, or their misdirections to the police, or simply their silence, served as a vocalisation of their own sense of disempowerment, granting the bushrangers tacit permission to act as their representatives. The bushrangers' primary targets were the sources of their grievances—if the bushrangers stuck to the outlaw hero script—so bushranging villainy offered a vicarious revenge against the amorphous 'them', a one-upmanship of sorts.

Of course, Fred had no genuine need for the community's support. He could have slipped across the border into Queensland and found work under an alias. His skills were always in demand, and his 'wanted' poster contained nothing distinctive: average height, average colouring, average build, along with a mole and a couple of warts that nobody would notice.

But the Eugowra gold escort robbery had also changed the social climate, dazzling the community with its daring, reminding everyone that the colony's highways were also paved with gold, and that riches awaited men who were skilled and courageous enough to seek a new way of mining it. The robbers had effectively held a gun to the broader community's astonished faces, forcing them to acknowledge that rural men were not simply an invisible, exploitable workforce. The robbers had also unintentionally thrown down a gauntlet for other rural workers, challenging them to mount their own horses and take charge of their destinies. In so doing they had dragged the spotlight towards their own majestic horse-mounted forms—man and horse as one, physically skilled, psychologically daring, the embodiment of the rural masculine ideal. A home-grown hero had just ridden onto centre stage and cracked his whip and, whether they approved or otherwise, the New South Wales community was enthralled.

Fleeing to Queensland and hiding under an alias? The gauntlet thrown down by Ben Hall and his gang was both a challenge and a temptation that Fred could not resist. And the rural community was waiting. They had another outlaw hero mould ready to be filled.

18

There are individuals of such peculiarly constructed minds ... that bushranging with all its perils and misery has a peculiar charm for them. They fancy apparently that there is a dash and an independence about it, which are not to be found in the ordinary lines of work, and that it gives them that notoriety which they seem to be so anxious to obtain, and which they could not acquire in a quieter and more laborious mode of subsistence.

Maitland Ensign, 1 May 1867

William Delaney had the first shift at the Campbell's Hill toll-bar, between West Maitland and Rutherford, early on the morning of Monday 21 December 1863. Daylight was peeping over the horizon when he opened the toll-house door a little after 4.30 am, then returned to the back room. The toll-bar itself was locked into place, so anyone wishing to head south-east along the main road towards Maitland or north-west towards Singleton would soon call for assistance.

But someone didn't. When Delaney returned to the front room around 4.45 am, he saw a man standing in the doorway pointing a gun at him. No mask, no fear, just cool hazel eyes framed by a determined countenance.

'Go into the corner near the dresser!'

The startled toll-keeper backed into the corner.

'Give me your money!'

'I have none.'

'Give me your money or I'll blow your brains out!' was the swift rejoinder.

'I have none,' came the quavering reply.

The highwayman edged over to a cupboard not far from the door and used his free hand to open it. There: a cash-box. Keeping his revolver aimed at the toll-keeper, he lifted out the box but didn't open it. That would require two hands. Instead he tucked the box under his arm and bade the toll-keeper a polite 'Good Morning', before backing out the door.

Delaney waited for a moment, then slipped over to the door and peeked outside. He saw the highwayman unlash a horse tied to a tree, then mount and turn the horse towards Singleton, glancing across at the toll-house doorway as he passed. Their eyes met.

'Captain Thunderbolt,' the man said politely.

The greeting was not just an acknowledgement of the toll-keeper's presence and a final salutation, it was a belated introduction of sorts, communicating a sense of equality, of shared human experience, the social niceties being preserved despite the nature of their encounter. It was almost an apology.

The day began early at Rutherford's Spread Eagle Inn, conveniently situated on the main road opposite the racecourse, about a mile north-west of the toll-bar. Sometimes Mrs Byrne had hungry patrons already waiting on her doorstep when she opened the door, although they were not usually armed with a belt of revolvers.

'Can I have something to eat?' the intimidating stranger asked.

Mrs Byrne hastily prepared a plate of bread and meat. The man ate contentedly, emptying his plate, then asked how much he owed her.

'There is no charge for a thing like that,' she assured him, hoping to be rid of the dangerous-looking stranger as soon as possible.

Seeming surprised, the man said bluntly, 'I came to rob you, but as you are so hospitable I won't do so.'

He paid for a bottle of rum and remained at the inn for a while longer. When he eventually returned to his horse he fastened the remainder of the rum to his saddle, along with some bread and cheese, and was about to mount when he spotted an acquaintance—if one could call him that.

'Well, you are the chap I stuck up this morning at the toll-bar,' he greeted Delaney. 'I suppose you have come after me!'

The toll-keeper assured him that he hadn't, that he was just heading to the pub. Such a traumatic start to the day required a stiff nobbler—no matter how early it was.

'I suppose your mate has gone for the crushers?'

'No,' Delaney replied. 'There's no one to mind the toll-bar.' He didn't explain why he had walked west to Rutherford for a drink rather than east to the Maitland police station, and the highwayman had seemingly enjoyed his own tipple too much to question him further.

Captain Thunderbolt proved a kindly drunk, sticking his hand into his pocket and pulling out a handful of coppers, four-shillings worth, the only money stored in Delaney's cash-box. Handing over the money, he confided: 'I am a bushranger but you might meet a worse one than me. I was put on a lay to stick-up your place. I was told there were 200 sovereigns there. I thought it was Young the flash fighting man who kept the place.' With grog-bolstered confidence, he added cockily, 'If I met him, I'd take it out of him!'

Delaney wasn't interested in the bushranger's pugilistic prowess. 'Where's my cash-box?' he demanded.

Captain Thunderbolt described its location, then farewelled the toll-keeper before riding off towards Singleton. Delaney found his cash-box exactly where the bushranger had said it would be.

Delaney had not needed to personally advise the police of the robbery. He had known that sooner or later someone would pass through the toll-bar heading towards Maitland. Tommy Moore the horse-breaker was charged with the news. Tommy told one policeman, who shortly before 6 am reported the robbery to Edward Purcell, one of West Maitland's eight foot constables who patrolled the main thoroughfare. Purcell returned to the Maitland police barracks and awoke Senior Constable Gordon—who was in temporary charge of the barracks that morning—and asked for instructions.

'Go to the toll-bar as quick as you can and find out if the report is true,' Gordon ordered, 'then return as soon as possible and report on the circumstance.'

Yet nearly two hours were to pass before Purcell reported back with the details.

Godfrey Parsons' wife needed medical advice. The Anvil Creek butcher bundled her into his spring-cart early that same Monday morning and trotted south-east along the main road towards Maitland. They were passing the intersection of the Anambah road when a horseman rode across the green towards them. The man reined in beside the cart and called out for them to stop.

Parsons agreeably pulled up his horses and looked over again at the horseman. That's when he noticed the revolver pointing at him.

'Give up your money!' the bushranger demanded.

'I have only £2,' the quick-thinking butcher replied, although he had pocketed £10 before departing that morning. He added beseechingly, 'I am coming to Maitland for a doctor's advice for my wife.' Beside him, his wife obligingly began to cry.

'If the money is needed for a doctor,' the bushranger sighed, 'I won't take it.'

Captain Thunderbolt's inaugural bushranging spree was not proving very successful. Three potential targets so far; no profits. A free breakfast, but Fred had felt obliged to pay for his rum because of the innkeeper's kindness. Lunch was packed in his saddle-bag, but the hunk of bread and lump of cheese were no substitutes for the bag of glittering gold sovereigns that should have nestled there. He would need to find some more customers.

A teamsters' camp. Too many brawny men—he could easily be out-numbered. He stopped for a chat, then continued on his way.

A woman, her two daughters, and their gentlemen companion. Nothing much there.

A woman on her own. He wouldn't rob her. He always treated the weaker sex kindly—and he had already faced one sobbing woman that day.

A lone horseman. Ideal.

But then he noticed another horseman, a man wearing a distinctive blue uniform.

James Troy was riding from Anambah to Maitland and was about to turn onto the Great North Road when he noticed—without really noticing—a lone horseman coming from the west. A moment later, the man called out: 'Hallo! You want me, don't you?'

Troy focused on the horseman and saw a pistol in the man's hand. He lifted his shocked eyes to the man's face. Their eyes didn't meet;

the highwayman was not talking to him. He followed the highwayman's gaze and saw a mounted policeman a short distance away riding towards Maitland. The trooper had swivelled around at the greeting but, strangely, didn't say or do anything.

Troy looked back at the highwayman. The fellow pointed his pistol at the trooper and demanded, 'Don't you want me?'

The trooper hesitated for a moment, then cried, 'No, I don't want you in particular. I am only giving my horse an airing.' And he dug in his heels and sped off.

The bushranger immediately turned his gun towards Troy and yelled, 'Stand!'

Troy looked hopefully towards the trooper, but saw only a stubborn back receding into the distance.

Captain Thunderbolt needed his own refreshments—and a chance to crow. He returned to the Spread Eagle and ordered the usual fare of bread and meat as well as a pot of tea, invigorating but not inebriating. Better to keep his wits about him as the police would probably return before too long. From his lofty perch—dismounting would also be foolhardy—he shouted drinks for the other patrons. Assured of a captive audience, he began to regale them with tales of his encounters with the colony's lily-livered troopers. His recent confrontation? Airing his horse, the craven constable had claimed. The northern troopers? 'They chased me near Armidale and when they got to the Big Rock they got afraid and went back, saying their horses got bogged in the Green Swamp!'

His audience delighted in his tale, enjoying the camaraderie as well as the bushranger's willingness to let them share vicariously in his triumphs over the scorned police. Free grog as well: he was instantly their mate.

Eventually, with stomach replete, the captain rode off again, turning right at the Anambah road intersection and heading north towards the Hunter River. He soon found himself at a bend in the road, with a good view in either direction. He was probably unaware of the location's ominous name: Skeleton's Hut.

Well-known cattle and station dealer, Henry Butcher, was travelling behind a mob of cattle when he noticed a horseman ride out of the bush and up to the lad driving the mob. Then the horseman pulled out a pistol.

Butcher was a strong man, brawny enough to manhandle recalcitrant cattle, tough enough to intimidate reluctant debtors. He was also a practitioner of the pugilistic arts. No bushranger was going to rob his lad. 'Stop there,' he told his two companions who were bargaining with someone else about cattle. 'I'll go to the bushranger alone.'

He rode towards the gunman and reined in just a couple of feet away. 'Why do you stick up a boy like that?' he challenged the ruffian. 'You ought to be ashamed of yourself. If you want to rob, why don't you go to Maitland and stick up a bank?'

The gunman immediately turned his pistol on Butcher. 'I think you look as if you want sticking up too!' he mocked.

Butcher wasn't having any of that. He knew how to manage disrespectful striplings. He clenched his fist and punched, knocking up the bushranger's pistol hand before landing a mighty uppercut to his chin. The man's head snapped backwards, almost tipping him off his horse. Butcher rammed his horse into the bushranger's, attempting to jam the man against the fence. The cunning outlaw backed his well-trained horse and managed to slip free from the vice. Unfortunately Butcher's momentum jammed his own foot into the fence. He tugged and tugged, but couldn't extricate it.

The bushranger didn't hang around to secure his profits—or to laugh at his attacker's misfortune. A moment later the man's splendid bay soared over the fence and disappeared into the bush. Butcher and his companions watched in awe.

'The road leading through Anambah,' replied the drinkers at the Spread Eagle, hands pointing towards the west. Captain Thunderbolt might have received their enthralled attention but they were a fickle audience, their devotion lasting only until it was time for another drink.

Four disguised troopers took the side road as directed, then spread out, determined to catch the bushranger before he robbed any more travellers. Constable Shannon of the Muswellbrook police continued north towards Anambah. He wasn't far from the village when he spotted a horseman talking to a tenant farmer. The description matched, man and horse, but he would need to get very close indeed to be assured of taking the villain into custody. Thinking quickly, he headed towards the two men, calling out as he approached: 'Have you seen any bullocks about?' He reined in a short distance away as the bushranger answered that they hadn't.

Shannon pulled out his pistol and announced triumphantly: 'You are my prisoner!'

But his prisoner thought differently. Captain Thunderbolt spun his horse and galloped off towards Anambah, as if the pistol pointed at him was merely a toy in the hands of a smirking child.

Shannon aimed at the bushranger's hunched back and pulled the trigger. The man didn't fall—or the horse for that matter. Shannon fired again, another distinctive blast, then sped after him. The two horsemen thundered through Anambah, pigs squealing, hens squawking as they skittered out of the way. Shannon closed to within fifty yards and fired again, but his bullet whizzed into the bushes.

The final explosive gallop had blown his horse. He had already ridden hard from Maitland, and the usual police horses weren't built for speed, or endurance, or much else for that matter. Little more than broken-down hacks, most of them, sold to the police by 'friends' with an eye to filling their own pockets. Yet the troopers were expected to catch a bushranger born to the saddle riding the best horse he could steal. Government economies!

Spotting a saddled and bridled horse dozing near the blacksmith's forge, he leapt from his exhausted, foam-flecked mount. Nimble fingers unlashed the fresh horse's reins and soon he was riding again, further behind than before, but still with the bushranger in his sights. His horse's canter stretched into a gallop and ate up the furlongs, cresting a few gentle slopes before beginning the run towards the Hunter River in the distance. Shrubs and trees passed in a blur as he kept his gaze fixed on the bushranger ahead. The man reached the river and slowed his pace to safely negotiate the ford, then raced off again. Shannon arrived at the river a short time later and glanced down as his horse splashed through the water.

When he looked up again, the man was gone.

Such daring outrages committed by an impudent scoundrel in broad daylight and within sight of the police! The press was aghast. 'Residents

of the Northern districts who have read the frequent accounts of the robberies committed in the less favoured west, could hardly credit the reports,
or believe it possible that one individual could, with impunity, stick up
from ten to twenty persons in a day.' Frustratingly, the press was unable to
report the bushranger's apprehension. The police had tracked him nearly to
Singleton before losing all trace of him, and had returned to their stations
on the Wednesday evening.

The 'impudent scoundrel' was evidently being kept informed of the
troopers' movements. He ventured out again on the Thursday morning,
closer to Singleton this time, holding up two travellers near Jump Up
(Belford) and stealing £1 from one, but finding little on the other. His
victims were certain of his identity: 'Captain Thunderbolt' was his arrogant
introduction before he robbed them.

'Captain Thunderbolt!' the awed community mouthed. What an evocative and intimidating nickname. A bolt from the heavens hurtling to earth
with a deafening crack and a brilliant flash of light, stunning everyone with
its supreme power, its potential for violence, then disappearing as instantly
as it had appeared. A thunderbolt in the hands of a captain no less—a leader,
a military officer who prided himself upon his planning and precision in his
efforts to outwit the enemy. Any intimidating adversary indeed.

'We fear these wretches are flattered by formidable names,' the *Sydney
Morning Herald* would write, 'and crime seems lessened in their minds when
performed under a grand sobriquet.' Some realised that such self-anointed
nicknames were a form of bravado, of self-aggrandisement, reflecting the
desperate need of the unworthy to be spectacularly noticed. Naturally,
however, the nicknames served to intimidate only if the bearer remained
intimidating. Spoils of a mere £1 from two days of robberies? The press's
tone gradually changed from awe at Captain Thunderbolt's impudence to
mockery at his meagre takings: the 'fruitless display of daring', the 'famous
exploit' that had netted him only a few shillings.

Even Parliament laughed. A few days after the robberies, the Upper
Hunter's member asked if the government was aware that a bushranger
had recently committed a spate of robberies within a couple of miles of
Maitland, that the man had remonstrated with a constable and had escaped
from four troopers after refusing to surrender. The Parliamentarian received
a dismissive reply. As far as the government was aware, the bushranger's

only booty was four shillings stolen from the toll-bar keeper, money he had later returned.

Of course, the community recognised the fundamental truth. Captain Thunderbolt's takings were not important. It was his audacity, his victims' terror, their own vicarious thrill in the events on their doorstep that made the bushranger the prime topic of conversation. Everybody was talking about him. Everyone knew someone he had bailed up, or knew someone who knew someone he had bailed up, or had seen him or thought they had seen him or thought they could identify him.

Who was he—this bushranger who had suddenly appeared in the neighbourhood, who had treated his victims with kindness and bestowed his largesse upon the inn's patrons, a superb horseman who had brushed off the troopers and shown coolness and courage under gunfire before disappearing as suddenly as he had appeared?

'He is believed to be an old offender bearing the name of Ward,' reported the *Maitland Mercury* early in January 1864, 'formerly connected with a gang of horse and cattle stealers who used to make Lambs Valley a favourite haunt.'

The gallant captain was incognito no longer.

19

What are fears but voices airy?
Whispering harm where harm is not.
And deluding the unwary
Till the fatal bolt is shot!

William Wordsworth

Money to be made bushranging? Not likely. For his mere pound or two, he had narrowly escaped being shot, had almost been knocked off his horse, and had only evaded the troopers' shackles because he had stolen a lightning-fast racehorse. Surely there were safer and more profitable ways to make money—but first he had to evade the troopers who had converged on the district.

Fred crept out of the Singleton area, leaving the easy visibility of the Hunter River flood plains and riding east into the heavily wooded Tangory Mountains. He knew the area well. The mountains lay only a few miles north-west of his family's old rustling hideaway at Lambs Valley. The peaks weren't as high as the ranges to the north, yet among the soaring gums on the ridges and the tangled thickets hiding the gullies were places inaccessible to strangers, particularly the British-bred troopers pursuing him.

The police soon heard that Captain Thunderbolt had been spotted heading into the mountains. Sparks of hope lit their previously glum faces—they had him trapped. The mountains were tucked within a horse-shoe of roads: Elderslie, Glendon Brook and Paterson. If they stationed some troopers in the vicinity, they could nab him when he came down from the ranges.

The press laughed: the police were surely jesting. The villain knew every inch of the terrain. How would they capture him if he remained in the mountains, and why would he leave their safety to risk a shoot-out?

The police waited, and waited, but there was only so much time they could devote to chasing a man who had merely bailed up a few local residents. He hadn't robbed a gold escort. He hadn't harmed anyone. The troopers had numerous other important duties to attend to, like collecting electoral rolls and handing out writs. Within a few days, they reluctantly steered their mounts south and west and returned to their stations.

The press refrained from crowing. The seemingly omniscient highwayman had outwitted the police again, but the whole community suffered when such a miscreant remained on the loose.

Marbles! That's all? Fred frowned at the two boys he had bailed up near Glendon Brook, on the road between Singleton and Gresford.

The lads proffered up their coloured balls of glass, assuring him that they had nothing else of value.

He looked at the toys disdainfully, then handed them back. 'Who is your father?' he asked, as an aside.

'Dr Glennie,' the boys chorused, referring to the well-known Singleton medical practitioner and magistrate.

'I know Dr Glennie well,' Fred nodded. 'He is a clever fellow.' And with that backhanded apology he continued along the road to the east, ever on the alert for customers as well as troopers.

'Captain Thunderbolt has been arrested by the Dungog police!' announced the *Police Gazette* on 13 January.

The report of a Thunderbolt sighting had reached the Dungog police two weeks previously, the same day the *Maitland Mercury* identified the bushranger as one of the Lambs Valley horse-thieves of nearly a decade ago. Many remembered the case; indeed, many had known the thieves. Which meant that they might be able to recognise him, and profit from the £25 reward offered by the government after Ward's escape from Cockatoo Island.

Where might he have gone after slipping down from the Tangory Mountains? Probably not south or west, given the busyness of the Great North Road and the police's continued vigilance. Probably not north, as that would force him into the impassable Mount Royal Ranges. Most likely east—which meant the Dungog district. Passing glances became focused stares, eyes that assessed and dismissed, or looked again. One pair of eyes looked back a third time, then turned towards the police station.

Senior Sergeant O'Sullivan from the Dungog police headed out after the suspect late on the evening of Sunday 3 January, riding east along the winding road to Stroud. Darkness fell and still he kept riding, turning north towards Gloucester when the road diverged. Around 10 or 11 pm, some fourteen miles from Dungog, he reached a camp by the side of the road.

'I am innocent!' cried the horrified incumbent after being rudely woken and informed that his accoster was taking him into custody on suspicion of being the toll-bar robber Captain Thunderbolt. 'I never did anything of the sort. I have driven a team down to Maitland from New England and am returning by Gloucester. I am a stranger and have never been this way before.'

O'Sullivan wasn't interested. Not only did the man bear a striking resemblance to the bushranger—as far as he could tell in the darkness anyway—there was a reward in the offing if he succeeded in capturing the outlaw. His policeman's pay was low and the reward system highly motivational. It wasn't his problem if some innocent people were caught in the net.

He searched the man, but surprisingly found no firearms, only a few caps. The absence of firearms wasn't enough to deter him.

'Mr Superintendent Lydiard deserves praise,' applauded the *Maitland Mercury* soon afterwards, reporting that the police superintendent and his men had succeeded in ridding the district of the scoundrel attempting to take control, the man who had evidently hoped to follow in the footsteps of his compatriots to the west. The unlucky drover, George Vitnell, knew otherwise. He was remanded from Dungog to West Maitland and thrown in the lock-up, only to be released after the toll-bar keeper swore that Vitnell was not the robber.

'The real offender is supposed to have crossed the country in the direction of New England,' the *Police Gazette* soon advised, reluctantly admitting that the latest king of the road had not been dethroned quite so easily.

Stephen Smith was not surprised to see the horseman again on the morning of 15 January 1864. The man had lodged at his cottage a few nights previously and had behaved oddly at the time, moving around restlessly rather than sleeping, and keeping his horse saddled all night as if he might suddenly need to flee. Smith had suspected something was amiss and now the fellow was back. This time he was making his intentions perfectly clear.

Smith was one of the many small settlers who had jumped on the 'free selection before survey' bandwagon, settling beside the Chichester River fourteen miles north of Dungog. Free selection was Liberal Parliamentarian John Robertson's brainchild—or idiocy, as many claimed then and later. His policy was intended to 'unlock the land', to break the squatters' stranglehold on the interior, and to allow 'poor men' to acquire farming land before the overworked surveyors had time to mark out new allotments for sale. In truth, much of the squatters' land was unsuited for agricultural purposes by reason of fertility or location, as many selectors would eventually learn to their great cost. In the summer of 1863/64 however, free selection was still in its infancy, and only the occasional track could be seen meandering off the main road towards a curl of smoke in the distance. These isolated dwellings, home to a family rather than a stable of stockmen, were ideal as short-term boltholes for those who ranged in the bush—unwitting though their hosts might initially be. The dwellings had other advantages as well.

A hundred-weight of flour, fifty pounds each of beef and sugar, some tea, a double-barrelled gun (albeit with a broken barrel), a bullet mould and lead, two saddles and a bridle. Food, arms and getaway gear. Smith's robber had no need to state his calling. Considering the goods taken and the IOU he didn't leave, the bushranger might as well have left his calling card.

Immediately after the bushranger departed, Smith headed south to Dungog to report the robbery to the police—and to everyone else he met.

The news spread quickly. Captain Thunderbolt? It had to be. The description matched: aged about twenty-six or twenty-seven, five feet eight or nine inches with light-brown hair, dressed in moleskin trousers and wellington boots, a blue shirt and a cabbage-tree hat.

By that time everyone knew Captain Thunderbolt and the Cockatoo Island escapee Frederick Ward were one and the same. Ward had been spotted in the district a few times in previous weeks. He was riding a grey horse and leading a bay, both fine-looking animals reportedly stolen from St Clair and worth a £10 reward. The locals were not surprised to see him, having suspected that he might be drawn back to the district by the presence of his woman, James Bugg's eldest daughter Mary Ann. They even knew his beat. He had been seen travelling from the mountains near the headwaters of the Williams and Chichester Rivers south to Monkerai, where Bugg lived, and on to Main Creek, where Bugg's second daughter lived. Scrubby country, difficult to traverse, but that was a policeman's job, wasn't it—to endeavour to catch criminals?

Evidently not in Dungog, jeered the *Maitland Mercury*'s Dungog correspondent soon afterwards. Their force consisted of two men—one an old hand of the old stamp, accepted from the previous corps into Cowper's new police force. Which was part of the problem. Unfortunately 'old' in this instance didn't mean able: the man should have long since been superannuated. As for the other, he was a Cowperite fop dressed in a suit of tweed, with rings adorning fingers that carried a silver-mounted whip. Definitely not the community's idea of a working policeman. 'Both took the report of the robbery quite coolly,' the correspondent complained, 'and never lost their evening's walk.' Indeed, in the twenty-four hours following the robbery report, they had taken no steps whatsoever to apprehend the robber.

Perhaps the correspondent was unaware that two weeks previously the Dungog police had chased another reported sighting and had arrested the wrong man. Admittedly, that was just a sighting. This was an actual robbery.

'We want working police, not gentlemen idlers!' demanded the correspondent, repeating one of the community's many gripes about the elitist police force. Officer appointments were based on social class rather than merit, 'gentleman' and 'officer' still being considered synonymous in the new police force. 'If the authorities do not immediately move in the matter and secure this scoundrel, it is to be hoped the quiet settlers of the district will rise up and capture him.'

Such a call to action would be echoed in many of the state's newspapers as the police continually failed to meet the community's need for protection.

Fred and Mary Ann knew they had to leave the Dungog district if they were to be together again. They were too well known and too distinctive a couple. It was only a matter of time before the police caught up with them and carted Fred back to Cockatoo Island. But where could they go? Fred's family revealed that his brother William was working on the Culgoa River out near Bourke, a lawless area, a real frontier land. The region straddled the Queensland border, a sparsely populated expanse with a minimal police presence, where nobody asked too many questions. It was perfect.

Which way? The easiest route to the north-western districts took them back to Singleton and along the Great North Road, but they might as well cuff Fred themselves if they took that route. North to Gloucester, then north or west across the mountains? Just getting through the Dungog district to Gloucester would be difficult. The police were on the alert and the eyes of potential informants everywhere. On his own, Fred could pull his hat down low on his brow and slip through the district largely unnoticed, but a stockman accompanied by a part-Aboriginal woman and two little girls lacked the same anonymity.

One by one, they considered their options and discarded them until they had only one left—the impossible: backtracking along Fred's usual beat and trying to push through the mountains near the mouth of the Chichester. It was not the usual route out of the district, as the rugged mountains were considered almost impassable. They would never have contemplated taking such a route in winter, but summer's warmth made it feasible. Worth trying, anyway. If they succeeded, they would exit east of Aberdeen, bypassing most of the police lookouts.

Mary Ann bundled up her two daughters and they began the journey north. Fred had already reconnoitred Stephen Smith's farm on the Chichester a few days previously, and decided to pop in again and stock up on supplies. With their saddle-bags loaded, they took one last look up at the vast heave of mountains in front of them, then squared their shoulders and set off.

The news filtered through to Dungog a week after the robbery at Smith's: Thunderbolt's horses had been found in the rugged mountains between the Chichester and Little (now Wangat) Rivers. The grey mare was dead, the bay dying.

'Downright slavery,' blasted a correspondent writing from nearby Bandon Grove. Desperation was the general conclusion. Why else would anyone attempt such a dangerous journey on horses unsuited to the rugged terrain?

Scattered nearby were items abandoned by the bushranger, who no longer had a beast of burden to carry them. A single saddle: Thunderbolt had evidently taken the other with him. Smith's stolen flour: the selector would be glad to have that back. A woman's jacket and some other female items. Thunderbolt had a companion? Heads nodded knowingly, as everyone realised who the woman must be.

Bandon Grove resident, Mr Conway, was determined to catch the horse-less bushranger and immediately called for volunteers to join a search party. 'Conway is a very energetic man,' the local correspondent reported, adding that his rallying cry had been heeded by other locals.

Conway's party set off on horseback soon afterwards, accompanied by some blacktrackers from the local area. Reinvigorated, the Dungog police and their own party of young locals headed north again on 25 January. Many community workers felt that the search parties had an excellent chance of capturing Thunderbolt. He was on foot and lugging a heavy saddle, whereas his pursuers were riding fresh horses. His woman might slow him down as well, although perhaps she would be more help than hindrance: her Aboriginal roots lay in the Dungog–Gloucester district.

The Bandon Grove correspondent, however, doubted that the search parties would be successful: while Thunderbolt would struggle to travel any further through the rugged mountains, the search parties would face the same difficulties. Moreover, Thunderbolt had taken a saddle with him, so he would probably head across the rivers to the west and steal a horse, thus baffling them again. 'In fact, as an experienced person in this rugged and broken country,' the correspondent continued, 'I cannot understand how this man can even travel anywhere over it and dodge the police. No doubt he is a thorough bushman and will be troublesome to catch. The rider who captures him on a horse will have to ride or hound in a masterly style through the mountains.'

Awe at Thunderbolt's remarkable horsemanship continued to seep through the various accounts, although there was one strange note in the Bandon Grove report. 'I believe Thunderbolt is pretty well armed now and after running the risk from Cockatoo one would imagine he would show pluck before he is captured, though from accounts he is spoken of as having none.'

Admiration for his horsemanship, yet scorn for his apparent gutlessness: it mirrored the heroic tug-of-war in the broader community. The people wanted heroes, even if heroic villains were the only ones on offer. Yet a villain who fled was no one's idea of a hero. Stand and fight like a man!

Of course, someone who fought 'like a man' risked killing police and bystander alike. Fleeing was the safest course for everyone, as the crafty bushranger had already realised.

A thorough-going bushman Fred undoubtedly was, but he was accompanied by a woman with skills of her own. Good hearing, for one. The steady drumbeat of horses' hooves, the distant hurrahs and raucous laughter of a hunting pack: the search parties were not going to descend upon them unnoticed. The threat of blacktrackers? Those who tracked had developed tricks to outwit other trackers and Mary Ann knew many of them.

They had abandoned the idea of trying to push through the mountains above the Chichester. Without horses or even a certain trail to follow, and with two young children on their backs, they could carry only limited supplies. Pushing on might kill them all. Instead, they decided to sneak back towards Dungog, stealing some more horses along the way. Then they would loop around and follow the trails towards Gloucester, attempting to cross the mountains from there.

If someone approached? Some hurried steps off the trail, children clutched in front of them as they crouched behind scrub and trees, a murmured 'hush, hush' and a gentle hand slipped across a youngster's mouth: hopefully, the unwelcome visitors would ride past none the wiser.

They were nearing Gloucester before someone spotted them—someone determined to report their presence to the police, anyway.

'Active and intelligent' was the new force's assessment of Constable Henry Finlay when they recruited him from the old police force. Only in his early thirties, he was neither an antiquated relic nor a Cowperite fop, so when news of the outlaw's sighting reached the Stroud police office, he and his partner started in pursuit.

More Thunderbolt sightings were reported when they reached the Gloucester area. Ward had apparently crossed the Gloucester River and was heading west towards Rawdon Vale. He was well mounted with two horses but no saddle, having evidently been forced to abandon his cumbersome saddle before managing to steal another horse. He was still accompanied by the woman and two children, although he generally kept them in the background when making enquiries.

As the two constables took the road to Rawdon Vale, they glanced up every so often to assess the weather. Heavy rain clouds were massing, an ugly blanket of greyness that stretched to the horizon. Gusts whipped at their clothing as they urged their horses faster. Fifty miles they had ridden and they were as tired as their mounts, but they would try to reach shelter before the rainstorm began.

The first drops stung them before they reached Rawdon Vale. Soon the rain bucketed down, a deluge heavier than they had seen in years. But when the dripping constables stood on the verandah of the first station house they came to, they received welcome news. Ward had been there—just the previous evening, in fact—and had asked the way to the adjoining station. Where might he be heading? Probably across the mountains to the Moonan Flat area or to Hanging Rock near Nundle.

One day behind him—that's all they were. Should they remain overnight when their prey was so close? The rain was also bucketing on Thunderbolt, and he was encumbered by two young children and was likely to stop and seek shelter. They would push on, they decided, but would be grateful for a warm meal first.

The residents directed them towards the road through the mountains—if it could be called a road. 'There could hardly be worse,' they warned, shaking their heads at such impetuosity, that the constables would even consider heading out at night along such a road during such a downpour.

Nobody realised that they were experiencing the first deluge of what would become known as the Great Flood of 1864, a flood so extensive that Noah himself might have considered pulling his ark out of mothballs.

Two horses plodded along the rough mountain road, twitching tail in front of patient nose, picking their way over rocks and around stumps, hugging the steep banks on one side while the riders tried to ignore the deep ravines on the other. As heaven's floodgates opened, each of the riders crouched protectively over a small whimpering body, taking the bullet-like stings of rain on their own backs, while glancing up every so often to seek an over-hanging rock or a cave that might provide shelter.

The pelting rain was like a blanket that smothered all other sound, silencing the defiant twitter of uncowed birds, even the raging current nearby. Once a brook gurgling merrily down the mountainside, brushing delicately at its banks and sliding politely around any protruding rocks, the river was now a torrent that smashed at the rocks and clawed at the banks, that dragged in shrubs and trees, crumbling the man-made tracks beside it and swamping the fords—nature reasserting its authority over man's supposedly God-given right of dominion. Yet nature's triumph would prove a blessing for the Ward family.

The rain continued from Tuesday night until Friday morning. As the rivers rose, the two troopers were soon stranded. Unable to continue their pursuit, yet also unable to return to Rawdon Vale, they were forced to seek shelter and wait out the rainstorm. When the rain finally ceased on the Friday, they were able to continue their journey, although without provisions there was no point following Thunderbolt. 'Alas the very elements have taken the miscreant's part,' lamented the local correspondent when the disconsolate troopers returned to Stroud.

Fred and Mary Ann's decision to bypass the lowlands was not only fortuitous, it possibly saved their lives. All of the rivers flooded, swamping most of the towns in the arc from Maitland up to Bendemeer. The towns had generally begun as teamster camps on river crossings, first a pub to meet the teamsters' voracious thirsts, later a store and a couple of houses; then the town grew from there. When heavy rains in the mountains sent torrents down the river beds, the towns naturally flooded. Sometimes weeks passed before the rivers could again be crossed—hence more pubs for the teamsters waiting on the river banks.

'So disastrous a flood no individual here has witnessed,' reported a distraught Tamworth correspondent as he surveyed the damage. Lives, livestock, livelihoods: so much destruction. Everyone was suffering, so few paid attention to a family of four travelling through the district on horseback. For the outlaws, it was indeed a strange sort of good fortune.

From the Denison diggings, the shortest route to the Culgoa River was along the Namoi River via Gunnedah, Narrabri and Wee Waa and on to Walgett, but the rain hadn't restricted itself to the eastern districts. 'It is my painful duty to chronicle one of the greatest misfortunes that has ever visited the Northern districts in the shape of a flood,' wrote a correspondent from the Namoi River district. Almost every house in Gunnedah destroyed, Narrabri flooded, Wee Waa entirely under water. Walgett? No one knew. They heard nothing for weeks. When news eventually came through early in April, the Walgett correspondent advised that the Namoi, Barwon and Castlereagh Rivers were one vast sheet of water, and that for weeks the only way through the district was by boat. The district had become the 'inland sea' early explorers such as Sturt and Oxley had sought—albeit with trees sticking up like signposts, and abandoned huts listing drunkenly.

Given the extent of the devastation, it wasn't surprising that someone would later report that Ward was seen around the time of the floods looking very miserable and hard-up. Fred and Mary Ann's journey from Gloucester to the Walgett district took three months, a long time to be living hand-to-mouth. By then the floods had eased and lives were more or less back to normal so people were paying attention again, noticing in particular the distinctive Ward family.

'Ward is now in Queensland,' reported the *Police Gazette* late in May 1864. 'He is supposed to have travelled with a half-caste girl and children, and the last few days in company with a Mr McKay to that gentleman's station on the Moonie River, and to have gone from thence to the Culgoa River.' Through the medium of the *Gazette*, the central authority in Sydney advised the police at Walgett, Fort Bourke and the other border stations in New South Wales and Queensland to keep a lookout.

Yet to police the north-western district—which covered every acre west of Wee Waa—the force comprised one sergeant and three constables. Millions of acres of land, four policemen, and the Queensland border a mere 75 miles away. The very idea was a joke. Spot a lawbreaker and they would simply flee north, pausing after they were well past the border to poke their tongues out at the lawmen, knowing that the New South Wales police had no jurisdiction beyond their own borders. Needless to say, the north-western troopers merely rolled their eyes and continued with their regular duties.

In the waterlogged plains near the Culgoa River, the Ward family made camp. It wasn't quite the Aboriginal lifestyle of Mary Ann's mother's ancestors. Instead, they would remain at their camp for as long as possible, rather than uprooting themselves after a few weeks to forage elsewhere, a survival instinct bred into her forebears after thousands of years living on the harsh continent. Yet a natural survival instinct would determine when the Wards too should gather their possessions and flee, although it wouldn't be nature's dictates they were heeding.

Nor did Mary Ann wear the attire of her Aboriginal ancestors. She had long ago realised that men's trousers were more practical for riding, gathering food and general everyday living. And there in the bush she appears to have given birth to another child—perhaps alone like her mother's people, yet evidently unsuccessfully, as the baby seems to have died soon afterwards.

For eight months, the Wards' life on the Culgoa was as different to Fred's previous years of confinement as it was possible to imagine. A ready-made family; the daily chores of child care and food preparation. Eventually he began to chafe at the mundane routine. Domestic happiness was not the only bliss of paradise to survive the Fall, according to those who revelled in the excitement of breaking in a difficult colt or plunging down a steep mountainside, who enjoyed the mateship felt by a group of weary men sitting around a campfire after a hard day's work, or lounging on a pub's verandah drinking away their earnings. There were other thrills and adventures to be had with a group of mates as well. So when opportunity knocked, Fred furtively opened the door again.

PART 5

RECKLESSNESS

My name is Frederick Ward,
I am a native of this isle;
I rob the rich to feed the poor,
And make the children smile.

Attributed to Frederick Ward

20

Men who ought everywhere to be regarded as ruffians, as outcasts, as curses to the country, have a circle of colleagues, a large circle of sympathisers, a still larger circle of admirers and a still larger circle of those who take a romantic interest in their achievements.

Sydney Morning Herald, 11 July 1864

'Have you seen two horses?'

George Davies and his assistant were camped on the banks of the Culgoa River, some 60 miles north of the Darling River junction (near today's Weilmoringle), when two horsemen trotted towards them. Davies was a businessman, a hawker who travelled the lonely country roads peddling his wares. He stopped in towns and villages, at isolated stations and cottages, accepting payment in cash or cheque or kind—a 'kind' he could at least eat if not sell. Travelling hawkers depended upon rural hospitality for their survival, and the pair had been cooking the fruits of this mutually beneficial relationship on the morning of 5 January 1865 when hailed by the horsemen.

Two horses?

The strangers began describing them, but Davies and his assistant were already shaking their heads. The strangers then sniffed the delicious aroma and hinted: 'We have not yet had anything to eat.'

Davies invited them to share breakfast, a convivial host and a canny salesman. The horsemen might be interested in some of his goods.

They were indeed interested—too interested, as it turned out.

After eating their meal, the men strolled over to Davies' wagon and looked through his goods, agreeing to purchase half a pound of tobacco. They picked up some other items and enquired about the prices, then put them down again, turning from the wagon and fumbling in their clothes as they walked back to their horses. Suddenly, two revolvers appeared, accompanied by a resounding 'Bail up!'

Rewarding his kindness by robbing him? Davies knew there was little point in resisting. He and his assistant walked over to two separate trees, as ordered, and stood there while the bushrangers lashed them to the sturdy trunks—indignity compounding injustice. Constrained in such a way, he couldn't stop them rifling his pockets and pulling out the precious cheques and orders he had carefully stowed away. He watched them examine the bits of paper, putting the cheques in one pile and the orders in another, then magnanimously handing back the orders. They evidently knew the difference. He tried to memorise their descriptions: one aged around thirty, the other about twenty-five, both around five feet seven or eight, the older man with brown curly hair, a sallow complexion and hazel-grey eyes.

He watched them amble over to his wagon and pick up his account book, adding it to the growing pile of clothes and other goods. A clever move: he would be hard-pressed to describe the stolen cheques without it. He noticed a bundle of women's clothes in their pile. They must have a female companion somewhere behind. As the pile continued to grow, he began to remonstrate with them: 'Why are you robbing a poor man?'

'The government drove me to it,' the older bushranger retorted.

'The redoubtable Captain Thunderbolt did not mince matters at all by seeking disguise but did his work openly *à la* Johnny Gilbert, saying that he was driven to it by the government,' reported a sarcastic press when news spread of Thunderbolt's return to the highways. 'I suppose that means that the Government will not let him rob the country with impunity.'

Fred had learnt the lessons of his unsuccessful Hunter River bushranging spree. The folk hero script wisely advised that he rob only the rich and not the poor. One hold-up had just netted him £150 in money and goods—and breakfast. Admittedly the hawker wasn't a member of the squattocracy and their lawmaking friends, but wealthy squatters and law-makers were rarely out on the country roads carrying money and goods, just asking to be robbed. It all came down to supply and demand. Hawkers, moreover, were simply travelling shopkeepers, members of the merchant class who toadied up to the squatters and set prices that workers were forced to pay. Poor men? Not likely.

The blacktracker carefully examined the area, the indentations where the hawker's wagon had been parked, the grassy expanse where the bush-rangers' horses had grazed. He regretfully shook his head.

Sergeant Andrew Cleary wasn't surprised. He had hoped that the bush-rangers' tracks might still be visible despite the recent rain, although he knew the odds were slim. Still, he wasn't going to give up that easily. It was only by chance that he and the tracker were examining the hawker's hold-up site in the first place. They had been returning home to Bourke after investigating a gunshot suicide when they stopped at a station on the Birree River and found Davies recounting his misfortunes. The sergeant heard the news with alarm. The north-western district hadn't witnessed any armed hold-ups by the likes of Johnny Gilbert and Ben Hall, nor did he want a new gang to be bred or succoured in his vast lawless district. It would be almost impossible to catch the culprits—chance more than anything else—and chance had just offered him such an opportunity.

They were only three days behind the bushrangers when they headed for the robbery site, with Davies directing the way. Their enquiries about sightings received instant nods of recognition and reports that similar men had been seen heading in this direction or that. When the robbery site failed to provide a trail, the sergeant decided to follow the most promising of the leads.

The bushrangers had been spotted riding towards the Narran River which, like the Culgoa, branched off from Queensland's Balonne River and headed south, following a parallel course to the Culgoa and Birree and Bokhara Rivers—although 'creeks' was probably a better description. That the bush-rangers should be heading towards the Narran was not surprising, as Hill's public house on the river was a drawcard for the worst characters in New South Wales.

More travellers were stopped for questioning; more sightings were mentioned. The search party followed these stepping stones north towards

Queensland, eventually reaching the police station at Curriwillinghi (near current Hebel) on the Ballandool River just a few miles north of the border. They were out of their jurisdiction: the bushrangers had foiled them.

Someone suggested that they question the local Aboriginals, just in case, and providence—in the form of the Aboriginal bush telegraph—smiled upon them again. The bushrangers were reportedly camped some 25 miles away, back across the border in New South Wales.

Sergeant Cleary called upon the Queensland police for assistance and the expanded posse headed out again, riding south-west towards Brenda, continuing as the last ruddy rays of sunlight disappeared, as dusk shaded the landscape. They would use the darkness as a shield. The area was flat—flood-plains flat—and they didn't want the bushrangers to see them coming.

A flicker of firelight; a plume of smoke discernible only to the eagle-eyed blacktracker. The policemen found the bushrangers' camp in thick scrub between the Culgoa and Birree Rivers not far from Brenda. They quietly retreated and hobbled their horses, settling down to wait out the night. They would rush the camp when the mantle of darkness lifted.

'A half-caste gin and two piccaninnies!'

Sergeant Cleary groaned in frustration. No bushrangers! Was it mis-direction, or rotten timing? As the woman gathered her children around her, Sergeant Cleary asked who she was.

'Ward's wife,' she answered, her English perfect. Two intelligent eyes appraised him.

Evidently they had found the right place, but where was Thunderbolt?

'Gone,' his wife reported helpfully. 'Five weeks ago.'

Davies' relieved cry at finding his property indicated otherwise. The bushrangers couldn't have been gone for five weeks: a few days—at the very most.

'Where has your husband gone?'

'To Mr Reynolds' station on the Paterson.'

Sergeant Cleary eyed the woman, who looked innocently back. He knew that Tocal bred the best horses in New South Wales; indeed the whole community was aware of that. Was she suggesting that Ward intended to steal some and overland them to Queensland? The cross-border trade in stolen horses was a thriving business and could prove a profitable enterprise for a man with Thunderbolt's horse skills. More so than bush-ranging, at any rate. But was she being naively honest, or taunting him? He could see the answer in her mocking smile.

A hobbled horse grazed nearby. Cleary examined the horse and noticed the brand $^{TM}_{WM}$. Her husband's favourite racing mare, the woman told him. Racing mare? Did the bushranger compete in horse-races? No doubt the horse was stolen, yet its presence suggested Ward was intending to return.

Ward's woman seemed happy enough to continue answering his questions. She mentioned that they had been camping on the Culgoa for the past eight months, having settled there after travelling all the way from the Maitland district.

The *Police Gazette*'s earlier report was correct, Cleary realised. Thunderbolt had indeed been heading for the Culgoa River. But the police couldn't spend time searching for a man who might be somewhere in the vast north-western expanse—or might not. Until the bushranger had declared his presence—had marked his territory so to speak—there had been little they could do.

As Davies began collecting his goods, including the all-important account book, the blacktracker continued to examine the area. He called the sergeant over and pointed to a well-beaten path heading off through the scrub. The bushrangers might have ridden off in that direction—might even be returning, unaware of the troopers' presence.

What should he do with the woman and her children? Cleary knew that he could arrest her on a 'possessing stolen goods' charge, but proving the case might be difficult. She had said she was Ward's wife and, as a married woman, she could disclaim all responsibility for the goods, putting the onus back on her husband. Moreover, it would mean transporting her and her children to the police station at Bourke, 120 miles away, which would prevent him pursuing the bushrangers. Capturing an Aboriginal woman and her two children, or continuing his pursuit of Captain Thunderbolt and his men? No contest there.

Mary Ann watched the hawker gather his goods and load them onto the horses—there went the variety added to their diet. She watched a trooper tie a lead to Fred's beloved racehorse. Fred would not be happy. She watched the party mount and begin to ride away, sitting tensely in their saddles, hoping they might cross paths with the unwitting bushrangers.

Did they really think that a party of horsemen, or even a single horseman for that matter, could come anywhere near her camp unnoticed?

One mile . . . two . . . three . . . five: the path continued until, eventually, seven miles from Thunderbolt's camp, the troopers exited the scrubby bushland near a homestead. They looked around in surprise. One of the troopers spotted a resident and asked where they were. 'Bunna Bunna,' was the answer—the cattle station owned by Thomas Moffitt.

Sergeant Cleary knew of the cattle station and its owner. Moffitt was reportedly the first squatter in the Walgett district and bore the nickname 'Red Tom'. To the police and the more respectable squatters in the district, he was 'the notorious Red Tom'. That a path from a horse-stealer's camp would lead directly to Moffitt's station came as no surprise at all.

'Is the horse yours?' Sergeant Cleary asked the station owner, showing him Thunderbolt's racehorse and pointing suspiciously to the 'TM' brand.

'No, the horse is not mine, but the brand is,' Red Tom said evasively. As for the bushranger camped at the end of the well-worn track leading directly from his homestead, he was afraid he was unable to help them at all.

Meanwhile, events further south suggested that Fred had picked a bad time to resume his bushranging career. The trigger was a cold-blooded murder committed by Gilbert and Hall's latest recruit, eighteen-year-old John Dunn. He shot father-of-eight Constable Samuel Nelson in front of his two young sons on 27 January 1865, the first day of the new Parliamentary session— the very day that the New South Wales Governor dissolved James Martin's conservative government after only fifteen months in office. Martin's team had failed to solve the state's financial woes, caused largely by a balance-of-payments crisis and an inefficient Treasury organisation. They had failed to curb the bushranging epidemic that began with the Eugowra gold escort robbery two-and-a-half years previously. The voters at the recent election had proclaimed their displeasure. News of Constable Nelson's death might have pushed Martin's teetering government over the edge if Sir John Young's bony finger hadn't already given it the final nudge.

'The first duty of every well-regulated government is to maintain its finances in a sound and solvent condition,' Sir John chastised Parliament.

It is? queried the *Sydney Morning Herald*. 'Surely the first *object* of Government is the security of life and property. And if the first *duty* is to secure a sound financial condition, it is because an insolvent Government cannot count on the means of attaining that primary objective.'

Clearly, even the Sydney press considered the rural bushranging epidemic the most serious of the state's problems.

Editorials dissected the government's failure to control the bush-ranging outbreak and berated the public for their complicity, either by actively helping the villains or by turning a blind eye to their activities or those of their supporters. Part of the problem lay with the law as much as anything, the *Herald* admitted. To apprehend a bushranger, the police had to first announce themselves—which would likely be answered with a deadly shot. If the bushranger himself happened to be killed, the communi-ty's saviour could be judged guilty of murder. 'How are we to suppose that in such a state of the law, any honest men will place their liberty as well as their lives in jeopardy?' As for the public's complicity: how could the courts punish harbourers when the harboured bushrangers themselves had not yet faced the courts, let alone been judged guilty of any crime?

Letters flooded into the newspapers proposing strategies for dealing with the problem. One letter-writer based his strategy upon a method used to prevent murder in ancient times, suggesting that they divide the state into districts and impose a heavy fine or tax on bushranging districts; the fine would be paid by the inhabitants, with the proceeds used to fund rewards for the bushrangers' apprehension and additional policemen for that district. The suggested strategy had a simple appeal, placing the onus on the community itself to take responsibility for its members, rather than whining to the authorities to solve all their problems. Of course, such a hip-pocket approach could soon rebound upon the Parliamentarians them-selves. Those most easily caught in the tax net—that is, the names on the electoral rolls—were those who had voted them into office. It would take remarkable political courage to implement such a strategy, effective though it might prove.

One letter-writer suggested establishing militias of able-bodied men who, in the event of trouble, could act as special mounted constables within their own district. Another proposed calling for fifty or sixty volunteers from the police force and dividing them into groups of five or six, each with a blacktracker, then sending them out to scour the countryside and hunt down the bushrangers. Both strategies could prove remarkably effective in eradicating the problem—most likely by the wholesale execution of the bushrangers. Such volunteers could easily turn into legalised vigilantes, with little accountability. Innocent until proven guilty? How many bushrangers would survive to face their day in court?

A person signing themselves 'Divide and Conquer' recommended offering a reward to the bushrangers for turning in their companions: £400 and a free pardon. Perhaps the letter-writer assumed that the bushrangers were, at heart, desperate to be responsible citizens, that whatever need or desire or grievance had pushed them into bushranging in the first place would be expunged if they were given a hand-out. And clearly the letter-writer assumed that they would have little compunction about sending their mates to the gallows.

'Justice' advised the authorities to reconsider the bushrangers' legal position. 'Why shouldn't the bushrangers who are guilty of murder and refusing to surrender for trial, be tried and convicted ex parte, and then outlawed' he queried. But not only outlawed: 'A reward of £1000 should then be offered for the capture of each of them, dead or alive.' Chief Justice Alfred Stephen had a similar suggestion.

'Just do something!' cried the remaining voices. And Charles Cowper's new government was listening.

21

When a chieftain presents himself who is willing to risk his life and liberty in an enterprise which presents large gains and a highwayman's glory, volunteers are to be found in abundance.

Lachlan Observer, 1863

'I have been authorised by his father to chastise the boy when he deserves it,' said John Brown, master of the brig *Venus*, to the Water Police Court in 1859 when brought up on charges of ill-usage. The prosecutor? His eleven-year-old apprentice, John Massey Thompson. 'He is a sharp but pert boy,' wrote the bemused court reporter as he listened to Thompson's testimony—no doubt understanding why the boy's father found him such a handful.

Thompson was the son of educated middle-class townsfolk, his father an official employed by the City of Sydney Corporation, his mother the daughter of an Irish protestant clergyman. Thompson Senior eventually sent his wilful son hundreds of miles away to the tough environment of a country station near Moree, but the lad continued to resist dictatorial authority. Early in 1865 he threatened to shoot the Terrihihi station superintendent. Then he stole a horse and headed west to pursue his long-expressed dream of joining a gang of bushrangers—the colonial equivalent of a disaffected youth lured seawards by tales of swashbuckling adventures under a Jolly Roger flag. He soon found his own buccaneer hero.

Thompson would later swear he was the innocent victim of a devilish plot, that Thunderbolt had ensnared him by claiming to be a wealthy

Narran publican and offering good wages and the chance to visit his family in Sydney, and that the bushranger's true calling was not revealed until he robbed a hawker and made the lad an unwitting accessory. Afterwards, Thunderbolt convinced him that any protestations of innocence would be ignored—he knew so from bitter personal experience—and that they must stick together until they had sufficient funds to leave the country.

Well, that's the story Thompson told his mother, anyway.

Thompson was only around seventeen at the time, just a few years older than Mary Ann's sons—not that he was the type to be mothered. Nor were the two men who also hitched their spirited horses to Thunderbolt's bushranging wagon. This little band of outlaws was the oddest bush-ranging gang to roam the highways and byways of New South Wales, not only physically distinctive but culturally diverse, a colonial melting pot in itself: Thompson a slight, flaxen-haired, blue-eyed, fresh-faced English-born lad of the butter-wouldn't-melt variety; McIntosh, a lanky Scottish giant over six feet tall with a cadaverous appearance; The Bull, christened Thomas Hogan, son of Irish Catholic parents, dark and swarthy, about Fred's age but taller, a tough mountain man; and Mary Ann, with her milky-brown complexion and Aboriginal heritage, and her two young daughters. Of the bunch, Fred—average height, average build, average colouring—was the least striking in appearance, but he was 'Captain Thunderbolt', the leader of this gang of misfits.

Fred had grown up with tales of bushranging heroes—the Wild Colonial Boy who preferred death to a life of slavery bound down by iron chains, the Jewboy who fought to the last—and of their British highwayman pre-decessors. With each retelling, these tales had become more exciting and romantic, more enticing. Now that he had discarded the law-abiding life-style and tasted the pleasures of bushranging—the thrill of danger, the intoxication of power, the anticipation of a windfall—he wished to bask in the same 'heroic' glory. With a gang backing him, both fame and fortune seemed within reach. Bolstered by each other's bravado, they decided to take the Walgett district by storm.

Fifteen revolvers and two rifles: the frightening array greeted the residents of Bagot's Mogil Mogil station, north of Collarenebri, after Fred and his gang rode up to the station on 16 March 1865. Threats of instant death followed if the residents moved without permission, although Fred soon allowed the cooks to prepare supper. Food and £7 from a broken-open chest proved their only rewards.

The gang robbed a traveller the following day, and a man returning from the Collarenebri races a couple of days later. On 20 March, they searched William Earl's Squatter's Arms pub at Collarenebri, although they didn't steal anything. As they departed, they announced that they were heading back to Mogil Mogil, then to Goondoobline station and on to the Monindie Inn and store, robbing everyone as they passed through.

Their successes were fuelling their daring. The weight of numbers and armaments had tipped the balance of power. Suddenly they were in control. Suddenly those who had once ordered them around were cowering before them. Drunk on grog and glory they were becoming reckless, taunting the community with their plans, challenging anyone to try and stop them. In a district so far from police protection, they realised that few, if any, would be willing to defy them.

Hugh Bryden knew that bushrangers were marauding in his district. A local magistrate as well as the managing partner of a large squatterage, he tried to keep abreast of the local news. When he heard that the gang had become so reckless they were announcing their robbery itinerary, he decided that enough was enough. Ben Hall's gang had behaved similarly in the Bathurst district, assuring their victims that the police could be relied upon only to arrive too late to prevent a robbery, even when given advance warning. And they had proved it. Each sign of the police's incompetence and cowardice had increased the Bathurst gang's fearlessness and magnified their sense of omnipotence. But the Collarenebri region had no local police force to protect it, incompetent or otherwise. It was up to him to make sure that Thunderbolt's gang did not take control of the whole district.

Gathering all the armaments he could find at his head station—an old dragoon, a revolver, and a gun for which he had only a single ball— he and another station manager rode towards Mogil Mogil where they collected the station's stockman, just a lad, and the local pound-keeper. They continued to Burn Burn station, only a mile from Mogil Mogil, where Bryden obtained two more guns and swore in the volunteers as special constables. Then they held a council of war.

Seventeen guns the bushrangers had carried at the initial Mogil Mogil robbery, according to the reports Bryden had received. Clearly his posse was not sufficiently armed to meet four desperadoes belted with revolvers. He left the lad to watch out for the bushrangers while he and the others raced to Goondoobline. There he gathered another three recruits—the manager and two stockmen, one an Aboriginal man who would also prove helpful as a tracker—and added a breech-loading rifle, a double-barrelled gun, a pistol and a French bayonet sabre to their arsenal. The larger posse then headed back towards Mogil Mogil.

Expecting to meet the bushranging gang along the way, they surrounded and surprised several camps, much to the alarm of the innocent occupants. When they eventually reached the station's young stockman again, they learnt that the bushrangers had robbed a hawker—while the lad was watching.

William Lawson was irate. Four horsemen had robbed his wagon while he was absent, stealing £50 of goods including five revolvers, twelve brown shirts, ten pairs of moleskin trousers, two dozen pairs of spurs, four bridles, four pairs of riveted hobbles, two loaded whips and two-dozen pocket knives, among other items. But what really infuriated him was that a magistrate and some troopers had reportedly seen the robbery from a distance, yet instead of rushing over to protect his goods and apprehend the villains, they had ridden off to a station sixteen miles away to get reinforcements.

His fury overflowed into a letter sent to a friend, a letter then forwarded to the *Maitland Mercury*. Like most second-hand stories, however, Lawson's was full of errors.

Unbeknown to Magistrate Bryden, or the angry hawker for that matter, Thunderbolt and his mates had retreated to the Barwon after robbing the hawker, and from the angle of the river had seen Bryden's party galloping up the road. Deciding they should put some distance between themselves and the Collarenebri district after all, they aborted their plans to rob the remaining stations and fled west towards the Narran River some 75 miles distant.

Bryden's blacktracker soon picked up the bushrangers' trail and the pursuit began. Unfortunately the search party had not planned on a cross-country journey and carried insufficient supplies; eventually, the men were forced to turn back. As they journeyed home, Bryden consoled himself with the knowledge that he might not have caught them, but he had at least sent them packing from his district. They were now someone else's problem.

William Beaumont's problem, as it turned out, but he too was not going to be robbed without taking a stand. The resident partner of the firm Messrs Macleay, Little & Co. of Talawanta, on the Birree River, was just the '& Co.' on the letterhead, but he wasn't merely a figurehead as many station owners were: top-hat doffing gentry who invested their wealth in land and livestock but kept their gloved hands pristine. When the four bushrangers rode up to his homestead on 26 March 1865, Beaumont refused to submit to their demands. He turned to the four or five station hands who had submissively raised their arms and begged them to join him in fighting the villains.

Risking their lives for someone else's financial benefit? Beaumont's men had little interest in resisting the demands of four gun-wielding bushrangers. Dropped eyes, sullen countenances: no words needed to be spoken.

The disgruntled station owner had no other option but to submit, although he cursed the bushrangers as they robbed him. Four new saddles, six saddle-straps, a bridle and a pair of saddle-bags, firearms and ammunition—including two double-barrelled guns and five boxes of percussion caps—three red blankets, five pairs of trousers, two pairs of wellington boots, two tweed coats, three water cans and a bay mare. The robbers had come prepared, leading two packhorses to carry away their booty. A station was an ideal supply depot for anyone living in the bush.

Thunderbolt again. With *three* accomplices?

Sergeant Cleary was horrified. The outlaw was indeed proving a beacon for the unworthy. Fortunately, William Beaumont had immediately sent a messenger to the Bourke police station, a hundred miles away, with news of the robbery so the gang's trail was not yet cold. If the rains held off, they might be able to track them.

Cleary's squad made their preparations and rode out the following morning: the sergeant himself and a constable, the Talawanta messenger, and Bourke's blacktracker, who happened to come from the Talawanta neighbourhood. If they failed to pick up the men's trail, the tracker's kin might be able to help them.

The troopers rode hard, reaching Talawanta on the Wednesday evening only three days after the robbery, where they rested for the night. At first light, the blacktracker picked up the bushrangers' trail. With the testy Mr Beaumont accompanying them, Cleary's party mounted fresh horses and headed out.

Blacktrackers were Fred's greatest fear. Forget the blustering station owners or the nag-riding troopers. He could outwit any of them. But the black-trackers? Inexorable hunters, tenacious and untiring. When they joined forces with the troopers, he could hear the hounds beginning to bay.

The hunt wasn't over that easily, however, particularly with Mary Ann on his team. His resourceful wife had taught him some clever strategies to outfox them.

Bourke's blacktracker wasn't fooled. The bushrangers had set fire to the grass for a distance of eighteen miles in an attempt to obliterate their tracks, but the tracker hadn't lost them. Up the Birree River and across country to the Bokhara. Dislodged stones, broken twigs, crushed grass, smudged hoof-prints, piles of fly-encrusted dung—seemingly nothing at all, yet somehow the relentless tracker still managed to follow their trail.

On the second evening, the troopers arrived at one of Thunderbolt's camps, probably the gang's resting place on the night of the robbery. The fire still burned and the carcass of a bullock lay nearby. The thieves had cut some meat from its rump, feasting on the succulent flesh before bedding down for the night. The police decided to rest as well, picking up the trail again the next morning and following it south-east towards the Narran Lake.

Into the Narran Lake, as it turned out. The bushrangers had tried another clever trick for evading their pursuers—and they nearly succeeded. For hours the tracker patiently searched the area, trying to determine where Thunderbolt and his men might have left the water. The lake was five miles across, some fifteen miles around if strictly circular. Where could they have exited? The troopers noticed a lone horseman galloping along the edge of the lake, but he was a long way away—too far away to question.

Eventually the tracker noticed a tiny path heading up the hill into the scrub. 'A piccaninny's track,' he told Sergeant Cleary. He continued searching. 'A gin,' he soon announced, adding that her track led up the same hill, that this was probably their path to collect water.

Dense scrub covered most of the area. Cleary and his men followed the tracks for about 300 yards until the path opened into a clearing. That's when they saw them.

A pair of amused eyes looked across at Sergeant Cleary. 'So you are here again, are you?'

Sergeant Cleary hadn't forgotten Thunderbolt's woman. She was fast becoming his torment. The Culgoa River a few months previously and now here, on the Narran. Had they just missed the bushrangers again?

'You're too late,' she taunted. 'They're off. We saw you when you came on the lake this morning.'

Glancing around, the sergeant saw a jumble of stores, the booty from the station robbery no doubt: tea, sugar, flour, tobacco, slops, three double-barrelled guns loaded to the muzzle, two pistols and spare ammunition. A bounteous haul indeed—and that was after the gang had eaten some of the supplies and equipped themselves before departing. His suspicions were confirmed when Beaumont pointed to his own possessions among the piles. That was when Thunderbolt's woman learnt the identity of the civilian at Sergeant Cleary's side.

'You were only showing off at the station when you wanted to show fight,' she jeered, directing her barbed tongue at Beaumont; Fred had enjoyed recounting the tale of the vengeful squatter. Her verbal emasculation continued for a while longer, then she resumed her attack on the sergeant, twitting him about his lack of success and enjoying his evident frustration and discomfiture.

Meanwhile, the tracker searched the camp's perimeter. He found that the fleeing bushrangers had used another trick for evading detection. They had separated, each riding off in a different direction.

Should they follow one of the tracks? Should they wait at the camp in the hope of surprising them when they returned? If they returned. Sergeant Cleary decided to retreat and discuss their options. Better that than hanging around listening to Thunderbolt's woman mocking them.

The police party crossed to the other side of the lake, where the men camped and rested for the remainder of the day. Late that evening, concealed by night's gloom, they crept back to Thunderbolt's side and hid themselves within sight of his camp, watching and waiting. The rosy light of sunrise eventually replaced the darkness, the birds warbled a greeting, but still the bushrangers didn't return.

Did they really think that Mary Ann wouldn't have organised to signal Thunderbolt and his gang when it was safe to return?

'I am taking you into custody for being in possession of stolen goods,' Sergeant Cleary informed Mary Ann later that same morning.

Too little sleep, too long a night and nothing to show for his endeavours. Again. He had decided not to arrest her at their previous encounter—even though she was surrounded by stolen goods—choosing instead to pursue the bushrangers. This time the men were long gone and wouldn't be coming back, not while the troopers were around. Mrs Thunderbolt would make sure of that. She was clearly a vital cog in their proficient bushranging machine—so maybe if he extracted the cog, the machine would falter. And arresting her would make her pay for her insolence. Ridiculing a thwarted policeman was never wise.

As Cleary's words died away, a remarkable transformation came over the mother standing in front of him. Her pretty features disappeared, replaced by glaring eyes and bared teeth. Her body tensed—then, with a primeval howl, she leapt at him. She clawed at his uniform with her fingernails, gouging long tears in his shirt as all the frustrations of her life coalesced into that one moment of pure rage.

'Coward!' she screamed. 'Bully!'

She pummelled at his chest, swearing that Fred would avenge her. Suddenly, she released him and backed off a few feet. Still glaring and panting, she crouched into a fighter's stance and lifted her clenched fists. Then she challenged him to single-handed combat.

Cleary's companions watched the ferocious attack with stunned immobility. Cleary barked at them to help him. They surrounded Mary Ann and grappled her into custody, lashing her hands so she couldn't attack them, trying to control her writhing torso and kicking feet.

Her body might have been restrained but her mouth wasn't. The taunts continued as they loaded the stolen goods onto the available horses, putting leads on the four horses grazing at the camp. Objections rang out as they packed up Mary Ann's possessions, then mounted her and her children onto the horses and set off on the long journey south-west to Bourke. More taunts; more vows of Fred's vengeance. The incessant torrent of abuse and derision continued for mile after endless mile.

Behind her busy mouth, Mary Ann's mind was working furiously. What was the one thing that terrified most men? Suddenly the stream of abuse stopped, replaced by a cry of pain, a hand clutching her well-rounded belly.

The troopers knew what that meant.

More gasps of pain from a doubled-over torso.

They couldn't take her with them, the troopers realised. George Forrester's Wilby Wilby station was nearby. They would detour there and leave her.

A short time later, from the safety of Wilby Wilby station, a complacent Mary Ann watched the troopers ride away. Now all she had to do was wait for Fred to come and rescue her.

'With the usual luck of our New South Wales police, the robbers escaped,' reported the *Maitland Mercury*'s Walgett correspondent. 'The police succeeded in capturing a half-caste woman and two children belonging to one of the robbers, some horses, saddles and stores. I feel sure you will think with me that great praise is due to them for their gallant conduct.'

The correspondent's sarcasm was noted by Sergeant Cleary and his men. Fail to catch anyone and the press rebuked them for their incompetence. Capture someone who was living off the proceeds of crimes—a criminal offence—and the press reviled them for their lack of gallantry. They couldn't win.

Visitors were usually a welcome sight at a lonely rural station, bringing news of the district and a fresh voice at the supper table. But not this time. The four horsemen who dismounted at Wilby Wilby station around 5 pm on Tuesday 4 April 1865 initially seemed little different to the average rural travellers. Quality horses, good equipment: a station owner and his men travelling up-country, perhaps. Until they pulled out their pistols and held them to the heads of the four men who ventured outside to greet them.

The Wilby Wilby stockmen stood by passively while the bushrangers searched them. The bushrangers' first demand wasn't surprising: the woman and her children. Sergeant Cleary had warned them; the woman herself had assured them—endlessly. The bush telegraph had proven its worth: only two days for Thunderbolt to find her.

Mary Ann was prepared. She had been watching and waiting, alert for the sound of horses coming towards the station house. Before the stockmen even realised what was happening, she had gathered the children and collected their belongings, ready to be taken outside.

A quick smile in greeting. The three of them tossed up onto the horses. The young girls knew the drill: Ellen, aged five, and Marina, three-and-a-half, had spent much of their young lives in the saddle.

Thunderbolt and his gang then made it clear that their demands weren't finished. They wanted gunpowder.

Were their guns empty? The bushrangers exuded an easy familiarity in their actions, a dangerous confidence. No one was willing to call their bluff. As the stockmen dutifully passed over the gunpowder, one of the bushrangers remarked conversationally, 'It is of more value to us than gold.'

After searching the residents but obtaining no money, the bushrangers mounted their horses and rode off, a surprisingly speedy visit for a gang whose booty had just been carried away on Sergeant Cleary's packhorses.

Around 8 pm that same evening, the thunder of hooves heralded the arrival of more visitors. Thunderbolt and his gang had returned, although without Mary Ann and the children this time. Having stashed them away safely, Fred and his men were getting down to normal bushranging business.

The Wilby Wilby residents knew that the bushrangers had a formidable arsenal and an augmented supply of ammunition. They offered no resistance and the gang made no threats, just demands. Supper was first on their list.

The cook hurried into the kitchen and began preparing a meal for them. The bushrangers' request wasn't surprising. What traveller didn't relish the thought of a home-cooked meal after eating the limited supplies available on the road? Bushrangers were permanent travellers, although worse off than most. They couldn't enjoy the hospitality of many of the roadside inns, forced by their notoriety to avoid towns with a police presence and innkeepers who might collude with the police, always on the alert in case a police patrol stopped by at just the wrong moment—or the right moment, depending upon the perspective.

Some of Fred's men searched the house, rifling through drawers and trunks, peering into cupboards and wardrobes. A good haul: £10 in coins and notes. Clearly the Wilby Wilby residents hadn't expected them to return. Another two visitors had arrived in the meantime, hawkers who intended bedding down for the night. Their accommodation decision proved a particularly expensive choice: £20.

Fred and his companions ordered all the residents to join them for supper, yet unlike the earlier Mogil Mogil robbery, they didn't fill their stomachs and stand up to leave. Instead they remained at the dining table chatting to their hosts, lolling back in their chairs as if they were honoured guests invited for an evening's socialising, flaunting their power. When their curious table companions mentioned the police, Fred laughed off the troopers' efforts to apprehend them, talking about the police with a dismissive contempt.

With every reason, the morose Wilby Wilby residents knew. The odds of the police arriving during a station hold-up were virtually non-existent at the best of times, even worse in this instance because the troopers had set off only two days previously on their 100-mile journey back to Bourke. Yet even when pursued by the police, Thunderbolt always seemed to get away. Sergeant Cleary had been concerned that the more the gang out-witted the police, the more audacious and arrogant they would become. His concerns were proving justified.

Eventually, three hours after arriving, Fred and his men loaded some clothes and rations onto their horses and bade their hosts a cool 'Good evening'.

Around 3 am that same night, long before dawn's rays began to lighten the sky, the Wilby Wilby residents were woken by the rhythmic pounding of horses' hooves again. Thunderbolt's gang had returned for a third visit.

They stayed for only a short time, offering no threats of violence, indeed providing no reason for their return. But a third appearance within twelve hours contained an implicit threat in itself, particularly when the visit occurred during the pre-dawn hours when defences were at their weakest. Do not relax, it warned. Do not assume we are gone for good. We are out here watching you and we are in control.

•

'I understand the police have gone back to Bourke and left us to our fate,' wrote a frightened local resident after news surfaced of the gang's activities and the police's failure—yet again—to capture Thunderbolt. 'I fear if the bushrangers are not put a stop to, they will be as bad as Ben Hall and his gang.'

The *Maitland Mercury* also expressed alarm at the gang's activities, reporting that the robberies had been executed with a proficiency and coolness which proved that the bushrangers were experts at their nefarious business. As for Thunderbolt himself, the editor warned on 18 April 1865 with remarkable prescience: 'This notoriety is not the *bruten fulmen* [empty threat] which some consider.'

Mary Ann and her children must not remain in the Walgett district, Fred realised. She had outsmarted the police once, but encumbered by pregnancy and young children was unlikely to do so a second time. She could still travel a long distance by horseback, but not for too much longer—as he had learnt first-hand during their journey to Dungog shortly before Marina was born.

Where should they go? Her father's place was not an option. If the police issued a warrant for her arrest, Monkerai would be the first place the Dungog officers would look. They would have to find somewhere else for Mary Ann to make camp.

The gang set off soon afterwards, riding 300 miles to the Tamworth district in less than two weeks. Fred had no intention of leaving Mary Ann alone, despite her bush skills. With her pregnancy well advanced, she would need a companion. Mary Ann had some contacts and Fred employed another part-Aboriginal woman to stay with her, a woman who could also help during childbirth. Soon after settling them somewhere in the Tamworth vicinity, Fred and his gang mounted their horses and rode off again, back towards the north-western plains.

Unbeknown to Thunderbolt's gang as they crossed the New South Wales countryside, Fred's name was on the clenched lips of many politicians back in Sydney. The bushranging problem refused to disappear, so it was time to act. On 8 April 1865, four days after Fred rescued Mary Ann from Wilby Wilby, the Felons Apprehension Bill passed into law.

Premier Charles Cowper knew that the bushranging terror had contributed to the previous government's demise, and that of his own government beforehand. In March 1865, in the first days of his new government's Parliamentary session, two important bills were introduced. The Robberies Suppression Bill drew upon some suggestions offered by the letter-writer who had proposed that districts with a bushranging problem be proclaimed 'disturbed districts' and placed under martial law. Under this Bill, anyone charged with armed robbery could be legally proclaimed an 'outlaw', and anyone convicted of armed robbery or even attempted armed robbery could be sentenced to death—or life imprisonment if it pleased the court. Those caught harbouring, feeding, arming or even writing to such outlaws, or refusing to provide the police with information or assistance, or providing false information, could themselves face hefty fines and long penal sentences, and fines could also be imposed on anyone carrying firearms without a licence. Properties could be searched upon 'reasonable suspicion', and all property in the disturbed district was to be valued and taxed.

Had Thunderbolt's gang heard about this bill? If it passed into law, Mary Ann's taunts alone could be enough to send her to gaol, on the grounds that she was refusing to provide the police with 'information or assistance'. And shouting 'bail up' with a gun in his hand, or even tucked into his belt, could send Fred to the gallows.

Not surprisingly it was the simpler second bill, the one that didn't impose martial law or levy a fine on voters in the bushranging districts, that Parliament wasted no time in enacting. Under the resulting Felons Apprehension Act, bushrangers charged with an offence punishable by death, generally murder, would be ordered to surrender by a certain date. If they chose not to do so, the courts would declare them outlaws, men no longer protected by the law, men no longer entitled to that fundamental right underpinning British jurisprudence: that they were innocent until proven guilty. If armed, or even suspected of being armed (what self-respecting bushranger wasn't armed?), they could be shot on sight—by anyone.

Not that there weren't some detractors. 'It is repugnant to our very instincts that men who have not undergone a formal trial before a court of justice should be surprised and shot down either by the police or by amateur ministers of justice,' wrote the concerned *Maitland Mercury*. Yet even the liberal press recognised that most community members were willing to put aside their concerns for a short time to rid themselves of the poisonous tree growing in their backyard. Desperate times required desperate measures.

The legislation also targeted outlaw supporters, allowing searches without warrants, arrests and convictions based upon flimsy evidence, extraordinarily long prison sentences considering the nature of the 'crime', and the seizure of all goods and assets of those convicted. We will prevail, the government assured the community.

As signatures were scrawled across the new legislation, the Attorney General prepared to invoke the legislation against the four names on his first list: Mad Dan Morgan, Bold Ben Hall, and Hall's two gang members, Johnny Gilbert and the ruthless young John Dunn.

For the other aspiring or active bushrangers like Captain Thunderbolt, Parliament intended the Act to serve as a warning: Kill anyone and we will shoot you down like a rabid dog!

22

The possession of a race-horse, the accoutrements of the road, the wild licence of the bush, the occasional revels enjoyed after a season of success, even the very terror inflicted are all attractions.

Sydney Morning Herald, 3 October 1867

Some stockmen must be playing a practical joke, thought Martin Hurley as his horse and mailbag-laden packhorse plodded south on their 120-mile journey from Warialda to Tamworth on Wednesday 19 April 1865. He was riding through the Manilla River valley, only four miles from the township of Manilla itself, when he spotted three mounted men galloping down from a nearby ridge yelling 'Bail up! Bail up!' He eased his pace to find out what was going on. That's when he saw their guns.

With the ease of familiarity, the trio were gripping their reins with one hand and a revolver with the other. All three revolvers were pointing directly towards him. Perhaps these were not pranksters after all, Hurley decided, and pulled on his reins. He eyed the men drawing closer. Heavily armed bushrangers, more likely. He could see another revolver tucked into each of their belts.

The bushrangers were unmasked and made no attempt to hide their identities, although they didn't introduce themselves when they halted nearby. One of them, a man aged about thirty and of middling height, appeared to be their captain, as he ordered another gang member, a tall man, to stay with the mailman. Beckoning the third, he wheeled his horse and cantered towards a buggy some 200 yards behind.

As Hurley continued to watch them, he saw that the captain's tweed jacket had a hole burnt in the back. A story there, no doubt. But who were they?

Rotten timing, Mr Ross of Myall Creek realised, as he watched the two armed bushrangers leave the mailman and ride towards his buggy. They were clearly intending to bail up the mailman, and he just happened to be in the vicinity. To make it worse, he was unarmed and had Mrs Redhead and her family travelling with him. He had little choice but to obey them.

As the men neared, Ross took mental notes. The older man was clearly the leader. He bore the darkened complexion of an outdoors man, framed by heavily oiled dark hair and a bushy black beard, and was wearing a tweed coat, breeches and long boots. He was also surprisingly civil.

'I must trouble you, Sir, to bail up,' the captain asked Ross politely, without even brandishing his revolver. Ross requested that they refrain from frightening the lady.

The bushranger looked towards Ross's companion. 'Don't be frightened, marm,' he said courteously. 'I never insult ladies nor allow any one that is with me to do so.' Turning back to Ross, the captain asked if he had any money.

'I never carry any now-a-days,' was the simple response.

'You gentlemen never do carry any with you,' the captain said dryly. 'I wish you did!' He spotted Ross's watch and hinted that it looked like a good one. Ross protested at having to hand it over and the bushranger didn't insist. Nor did he search Ross or the buggy, simply asking him to drive off the road into the bush until his men had searched the mail. He promised not to detain them for long. Then he and his offsider, a fresh-faced young lad, headed back to the mailman.

Mailman Hurley had also led his packhorse off the road by this time, having been ordered to do so by the tall bushranger who remained with him. They waited in a little gully until the captain and his young offsider rejoined them. The captain told his mates to lift the mailbags from the packhorse, while remaining on his own horse, guarding the mailman. His minions opened the bags and dumped the letters on the ground, then picked them up one by one and began slitting them open, pulling out the contents and handing up any cash, cheques and orders to their captain. They also handed up a small parcel containing eight or nine ounces of gold.

The mailman saw the captain tuck the little parcel carefully into his pocket: a treasure indeed. Hurley knew that people were increasingly reluctant to send valuable goods via the postal service—alarmed not only at the number of mail robberies, but at the reported thefts by postal workers. Ten years previously, the Postmaster General had recommended cutting notes and cheques in half and posting them at separate times to foil any thieves, the double postage charge serving as an insurance premium of sorts. Hurley could see from the dozens of half-cheques and half-notes the bushrangers were extracting that many postal customers had heeded this wise advice.

'The halves will be no use to you,' Hurley taunted the captain.

'We'll stick up every mail that comes along the road for weeks until we find the other halves!' was the swaggering response.

After the bushrangers eventually rode off towards Manilla, Hurley gathered all the letters and stuffed them back into his mailbags, pleased that the scoundrels had not wilfully destroyed them. He loaded the bags onto his packhorse and climbed up himself. His own horse was gone, the bushrangers having stolen that as well. 'We want it for a mate who is in the bush with a knocked-up horse,' they had explained. He had nearly lost his waistcoat as well, as one of the bushrangers had taken a fancy to it and the valuable gold watch pocketed inside, yet surprisingly the man had returned both before departing.

Fred and his gang waited until after sunset that same Wednesday evening before stealing two of the best horses from a paddock belonging to Parliamentarian John Charles Lloyd. An intentional swipe at the government, or just a side benefit? From there, they headed 28 miles north to Barraba, where the residents awoke at midnight to the pounding of hooves. Another two horses were stolen, but two were left in their place, including one of Lloyd's own horses—a personal snub, if he chose to take it that way, on the quality of his 'best' horseflesh.

The following morning they bailed up Job Cheeseborough's Tareela station on the Manilla River, some twelve miles from Barraba. After ransacking the house, Fred turned to one of the stockmen and said, 'Bring me Glendower.'

'He is in the bush,' the cunning stockman replied, knowing that the celebrated Arabian stallion was actually in the yard only a short distance away.

Forced to make do with a less able horse, the gang left soon afterwards, taking with them rations, a revolver, a rifle, and ringing ears from the earbashing Fred had received from one of the station women who remembered the young horse-breaker from a decade ago and wondered that he dared show his face again.

The news of the robberies sent Tamworth into an uproar. The bushrangers were strangers in the district. Who were they? Rumours spread that Ben Hall and his gang had slipped away from the Bathurst district to find a new hunting ground. Some of the police primed their guns, keen to have a chance at capturing the notorious gang, to prove that the ranks of the new police were not riddled with men as cowardly and incompetent as the Bathurst troops. Others who read the bushrangers' descriptions thought it more likely that Thunderbolt's gang had ridden into the district, although no one had previously described the young lad, Thompson, as 'stupid looking'. While the gang's last-known robbery was only a couple of weeks previously in the Walgett district, Thunderbolt was known to be an exceptional horseman. Moreover, thunderbolts by their very nature were unpredictable. If Thunderbolt and his men had found fresh pastures, the captain was proving a wily leader indeed.

Tamworth's police superintendent despatched two policemen to the Manilla district. Constables Dalton and Lynch left Tamworth the day after the mail robbery and followed the sightings north to Barraba, where Constable Charles Norris of the Barraba police joined them. Three 'old force men', experienced and capable, were at last on the bushranger's trail.

The Barraba correspondent who watched them depart reported that they were suitably disguised as bushmen; however, their wretched horses would be incapable of overtaking Thunderbolt's gang, particularly if the bushrangers headed back to the Barwon River district. 'Ward is quite at home here in these mountains,' the correspondent warned, 'and can easily evade the police, the country being very rough from the Gwydir to the Namoi.'

Hugh Munro had no intention of meekly yielding to the gang of bushrangers who strode into his Boggy Creek Inn on Monday 24 April 1865 demanding that he and his customers 'bail up'. Faint-hearted publicans didn't survive long in the world of bellicose drovers and bullockies with a craving for more than their pockets could finance.

Munro's inn was off the well-beaten track from Narrabri to Moree, tucked on a parallel road used by drovers and travellers. His was one of the many roadside shanties that dotted the landscape every dozen or so miles throughout the interior, the inn itself a watering hole for the drovers, and the creek for their livestock. Bushrangers were not among Munro's usual clientele, however, and he wasn't about to offer an open invitation to rob him. So he held up the twin badges of his courage and bravely offered to tackle them, man to man, one at a time.

The bushrangers rolled their eyes and waved a dismissive pistol.

Rations, clothing, cheques and cash: a good haul worth between £70 and £80. To add to Munro's woes, the youngest rapscallion pocketed his precious gold and silver watch. Then the gang sat down to enjoy their takings.

A few drinks later, one of the roisterers decided to prove his marksmanship. He pulled out his pistol and aimed at Munro's dog. And fired. Fortunately the dog survived the assault. Thereafter the bullet protruded from its belly like a tumour, bearing testament to the shooter's drunkenness or depravity.

Some time later the bushrangers swung themselves back onto their horses and headed north again, towards the quiet little hamlet of Millie.

William Walford was in a hurry. The bush telegraph had reported that Thunderbolt's gang were carousing at the Boggy Creek Inn only fifteen miles away, and were likely heading in his direction. He knew Boggy Creek well, having been the first innkeeper there when it opened the previous year. He had only recently taken over the Sportsman's Arms at Millie, refurbishing the place and adding a bagatelle table to draw in the customers. Bushrangers were not the type of customers he had in mind when he invested in his new premises, however.

Walford grabbed his valuables and other portable items and stashed them away safely. This was a bad time for him to receive a visit from bushrangers—not that any time was good. As Honorary Secretary for the Millie Annual Races to be held a fortnight hence, he had more goods than normal on his premises. But forewarned was forearmed. No need for any show of bravado if there was little to steal. And there was only so much grog the wretches could drink, particularly as they had already been tippling at Munro's.

The sun had slipped past its zenith by the time the bushrangers crossed the vast treeless plain and dismounted at the inn's verandah. They lost no time in bailing everyone up and pocketing anything worth stealing—although they seemed surprised at finding only a small amount of cash and little else to add to their saddle-bags. Thunderbolt ordered one of his men to stand guard outside while the other three settled down for some more carousing.

Walford happily supplied the drinks, continuing to watch them closely. Drunk men often fell asleep, as any publican well knew. Drunk and sleepy men could easily be tied up, turning a robbery into a reward windfall.

A piercing whistle soon interrupted the jollity. The three bushrangers slammed down their drinks and hurried outside. Their lookout was gazing into the distance, gesturing in the same direction.

Four horsemen were riding towards them, a billowing dust cloud like a halo behind them. These men were clearly in a hurry. They were dressed as bushmen, but as they neared, Fred could see three white faces and a black one. Three troopers and a blacktracker. No doubt whatsoever.

The gang quickly untied their horses. They had time to flee—time for their fresh horses to outdistance the troopers' tired hacks. But pot-valiance was bolstering gang bravado. And as in all gangs, tension had been gnawing under the surface as the men jockeyed for position in the power hierarchy. The dog-shooting had been a tacit show of strength, a test of sorts, one set of cards laid down on the table with an implicit summons to the others to show their hands. It was an unspoken leadership challenge as well, colts bucking at the herd stallion. The stripling might be too callow and the cadaverous McIntosh unassuming, but The Bull? Even his nickname was a threat.

Sitting astride his magnificent chestnut horse, Fred lifted his arm and pointed his revolver skywards, like a sword raised to the heavens, a symbolic warrior's cry urging his men into battle. His three companions drew out their own revolvers. Fred wheeled his horse and cantered around the inn towards the open plain at the rear, choosing a battlefield a safe distance from the inn's innocent patrons.

Naturally, the innocent patrons raced through the inn and out the back door. The Sportsman's Arms was about to offer the most exciting sport of them all—a gun battle, a modern gladiatorial contest—and they wanted the best seats in the stadium.

The astonished troopers also recognised Thunderbolt's challenge. They dug in their spurs, urging their exhausted horses faster. Two hundred and fifty miles they had travelled in just a few days and they were as fatigued as their horses, but this was a challenge they could not refuse. They galloped around the inn, coming within firing range just a short distance behind the building.

Was it Thunderbolt who fired the first shot, trying to prove his valour as the leader of this band of brigands? His demand that the police prove their worth was answered by a volley from the troopers. Fred's second gun battle had begun.

The awed spectators watched the contest unfold in front of them like an unrehearsed dance performance. Horses pranced and lunged, twisted and circled, moving around and between each other to the accompaniment of an intermittent drumbeat of gunshots. Each blast was followed by a rider pointing his revolver skywards as if announcing his feat, as if demanding their applause, but it was only to prevent jamming, to allow the percussion cap's remains to fall out as the hammer was cocked.

Their eyes flickering between the bushrangers and troopers, the spectators began to discern a rhythm in the ebb and flow of the gun battle. The troopers had assessed their prey: like wolves, they were endeavouring to separate the weakling from the herd.

Fred had also recognised their ploy. Young Thompson was mounted on the weakest horse and his youth and inexperience were beginning to show. Two of the troopers were homing in on him, while the remainder tried to keep the other three bushrangers at bay.

With a burst of speed, Fred rode between the troopers and Thompson, firing at the policemen, trying to draw their fire, but the lad couldn't get away. Again and again, he courageously rode between them; again and again his gun blazed. Thompson wheeled his horse and began to flee. A gap opened.

One of the policemen raised his revolver again and fired. Thompson tumbled from his horse and lay crumpled on the ground.

Constable Dalton checked the lad was conscious, demanding his surrender. After getting the agreement he wanted, Dalton yelled to Norris, 'Take charge of him while I go after the others!' As he urged his horse on, he suddenly stopped and looked back—just in time to see the lad cock his gun.

Dalton threw himself along his horse's neck and the bullet whizzed past, over his back. Norris rode up to the wounded bushranger a moment later and aimed his own revolver at the immobile target. His bullet slammed into Thompson's face.

What had their sozzled brains been thinking? No doubt they were sick of turning tail and running, as if they were terrified mice fleeing an artful cat. Was this just a drunken game, a chance to prove their worth to each other with the police their unwitting foe, a chance also to cock a snook at the authorities by displaying their better guns and horses and horsemanship? The sight of the blood-soaked lad sprawled on the ground was the dose of common sense they needed. They fled.

The police attempted to follow, but their horses were exhausted, and they had little remaining ammunition. For once they turned back with a sense of achievement. Thunderbolt and his remaining gang members might have eluded them, but at least they had something to show for their efforts—including a reward.

'Thompson is in a very weak state and it is doubtful if he will recover,' warned the press.

It was astonishing that he lived at all. Dalton's shot had hit him in the back and ploughed through his body, exiting near his stomach. Norris's bullet had smashed through his jaw and out his neck. Each bullet could have killed him outright, or spawned a deadly infection, as could any of the other bullet wounds in his rump and right leg. But the lad was tough and, as the days passed, his wounds gradually healed. He was as lucky as the dog shot at Munro's.

Unfortunately he was too reckless and defiant to appreciate his good fortune. After his release from gaol seven years later, he armed himself with a gun and an alias and returned to his criminal ways.

The alias he chose?

'Thunderbolt.'

A posse of police and volunteers set off soon after the Millie shoot-out, emboldened by their efforts in capturing one member of the notorious gang. They followed the bushrangers' tracks towards Fred's old haunts near the Barwon until the rains came and washed the tracks away.

The police suspended their search, but only temporarily. Like stubborn hounds refusing to give up the hunt even when the scent was long gone, they waited until the rains cleared, then set off again, following verbal reports until they crossed into Queensland and were forced to give up the search.

'It is evident that Mr Thunderbolt and his brother ruffians have found the country about the Barwon and Narran Rivers too hot for them,' reported a gleeful New South Wales correspondent. Hopefully the gang would now become the problem of the Queensland police rather than their own.

23

Let us amend the law with reserve and hesitation, but let us never set it at naught. It is all that remains as our refuge and shield.

Sydney Morning Herald, 6 April 1866

Mad Dan Morgan: dead. Brave Ben Hall: dead. Johnny Gilbert: dead. What possessed Fred to deliberately challenge the police to a shoot-out only two weeks after the Felons Apprehension Act had been legislated?

Admittedly, neither Morgan nor Hall had been legally outlawed at the time they were killed. Morgan was shot only days after the legislation was enacted, falling victim to a police and volunteer ambush after he left his usual territory and headed into Victoria. Ben Hall was shot in the back during a police ambush on 5 May, after the Attorney General had announced that his gang would be officially outlawed the following week, but before the paperwork was signed. His two accomplices were outlawed on 10 May; three days afterwards, at Binalong near Yass, they too were ambushed by the police. Gilbert was killed by a hail of bullets, while Dunn managed to escape and went into hiding.

Was the Felons Apprehension Act truly responsible for ridding New South Wales of three of its worst bushrangers in such a short time? asked the community, particularly those who still considered that tampering with the laws affecting personal liberty—indeed life itself—was too dangerous an experiment.

The *Sydney Morning Herald* admitted that, considering the timeframes, the outlawry component of the Act couldn't be afforded such credit, although it must at the very least have made the state's bushrangers more aware of their increasingly insecure position.

Evidently the reporter hadn't noticed that Thunderbolt's gang's first shoot-out with the police occurred *after* the law was enacted, not before.

Moreover, added the *Herald*, the reports about the Act had been anxiously read in slab huts and weatherboard cottages across the countryside, and bushranger supporters were now realising that it would be a dangerous game to continue helping outlawed murderers. Without such support, the bushrangers would soon be brought to justice.

Apparently those who were hiding John Dunn—severely wounded in the shoot-out, according to some reports—were among the many bush folk who were illiterate.

At the very least, continued the *Herald*, Hall's gang had been destroyed and Dunn was unlikely to become the nucleus of another gang. Only Captain Thunderbolt and his men remained in the north, although thinned by Thompson's capture. Having been chased into less populous parts, they would struggle to find as much local assistance and were unlikely to survive for long. 'When they are disposed of'—with the dash of his pen, the *Herald*'s reporter summarily eradicated Thunderbolt's gang—'the chief cause of anxiety will be the prevention of bushranging.'

Therein lay another serious problem. The *Herald* admitted that the Act merely treated the symptoms and not the cause, that the bushrangers' long impunity had led many community members to admire what they ought to detest, and to despise what they ought to revere. It would take time and effort to cure such a chronic disease. Understanding what led the bushrangers to transgress in the first place was essential if they were to effect a cure, and they offered as a cause the Lambing Flat riots.

The Lambing Flat riots? queried some readers. The clashes between Europeans and Chinese early in 1861 over the right to mine gold? The *Herald* conceded that the bushrangers themselves might not have actually participated in the riots. Rather the 'morale' of the riots had taken possession of them: the mob's success, the police's retreat, the court's failure to convict. Evil had triumphed and the bushranging epidemic was the consequence.

Many readers nodded their well-coiffed heads: money, as always, was the root of all evil. In truth, the goldfield riots did not cause the bushranging epidemic, although the social destabilisation caused by the gold rushes, as well as the increased wealth travelling on New South Wales' roads, made bushranging more enticing and profitable. But when the influential *Sydney Morning Herald* failed to understand the causes, there was little chance that most of the politicians or broader community members would do so either.

The Felons Apprehension Act had painted a target on Dunn's back and warned other bushrangers against committing murder. Otherwise nothing had changed: not the circumstances that led to bushranging or to the support of bushranging, nor the recruitment, training, arming, mounting or deployment of the police needed to control the bushrangers. Failure to understand the causation led to a consequent failure to act effectively to curb it. Once the Act was legislated, the Parliamentarians seemingly stuck their collective heads in the sand and hoped for the best. When their only strategy for dealing with the problem within the law was to suspend the law, it was a difficult time indeed.

The state's northern neighbour was not happy. 'We on the Warrego are besieged with criminal refugees from New South Wales, including Captain Thunderbolt,' complained the Queensland press.

Thunderbolt was on his own again. Safety in numbers was no advantage with such a physically distinctive trio, and soon after the Millie shoot-out, the gang split up. McIntosh disappeared, but The Bull was foolish enough to drink too much and brag of his illustrious connections.

Their arrogant captain showed no reluctance to reveal his own identity in his new hunting ground. Among the Queensland properties he visited was Rutherford's Warrego station, where he helped himself to horses and rations and expressed his disappointment that the overseer was not at home. 'I came to stop him "blowing",' Thunderbolt told them, with an ominous jerk of his revolver. Many a station overseer liked to boast about how *he* would triumph over the bushrangers if they showed their faces at *his* station—and Fred was always happy to deflate such pretensions to bravery.

The press warned that prompt action must be taken against Thunderbolt or he would add murder to his tally of crimes, but the police remained as impotent as the press. The distances were too vast and police numbers too small. Moreover, the wretch kept skipping backwards and forwards across the border laughing at the police. Until he ventured further south to the New England or Liverpool Plains districts in particular, they would have little chance of apprehending him.

Not again! Mailman Martin Hurley spotted the horseman as he neared the Oakey Creek crossing (now Upper Manilla) around 8 am on the bitterly cold morning of Wednesday 9 August 1865. Mounted on a brown horse, the man wore an old pilot-cloth coat, with well-worn brown trousers tucked into wellington boots and an old cabbage-tree hat. He also had a handkerchief drawn over the lower half of his face, seemingly to keep his face warm rather than to mask his identity. Of course, if his intention was to conceal his identity, he had picked the wrong mailman to rob. Hurley instantly recognised the captain of the gang who had bailed him up near Manilla only four months previously. The drill was essentially the same, although this time Hurley noticed that the small pile of booty next to the seated bushranger contained little cash and gold. The public was learning.

'Were you not bailed up some time ago?' Thunderbolt asked nonchalantly as he continued opening the letters.

Hurley replied, carefully, that he had indeed been bailed up, without disclosing that he recognised his captor—although the question itself was a giveaway.

Near his pile of cheques and half-cheques, Thunderbolt added a bundle of newspapers. 'They will do for me to read in the bush,' he added conversationally. No doubt he was keen to know if they contained any reports about his own activities. In fact, they didn't. All had been quiet on the Thunderbolt bushranging front for the previous two months.

As Hurley recommenced his journey towards Tamworth, he noticed two hobbled horses in the bush a short distance away. Had Thunderbolt a new companion or two? Maybe his woman was out there hiding, watching his back. Or maybe the bushranger was beginning a long journey and wanted fresh horses to call upon if he needed a speedy getaway.

Mary Ann tugged at the makeshift spear, checking that her large butcher's knife was firmly lashed to the end of the long stick. Then she threw her trousered leg over the back of her horse and gathered up the reins. She was on her own again, without a man to help feed her little band of bush dwellers, and it was time to broaden their diet.

Fred had visited and departed again, keen to welcome another of his progeny into the world, but aware of the dangers of staying in one place for too long. After his foray into Queensland, after he had set the northern state's police and press onto his tail, he had slipped back across the border and made his quiet way south to the Tamworth district, to the camp where Mary Ann, the midwife and the girls were residing. Collecting their possessions, he moved them to a new camping site near Parnell's station, in the vicinity of the Borah Ranges near Manilla. He remained with them for the next couple of months, the coldest months of the year, a bleak time to be living in the bush on the north-western slopes. Early in August he farewelled his family again, including his newborn daughter. After replenishing his finances with the Oakey Creek mail robbery, he vanished again along his well-trodden trail to the north-western plains.

Mary Ann was now hunter, gatherer and milch-cow for her little horde. The midwife's services were no longer needed, but Fred had employed the woman to remain with her as a domestic servant and nursery maid—and a companion. It was lonely living in the bush with no other company than three young children, particularly when she was solely responsible for their welfare. Even her Aboriginal forebears had not lived in such a way. But Mary Ann managed, of course—she always managed. She dug wild yams from the creek banks as her mother had taught her; a nutritious foodstuff like the potatoes that had fed the Irish, the yams were a staple of her family's diet. She gathered the gum that oozed through the barks of the wattle trees, sweet and chewy. Flour was a rare delicacy, but meat practically walked into her bush kitchen, or at least into her large backyard, requiring only her skills and fortitude to harvest it.

She looked around, seeking a docile cow grazing on its own. She had learnt to stay on the outskirts of the herd; she didn't want to start a stampede and find herself caught in the middle. She rode up slowly, unthreateningly, making sure she had the makeshift spear grasped firmly in her hand. As she neared, she leant out of the saddle and used her horse's momentum to slash at the beast, cutting a deep gash across the back of a hind knee. The beast's leg collapsed and it crumpled to the ground. Wheeling her horse, she rode back. From her raised height, she thrust her spear into the beast. Meat for dinner.

Meanwhile, rumours were spreading that the outlawed John Dunn was heading towards the north-western plains, towards the Culgoa River in particular, in the hope of finding Thunderbolt's haunts. Reportedly, the young killer wanted to join forces with the most notorious of the remaining bushrangers.

Dunn had surfaced again near Cowra late in June, demanding some property previously left by Hall's gang, before he and a new partner rode off towards the Lachlan River. The Lachlan police managed to pick up his trail and followed him across country to the Bogan River, then north-west along the river. There they lost him. By late September he had been spotted on the Darling and was believed to have crossed the river in the direction of the Culgoa.

'The police are all out,' reported the local correspondent, 'and the greatest alarm prevails.'

24

Thunderbolt's incurably restless and reckless disposition would not long allow him to remain eating the bread of peace.

William Monckton, *Three Years with Thunderbolt*

Magistrate Hugh Bryden must have groaned when he recognised one of the men holding a gun to his head. He was near Collarenebri in October 1865 when he spotted two men riding up from the river. Thinking they might know something about a mob of fat cattle travelling a short distance behind, he rode towards them. Before he could open his mouth, he found himself looking into the wrong end of a brace of pistols.

Was that a mocking smile twitching Thunderbolt's lips as he introduced himself to the magistrate? Bryden announced his own identity, but he needn't have bothered. The bushranger clearly recognised him, clearly knew that he was responsible for driving the gang from the district the previous March. Presumably Thunderbolt also knew that Bryden had ridden with the posse of police and volunteers who had pursued the gang across the Queensland border after the Millie shoot-out in April, forcing them to separate. As for his many vehement declarations that he wouldn't countenance villains like Thunderbolt in his district and would use whatever means he could to suppress such criminal activity, there was not the slightest doubt that the bush telegraph had passed on that message. The devil must be laughing.

Yet he noticed that Thunderbolt and his companion showed a surprising graciousness—for bushrangers, anyway. Thunderbolt relieved him of his pistol with the panache of his famed British predecessor, Claude Duval, and amiably—as if requesting the loan of a handkerchief—asked him to turn out his pockets. Cheques? No, the bushrangers reassured him as they divided up his coins and handed back the coppers. His watch? They examined it closely but also handed it back. Bushranging etiquette, no doubt.

All the while Thunderbolt talked, gloating about his own achievements, ranting at others' failings. Likely, the bushranger thought him the perfect audience, a magistrate charged with enforcing the law, a man of status in the community who had the ear of others in positions of power. Better by far than the lowly troopers and settlers the bushrangers usually encountered. Bryden had no choice but to listen to the fellow's jeers as Thunderbolt asked—rhetorically—if the police truly believed that they could capture him, that they could outwit him?

At that very moment, as if the gods decided to answer that question in their own playful way, Thunderbolt's companion committed the bushrangers' cardinal sin. He dropped his gun.

Time lurched and slowed. Six eyes watched the gun falling. Would it fire? Would a bullet hit someone? The gun clunked to the ground and an ear-shattering blast followed. Thunderbolt's horse collapsed. Dead.

Three astonished faces looked at the horse and at each other. Thunderbolt pulled out a bottle of rum and took a swig, then companionably offered it to Bryden. Soon afterwards he wished him a courteous goodbye then mounted his companion's horse and rode away.

As the bemused magistrate watched them depart, he realised why Thunderbolt had been nicknamed the 'gentleman bushranger'. But who was his new companion? Not Dunn, hopefully.

Patrick Kelly, alias William Long, was his name, a fine-made man over six feet tall—good-looking as well except for a broken nose. The Irish-born Catholic from a large Maitland family was a Ben Hall type who had suffered a personal misfortune, leading him to desert his wife and two children and head for the lawless north-western plains. He first came to the police's attention in August 1865, when he held a gun to a trooper's head and rescued a friend facing charges of uttering forged cheques. A couple of months later, he found himself in the orbit of the district's bushranging beacon, Captain Thunderbolt.

Jemmy the Whisperer soon joined them. London-born most likely, the horse-breaker hid his identity behind a multi-layered cloak of nicknames: 'Little Jemmy' or 'Little Jimmy', not surprising considering that he was short and somewhat effeminate-looking; 'Flash Jimmy', suggesting that he was either vulgarly showy, or well known to be criminally inclined; 'Jemmy the Whisperer', likely an allusion to his dulcet tones, to the voice that could reduce grown men to tears when he sang his favourite tune, 'The Unfortunate Man'. Friendship had transformed Jemmy into a bushranger. Back in 1862, two constables had tried to arrest his drinking companion, Patrick McManus, and in the ensuing scuffle, McManus had shouted at Jemmy to shoot the constables. Instead Jemmy fled from the hotel, although he had the courage to return a short time later. Seeing McManus held down by one of the constables, he shouted, 'You eternal wretch, if you don't let him go I'll blow your brains out!' He didn't wait long for an answer. The constable survived, but Jemmy remained on the run thereafter, his many nicknames an undoubted advantage when he returned to living quietly in the north-western district. In October 1865, something triggered his decision to join forces with Thunderbolt and Kelly. Thunderbolt's second bushranging gang was in operation.

'About a fortnight ago, Captain Thunderbolt of the Warrego Mounted Patrol accompanied by Sergeant Kelly and one trooper crossed the Barwon en route for head quarters,' wrote a facetious correspondent for the *Toowoomba Chronicle* soon afterwards. The correspondent's informant had ridden part of the way with the gang and reported that the bushrangers were cautious about going on the road, always keeping to the side or riding in the bush. They claimed to have been to the Namoi for fresh mounts, and their five splendid horses confirmed the success of their raid. 'The captain had a cloak loosely thrown over his valise in front of him,' the informant added, 'and whilst riding along the wind blew it up and displayed a formidable battery of revolvers. He merely smiled and put the cloak down over them again.'

A formidable armoury. Five splendid horses. The news should have served as a warning that Thunderbolt's new gang was on the rampage, but by the time the report was published it was too late.

They struck on 7 November 1865, honouring the almost completed Bokhara Creek police station with their inspection before bailing up stations and individuals on either side of the Queensland border. 'Thunderbolt has been electrifying the Bokhara creek residents,' quipped one correspondent, but few were laughing.

Demands for rations were noticeable by their absence, evidence that supporters in the district were feeding them. The two extra horses Thunderbolt had brought back from the Namoi were not needed to carry plunder. Rather, each carried a new recruit on its back. One was described by an attention-seeking victim as having fair hair, thin whiskers, a moustache and a name: the outlaw John Dunn.

Thunderbolt and Dunn together? Police Inspector Henry Zouch was aghast. Snapping out orders, he gathered a detachment of Bourke troopers and raced towards the lower portions of the Culgoa, Birree and Bokhara rivers, while Sergeant Flynn and the Walgett police sped towards the upper parts. Up and down the rivers they searched, following sightings from one place to another until it became clear that the bushrangers' supporters, and those who delighted in undermining the authorities, were again playing games at the police's expense. Early in December, they were forced to return to their stations, frustrated and fatigued by the search and by their easily jaded police horses—'carrion' as one bitter correspondent would call them.

The police search for Thunderbolt had not been a total failure. Their presence forced the gang to flee the district, to find 'fresh fields and pastures new'. Rumours circulated that the bushrangers had gone back to the mountains, that Thunderbolt's woman and children were concealed in an isolated spot they used as a rendezvous when not out plundering. Chasing them from the district offered only a pyrrhic victory, however. Everyone knew they would soon return to continue their depredations, drawn back by the support they received, more arrogant and audacious because of their previous triumphs. And if the murderous Dunn was indeed among them, their return might usher in a reign of terror previously unknown in the district.

The bushranging support was the biggest problem, a letter-writer lamented, and it came from all classes of society, even those whose position in society should guarantee their hostility towards the villains.

Few squatters were like Magistrate Hugh Bryden, committed to the interests of their broader community and willing to take an active role in thwarting the bushrangers. To ease the threat to their own properties and families, most squatters pursued a policy of neutrality: leave me alone and I'll leave you alone. Which meant, the letter-writer bitterly translated: 'Murder and rob my neighbours, waylay and plunder unarmed travellers, evade the police, use any man in my employ for a telegraph, but leave me and my interests alone.'

Naturally, it was also in Thunderbolt's interests to abide by this unwritten accord. There was no advantage in making enemies of men who had the power and resources to make trouble for them. Until, of course, necessity demanded that they sacrifice the accord in pursuit of their own interests.

Yet the squatters were not alone in feeling threatened. While many rural workers willingly supported Fred and his men—women supposedly hung red blankets from their washing lines as a sign to the 'gentleman bushranger' that the police were in their neighbourhood—others feared crossing them. One shepherd who supplied Thunderbolt with supper would report that he'd had his suspicions about his guest's identity, yet there was little he could do. 'You see, I have to be out alone in the bush, miles from any living soul, and who'd know anything about it if a bullet was put through me.'

The bushrangers didn't have to threaten anyone personally; their continued existence was enough of a threat. By contrast, the central arrangement of the new police districts meant that the troopers were little threat to the bushrangers: indeed most rural towns and villages had no police presence at all. When a robbery was reported, the troopers had to travel long distances to the scene of the crime, eventually returning a week later having failed to find the villains. During that time their own town was left without police and exposed—most invitingly—to attack. 'Are we to have a repetition of the disgraceful scenes enacted in the Western districts?' the same letter-writer demanded. Appearances suggested so. In addition to his robberies, Thunderbolt had introduced himself to the very magistrate who had tried to apprehend him and had stolen his weapon and mocked the police's efforts to capture him before graciously allowing the magistrate to proceed.

Which created a new set of problems. Such behaviour tended to elevate him in the public's opinion, particularly as he didn't resort to violence. A halo of approval was growing around him and the broader community was becoming enthralled—mirroring the reaction to Hall's gang in the west.

Which brought the letter-writer to the next problem: the government. What were they doing about the bushranging problem? Surely they didn't want a repetition of the crisis in the western districts. Surely that was enough of an incentive for them to act decisively. Shouldn't the suppression of such an evil be one of the government's priorities? Instead, its failure to grapple with the problem was exposing New South Wales to the derision of the rest of the country.

Admittedly, capturing Thunderbolt and his men would not be an easy task, but the difficulty was not insurmountable. The most suitable method, the letter-writer advised, would be to employ a type of guerilla police force, using experienced men who were able to ride over a trackless and waterless waste for 60 or 70 miles with nothing but the gang's tracks to guide them. They should employ men with a background like the bushrangers themselves, the type of men the establishment was still reluctant to employ. If they adopted these measures, the squatters would see that they were again within the pale of protection. With their consequent cooperation, Thunderbolt and his gang would be speedily eradicated.

But the government ignored all the demands and pleas. Instead, on 4 December 1865, it raised the reward for Thunderbolt's apprehension to £100, and to £50 for his accomplices. The government clearly hoped that the good citizens of New South Wales—or more likely, the not-so-good—would stick out their hands. Of course, the sum was a pittance compared with the costs incurred by the police and the community during the two years Thunderbolt had already roamed New South Wales. Moreover, it would be paid out only if Thunderbolt was apprehended and convicted.

The government wanted the problem solved, but was unwilling to invest in its solution. All it would do was offer a bribe. The community was begging for leadership, but the authorities effectively tossed the problem back into their hands. You make it go away, was the government's rejoinder.

25

In the excitement and hilarity of their career they lose sight of its terrible end.

Sydney Morning Herald, 3 October 1867

'**B**ail up!' Two simple words. Mad Dan Morgan had shouted them at his victims before the bushranger, arsonist and murderer was shot dead a few months previously, a battle cry repeated by the many bushrangers who still roamed the New South Wales countryside. The once-imperious demand to stop and identify oneself had been commandeered by the bushrangers; 'Stop and allow yourself to be robbed' was its current meaning. A quintessence of economy, it contained an implicit threat, unspoken but instantly understood. 'Bail up or else . . .' No one knew what the trigger might be, when threat would transform into bloodshed.

The good citizens of the town of Quirindi—if anyone could call an inn, a pound-keeper's residence and a few dilapidated huts a 'town'—looked around on Friday 8 December 1865 to find the jester responsible for the frisson of fear that had momentarily turned their insides to jelly. That's when they saw the three strangers at Benjamin Cook's inn.

The strangers had trotted into town on magnificent horses, racehorses from the looks of them, one bearing a surprising resemblance to the famed Eucalyptus belonging to Mr Duff of nearby Werris Creek. Like most travellers they dismounted at Cook's Bird in Hand, the usual bush pub and store with its display of mangy characters on the verandah. Dressed in Bedford cord pants, wellington boots and cabbage-tree hats, the trio received little more than idle glances—until one of them yelled out the chilling words.

Time hiccupped. Memory's ink flowed more heavily, dark strokes scored on the day's page. The bushrangers were not just pointing their guns at the innkeeper and his customers: they were signalling to everyone in sight, just like Ben Hall had done.

Me? Heads twisted to look beside and behind, then back at the bushrangers.

Yes, you—with an unequivocal jerk of the gun.

Everyone knew the drill, from newspaper reports and gossip if nothing else. Do exactly as they demanded! Obediently they climbed the steps to the inn's verandah and meekly stood in line, husbands planting themselves in front of families, wives clutching children to their skirts, all expecting to be ordered to turn out their pockets. No? The bushrangers were interested only in the publican's takings.

Among the faces blanched with fear, a few secret smiles of satisfaction watched the publican hand over his money, around £9 or £10. Clearly, the bushrangers were not Dan Morgan's brothers-in-arms. They abided by the bushrangers' code of honour. Publicans and shopkeepers were among the 'rich', no more worthy of sympathy than the squatters and the banks. Shoulders relaxed; stomachs unclenched. So long as they did exactly as the villains demanded, they should all live to tell their grandchildren of the day a bushranging gang held up the town of Quirindi.

Heavy with child and trepidation, Mrs Eliza Cook lumbered towards her neighbouring store and unlocked the door. It opened onto an Aladdin's treasure cave—for the bushranger who accompanied her, at least. Goods lined the shelves: food, clothes and footwear, household utensils, medicinal products, farming tools and the staples required by horse and horseman.

The bushranger rifled through the shelves, pulling out a hat and two alpaca coats—deliciously warm for the cold mountain evenings—as well as some knives, three bridles and a new saddle. Mrs Cook noticed with surprise some of the other items he stashed in his pockets: a flower-scented hair cream to make hair long and thick, a few pretty hair-combs for adornment, a couple of blocks of scented soap and some perfume. Someone wanted treats for his lady.

Back at the pub, the bushrangers ordered John Ross, Quirindi's licensed pound-keeper, to round up his horses. Ross was responsible for impounding stray livestock, so he had horses aplenty grazing in his paddocks.

More hidden smiles of satisfaction greeted the bushrangers' latest demand. Pound-keepers were just another arm of the police, human tentacles that reached into every resident's paddock. Their government-sanctioned right to round up stray livestock and charge a fee for its release was little more than legalised cattle-duffing. Robbing the pound-keeper as well? It was another gratifying swipe at authority.

Ross returned with some horses and tethered them near the verandah. The bushrangers' boots clattered down the stairs. The men inspected the horses, discussing their merits as if they were bidders at a county horse sale. A calm disposition—essential in a packhorse, both for easy loading and quiet plodding: any horse showing signs of temperament was instantly sent back to the paddock. A willing disposition, content to be led on a rope, to follow closely behind another horse: one averse to having a tail twitching in its face was not what they needed on a narrow mountain pass. The bush-rangers picked two, crossing that item off their shopping list.

Money was always the first priority. Bushrangers who paid their supporters had a better chance of evading the law's grasp. An unspoken pragmatism underpinned such support, a bushranging bottom line. If the financial burden of feeding the bushrangers became too heavy, or the danger inherent in hiding them from the police became too great, there was always the government's reward as compensation. Supplies were nearly as important as money, yet harder to carry, hence the need for the packhorses.

The final item on their shopping list was the most pleasurable: grog.

Laughter rang out across the plains surrounding the inn, startling the chickens scrounging in the dirt, the dogs scratching their fleas. The bush-rangers were now the drinkers' best friends. Thumps as tankards were slammed onto benches, shouts to the publican for another round, shrill voices talking over each other in their excitement to tell the next tall tale. The bushrangers hadn't introduced themselves, but few cared when the drinks kept coming. Christmas had arrived early at Quirindi.

Bushranging? The curious couldn't help asking. One brigand spoke familiarly about Thunderbolt's encounter with the police, when the lad Thompson was shot and captured. Those who had kept their wits about them had little trouble identifying their self-anointed host.

One sharp-witted onlooker was the pound-keeper's boy. As the other children frolicked around the inn, he noticed that the bushrangers were paying little attention to them. He kept a surreptitious eye on the gang as they swigged their rum and chortled at each other's jokes. When they were looking elsewhere, he slipped out of sight and hurried back home. Grabbing his old saddle, he strapped it to one of the horses and rode across the back paddocks until he reached the Wallabadah road, then he kicked his horse into a gallop and headed east. Twelve miles to the nearest police station, then twelve miles back again with the troopers—if he was lucky enough to find them at the station.

Fred and his two accomplices did not notice that a child was missing. It never occurred to them that their nemesis might walk in the shoes of a twelve-year-old boy.

None of the Quirindi residents lounging on Cook's verandah said anything as the horseman rode up to the inn and dismounted, looping his horse's reins over the railing. As he looked up, a voice ordered him to bail up, to step onto the verandah and join the others.

Mr Davis of the Liverpool Plains was a man who bristled when others tried to order him around, a man more used to giving orders than taking them.

'I will not,' he retorted.

'Take off your saddle,' the voice then ordered, 'as we want it.'

'No, I will not,' the angry newcomer repeated. 'But if you come out one at a time, I will fight the lot of you. If I had a revolver, I would take you all.'

The bushrangers jumped down from the verandah and grabbed Davis' horse, trying to push him aside and untie the saddle. Davis resisted and began tussling with them.

'Give us the saddle or we will shoot you!' one of the bushrangers yelled.

'I dare you to do it!'

Everyone froze. In the ominous silence, their victims could almost hear the termites gnawing at the verandah's wooden railings.

It was just a bluff, as it turned out. Thunderbolt and his gang were having too much fun to shoot anybody. They shoved Davis aside and pulled off his saddle. 'We won't forget you,' they warned, pushing him up the steps onto the verandah. 'We will visit your place sometime in the future.'

'Quirindi is under siege!'

The news spread as quickly as the recent bushfire in the hills opposite the beleaguered hamlet. The bushrangers were allowing teamsters to pass through, men whose tediously slow journeys had just been enlivened by a first-hand encounter with a gang of bushrangers—a gang, moreover, who was holding up the whole township. Naturally they were telling everyone they encountered in the aftermath.

Squatter James Seville Junior was at Loder's woolshed just a mile away when he heard the news. Three bushrangers bailing up the town? He had fifteen brawny shearers with him and one at least had a gun. The bushrangers wouldn't stand a chance.

'Turn out with me,' he asked, half-request, half-demand. Naturally, he couldn't order his men into battle—for all that he might have wished to.

They refused.

'Please,' he begged, confused and appalled by their disinterest.

'They have not hurt us,' the shearers said, shrugging with indifference. They knew Thunderbolt's gang posed little threat to men like themselves—unless, perhaps, they were drinking in a pub that was robbed.

For several hours Seville entreated and cajoled, to no avail. Finally, he sent a lad over to Quirindi with a message for the villains: 'I want you and defy you!'

'We will wait upon you another day,' was the warning that came back via a different messenger, the bushrangers having kept Seville's lad as a hostage.

Meanwhile, Fred and his men kept carousing, strutting around the inn as if it were their own, as if they were feudal lords hosting a village picnic. These were men who lived only for the moment, like itinerant bush workers whose greatest pleasure lay in 'knocking down' their cheques after they were paid. They had no homes to build or repair, no clothes or household goods or farm equipment to buy, no families to please—except for Mary Ann, but she was living in the bush and her needs were simple. At this moment they were the monarchs of all they surveyed and they would revel in it for as long as they pleased.

The boy slid from his horse and ran into Wallabadah's police station. Senior Constable William Lang and Constable John Aggett were there. Breathlessly, the boy recounted his tale, reporting that he had slipped away while the bushrangers were drinking, that they might still be there.

The troopers saddled their horses and the party headed back towards Quirindi. They took little notice of the picturesque beauty of 'the most romantic and outlandish piece of road', as one traveller would describe it. The outlandish bits were the problem—the twists and turns as the road looped between hills and snaked around large stumps and rocks; the numerous fords across the Quirindi Creek, many in such a bad state that the party had to gingerly walk their horses through the water. The bushrangers would likely be long gone by the time they arrived, but hope urged their horses faster.

The uniformed figures hurtling towards the inn were easy enough to identify. The troopers had arrived.

Fred and his men knew they had pushed their luck by lingering for so many hours, but they also knew they had an advantage over any troopers determined to catch them: well-rested racehorses. Casually, they mounted and cantered away. Fred knew the area well, the roads and bush tracks, the paddocks with the beginnings of rude fences as selectors met their obligations to 'improve' their conditional purchases. Fortunately the fences were few and little impediment to daring horsemen who knew exactly where they wanted to go.

They had no idea how the police had learnt of their presence, but when they did discover the truth they must have wondered why the troopers had not taken a leaf out of the lad's book and crept up on them from the back paddocks.

They had lost them. Darkness had long fallen by the time the troopers stopped searching. They had continued the hunt despite losing sight of their prey hours previously, aware that the felons' racehorses could have carried them as far as Gunnedah, but hoping they might have slowed down on the assumption that the troopers had returned home.

The witching hour was fast approaching by the time the two troopers plodded into Quirindi, as bone-weary as their exhausted mounts, and as hungry. They would rustle up some supper and find somewhere to sleep and, in the morning, begin taking statements from the witnesses. Then they noticed the lights blazing from the inn—the sounds of music and laughter and revelry they had been too tired to heed.

Fred and his men were still crowing. They had led the police on a merry dance, far enough ahead to be out of gunshot range, but close enough that the eager troopers kept digging in their spurs. Slower they went, as the troopers' horses began to visibly tire. Even slower again, as the troopers' horses stumbled with exhaustion. Eventually, they grew bored with the game and rocketed away. Once out of sight, they circled around and headed back to Quirindi to continue carousing. Their day's entertainment had been rudely interrupted by the troopers' arrival, and the last place the police would expect to find them again was back at Quirindi.

Two more hours of revelry followed before the watch announced the return of the troopers. Pocketing some additional bottles of spirits, they farewelled their latest friends and mounted their horses. With a mocking salute to the troopers, they rode off.

The troopers were too tired even to care.

'When I saw in the *Herald* a telegram to the effect that the "township" of Quirindi had been stuck up by bushrangers and *all* the inhabitants robbed, I could not refrain from bursting into an involuntary fit of laughter,' wrote a travelling reporter who had recently visited the district. So much fuss about a bunch of hang-dog ruffians sticking up less than a score of people not in the least prepared to defend themselves, he added. Even the publican himself wrote to the newspapers to correct the statement that sixteen or seventeen men had been taken hostage and six new saddles stolen.

Exaggeration or not, the consequences were tragic for some of the partic-ipants. Cook's pregnant wife died three months later shortly after giving birth, traumatised by the robbery and never fully recovering. Another of Cook's children began having epileptic fits soon after the robbery, and fears were held for the child's future.

There were always consequences—unintended or otherwise.

26

The greatest crimes do not arise from a want of feeling for others but from an . . . over-indulgence to our own desires.

Edmund Burke

'There are bushrangers in the neighbourhood,' reported Postman Acheson as he climbed up the steps of Carroll's Albion Inn around four o'clock on the Sunday afternoon, two days after the Quirindi hold-up. Acheson was travelling his usual route from Gunnedah to Tamworth and back again, with his mailbags loaded onto his packhorse. He had just arrived at Carroll, twelve miles into his journey, and was glad of the momentary respite from the wild summer storm.

Fifteen or so people congregated on the inn's verandah—men, women and children, all mesmerised by the bucketing rain and the sudden flashes of lightning, glad to be enjoying the inn's comforts until the afternoon storm passed over. The postman's warning caught their attention. They knew that the Breeza road ran directly from Quirindi to Gunnedah, a 50-mile journey, so it was not surprising that the postman had heard the news before he set off from Gunnedah a few hours before. Naturally, Acheson would need to be careful—his mailbags were prime targets—but Carroll itself? After discussing the situation for some time, the locals decided that there was no cause for alarm, that of course the bushrangers would not trouble them at Carroll.

Half an hour after Acheson left, those lounging on the verandah noticed a tall man coming towards them, riding a black horse and leading another.

He lashed his horses to the verandah post and hurried up the steps out of the rain, glancing across at the verandah dwellers as he did so. 'Have two horsemen passed during the last quarter of an hour?' he asked. A few voices answered in the negative.

As the fellow stripped off his oilskin they could see his dark suit and Napoleon boots. He cut an impressive figure, over six feet tall, with a large beard and moustache, good-looking, rather genteel-looking in fact—a real ladies' man. He went through the door into the tap room and called for a glass of brandy, handing over some money in payment. After drinking for a short time he asked the barman, owner William Griffin himself, if he had spotted anyone on the road: 'I've lost my two mates. Have you seen them?' Griffin said that he could not help him and the stranger continued to sit there quietly, drinking his brandy.

Half an hour later, another two men rode up to the inn, each leading a spare horse. As they dismounted, the taller man said to the shorter one, 'Let us go and have a glass of brandy. We want it this wet evening.' They hurried up the steps out of the rain.

As the locals idly watched, they saw the taller man slip his hand under his mackintosh. A moment later a pistol was pointing directly towards them. 'I will trouble you all, ladies and gentlemen,' the man said politely, 'to bail up.'

The rain drummed through the shocked silence. Bushrangers! The threat they had so casually dismissed. One of the hostages peered at the two villains, recognising the features of the taller man holding the gun. Not just any bushrangers: Captain Thunderbolt himself.

Hands rose tentatively into the air as the man's shorter companion pulled out his own pistol and pointed it in their direction. 'Money we have come for,' Thunderbolt continued, 'and money we must have.'

Seeing terrified faces, the beginnings of tears, he turned to the women and said reassuringly: 'Fear nothing. We won't injure anyone. All we want is your money.' He then ordered everyone onto the verandah.

Thunderbolt's companion went into the bar and brought out Griffin and the stranger, telling them to line up on the verandah as well. The stranger stood there for a moment, as ordered, then began walking towards the bushrangers.

Confusion furrowed the brows of the other hostages. Was he about to defy them?

The stranger continued walking until he stood in front of the bush-rangers. 'Put them by,' he said to the two men, indicating the revolvers, 'they are not wanted here.' Then he turned and stood beside the bushrangers, facing the hostages. His lost mates had evidently been found.

Signalling Kelly and Jemmy to remain on guard, Fred entered the house and quickly searched all the rooms to make sure they hadn't missed anyone. Spotting the kitchen boy, he ordered the lad to accompany him. He had learnt his lesson from Quirindi. He stopped for a moment to rifle through Griffin's desk, picking up the account book and tucking it under his arm before heading back towards the verandah. Satisfied that he had gathered all the residents, workers and drinkers, he ordered the men to line up in a row. Then he stood guard as Jemmy took Griffin by the arm.

'Into the bar!' Jemmy ordered. 'I'll do you first.'

Jemmy's light hair and straggling beard were a marked contrast to the tall good-looking Kelly, but he was the more determined of the two—and the more frightening. He urged Griffin into the bar, then pawed through his pockets, pulling out £2.5s before ushering the publican back out to the verandah and ordering him to line up with the others.

Fred then handed his gun to Kelly, and he and Jemmy began searching the other men's pockets. From one hostage they took a watch and chain and about £6, although they soon afterwards returned £1.10s and the watch and chain. From another they took £2, returning £1 later. No one else was carrying any money.

They then tipped a mailbag of letters onto Griffin's counter and began ripping them open. It didn't take the hostages long to realise that Acheson himself had been graced with the bushrangers' company—although only for a short time. Drenched by the torrential rain, Fred and his men had decided to take the mailbag with them, leaving Acheson to gather up the opened letters. At Griffin's they dealt with the remaining letters, sticking any cheques in their pockets and ripping some letters to shreds. When the hostages rebuked them, Fred and his men explained that they were destroy-ing bills and summonses—both a thank-you to their bush supporters and a gesture of defiance to the establishment. Otherwise considerate, they gave the remaining letters to one of the hostages, who agreed to take them back to the post office for their eventual delivery.

'Grog all round!' announced Fred. So big an audience; so small a chance that the troopers would continue searching in such a storm. But he sent Jemmy outside to keep a lookout, just in case.

Music? Mr De Vere plays the fiddle, a keen local reported. Urged on by the gun-toting bushrangers, the fiddler started to play a ditty. Music, grog, laughter: the atmosphere quickly became lighter. Fred walked the boards with his pistol at the ready, while Kelly stole the limelight. As the fiddler began another ditty, the Irishman stuck his revolver into his belt and began to dance a reel. A smattering of spontaneous applause followed the impressive display. He flourished a mocking bow, then stepped over to one of the young ladies and invited her to dance a schottische with him. Fred and the hostages looked on benignly as the couple moved across the floor in the slow polka-like dance usually performed in ballrooms.

Fred allowed the hostages the run of the bar and adjacent verandah, but he stopped anyone from entering the house. A firm look and a jerk of the gun was message enough. It might be a party, but he was dictating the terms.

Darkness had fallen when a shout interrupted the festivities: 'Oi! Here's a mob!'

Wet and weary, the two Wallabadah troopers and Tamworth's Constable Jacob Shaw had been content to call off their search and rest at Griffin's inn for the night. Lang and Aggett had learnt one lesson at least from their failure to catch the bushrangers at Quirindi: all three troopers had shed their uniforms and were disguised as bushmen. There was no point in adding to the bushrangers' many advantages.

'Landlord, attend to our horses,' Senior Constable Lang called out imperiously as they rode up to the inn.

Griffin stepped through the door and hurried over to the horsemen, failing to recognise the troopers in the gloom. Thinking they were travellers, he took the head of Lang's horse and whispered, 'We are all bailed up here.'

Startled, Lang whispered back, 'We are the police. Where are the bushrangers?'

Griffin turned around and pointed. 'There's one of them on the grey horse.'

It was Thunderbolt, just a few yards away. Lang grabbed his carbine and fired.

With their well-developed sixth sense, Fred and his gang had suspected trouble as soon as they saw the three horsemen approaching. Kelly was not waiting around to find out if they were indeed troopers. He dashed out the front door and threw himself onto his black horse, racing off between the pound-yard and stable before the horsemen had noticed him.

Jemmy made no attempt to get away. He slunk to the end of the verandah and waited in the darkness for the horsemen to draw closer.

Fred watched for a moment longer, then decided that he too would flee. He bounded down the inn's steps and leapt onto his grey horse, grabbing the reins and digging in his spurs. A second later, he realised that this was the worst decision he could have made. His initial hesitation had delayed him for too long. He was suddenly exposed, within range of the carbine being raised in his direction. Frantically he kicked his horse, but there simply wasn't enough time to get away.

An almighty blast rent the air. Fred stiffened but didn't feel anything. Astonishingly, the trooper had missed.

From the darkness of the verandah, another shot. Jemmy was protecting his mate.

The trooper firing at Fred was easy to see in the light cast by the inn's lamp, perched atop his horse with his arm outstretched. Jemmy's first shot had missed but he was getting a second chance. Instead of fleeing for cover, the trooper had continued to track Fred with his carbine and had fired off another shot, but the second bullet also missed its target.

Jemmy aimed carefully and fired again. The trooper's body bucked and began to fall. The bullet had punched through the fleshy part of his firing arm, embedding itself near the bone.

A moment later the trooper's horse whinnied in surprise and anger. Jemmy's third bullet had hit it in the neck.

One trooper down. Two to go.

•

Fred urged his horse faster, looking for a gap where he could leave the road, where the bush would conceal him while he made his escape. He spotted one and tugged on the reins, urging his horse through the trees—straight into the river's muddy backwater.

At each squelching movement, his horse sank deeper into the bog. He tried to urge it forwards, without any success. He tried to pull it out of the bog, but the darkness enveloped them and he couldn't see his way to firmer ground. Eventually he decided to abandon the horse and flee on foot. Humping the heavy saddle, he stumbled into the darkness.

The news that Thunderbolt's saddle-less horse had been found abandoned in the bog reached the troopers the following day. That Thunderbolt had been almost within their grasp a fourth time—struggling to release himself from the nearby bog as they unwittingly galloped past—was a source of bitter frustration.

No one else had been injured during the gun battle which continued for another fifteen minutes after Lang was wounded. About twenty shots were fired. Eventually, Jemmy retreated through the inn and slipped out the back door, managing to escape.

The good news was that Senior Constable Lang should survive the shooting; Thunderbolt and his gang might not add murder to their list of misdeeds. But the wounding of one of their own had increased the constabulary's ire.

Another six troopers from Tamworth took up the pursuit, determined to catch these latest aspirants for the country's gallows.

27

We fear that much mischief is done in the mode of describing their exploits, by flattering their vanity as well as by diminishing the sense of horror with which they should ever be regarded.

Sydney Morning Herald, 3 October 1867

So much for the thunderbolt strikes: the quick raids into a district before the police worked out what they were doing, then the headlong dash across the countryside before striking unexpectedly in a new quarter. Instead the raids kept being prolonged as the gang delighted in the revelry, while the police kept barging into their festivities uninvited and unwelcome.

Carroll couldn't be considered a successful raid by any means—and if the wounded policeman died, the government would not hesitate to paint an outlaw target on their backs. With enraged troopers hot on their tail, the gang was down to two horses from the six they had ridden into town—and they had also lost two saddles and bridles, half a pint of brandy, a pair of dirty cord trousers, two Crimean shirts and a pair of socks, among other items. At least they still had £6 or so of the stolen money.

As for their transport, horses were easy enough to steal.

Usually.

'Thunderbolt has been seen by a black-fellow on the Wallah run, searching for horses,' reported the *Tamworth Examiner* a short time later. Despite his skills, Fred wasn't having much luck. After he and his mates met up again, they headed north-west towards Narrabri. They desperately needed more horses if they were to evade the police and return to the safety of the north-western plains, and Fred knew where to find some: the Wallah run next door to Baan Baa. Except the horses didn't want to be found. Stealing horses could be fun—the thrill of sneaking onto another's territory and taking a valuable possession without anyone being the wiser, the battle of wits with the horses themselves—but not when speed was of the essence.

Fred saw an Aboriginal man on the Wallah run so he sang out for help. The man refused. Fred called out again, an imperious white man's demand for a 'black boy's' compliance. Again the fellow refused. So Fred pulled out his revolver and fired. Twice.

Did he intend to hit the man? Most likely he deliberately missed, the gunshot blasts serving as both a warning and an expression of his general annoyance rather than a malicious attack on an innocent bystander. Or maybe he was just a rotten marksman. But the unwarranted attack communicated a cogent message to the Aboriginal people: that the 'gentleman bushranger' was not necessarily a gentleman in his dealings with their kind.

John C. Bagot was feeling rather vexed. His stations had just received a second visit from the troublesome bushranger. Thunderbolt's first gang had raided his Mogil Mogil station near Collarenebri the previous March, and had declared their intention of robbing nearby Goondoobline until Magistrate Bryden thwarted their plans and sent them packing to the west. Now Thunderbolt's second gang had bailed up both of his stations.

It seemed like Thunderbolt was deliberately targeting him.

Four horses, one or two saddles and a Wilson's patent breech-loading carbine rifle: Goondoobline had taken a hit. Fortunately the only thing that had interested the bushrangers at Mogil Mogil was the pound-keeper's copy of the *Tamworth Examiner*, which provided a detailed report about the gang's activities in the Tamworth region. Thunderbolt asked him to read the report to them.

'We have this week to record the doings of a new gang of bushrangers,' the pound-keeper began, 'for we believe, from all we have been able to learn, that Frederick Ward, alias Thunderbolt, is not of the number who have stuck up and robbed many persons in the district and wounded one of the police—Senior Constable Lang—in the right forearm.'

The bushrangers howled in disgust. Not Thunderbolt? A new gang? Fred in particular was incensed. Where was the glory if the press didn't accurately report his achievements?

Not surprisingly, when he robbed Edward Fletcher's Collarenebri store later the same day, his first action was to announce his identity. 'I'm Captain Thunderbolt,' he said. 'I've come to stick you up.'

The evening was unfolding like a well-rehearsed play, which indeed it was after the sessions at Quirindi and Carroll. After Thunderbolt and Jemmy had stolen over £20 in cash and goods from Fletcher's store, they ordered the storekeeper and his lads to accompany them to Earl's pub on the other side of the Barwon, collecting Kelly along the way. Kelly had been left to stand guard over the nearby Aboriginal camp, to make sure that the inhabitants did not give the alarm.

'We've come to enjoy three or four hours sport if we are allowed,' Fred told the innkeeper and his guests, although the guns he and his companions were holding assured them they would enjoy their sport, whether allowed to or not. But first, of course, they had to rob them.

'Have you any money about you?' Fred asked the ladies gently, explaining that he wouldn't lay a finger on them—not this time, anyway. 'Next time, I'll have my good lady with me so I can then have the ladies searched as well as the men,' he warned.

From the men's pockets the gang plucked a tidy sum, about £14 or £15, and added it to the notes and coins swelling their own pockets. Business now completed, it was time for the festivities to begin.

Kelly took centre stage again, asking Earl's young barmaid to join him in another impressive schottische. Fred was more of a conversationalist: he began talking about his bushranging career, a long discourse showing how one crime leads to another. Those who were not admiring Kelly's dancing listened and wondered. On the surface, it seemed like a morality tale, a warning to others against stepping onto the criminal pathway, although a hint of self-justification coloured his words. But underneath they could hear a braggart taking ownership of his many criminal deeds. No longer would the community have any doubts if Captain Thunderbolt was responsible or not.

By 2 am, storekeeper Edward Fletcher was exhausted, as were all the other hostages. His considerate host noticed Fletcher's weariness and said kindly, 'As you seem tired, you may go on a parole of honour.' Maintaining his benevolent air, Thunderbolt also informed the publican that he was permitted to go to bed, although he refused to allow the inn's staff and patrons to leave until after his own departure.

Soon afterwards, bidding this 'guard of honour' a gracious adieu, Thunderbolt and his gang rode off into the darkness.

East they headed towards the Mehi station on the Gwydir River. They made a quick stop at Henry Chambers' Meroe inn (current Moree), where they took three pairs of Bedford cord pants—a particular favourite— along with some cash and other goods. They missed the £90 roll of notes Chambers had tossed through the window into the woodpile when he noticed the suspicious cloud of dust warning of a rapid approach. Then they headed south again, back towards the Tamworth district and Mary Ann. But something happened during that journey.

No one knows what triggered the gang's separation. Seemingly, the men were still together early in January 1866 when they stole a horse from Eulowrie station, south-west of Bingara. From there, however, they apparently headed in separate directions.

Neither the press nor the police realised that the gang had split up—not for some time, anyway. 'The doings of Thunderbolt and his Gang' was among the newspaper headlines after Kelly and Jemmy's first solo robbery: bailing up the Turrawan hotel fifteen miles south of Narrabri. The pair had learnt their mentor's lessons well, behaving politely and treating the women and children kindly. When they robbed the Wee Waa mail the following day, they fired a shot into the rump of the mailman's horse because the mailman would not stop at their demands. Cunning joined ruthlessness when they cut the telegraph wires in several places after robbing the northern mail near Murrurundi. From there, they headed back to Collarenebri, where the patrolling police heard that Kelly was lording it over everyone at the local pub. That was his last night of freedom.

One newspaper would suggest that Thunderbolt's gang broke up because Kelly was so reckless in his robberies that even the Captain would not associate with him. However, the witnesses at Kelly's eventual trial testified that during the Carroll robbery he had urged his companions to put away their firearms, that he had shown no violence in word or deed and had played little part in the actual robbery. Apparently his recklessness resurfaced after leaving the steadying influence of the more experienced Thunderbolt. He paid a severe price. After serving seven years of his nineteen-year sentence he, like gold escort robber Frank Gardiner, was released to exile in America. The Crown was still happy to offload its refuse onto the upstart Americans.

The police continued to patrol the northern districts, determined to apprehend Kelly's colleagues. They soon received word that bushrangers had been seen at one of Thunderbolt's camps on the upper Barwon. The men fled upon the troopers' arrival, leaving some exhausted horses behind. One proved to belong to Mr Bagot, stolen from Goondoobline station by Thunderbolt's gang two months previously. Thunderbolt must be back, the police decided. Troopers and volunteers descended on the district, police from Queensland as well as New South Wales, but the bushrangers managed to elude them yet again.

In fact, Thunderbolt was not among the Barwon bushrangers. Jemmy the Whisperer had taken his new mates to the camp there. Jemmy began another bushranging spree in mid-1866, robbing a hawker and some stations in the Barraba/Bingara district, even having the audacity to steal a policeman's horse. Then he disappeared, presumably hiding behind another nickname.

Meanwhile, as the weeks passed, everyone was beginning to ask the same question: where was Thunderbolt? He was not in the Walgett district. He was not in the Tamworth district.

Fears that he had joined forces with the outlaw killer John Dunn had long been allayed: the robbery victim's claim that Dunn was a member of Thunderbolt's gang proved a case of false identification. Early in December 1865 the police had received word that Dunn was on the Commerawa Creek, only 60 miles south-west of Walgett, and that he had been quietly horse-breaking there for the previous three months under an alias. Another hempen rope would soon be thrown over Sydney's gallows.

But where was Thunderbolt?

PART 6

INJUSTICE

No small part of the antipathy to law and hatred of 'respectables' found among many of the humbler classes, results from their exposure to magisterial tyranny and from their frequent observation of the perversion of justice when the weak and poor are concerned, and where no Press watches or reports such proceedings.

Sydney Morning Herald, 28 July 1864

28

Whatever our souls are made of, his and mine are the same.

Emily Brontë

Just a commonplace crime: that was the general assumption after John Higgins' Berrico hut was robbed during his absence late in February 1866. Flour weighing 158 pounds, 20 pounds of sugar, a side of bacon and a pair of blankets: the robbers would need transportation to carry such a weighty haul. Suspects? Probably the brothers O'Brien.

The rumours began after Higgins realised that a horse was missing as well, a bay with a crossed LL brand. Forget the brothers O'Brien: Captain Thunderbolt, most likely. As none of his brethren had ever visited the district, all bets were on the return of the 'gentleman bushranger'. The *Manning River News* speculated that his previous neighbourhood had become too hot for him, leading him to rusticate on their turf for a season—but if so, he would be wise to rethink his plans. The Port Macquarie police were after him, under the leadership of the indomitable Sub-Inspector Henry Garvin.

The one-time Chief Constable of Maitland knew Thunderbolt well from his previous incarnation as the Lambs Valley horsethief. Garvin's decision to pursue him had initially been based upon weak information; however, it was now proving a wise move. 'The fugitive was not far ahead when last heard from,' the *Manning River News* advised, 'and there is at least a fair probability the police will come up with him shortly.'

•

Thunderbolt was indeed responsible for the robbery, reported a part-Aboriginal woman who stumbled into Stroud's police office on Thursday 22 March 1866. Her connection with the bushranger began nearly a year previously, she told the intrigued yet suspicious policemen, when she was employed to assist his wife during childbirth. In June 1865, they made camp near Mr Parnell's station, where they remained undisturbed until January. Thunderbolt returned alone at that time, saying that they needed to move to a new camping site. They travelled across the mountains and settled near the headwaters of the Little Manning (Upper Manning River). Recently he had said he was going to stick up Higgins' station and was gone three days, returning with flour, tea, sugar, soap, spoons, blankets, two butcher's knives and a horse branded LL.

Her description of the stolen goods matched the details provided by Higgins himself, the police realised. What else could she tell them?

Thunderbolt has ten horses in his possession, she reported, but all are in low condition. And he is injured, having hurt his back falling from a horse. He also has a bad knee, requiring assistance from Ward's wife and herself to mount his horse.

Her own assistance?

Involuntary, she told them—at least for the last few months. Thunderbolt had refused to allow her to leave, tying her up when he and Mary Ann were away. She had escaped nine days previously while Mary Ann was out hamstringing cattle, and had wandered through the bush for six days until eventually reaching an inhabited area. Another three days travel had brought her to their doorstep. And she could take them back, right now, directly to Thunderbolt's camp.

Informer or decoy? the police asked themselves. Naturally, Thunderbolt's woman would require assistance during childbirth, as well as a safe encampment where she could recover and look after three young children. Long-term assistance would be helpful too, as Thunderbolt was away bushranging much of the time. Changing camps after his gang broke up in January would also be wise, in case Kelly or Jemmy were motivated to talk. But was the woman's assistance truly involuntary—and why was she declaring herself willing to help the police?

Four horses rode out from Stroud the following day, three carrying troopers disguised as bushmen, the fourth carrying the woman, also heavily disguised. Among the troopers was Constable Henry Finlay, who had been foiled in his attempt to follow Thunderbolt during the Great Flood rain-storm two years previously. Finlay was particularly keen to have a second chance at catching the miscreant.

At Gloucester, the police party acquired the services of a blacktracker. They then headed into the mountains towards the upper reaches of the Little Manning. 'We hope shortly to be able to report the capture of the whole of them,' advised the *Maitland Mercury*'s Stroud correspondent. 'But we fear that by the time the police arrive at the spot he will have shifted his quarters in some other direction as it was nine days before the woman reached here.'

Meanwhile, Sub-Inspector Garvin and his troops were closing in on Thunderbolt from the north-east, while Maitland's Senior Sergeant Kerrigan and his men were also heading into the same mountains from the south-east. As the net began to close around the unsuspecting bushranger, the community asked if the power of this particular thunderbolt was about to be extinguished at last.

A barefooted Fred leant over a dead bullock lying belly-up on the ground, carefully cutting a straight line from the tailbone via the belly to its neck. Bloody work, so he had discarded his heavy coat and was dressed only in light pants and a faded Crimean shirt with its sleeves rolled up—and, of course, the eye-shading hat beloved by all bushmen. He gently wielded his knife, cutting around the legs and throat, pulling back the skin. A sudden noise caught his attention and he looked up.

Fred wasn't blessed with Mary Ann's excellent hearing. Only the quiet-ness of the bush allowed him to hear the intruders just a few moments before they spotted him. Three white men and a black man: a police posse! In that one shocked moment before he took to his calloused heels, he didn't have time to recognise his old nemesis, Chief Constable Garvin—not that any of the troopers were recognisable with their hats pulled down low over masks of determination. A few paces and a clumsy scramble had him astride the horse grazing nearby. Heels thumping into its flanks, he tugged on the reins and began crashing through the bush.

Alerted by the flash of movement and the thud of hooves, the police kicked their own horses into a gallop. They raced after the fleeing horseman, following in his tracks until suddenly the bush thinned and opened onto a grassy clearing. An astonished young man and some children stared back at them—no, not a young man, but a woman dressed in men's clothes. Horses, supplies, a fire: Thunderbolt had led them back to his own encampment.

Their eyes found Thunderbolt again. Fingers deft with experience were untying the reins of a blue roan grazing on the camp's outskirts. A moment later, the horse's long fluid strides carried the bushranger away from the camp.

The troopers knew Thunderbolt had lost vital time in the changeover. His racehorse was clearly fast, but not yet warmed up, not yet settled into its stride. Senior Constable Buckland and the blacktracker began to gain on him. Buckland yelled out 'Police!' as he edged closer, then 'Stand!' Thunderbolt ignored the summons, continuing to drum his heels into the roan's flanks.

Buckland pulled out his gun and aimed at the fleeing bushranger. He cocked the hammer and curled his finger around the trigger. He was about to snap off a shot when his horse began to leap over a log. He held fire for a moment, waiting for his horse to land, waiting for the rhythmic strides to continue, the moment when all four iron-clad hooves were in the air and nothing could disturb his aim. Suddenly there was a jolt, a stagger. The horse began to fall, taking Buckland and his cocked gun with it.

Buckland hit the ground, his hand still clutching the gun, deliberately keeping it pointed outwards just in case the jolt triggered a shot. The horse landed on top of him, all 800 or 900 pounds, then rolled over him and staggered to its feet again. Buckland lay still for a moment, shocked and injured, before struggling to his feet and pulling himself back onto his horse. Doggedly determined, he urged his horse onwards.

With Buckland now a distance behind and the other troopers' slower horses even further behind, only Peter, the blacktracker, continued to gain ground. In a moment Thunderbolt and his Aboriginal pursuer were both lost to sight.

•

'I thought he was going to shoot,' Peter later told Sub-Inspector Garvin when asked why he had turned back after almost catching up with Thunderbolt. 'I was afraid.'

He had seen the swift look behind, the swivelling body. He had seen, or imagined, a gun raised and aimed towards him. Low pay and only a minuscule fraction of the reward the other troopers would receive for apprehending a bushranger—if they succeeded. Little wonder he had pulled his horse to keep out of gunshot range.

Mary Ann was expecting the troopers to return to her camp, with or without Fred in cuffs or slung over the back of his horse. The police wouldn't just ride away after discovering Thunderbolt's camp. They would return to collect the three remaining horses, knowing full well that all were stolen. At least then she would learn of Fred's fate.

With relief she saw only four disgruntled faces returning, heard the staccato command to pack up her belongings. They had failed to catch Fred, but they were taking her with them. It was happening all over again.

Sub-Inspector Garvin knew that he couldn't leave Ward's woman alone in the mountains with three young children, no transportation and no supplies. Her campsite lay on the Pigna Barney Creek in rugged countryside 50 miles east of Murrurundi, an unfrequented area at least 25 miles from any homestead. Simple humanity dictated that they take her with them. Moreover, the press would crucify the police if his men rode off and abandoned her. No point in giving them any more grounds for complaint or derision.

As they gathered Thunderbolt's supplies and loaded the horses, Garvin tried to console himself with the thought that the barefooted and lightly clad bushranger was now alone in the mountains in the autumn's chill, without a spare horse or supplies or even a gun. They had found a revolver he had dropped in his haste—or perhaps thrown away for some reason. Considering the circumstances of his flight, it seemed unlikely he would be carrying a spare. If they could find him again, he would be at their mercy.

The party, now double in size, set off soon afterwards, heading northeast towards Nowendoc. Ward's woman rode astride, still dressed in male attire; the troopers could understand why, but were nonetheless askance.

She carried an infant about nine months old cradled in a pouch and had a little girl tucked in front of her. The oldest girl rode another horse. The lass was a good rider, the men noticed, more than capable of managing the horse on her own. Still, it would be a long, slow journey, their speed curtailed by the apron strings of motherhood.

As the seven horses plodded along the narrow mountain trail, through grassy glades with sunlight dancing through the leafy canopy, beside gloomy ravines that cut a swathe through the mountain itself, Sub-Inspector Garvin had plenty of time to think. Ward was obviously devoted to his woman and she to him. Surely they must have made arrangements to meet somewhere in the mountains in the event they were separated. If a police raid forced him to suddenly flee the camp—as had just happened—they would not have time to organise a meeting place. Nor would the crafty villain risk returning in case the police were waiting in ambush.

So what if they used Ward's woman as bait? They could stop at the nearest homestead and leave her there with the children, guarded by a constable and the blacktracker. He would explain to the woman that the pace was too slow and that he needed to return to his station—she wouldn't have any reason to doubt he was telling the truth. Meanwhile, he would order his men to allow her to escape, to allow her to think she had outwitted them. Hopefully, she would head towards their meeting place while the blacktracker followed at a safe distance.

If they were lucky, his men might have another chance to capture the charmed bushranger.

Augustus Hooke of Curricabark station was a man of faith who believed in helping needy widows, ailing pastors and horse-race organisers. While the squatter and racehorse-owner might deplore Thunderbolt's criminality—particularly his penchant for stealing good racehorses—as a horse-race lover himself, he could not help a sneaking admiration for the fellow's horsemanship. So his feelings were mixed when he opened his door to Thunderbolt's woman and her three young children.

Curricabark station lay halfway between Tomalla and Nowendoc. It was connected with civilisation by a rough track the police could follow until they reached the Gloucester–Walcha thoroughfare, a windy mountainous track that would later become known as Thunderbolt's Way. From

Gloucester they could follow the road east to Taree. Curricabark was as good a place as any to leave Thunderbolt's family.

It was only for a short while, the troopers assured Hooke, knowing that her stay would probably be even shorter than they were suggesting.

More policemen! The four horsemen riding towards her camp near Pigna Barney Creek were dressed as bushmen, but she wasn't fooled. Three white men and a black man riding through isolated Thunderbolt territory? They needn't have bothered discarding their distinctive blue uniforms.

The faces were unfamiliar, however. Not the Port Macquarie police again, that was clear. She had managed to hide her trail too well for their blacktracker after slipping away from Hooke's not long after the police left. Not that it mattered where this lot came from. They were trouble, whoever they were.

The woman was standing near a derelict hut when Senior Sergeant Thomas Kerrigan and his Maitland force spotted her on Thursday 27 March 1866. She eyed them warily as they rode closer, yet appeared not to be frightened, making no attempt to run away or to pick up and protectively cradle the infant lying on the grass nearby.

Kerrigan and his three companions had been scouring the district for the previous few days, following reports of Thunderbolt's return to the mountains between Gloucester and Tamworth, but their search had been fruitless—until now.

Kerrigan climbed down from his saddle and walked towards the light-skinned Aboriginal woman. 'What is your name,' he asked, 'and who are you?'

'Mary Ann Ward,' she said. 'I am the wife of Frederick Ward.'

'Alias Thunderbolt?' enquired the hopeful copper.

'I don't know about Thunderbolt,' was her cautious response.

Kerrigan had not seen a fleeing horseman or any sign that the bushranger had just departed. 'What has become of Ward?' he asked curiously.

'Last Friday, the police from Port Macquarie chased him,' she told him, adding that the police had left her at Mr Hooke's Curricabark station, but that she had returned to the mountains soon afterwards. 'For the last two days I have been looking for him in the bush but I cannot find him.'

The trooper looked around the camp, at the single horse and meagre supplies. 'Do you have any means of support?' he asked.

'No,' she said, 'but what I have got, I got from Mr Hooke which he gave me for charity.' Her words were deliberate, defiant. They would not find stolen goods in her camp.

Kerrigan noticed an odd-looking implement lying on the ground near the infant, a blade fastened to a long stick. He pointed towards it and asked what it was.

'We kill cattle by having a shear blade tied on the end of a pole and hamstringing them,' she explained, acknowledging that beef was their main food source.

Kerrigan appreciated the ingeniousness of the simple weapon. Much easier to kill cattle after they were lying on the ground with their back legs paralysed. As he continued asking questions, the woman acknowledged that she had no permanent residence, now or for the past two years.

Living in the bush; no fixed address; companion of a reputed thief: there was a law that covered individuals like her. 'I am taking you in charge for vagrancy,' Kerrigan announced.

Senior Sergeant Kerrigan was one of the smartest, most intelligent and plucky officers in the police force, a letter-writer would later praise, and naturally the lawman made the most of their journey from the mountains down to Stroud. His party encountered the Dungog–Stroud party soon after setting out, the female informer having led the troopers from one Thunderbolt camp to another without finding him. The officers decided to separate Ward's family, making it harder for Thunderbolt to rescue them or for Mrs Ward to escape. The woman and her infant continued the three-day journey with Kerrigan's men, while the two older girls travelled with the female informer and some of the Dungog–Stroud force.

As they journeyed towards Gloucester, where the Australian Agricultural Company now ran thousands of celebrated Durham cattle on its rich pastures rather than the docile sheep of her childhood, Kerrigan asked why they had camped in those particular mountains.

Mrs Ward seemed happy enough to answer his questions, in addition to boasting about some of her husband's remarkable achievements. 'We went to where I was taken as a sort of refuge,' she explained, 'to be out of danger while my husband rested and recovered the use of his leg.'

Kerrigan asked what had happened to his leg.

'Some time ago he was wounded by a bullet in the leg, and recently his horse fell on him, on the same leg. Since then I've had to lift him onto his horse. He is hurt so much that I do not think he can long survive.'

Thunderbolt seriously injured? Sub-Inspector Garvin would later report that he had seen nothing to suggest so. 'It is not quite true as regards Thunderbolt being crippled. He may be hurt in the leg and back, but it does in no way incapacitate him. He can still mount his horse well, and ride like the wind.'

The press began speculating about the charges to be laid against Mary Ann. 'Possessing stolen goods,' a Gloucester correspondent suggested, having heard that Higgins' property had been found at the original campsite. However, the Port Macquarie police had shown no interest in laying such charges against her, abandoning the hunt and returning to Taree with Thunderbolt's revolver and the three camp horses.

The press was not alone in discussing the possible charges. The Stroud police knew they hadn't enough evidence to bring a 'possession' charge against her. Nor could they charge her under Section 4 of the Felons Apprehension Act—harbouring or aiding an outlaw—as Thunderbolt had not been legally declared an outlaw. Vagrancy it must be, they decided, the all-encompassing act that covered myriad minor sins and predicaments.

Had Kerrigan failed to read the fine print? Ironically the Vagrancy Act was first legislated in 1835, just a few months after the murderous attack against Mary Ann's father. Some powerful figures in the community had demanded the law in the aftermath of the Whattonbakh murders in an attempt to ease tensions in the outlying districts.

But the law made allowances for Aboriginal people living in the bush.

29

He who profits by a crime commits it.

Seneca

Mary Ann stood before the magistrate's bench in the Stroud police office on 31 March 1866 with her infant perched on her hip, its tiny fists clutching the bodice of her gown. She looked across at Thomas Nicholls, the presiding magistrate, the public face of Stroud, and saw a countenance she knew well.

Nicholls was about her father's age and had lived in the Stroud district for as long as she could remember, also an employee of the Australian Agricultural Company, but a 'pure merino', unlike her emancipist father. He had been honoured with a magistracy while she was living in Mudgee, and took his community responsibilities seriously indeed.

Seated near the magistrate's bench was the Clerk of Petty Sessions, who self-importantly read out the charges: 'Mary Ann Ward is charged by Senior Sergeant Kerrigan with being an idle and disorderly person and a companion of reputed thieves, and having no visible means of support or fixed place of residence.' He then called Kerrigan to testify.

The experienced police officer knew the drill. Kerrigan described his encounter with Mrs Ward and his decision to charge her with vagrancy. 'The prisoner, I have no doubt, has accompanied the man Ward and has assisted him to plunder,' he reported to the magistrate, 'as she has spoken of several robberies committed by Ward.'

Mary Ann stood there silently, mentally grimacing as she realised that her boasts about Fred's activities had come back to haunt her.

Kerrigan reported that beef was the Wards' chief support, according to the prisoner's own claims, and he recounted her description of how she hamstrung cattle. Then he added a final piece of telling evidence: 'When I took her into custody, she had a swag nearby containing a pair of men's pants and regatta shirts. She also stated that when the police chased Ward, she was dressed in men's pants.'

A woman dressed in men's pants? Who else but a vagrant would clothe themselves in such a way? All eyes turned towards the suitably frocked woman standing demurely in front of them.

Mary Ann was well attuned to the dress code of 'civilised' society. She knew how the community would react to Kerrigan's report. 'I was not dressed in men's clothes!' she cried. 'I didn't say that!' Then she vehemently denied the charge that her family's main food source was beef—because there was only one way her bush-dwelling family could live off beef, as everyone in the courtroom well knew.

'You did say that when the police chased Ward you had pants on,' Kerrigan declared firmly, 'and you did tell me that you lived chiefly on beef.'

The magistrate looked over at Mary Ann and asked if she had anything to say in her own defence.

'I am no vagrant,' she told him proudly, defiantly. 'My husband Frederick Ward keeps me.' In the silence that followed, they could almost hear the unspoken words, 'by the proceeds of crime'.

Could she have provided a worse answer? If she had told the magistrate that she lived in the bush like her ancestors lived, that she supported herself and her children as her ancestors supported their own families, she might have stood a chance. But Mary Ann never publically claimed an Aboriginal heritage, and Nicholls, of course, knew both her family and her personal history. Instead, by invoking Fred's name, she had reminded the magistrate that she lived with and was supported by a thief—and was proud of it.

'The Bench finds the prisoner guilty of being an idle and disorderly person, and a companion of reputed thieves, and having no visible means of support or fixed place of residence,' Nicholls announced. With a hammer of his gavel, he sentenced her to six months' imprisonment in Maitland Gaol.

It squatted dour and forbidding on an eminence overlooking East Maitland, a deliberate focal point for the whole district, a stern warning to lawbreakers that the eyes of justice were watching them. Two decades old, the gaol had been praised as handsome and well-finished soon after its completion, yet Mary Ann and her daughters had little appreciation for its structural splendours as the gaol gate squealed its welcome.

Cell walls two-and-a-half feet thick, ceiling and floor one feet thick, stones so closely dovetailed together that any would-be escapee would effectively have to tunnel through solid rock to escape. Small glass-less windows for ventilation at the top of ten-foot-high cells. Two doors to each cell, the inner made of iron bars and the outer of hardwood sheeted with iron. It was no place for a woman used to living in the bush, or especially for three young children who had committed no crime whatsoever.

At 3.25 pm on 5 April 1866, the New South Wales Speaker of the Legislative Assembly took his chair. As voices died to a murmur, a tousled head rose above the crowded benches. David Buchanan was on a mission. The Scottish-born barrister and radical liberal had a battle to fight, an underdog desperately needing the power of his advocacy, the eloquence of his oratory. Voice emboldened by passion, he announced: 'I wish to bring under the notice of the Government an act of the most cruel injustice perpetrated by the Bench at Stroud.'

Papers stopped rustling as his colleagues lifted their own heads. Was this simply Buchanan histrionics? What cause had the champion of the working classes taken up now? A new one, presumably—unless he had jumped the fence again, advocating something else that he had recently been railing against. His political seesawing left them reeling, while his violent passions and extreme views were often persuasive—in uniting the opposition! Or had he simply lifted one glass too many, again? But the man was unflinching in his attacks upon the wealthy and influential, fearless despite their frowns. He might be tiresome and unruly—and largely responsible for Parliament's nickname 'the bear pit of Macquarie Street'—but he was a kindly soul, his outspoken honesty well-meant, despite his bombastic style. What was this latest passion?

The Stroud Bench had convicted an *Aboriginal* woman under the Vagrant Act on the grounds that she had no fixed residence and was without visible means of support, Buchanan told his fellow Parliamentarians. A party of police had reportedly been pursuing the marauder Captain Thunderbolt when they came upon the half-caste woman at her camp in the bush. They had taken her into custody and marched for three days to Stroud, and had brought her before the Bench where the magistrate, without even charging her with any other crime than vagrancy, had sentenced her to six months' imprisonment. 'I would ask the honourable members to reflect seriously upon the enormity here committed,' Buchanan entreated. 'Had the police gone into the house of an honourable member and dragged him from his home, they could not have done a greater wrong than has been done in the case of this poor woman, for the wilderness is her home and the whole bush the only residence she possesses.'

His honourable colleagues knew that an exemption of some sort existed for bush-dwelling Aborigines in the New South Wales Vagrancy Act, both the initial 'Act for the Prevention of Vagrancy and for the punishment of Idle and Disorderly Rogues and Vagabonds and incorrigible Rogues', as well as its later incarnation. What had the Stroud Bench been thinking?

'If there had been any other charge legally proved against her—if she had been found guilty of aiding and abetting the bushranger Ward, then indeed, the matter would have been different, and I would certainly never have raised my voice in her favour,' Buchanan assured his listeners. 'But here she was charged with nothing that could be construed as a breach of law, and to send her to gaol for living as her ancestors had lived before her in the wide bush is an act of the grossest tyranny and injustice.'

Buchanan glanced around at the members seated in the horseshoe-shaped tiers of benches surrounding him: the elected representatives of the people. He reminded them that such a judgement reflected a wilful and culpable ignorance of the law and would seriously weaken the public's confidence in the administration of justice. 'I hope that the Government will do full justice in the case, not only to the woman by liberating her, but upon the bench of magistrates for their illegal and ignorant act,' he concluded. 'It would indeed be a very serious thing for this country if oppression of this kind could be for a moment tolerated.'

Buchanan's charge was a subtle reminder that the original inhabitants of the land now governed by their new democracy had no political representation and that Parliament had a duty of care for all who lived under the umbrella of its governance. It was also a reminder that oppression was the dark side of power, and that voters would not want to have them wielding that particular club, whether it be in the local courts or in Parliament House itself.

James Martin doffed his Premier's top hat and donned his Attorney General's helmet when he stood up to respond. He had heard nothing about the case until Buchanan alerted him to the woman's situation, he advised his colleagues; however, he would make enquiries. Whatever remedy was required would be applied, he assured them. Then he sat down again.

Cowper's liberals refused to let the issue rest. 'In no instance have I ever met with so gross a perversion of justice,' cried solicitor James Hart, who had experienced both town and country life as he hopscotched across the state in his attempts to secure a Parliamentary seat. 'This woman was sent to gaol and her three little children torn from her and all this was done because it was suspected she was the paramour of the bushranger Ward. Thus she was found guilty of one offence because she was thought guilty of another.'

The Parliamentarians were not to know that Mary Ann proudly claimed the connection; however, they did know that the police and courts should not be conspiring to make a woman—wife, paramour or otherwise—suffer for the crimes of her felonious spouse. The law allowed married women few rights over person, property and progeny, and accordingly, the law sometimes allowed married women to disclaim all criminal responsibility along the lines of my-husband-made-me-do-it. Not that Mrs Ward had been convicted of an actual felony, merely of being a 'companion of reputed thieves'.

Hart then reminded his colleagues that the courts could not convict Mrs Ward of 'aiding and abetting' either, as Ward had not been formally declared an outlaw under the Felons Apprehension Act.

James Martin's conservative ministry silently muttered that this was hardly their fault, that the Act itself was legislated by Hart's own colleagues during their administration and only targeted murderous bushrangers. Hart's colleagues had failed to introduce either legislation or strategies to rid the state of the many less brutal bushrangers like Thunderbolt, and so the bushranging epidemic continued.

Not that Martin and his men had been happy about the legislation in the first place, appalled at the idea of shooting men down like wild beasts. It was un-British. Nor in the two months since their return to office had they introduced any strategies that could deal with the likes of Mr Thunderbolt, or indeed Mrs Thunderbolt for that matter. But it was only early days.

The pitbull of the bear pit, Dr John Dunmore Lang, added his Scottish brogue to the pleas. The fiery Presbyterian minister was regularly outraged by injustice and oppression, particularly when directed towards the power-less in the community. He told the chamber he thought it monstrous that the woman should have been taken into custody under such circumstances and treated as a criminal. 'Even though she is the paramour of this outlaw, such conduct is not justifiable.'

Meanwhile a 'Lover of Justice' was penning an outraged letter to the *Herald*'s editor, unwittingly confirming Buchanan's warning. 'This unfortunate woman suffers in being so imprisoned for the deeds of her reputed husband, and committals of this kind only bring the law into contempt.'

The paperwork associated with Mary Ann's conviction was lifted from Attorney General Martin's mailbag a week later, along with a letter from the Stroud magistrate containing additional information about the woman who had suddenly become the focus of so much political attention. Thomas Nicholls reported that he had known her father for more than thirty years and the prisoner herself since childhood, and he provided details about her family background, baptism, education and marriage. As for more recent years: 'Her career as the companion of Ward is perhaps better known to the Police than to myself,' he advised, 'but, it is to be feared, it is one of crime—at least, her presence in the upper parts of this district was dreaded, where dressed in man's attire, she assisted Ward in carrying on his nefarious pursuits.'

When the paperwork reached his in-tray, the Attorney General and future Chief Justice immediately applied his formidable brain to the problem. He pulled out the current Vagrancy Act and read the wording, finding a single reference only to the colony's original inhabitants:

> . . . and every person not being an aboriginal native or the child of any aboriginal native who being found lodging or wandering in company with any of the aboriginal natives of this Colony shall not being thereto required by any Justice of the Peace give a good account to the satisfaction of such Justice that he or she hath a lawful fixed place of residence in this Colony and lawful means of support and that such lodging or wandering hath been for some temporary and lawful occasion only and hath not continued beyond such occasion . . .

The wording was obscure to the point of being ungrammatical, and the reference to Aboriginal exemptions implicit. He pored over the section again, forced to read between the lines, to seek the legislature's intentions. Eventually he inked his nib. 'I have no doubt that Mary Ann Ward is a person who may be lawfully punished under the Vagrant Act,' he wrote to the Under Colonial Secretary that same day. He agreed that the bush-dwelling progeny of Aboriginal natives were not, strictly speaking, answerable to that particular law, yet he believed that there was nothing to prevent an Aborigine who had 'acquired civilised habits' from being charged with vagrancy. 'Still less,' he advised, 'is there anything to prevent a person educated like Mary Ann Ward from being punished for a violation of that Act.'

Baptised, educated: the woman had been granted every social advantage and should have known better than to return to a bush-dwelling lifestyle, was the Attorney General's intimation. Nor should she have wanted to. Indeed, the Vagrancy law allowed her to be convicted simply for having done so, irrespective of whether or not she was the companion of a 'reputed thief'. Those who failed to appreciate the benefits of the civilised life graciously bestowed upon them could, under the law, pay for their ingratitude.

The Attorney General had essentially hung Mary Ann's Aboriginality from one arm of a set of balancing scales and her 'civilised habits' from the other and had decided that 'civilised habits' outweighed Aboriginality. In making this decision, he had delved much further than the legislature's intention, because the legislature had seemingly given no thought as to how the Act should treat Aboriginal or mixed-race bush-dwellers who had been baptised, educated and otherwise brought up 'within the pale of civilisation', let alone those who 'lodged or wandered' in the company of a white spouse and mixed-race children rather than an Aboriginal tribe. No doubt there were no more people who fitted this description when the legislation was initially crafted than there were when Mary Ann's case came to Parliament's attention. Mary Ann was probably one of a kind.

While the Attorney General argued that her Aboriginality was no bar to a vagrancy conviction, this didn't mean that he was allowing her conviction to stand simply because she was an educated Aboriginal woman living in the bush. It merely pushed issue aside that preclusionary clause. The other charges were still the issue. Therein lay another problem: the charge was inaccurately drawn up. Mrs Ward had not been described as an 'idle and disorderly person within the true intent and meaning of the Act', which would have sufficed. Moreover, the charge described her as the 'companion of reputed thieves', whereas the Act's specified offence was that of being 'in a house frequented by reputed thieves and in the company of such reputed thieves'. Indeed, the problems with the paperwork were legion, so much so that her case would almost certainly be discharged if brought before a Supreme Court Judge. Yet it was unlikely that the woman would have either the means or the friends to take up her cause. 'I think the best course to take,' Attorney General Martin counselled, 'would be to submit the matter to His Excellency the Governor as one in which he might properly interfere by directing the prisoner's liberation.'

Would he have recommended such a course of action if Mary Ann had not been an 'Aboriginal' woman? His paternalistic concern reflected an awareness of the difficulties Aboriginal people faced in the colonial justice system. It was probably the only time in Mary Ann's life when her Aboriginal heritage actually worked to her social or political advantage. But Martin's decision was not purely altruistic. Picking up his Premier's hat again, he knew he would be best rid of the problem. Less than three months old, his government did not need the fiery Dr Lang and his radical colleagues pestering Parliament about Aboriginal rights.

Matters moved surprisingly swiftly after Martin's letter reached the Colonial Secretary's clerks on 17 April. The following day, the governor of Maitland Gaol called Mary Ann to his office. The New South Wales Governor had remitted her sentence, he informed her. She was free to leave.

Mary Ann grabbed her belongings and her three young children and scurried through the gate. She had been locked behind the gaol's sandstone walls for fourteen days, only a fraction of the time Fred had been on Cockatoo Island, but it was long enough. No wonder he refused to sleep indoors ever again.

Many disapproved of the Parliamentary support Mary Ann received. 'She is a very smart woman, intelligent, and can read and write pretty well,' wrote the *Tamworth Examiner*'s editor with a touch of admiration, adding that Parliament's fuss over her vagrancy conviction was quite unnecessary, that sympathy for the 'poor Aboriginal woman' was misplaced. 'She may have some black blood in her veins,' he argued, 'but she is not darker than many European women who might easily be amenable to the Vagrant Act.'

Of course, the colour of her skin was not the real issue; rather it was the colour of her companion's skin. Had the police encountered her living in the bush with an Aboriginal husband, they would likely have left her alone. Instead, she was living in the bush with a white husband, allowing the Vagrancy Act's tentacles to wrap around her, irrespective of her husband's roguery.

'Such wretched stump oratory!' blasted a *Maitland Mercury* letter-writer, disgusted at the Parliamentarian's support. The facts were simple, he proclaimed. Ward was a lawless scoundrel who supported his half-caste woman by robbing anybody and everybody he could. The wretched woman was used by the robbers as a scout—that is, she was legally aiding and abetting, so she was to all intents and purposes an accomplice. She was undoubtedly a thief herself and, what was worse, she was breeding more of them!

A Parliamentary correspondent agreed. 'The facts have been very grossly distorted,' he advised the public. 'The poor ignorant Aboriginal woman turns out to be a well-educated half-caste who can read and write far better than most European women. Far from being the "poor harmless creature" who "roamed through her native home, the bush", she was Thunderbolt's chief lieutenant and right hand man.' Indeed, she dressed in men's clothes and rode *en cavalier* as she gathered horses, information and supplies for Thunderbolt and his gang, and her importance in keeping the bushranger alive and outwitting the police could not be underestimated. 'Turning her adrift to join Thunderbolt again would be far worse for the country than if half a dozen of the most hardened ruffians on Cockatoo were granted permits for his gang.'

Lady Macbeth in the Antipodes? The power behind the golden saddle? Yet Mary Ann hadn't ridden beside Thunderbolt shouting 'bail up', hadn't held a gun to a victim's head, hadn't searched the female hostages as Thunderbolt kept promising, hadn't fired at the police, hadn't robbed or raided or swindled. Could she really be considered more dangerous than half a dozen hardened criminals?

The underlying venom revealed a miscellany of emotions. Anger that Parliament's kindness towards what was thought to be a poor ignorant bush creature who could know no better had in fact been bestowed upon a 'half-caste', whose European blood alone was seemingly a source of knowledge and empowerment. Contempt at those of mixed race in general. Outrage that this particular conniving 'half-caste' refused to appreciate her superior education and behave as a civilised woman should. Anxiety at her chameleon-like qualities, that she was capable of adapting to both worlds, rather than straddling both without being accepted by either. And fear: not just the typical misogyny that branded such a woman as Eve the temptress or Jezebel the harlot, but the deeper, primitive fear of a woman with special powers. This woman was not only better educated than most, she possessed the Aboriginal abilities that the worthies of colonial society respected and the unworthy feared: the skills of a black-tracker. Seeing and hearing what was invisible to others seemed almost like sorcery. A witch—a malevolent black witch—was the most feared of the female incarnations.

No wonder Mary Ann seemed like a more formidable foe than any number of hardened Cockatoo Island criminals. And she was helping one such criminal to evade justice.

30

The [old policing] system had grown out of the penal times and it embraced the matured art of thief catching in the bush of Australia as practised by experienced officers who in their respective districts were like spiders in the centre of their webs, cognisant not only of every illicit movement but of every flutter of their lawful prey. But all this having been swept away, bushranging became rampant at once.

The Empire, 17 February 1863

'I fear bushranging will not be put down until all honest men adopt our American cousins' plan,' wrote 'Crito' to the *Maitland Mercury*, his pseudonym meaningful only to the literati, but his intent clear to all. While Socrates believed that the response to injustice should never be further injustice, his friend Crito—and the latter's namesake—had no such compunctions. 'Run the bushrangers down and to prevent any legal quibbles being raised to let them loose again, have ropes and tar barrels near every river!'

'Crito Jnr' responded disappointedly, yet with a trace of John Bull superiority, that lynch law justice would never be tolerated on British soil. Moreover, the vigilance committees who meted out such justice could end up targeting others, 'which would be considerably unpleasant to the actual sufferers'. He suggested instead that the government proclaim all bushrangers to be outlaws and offer rewards to private individuals who captured them.

Evidently Crito Jnr had wilfully forgotten that his beloved British justice system decreed that bushrangers, like any other alleged offender, were deemed innocent until proven guilty in a court of law. He was also ignoring the lessons of history, that injustice countered with injustice risked begetting further injustice. What if the bushrangers were not captured but killed, or if someone was mistaken for a bushranger and killed, or if an innocent passer-by was killed in the process of capturing a bushranger?

The Critos were not alone in demanding new solutions—radical solutions if necessary. 'The evil seed has been sown too widely,' lamented the *Maitland Mercury*'s editor after a new bushranging gang, the Clarke brothers of Braidwood, murdered a policeman. He feared that bushrangers threatened to become a permanent and recognised class in society, that the circumstances that spawned the bold, reckless banditti in the half-civilised countries of the world were also present in New South Wales, embedded deeply within the structure of colonial society. He recognised that the problems began with the colony's penal settlement origins and were exacerbated by the current laws and practices governing land occupation, while the physical nature of the countryside compounded the difficulties. And he wondered not that bushranging should have gained such a hold on the community, but that its development had been so recent and its prevalence so limited—to date, at least. 'Painful as the admission may be, there is opportunity and scope for much more of it. The time is now past for treating this evil as something exceptional or temporary.'

The *Maitland Mercury*'s insightful editorial was ignored. In May 1866 James Martin's conservative government tossed aside its own qualms about handing the public a licence to kill unconvicted criminals and invoked the Felons Apprehension Act to outlaw the Clarke brothers. Martin's men had examined the statistics—the four bushrangers previously outlawed were all in their graves—and had decided that it was the cheapest and easiest solution after all. The costs of any other solution would risk financially crippling the government again.

Far from having the salutary effect of deterring other bushrangers like Thunderbolt, as short-sighted governments continued to hope, invoking the Act merely reinforced the bushrangers' sense of their own omnipotence. They could rob and pillage as much as they liked: evidently, the government would react only if they committed murder.

Had Thunderbolt surfaced again? No one was sure. 'Repulsive appearance,' noted a report about the bushranger who held up the Tenterfield mailman near Deepwater on 14 June 1866. However, the fellow's curly hair and splendid chestnut mount invited suspicion—not that the local residents were likely to discover the truth.

'The praiseworthy conduct of the police in remaining at home ever since the occurrence will no doubt be a warning to the bushrangers,' wrote a sardonic Tenterfield correspondent. 'If however the thieves should wish to meet the police, I can assure them their best, indeed their only plan, will be to come into town and lay siege to the police barracks!'

Their quiet little township had not previously encountered any bushrangers, the correspondent explained, yet he was still surprised at the police's antipathy towards meeting the bushrangers, at their decision to cower in their barracks rather than chase robbers, as they were employed to do. Nonetheless, he assured his readers: 'Should Captain Thunderbolt be caught in the police paddock, I will immediately communicate the gratifying intelligence to you by telegram.'

The correspondent's sarcasm reflected the broader community's attitude to the police. They understood the problem, implicitly at least, yet the government still refused to accept the significance of the timing: the bushranging epidemic began in 1862, the same year the new police force donned their blue uniforms.

The new force was established in the aftermath of the Lambing Flat gold riots, and was modelled on the military-style English and Irish police forces so it could more effectively deal with mass uprisings in localised areas. Instead, the force found itself coping with guerilla-style warfare across vast tracts of harsh, unfamiliar terrain.

The old system was not perfect, by any means; it wouldn't have been replaced if it was. But when the authorities booted out the old, they booted out the good with the bad: men experienced in rural policing who knew their local environment and everyone in it. Only one-third of the new officers were 'old force' men and these were moved to new districts to prevent corruption. Two-thirds of the troops were Irish-born, many recruited from the Irish constabulary and mainly followers of the Roman Catholic faith, whereas colonial society was largely Protestant and often deeply antagonistic to the 'Papists'. Most of the remaining troops were from the English constabulary or the military. Only one in fourteen was colonial-born: the establishment thought rural workers were too closely allied with convictism to be trustworthy, while the rural workers themselves were wary about accepting employment in such an alien, authoritative body.

If the recruiters had filled the ranks with rural bushmen and black-trackers, the bushranging 'epidemic' would have been over before it started. Instead they provided a mere two weeks' training—mainly devoted to riding in cavalry formation—to British and Irish bobbies, red-coats and agricultural workers, then sent them into the bush to learn on the job.

If the troopers had made an effort to befriend the locals and benefit from their knowledge and experience, the new force's disadvantages would not have been so crippling. However, the new force's culture dictated that the men keep themselves aloof from the community; intimacy was believed to increase the risk of corruption. As conversations between troopers and locals were consequently rare, any approach was looked upon with suspicion. Who would risk providing information about a bushranger's whereabouts under those circumstances?

Poorly trained, treated with contempt by the broader community, facing armed bushrangers who knew how to survive in the harshest terrain: it wasn't surprising that the Tenterfield police preferred to hide out in their barracks rather than risk their lives in such a pursuit.

Fred wisely steered clear of the Tenterfield police paddocks. In July 1866, the *Sydney Morning Herald*'s monthly 'State of the Colony' column observed that bushranging had lulled for a time, that Thunderbolt in the north and the Clarke brothers in the south were keeping their heads low. The August column foolishly remarked that bushranging appeared to have received its death blow as no daring exploits by the 'Knights of the Road' had recently been reported.

The telegram section of the following day's issue revealed otherwise. Thunderbolt had 'come out' again on 22 August, sticking up the Warialda–Tamworth mailman near Manilla and stealing a packet containing £40 in gold. 'Needless to say,' reported the *Herald*, 'the police are in search of him.'

So was Mary Ann.

•

A wispy plume of smoke rose from a patch of nearby scrub as a young woman rode across the drowsy plains near the Borah Gap. Steering her horse towards the smoke, she discovered a clearing between the woody trees and mounds of shrubs. Near a tethered piebald lay a lad on his saddle-cloth, his head resting on his saddle. He was reading a book while waiting for his billy to boil.

The young woman called out a greeting and the two began talking. It wasn't long before she realised that the lad wasn't a boy at all, but Thunderbolt's woman, no less.

Chatty as always, Mary Ann talked a bit about herself, mentioning that her father was an Englishman and her mother half-Maori—a convenient fiction that made her more acceptable, somehow, in colonial society. She recounted the tale of Fred's dramatic escape from the police back in March, embellishing the story by claiming that she had shot at the blacktracker herself. She talked about her own apprehension and imprisonment and how, upon her release from gaol in April, she had stayed with some of Fred's relations in Maitland, hoping he would come to collect her. The news of her release was not published in the newspapers, however, and he failed to return.

Never one to leave fate to pull her strings, Mary Ann had borrowed some money from her sister-in-law and had purchased the piebald mare from the Maitland saleyards for £3.10s. Cutting off her black locks, she dressed again in men's attire and took to the highways, leaving her children in the care of relations.

'I have not seen him for a time,' she told those she encountered along the way, adding a message to be passed down the bush telegraph: 'If he does not turn up soon, I will have to secure a fresh settlement in life!'

Mary Ann reached Tamworth early in August, where she enquired again about Fred's whereabouts. Then she headed north to Manilla, and settled to wait near their old camp in the Borah Ranges.

The editor of the *Tamworth Examiner* was amused. Fancy sending a message to a formidable bushranger that the clock was ticking—that he must soon return to his little woman's side or she would find herself another lover. This was no hearth-bound wife meekly waiting for her man to return and take charge.

Did the editor realise, when he mentioned Mary Ann's comments in a report soon afterwards, that he was providing the 'come hither' appeal that she so desperately needed—a free advertisement that would spread the news across the countryside until it eventually reached her man? Or perhaps he assumed that her message had already been received. He published his report on 25 August 1866, three days after Thunderbolt robbed the Manilla mail, only a few miles from where Mary Ann was patiently waiting.

'The distinguished ruffian has again gone into retirement,' advised the September 'State of the Colony'. Eyes continued to watch out for him, however. Thunderbolt's was a recognisable countenance in the northern districts, even more so now that his woman had rejoined him.

31

When justice is administered by ignorant and unprincipled men who are incapable of understanding the law, or indifferent to the justice they profess to administer, it is the humbler classes that writhe under the consciousness of an unsupportable tyranny for which there is no expiation, and from which there is no deliverance.

Sydney Morning Herald, 16 November 1865

The news of a Thunderbolt sighting in the vicinity of Allyn Vale reached the Paterson police office around 1 am on Sunday 5 January 1867. Some of the locals had suspected he might be in the neighbourhood again, having seen his calling card: one or two cows killed and a few prize joints cut off—an expensive meal for those who owned the cattle. Nobody bothered alerting the authorities, however, until Henry Jarrett sent a messenger from Allyn Vale around dusk on the Saturday evening.

Perhaps the community had been graciously allowing the Wards a Christmas holiday with their family. Mary Ann's ties continued to tug her back to the district, not only her father and siblings, but her daughters in particular: Ellen was living with members of Mary Ann's family and Marina presumably as well. But Mary Ann's ties to Fred were stronger. She chose to leave her elder daughters and ride off with him again, carrying only their infant. They were nearly out of the district when Henry Jarrett decided that their Christmas holiday was over.

If Paterson's Senior Constable James Johnstone had been hoping for a full night's sleep and a quiet Sabbath, the ringing of the barrack's bell was an ominous signal. Not that the Sabbath would be a day of rest. He worked every Sunday—and Saturday for that matter—indeed, at least eight hours every day, unless enjoying one of his fourteen days of annual leave. Nor would he receive any overtime for the hours of sleep he was about to lose as he saddled his horse and rode through the darkness towards Allyn Vale with the messenger leading the way. What motivated him to leave at that hour instead of waiting until daylight—what kept him awake as he swayed gently in the unyielding saddle—was the thought of the £100 reward and the likely promotion.

The pair arrived at Allyn Vale around 6 am, where Johnstone immediately sent out an appeal for help. Naturally, the young bloods were the first to rally. Hunting a bushranger? It had to be more fun than hunting kangaroos. The police party set off soon afterwards, following one track after another until, around 9 am, they spotted two horseriders.

Deft fingers hastily unbuckled the pack fixed to his saddle and tossed it into the bushes, then Fred pulled out his revolver. He had no intention of firing at the posse descending upon him—unless he had to, of course. The shooting of young Thompson had taught him a better survival strategy than 'he who fights and runs away . . .' Run first. Police nags versus a racehorse? He could outride the troopers any day—and the howling young bloods among the swiftly approaching posse as well. Only a fool would turn to face men baying for his blood when he sat astride a racehorse. But the sight of his gun might deter his pursuers from getting too close, and a quick shot in their direction, if needed, might slow them for a moment, the very moment he needed to get away—so long as he didn't drop his gun again.

Clasping his revolver firmly, he slammed his heels into his chestnut's flanks and bolted.

The sight of the chestnut exploding into a gallop lit a fuse under his pursuers. No innocent family travelling home from Christmas would react in such a way, terrified though they might be of the whooping horsemen descending upon them. The senior constable yelled out the usual police warning, knowing that the fleeing horseman would ignore his command. He wasted no time in calling out a second warning. The distinctive crack from his pistol echoed through the trees: once, twice.

The horseman seemed to ride even faster, never hesitating for a moment in his headlong gallop, never looking back at his pursuers as his horse ate up the furlongs, keeping him out of gunshot range. He crouched over the chestnut's neck, his body swinging so easily with the horse's rhythmic gait that it seemed as if man and horse were fused as one, a new breed of centaur.

The track turned slightly and began to wind up a hill. The bushranger followed the track, urging his horse up the slope. A crafty youth shot away from the pack and took a shortcut through the bush, an oblique line that reduced the distance between hunter and hunted, a gentler slope that helped him gain ground. The bushranger didn't look back. The youth advanced closer and closer. Suddenly, a scrubby thicket forced him to pull on his reins and skirt around it. When he looked up again the bushranger had stretched the distance slightly.

Soon afterwards, Fred steered off the track. Pressing tightly with his knees, he urged his horse forwards. The horse's sweaty flanks rippled with a convulsion of muscles. Bunching its legs, it soared into the air, leaping over a jumble of large rocks and disappearing into the bush.

His pursuers slowed and watched, jaws agape. They didn't follow: the reward was not worth a broken neck.

Fred had not expected his pursuers to leap after him. Only the courageous or the reckless would attempt such a jump, and only a skilled rider mounted on a nimble horse would survive it. Horses were intuitive; they could sense fear and uncertainty. Unless the posse included a horseman as game and able as he was, he had lost them for sure.

A quick backward glance confirmed that none of the police party had tried to make the jump—or had survived it. He eased his reckless pace and turned his horse towards a local farmer's homestead.

'It's become as hot as a nest of hornets for me,' he complained to the farmer, after asking for meat and provisions. Then he rode off into the bush, back across the Great Dividing Range to the north-west, leaving Mary Ann alone and at the mercy of the frustrated police.

'Is this your property?' Senior Constable Johnstone asked Mary Ann as he pulled seven yards of unbleached calico, five-and-a-half yards of derry cloth and two yards of tweed from her saddle-bags.

Mary Ann had not travelled far since dragging her bay mare off the track and watching the vigilantes tear past. Best to steer clear of men driven by bloodlust. Like dingos in a sheep paddock, their hunger for one kill could easily lead to the destruction of many. Nor was there any point in attempting to flee herself. The police would return to find her—they always did.

Mary Ann was near the Allyn River not far from Eccleston when she heard the police party returning, just the occasional mutter of voices above the tired plod of horses' hooves. No excited refrain; no triumphant chorus.

The trooper identified himself and demanded that she dismount. She offered her name when asked, but otherwise stood by her horse with her young daughter on her hip, watching him warily. Her previous conviction and weeks of incarceration had taught her many things, among them that it was better not to volunteer information and, in particular, not to tease or taunt disgruntled policemen.

'Is the horse your own?' the trooper asked.

'No.'

'Your saddle? Your saddle-bags?'

'No.'

Johnstone opened her saddle-bags and began pulling out the contents, some lengths of fabric among them. 'Are these yours?'

'Yes.'

'How did you get them?'

'They are mine,' she said stubbornly, side-stepping the question.

He didn't believe her—not about the fabric, or the horse, or anything else for that matter. 'I am taking you into custody for having property in your possession that is suspected of being stolen,' he announced, and ordered her to mount again.

Thunderbolt's youngest child was in court again, the first time just an infant when Mary Ann was convicted of vagrancy, now a squirming youngster as she faced the latest 'possession' charges. Mother and daughter had been sweltering in the Paterson lock-up for over a week, released from its stifling confines shortly after their incarceration so her case could be brought before the magistrate, then returned again when he remanded it for a week to allow evidence to be gathered. Bail? Not Thunderbolt's woman. She would be gone in an instant.

Magistrate Edward Gostwyck Cory Esq. was again sitting on the bench when Mary Ann walked into the courtroom on Tuesday 15 January. His name was familiar to most northern residents, one of the purest of the pure merinos (British-born gentry, no less). He was a one-time explorer who had discovered the route through the Moonbi Ranges that allowed sheep and cattle onto the New England tablelands, a squatter honoured with a magistracy before the hoi polloi polluted the benches, a political man of influence whose failures were attributable to conservative principles 'untenable amongst the great body of the community', according to a blunt biographer. He was not the type to look kindly on the woman standing in front of him, the part-Aboriginal paramour of a bushranger who had begun his life of crime by stealing horses from Cory's Paterson neighbours, and who had begun his bushranging career by robbing a hut on the Gostwyck run that Cory had once owned and named.

That morning in the courtroom there was a subtle variation in the usual magistrate–prisoner dynamic, a third presence that was invisible but pervasive, unmentioned yet impossible to forget. Everyone in the courtroom knew that this arraignment was not about a single case of theft or possession or whatever charge the court would decide to lay against Mrs Thunderbolt. Indeed it was not about Thunderbolt's woman at all. Nine months previously, Parliamentarian James Hart had said, 'Thus she was found guilty of one offence because she was thought guilty of another.' It was happening all over again.

Mary Ann answered when her name was called and listened to the charge. Not vagrancy this time, but horse-stealing, or failing that, being in possession of a stolen horse knowing it to be stolen.

'Not guilty!' Mary Ann announced firmly, aware of the seriousness of the charges and the ramifications of a conviction. Three years' imprisonment was Fred's sentence after his own Mudgee conviction.

As Senior Constable Johnstone presented his case, Magistrate Cory realised that the grounds were shaky. The woman claimed to be Ward's wife and was found in his company, and stated that the horse she was riding was not hers. Married women had no property rights. If Ward purchased the horse, it was his, not hers. If he stole the horse, it was arguably still his, not hers. If she was caught stealing the horse in his company, she could defend herself by claiming coercion—and possibly even be acquitted.

Without proof that the horse was stolen, without the woman's admission of possession, the evidence was weak.

'Case dismissed,' Cory announced to the frustrated trooper and the relieved prisoner.

Senior Constable Johnstone refused to give up, although he wouldn't attempt to charge her with vagrancy again after the outcry in Parliament the previous year. Not that he could support such a charge, anyway, as he had encountered the Wards while they were travelling through the bush, rather than dwelling there. In fact, his only proof of their criminality was that the woman's husband had bolted. What law-abiding citizen would behave in such a way?

'On 6 January 1867, I apprehended the prisoner at Allyn Vale, near Mr Jarrett's house,' Johnstone began again after the clerk announced the next charge: possession of fabric suspected of being unlawfully obtained. Johnstone described the three lengths of cloth found in her saddle-bags and her admission that the goods were her own. 'She was in company with Thunderbolt when I first saw her,' he reminded the court.

The magistrate turned to Mary Ann and asked her about the fabric.

'I purchased it at the stores of Messrs Wolfe and Gorrick in West Maitland in December,' she told him.

Receipt?

She didn't have one, she admitted, however if they asked at the store they would learn she was telling the truth.

'I will remand the case until the 24th to enable you to produce evidence as to your legal possession of the goods,' Magistrate Cory told her. Witnesses; a receipt: the bushranger's notorious accomplice would have to find something to prove that the fabric was not stolen. She had opened the gaol door herself by claiming possession of the goods. Without proof, they would soon push her through and turn the key.

The Paterson petty sessions clerk waited patiently as Mary Ann fumbled for an answer. The magistrate wanted proof of her purchases, but without a receipt her only option was to call witnesses. The court would subpoena the witnesses, but needed names to do so. 'I purchased the fabric from Wolfe and Gorrick's Maitland store,' Mary Ann repeated despairingly.

The clerk asked for the name of the salesman, his pen hovering over the subpoena paperwork.

His name? That was the problem. How could she know his name?

No name, no subpoena, explained the seemingly indifferent clerk. Then he advised, helpfully, that she could write to her friends, that the court would pay for the pen and ink, the paper and postage.

She wrote two letters to friends or family members in the Maitland district and handed the letters to the clerk. He said her letters would be stamped by a local Justice of the Peace and posted by the police, then he told her escort to return her to the Paterson lock-up.

No one wrote back. No one came to visit. She had seemingly been abandoned by family and friends, as well as Fred.

Mary Ann still had no proof of her purchase when the lock-up door reopened on Thursday 24 January. Carrying her little daughter, she was ushered back into the Paterson police office and again faced Magistrate Cory's determined frown.

The clerk repeated the charges. The magistrate asked for Mary Ann's evidence of purchase.

'I purchased the property at Wolfe and Gorrick's store at Maitland,' she repeated stubbornly.

'You will need to call witnesses,' he told her.

She remained silent, having nothing else to offer in her own defence. The system had finally cowed her.

'Is there anyone you would like to subpoena?' the magistrate urged.

Silence.

'This is not satisfactory,' Cory remonstrated. 'Is there anyone you would like to subpoena before I sentence you?'

Still she said nothing.

'I sentence you to three months' imprisonment in Maitland Gaol,' the magistrate ordered. And in the echo of his gavel, she heard the Maitland Gaol gates clanging behind her for the second time.

The law offered many brooms for sweeping the 'unworthy' from the streets and bridle-paths—as Mary Ann was learning.

32

She gave me eyes, she gave me ears;
And humble cares, and delicate fears;
A heart, the fountain of sweet tears;
And love and thought and joy.

William Wordsworth

'They would not leave me alone when I was quiet so I was determined to go out and torment them,' Fred would later bitterly exclaim when questioned about his return to bushranging. He had remained in retirement for nearly five months following his lucrative £40 gold haul from the Warialda–Tamworth mailman back in August 1866, after he had found Mary Ann again. She was a calming spirit, a curb on his daring, and the community—and Fred himself—was safer when they were together. With her apprehension, however, the Thunderbolt bushranging lull ended. Fred was angry, and anger made him reckless.

He surfaced around noon on Sunday 3 February 1867 about a mile past Manilla, ordering mailman Abraham Bowden into the bush where a chestnut packhorse was tied up. He rifled through the mailbags, taking the usual halfnotes, cheques and orders, and then told Bowden that he was taking his saddle as well, although he promised to return it. With his own packhorse in tow, he rode off again towards Manilla.

Short of a saddle, mailman Bowden decided to return to Manilla rather than continue a further 27 miles to Tamworth. As he rode through the town, he noticed two horses tied up on the opposite side of the river—horses that looked suspiciously like the bushranger's.

Despite Thunderbolt's evident fondness for the Manilla district, the authorities had not seen the wisdom of posting a policeman in the town, so Bowden could report neither the robbery nor the horse sighting. With the usual mutters about police incompetence, he saddled up and took to the road again to continue his long journey south to Tamworth.

John McKinnon, superintendent of the Manilla pastoral station, was also travelling to Tamworth that Sunday afternoon. After a quick meal and drink at Mr Hill's pub on the Namoi's northern bank, he crossed the river to continue his journey. He was riding past George Veness's Manilla inn when several voices hailed him.

'The mail has been stuck up by Thunderbolt,' the innkeeper's wife cried out, 'and he went across the river to Hill's house a short time previously.' Then her eyes glanced past him and widened. With a shrill scream, she backed up and ran away.

McKinnon spun round and saw a pistol barrel pointing in his direction. He gaped up at the face above the pistol and saw a man he had seen at Hill's inn a short time before, a man now mounted on one horse and leading another.

The man's mouth opened. 'Bail up!' he told McKinnon and everyone else present.

'What the devil do you want with me?' McKinnon demanded, not realising—as he later recounted—that he was being held up by a bushranger.

Thunderbolt ignored the question and demanded that he dismount.

McKinnon refused.

'I'll blow your brains out if you don't,' the gun-toting bushranger said equably.

McKinnon complied.

'Do you have any arms?'

'Look and see!'

Thunderbolt ordered the surly superintendent to untie his waterproof coat, which was hanging from the side of his saddle, saying it looked like it might contain arms so he must hand it over along with his saddle and pouch. After examining McKinnon's coat and pouch he returned them both, keeping only the saddle. Then he graciously invited everyone to join him in the pub for a drink. None of his hostages were naive enough to demur.

For nearly an hour Fred kept everyone bailed up, paying for some grog and boasting to McKinnon that he knew the country even better than the station superintendent himself. Considering the frequency of his mail robberies in the district, his hostages knew it was no idle claim, vainglorious though it might be. As the hour passed, as he downed one drink after another, his attitude changed. He didn't become more arrogant or aggressive or opinionated, as his hostages noticed with surprise; he became more polite and civil, the epitome of the gentleman bushranger he was reported to be. Eventually McKinnon asked if he could leave, explaining that he was on his way to Tamworth to visit a doctor. Fred complacently agreed and remained seated under the verandah. He was pleasantly, foolishly, recklessly drunk.

McKinnon was tying on a loaned saddle and reattaching his pouch when Fred suddenly exclaimed: 'Who the devil's that?' As he stared down the road, McKinnon followed his gaze. A uniformed trooper leading a packhorse was riding towards them.

Fred jumped up and mounted his own horse. With his packhorse in tow, he trotted around the gable of Veness's house and along the paddock fence at the back.

'Bushranger!' bellowed his erstwhile drinking companions to the trooper who was now only 60 yards away. 'After him!' they urged, hands eagerly pointing in Fred's direction.

Senior Constable Norris had been returning to his Barraba station after attending the Tamworth Quarter Sessions when he encountered mailman Bowden about eight or nine miles south of Manilla and heard about the robbery and sighting. His was the pistol that had nearly despatched young Thompson to an early appointment with Lord Lucifer two years previously, and he was delighted to hear that his seemingly invincible adversary had surfaced just a few miles away. He spurred his horse on towards Manilla, fully expecting that Thunderbolt would be long gone by the time he arrived, so he was startled when he heard the raucous cries from the inn. He paused for a moment to get his bearings, then sped off in pursuit.

●

They stood like spectators at a cross-country steeplechase, their bodies tense with excitement, their eyes peering into the distance, unsure of the riders' route, uncertain when or where or if they would suddenly appear in view. Someone called out that Thunderbolt had reached the other side of the river and all eyes turned to watch his progress. Every so often the eyes glanced behind the bushranger, expecting to see the trooper in pursuit. But the trooper didn't come into sight—not on that side of the river at least. A short time later he rode towards Veness's pub again.

What had happened? Another inept police horse most likely, the inn's patrons decided. They could see that his mount was difficult to manage and that it was too slow to keep pace with Thunderbolt's stolen racehorse. But one of the patrons was eyeing the trooper with confusion. David Hartley had ridden after the constable, knowing that helping to capture the bushranger would make an even better story than 'the day I was held up by Captain Thunderbolt'. He had seen Norris closing in, forcing Thunderbolt to drop the lead to his packhorse and speed up. Yet, strangely, Norris didn't raise his gun, didn't send a bullet whistling after the fleeing horseman. When Hartley caught up with the trooper and asked for the loan of a revolver, saying he had a better chance of capturing the bush-ranger on his own fresh horse, Norris refused. He had only the one gun, he told Hartley, and insisted that they return to Veness's inn for additional firearms and assistance. It was strange behaviour indeed for a trooper. Was he another coward like the Bathurst lot?

As the Manilla inn patrons muttered among themselves, disappointed that they would not see the bushranger captured after all, a voice called out that they had another visitor. A man and two children were drawing up in a buggy.

'Thunderbolt is on the other side of the river,' Constable Norris called out to Constable Jacob Shaw, having recognised the buggy-driver as the Moree trooper. Shaw had also been returning to his station when he encountered mailman Bowden journeying south to Tamworth.

'If you go over, you will get stuck up,' Norris advised. 'He is blind drunk!'

Everyone began talking over each other, a clamour of excited voices: comments, suggestions, criticisms. Everyone wanted to be involved, to participate in the hunt—from the security of the inn, at least.

'You had better mount and follow me,' Shaw told Norris.

'Jump in and go over in the buggy,' McKinnon suggested. When Norris seemed reluctant, he urged, 'If you don't go over in the buggy, give me your pistol and I will go.' He knew the bushranger would not expect to be pursued by gunmen travelling in a buggy.

The strangely reluctant Norris eventually agreed to travel in the buggy himself. He tried to disguise his uniform, then tucked himself behind one of the children. Shaw jerked on his reins and the buggy jolted down to the river, then its large wheels churned through the shallow water before lurching up the opposite bank. Shaw whispered that he could see Thunderbolt astride his horse on a rising piece of ground ahead, that the bushranger had retrieved his packhorse and had it on a lead again. Evidently the reckless bushranger cared little that a trooper was in the vicinity.

A voice hailed the buggy. 'Bail up!' Thunderbolt yelled, a mock toll-keeper charging a fee to travel north, a colonial Charon whose pointed gun threatened to despatch their souls to Hades if they refused to pay his fee.

'All right,' Shaw called back, but he kept driving, surreptitiously pulling out his own revolver.

Thunderbolt rode towards the buggy, unaware that the hunter was now the hunted. The distance between them closed rapidly. When they were about 80 yards apart, the eagle-eyed bushranger spotted Shaw's companion and recognised him. 'It's the bloody traps!' he yelped. He let go of his pack-horse again and galloped into the bush.

Shaw scrambled out of the buggy and bounded after Thunderbolt, keeping his gun by his side until he was far enough away from the buggy for his children's protection. Then he fired. Bullets whizzed like agitated hornets, burrowing into bark and whipping at bushes, but missing their target.

Instead of escaping to safety, Thunderbolt began circling through the trees and shrubs, seemingly intent upon reaching his packhorse. Shaw tried to keep track of him, listening for the rustle of shrubs, the gentle slap of branches after the horseman disappeared from sight.

The bush noises were suddenly interrupted by a cry from Norris. 'The packhorse is mine. Someone catch it.'

Shaw turned to see Norris chasing the packhorse rather than the bushranger. What was going on? After Norris reached the packhorse and brought it back to the buggy, Shaw took one last look around, but he couldn't see Thunderbolt. The chase was over. Buggy-bound, they had little chance of catching the miscreant. They lashed the packhorse to the back of the buggy and drove towards Hill's inn on the same side of the river.

As they neared the inn, they were astonished to see a regal, horse-mounted figure. It was Thunderbolt again. He hadn't escaped into the bush after all: he was waiting for them, seemingly taunting them, almost begging to be caught.

The two troopers hopped down from the buggy and fumbled at the straps, attempting to untie their own horse so they could saddle it and ride after the ruffian. One buckle. Another. It was taking too long. Norris decided that his own brute would have to do. He loped back to Veness's inn to collect it.

As Shaw impatiently waited, he saw Thunderbolt ride down to the river and pick up the lead of a packhorse grazing on the river bank, then ride off again. But Thunderbolt's packhorse was lashed to the back of his own buggy. Or was that Norris's packhorse? What was going on?

Meanwhile, another saviour had just arrived at Veness's inn. Sergeant John Doherty of the Warialda station had also encountered mailman Bowden on his own trip north from Tamworth. He ordered the now mounted Norris to accompany him, and the pair crossed the river before continuing along the northern road in pursuit of Thunderbolt, with the sergeant setting a fast pace.

'Don't ride so quick or my horse will bolt,' Norris begged.

'This is the time to make a bolt!' Doherty snapped. 'Push on!'

A mile past Manilla, they spotted Thunderbolt about 300 yards ahead. 'Rush him!' Doherty barked, hoping they could sandwich the bushranger between them.

But Thunderbolt had been glancing over his shoulder every so often, keeping an eye out for any pursuers. Spotting the troopers, he dropped the packhorse lead again and sped away.

Doherty followed for a few miles, firing shot after shot—five in all—but he was never close enough to do any damage. He followed Thunderbolt into the bush, then waited on the bank of the Manilla River for Norris to catch up. 'Why didn't you come on quicker?'

'My horse won't stand fire,' complained Norris, 'and if I came quicker, he might knock me against a tree.'

They rode along the river bank for a mile, trying to find a suitable crossing. Doherty's horse jumped off a rock into a hole and both horse and rider fell into the water. By the time they reached the other side they had lost sight of the bushranger.

Three times the drunken bushranger had been within the troopers' reach; three times he had evaded them. Sergeant Doherty was irate, particularly at Senior Constable Norris. He would later bring charges against Norris for neglect of duty.

In the packhorse comedy of errors, Fred had ended up with Norris's horse and the troopers with his own. Norris's loss was Fred's questionable gain: a new colonial saddle (a bushranger's buttocks particularly loved a new saddle), an old bridle and some dirty washing. Fred's loss, however, was many people's gain: his saddle-bags contained £427 in cheques and orders stolen from mailman Bowden that very morning. No wonder he had wanted his packhorse back. As for any cash or gold found in the mail, he must have tucked those treasures into his clothes or saddle-bags. At least he had something to show for his first robbery in nearly six months.

'This is the main source of attraction,' the *Tamworth Examiner* remonstrated with its readers, adding that the mail robberies would cease only if they proved unprofitable for the bushrangers.

But how could rural residents and businesses convert cash and gold into money orders if they lived nowhere near a bank? And how were businesses and banks to otherwise move cash and gold unless they paid for an armed escort? In the grand scheme of things, bushrangers stole only a fraction of the financial assets travelling around the countryside, and the occasional loss had to be factored in as one of the regrettable costs of doing business.

Of course, if the police could catch the bushrangers, the problem of the financial transfers would largely disappear.

33

Every week longer that Ward escapes capture, every fresh mail-coach he robs, he is exercising the more evil fascination over youthful minds— he is practically training up additional bushrangers.

Maitland Mercury, 4 June 1867

'Take off all your clothes!' the bushranger demanded angrily.

The astonished shopkeeper stared back at him, wondering if he really meant it. Surely this curly-headed highwayman could not be the man generally known as the 'gentleman bushranger'.

Samuel Cook, shopkeeper at Moonan Brook, had been driving his team to town when the more usual bushranger greeting assailed him. Two horsemen were riding up to him, a man carrying a double-barrelled gun, and a blackened-faced lad dressed in a red Crimean shirt and riding a white horse. He recognised the lad, a visitor to his store that very morning— although without the facial disguise. Aged around fifteen or sixteen, the boy had mentioned he was going travelling and had asked the storekeeper about his own travelling plans. Cook had answered without any compunction as his preparations were obvious.

'Turn out your pockets!' the older bushranger had first demanded after bailing him up. Cook handed over the seven shillings he was carrying.

'I know you have money on your dray and I'll have it!' said the annoyed bushranger. 'If you make no resistance it will be better for you.'

'I will make no resistance,' the frightened shopkeeper assured him.

•

Fred was not having a good day, or month, or year for that matter, and he wasn't happy. Mary Ann was still in gaol and he didn't like being on his own. He was a sociable man, a hail-fellow-well-met type, garrulous and opinionated, a conversation monopoliser with no interest in hiding his thunderbolt under a bushel. Gloating over his successes was as pleasurable as the deeds themselves, so the lack of a companion left him without an audience. With Mary Ann gone, he also had no one to mind his back. Yet the Millie and Carroll shoot-outs had taught him the dangers of having adult accomplices—men who were quick with the trigger, men who vied with each other for leadership and glory.

In the aftermath of the Manilla robbery, he had decided to fool the troopers by heading south-east rather than to the safer north-western districts. He took the scenic route across the Great Dividing Range and stopped at Moonan Brook, the township that supported the gold-seekers at the Denison diggings. There he encountered a fifteen-year-old Queensland-born youth named Thomas Mason.

Mason had a troubled past: father dead, mother a prostitute, step-father a bully. A plucky lad, he had fled to the bush a few years previously and found work as a stockman, but he wanted more from life: adventure, excitement, riches. He decided to try his hand at gold-digging—then bush-ranging. His first job as Thunderbolt's apprentice had been to scout Cook's shop and determine when the shopkeeper was beginning his journey, his second to assist Fred in robbing the shopkeeper. Their expectations of an easy windfall, however, were not being met.

Mason led Cook's horse and dray into the bush, then untied the ropes securing the load and threw everything off the dray. He searched through the boxes and bundles, extracting a couple of cheques worth around £72 and handing them up to his master.

Fred looked at the pathetic takings. As if a goldfields shopkeeper would be driving his team to town carrying only a handful of silver and a couple of cheques. That's when he told Cook to strip off his clothes.

The stunned shopkeeper chose not to resist the humiliating demand. He took off each piece of clothing and handed it over to be searched, but the bushrangers found nothing else tucked into the folds or sewn into the seams.

'I'll go to your house,' Fred threatened before dismissing him.

For once, Fred actually meant it. He ordered Cook's employees to wait under a willow tree while he sent young Mason in to search the house. Mason was clean-faced by then, having sheepishly washed his face after one of Cook's men dryly remarked that he recognised the lad from the store earlier in the day.

Mason came back a short time later saying that he couldn't find anything. 'You're a greenhorn,' Fred said disgustedly, and told him to guard the hostages while he searched the house himself.

One of the female hostages seemed mesmerised by the sight of Mason's gun. She asked him nervously if he would shoot a woman. 'Yes,' said the greenhorn firmly. 'I would blow her bloody brains out!'

Fred found little more, only £2 in silver from both the house and the store. 'I know there is more money somewhere on the premises,' he raged, 'and if I do not get it, I will make someone pay for it before sun-down.'

His terrified hostages remained silent.

Eventually Fred realised there was little point in threatening them further. Perhaps he would have more luck at the innkeeper's.

Thirteen people were sitting down for dinner at Richard Simpson's inn, the Reefer's Arms, when Fred and his apprentice walked into the room. Presenting his pistol, Fred ordered them to remain in the room with him while his lad searched the premises. A short time later the boy brought out a small box and ceremoniously placed it on the sill next to the door where his master was standing guard.

'I have made a touch,' Fred said delightedly as he lifted out the contents and pocketed them, before sending the lad back to search some more. Some £90 in notes and sovereigns, as well as 32 ounces of gold: his day was improving.

Meanwhile, Neil McInnes was standing under the verandah at the Reefer's Arms, oblivious to the drama unfolding above him, when the tantalising aroma of dinner wafted down to him. Hunger sent him up the stairs and into the inn a short time later. The atmosphere seemed odd as he entered the dining room, strained somehow, tense. Then he noticed the stranger pointing a double-barrelled gun towards the other dinner guests.

McInnes' roots lay among the kilted Scottish highlanders who roared their battle cry then hurled themselves into battle. Giving little thought for his own safety—or that of the hostages in the line of fire—he threw himself at the gunman. The suddenness of the attack gave him the benefit of surprise. He managed to pinion the man's arms, and hung on as if his very life depended upon it. No gun-toting robber was going to get the better of a Scotsman.

Apart from a few disgruntled victims who had impotently stuck up their fists, none of Fred's victims had ever physically challenged his authority. He was tough and wiry but he had met his match with the mighty Scotsman. And he was afraid.

Under his usually convivial exterior was an explosive temper that could suddenly erupt like a seemingly dormant volcano. He had been in a bad mood for the previous few weeks as it was: Mary Ann in gaol, most of the mail robbery proceeds lost, a paltry booty from the storekeeper, and now this.

'Rip him with your knife!' he screamed at his young apprentice. 'Rip his belly open!'

Paralysed by shock and indecision, Mason had been watching the drama unfold in front of him. He had signed up for bushranging, for riches and glory, not murder. He watched Fred struggling against the unyielding arms, then he made his decision. Pulling out his knife, he charged towards the assailant, intent in every bone of his stocky young frame.

McInnes saw the deadly knife, the glare of determination. The lad was about to skewer him unless he released the gunman and defended himself. None of the other hostages had come to his aid—or even looked like they were planning to assist him. Only he could save himself.

He loosened his arms, releasing his grip on the robber, and shot out the door. Leaping from the verandah, he bolted for the cover of the trees.

Fred fumbled for a grip on his gun and raised it. He fired after his attacker, cursing him and screaming vengeance. It was the closest he had come to being captured in his four years of bushranging. If he had been bushranging on his own, he wouldn't have stood a chance.

Eventually he calmed down. 'I'm not a bloodthirsty man,' he grumbled to his terrified hostages. 'I'll be satisfied with the man's ears.'

When the ears failed to present themselves, he called for a bottle of ale and gulped part of it, then he and Mason stole another two horses, and mounted their own. They turned to farewell their victims.

'I promise to visit you again shortly,' Fred threatened—in the politest possible tones—as he gathered his reins.

'We'll be better prepared,' was the spirited response. 'We'll have more arms.'

'I'll bring more soldiers,' he countered as he rode away, leaving his host feeling all the worse for the loss of his £200 stash of cash and gold.

So foolish for anyone at the diggings to keep large sums of money in their houses, chastised the *Maitland Ensign*'s local correspondent, reminding his readers that Thunderbolt was known to frequent the neighbourhood. 'As there is a mail twice a week, they could easily forward it to the bank.'

Evidently he had forgotten that the mail was Thunderbolt's favourite target.

The correspondent was not surprised when the police returned from their search a week or so later, failure etched into their despondent faces. Not only had Thunderbolt eluded them, they hadn't found the bush telegraph who they assumed must have supplied the information about the storekeeper's impending journey; otherwise, why would Thunderbolt have been so convinced of the man's riches that he forced him to strip? He had never treated his victims in such a demeaning fashion before.

'It is of no use strangers going after him in country where he is at present,' warned the correspondent with annoyance, adding that McInnes' attempt had been their best chance to apprehend the bushranger, and that his companions should have assisted him.

In fact, the initial newspaper accounts had advised that McInnes' companions had leapt to his aid—valiant by report if not by deed. Faced with guns, knives and the recklessness of desperation, however, it was not surprising that they lacked the courage to do so.

'This daring marauder is certainly making a fine game of both the police and the country,' lamented the *Singleton Times*. 'Surely it is high time that some extraordinary means were adopted to dispute his liberty and stay his determined unopposed career.'

Magistrate George Lethbridge had been having similar thoughts. Extraordinary? Yes, indeed. His idea was definitely outside the ordinary. 'It is not philanthropic motives alone which induce me to address your Excellency,' he wrote to the New South Wales Governor before presenting his extraordinary proposal: that the Governor should consider offering the bushranger a conditional pardon.

Lethbridge's four-page letter explained why he considered Ward's situation to be worthy of such consideration. The bushranger had said he was thoroughly tired of his present mode of life and was willing to give it up; he had never shed human blood, a notion that was reportedly highly repugnant to his feelings; he had proved himself a consummate horseman and a man of the most undaunted courage; and he had shown the greatest contempt for the police whenever they fell in with him—understandably so, considering their failure to catch him, largely through their own lack of horsemanship skills.

'Would it not be well, therefore, before he is induced to shed human blood (in order to preserve his liberty), to offer him a conditional pardon, the condition of his pardon to be that he remains in the police force for life?' Lethbridge begged to suggest. 'There is no doubt that the service of such a man to the Government would prove in a short period highly beneficial to the colony.'

Lethbridge proposed that Ward would make an invaluable riding master, that he was both an excellent horseman and bushman and could strike across the most difficult country without the aid of either road or track—'a peculiar gift!'—and that he had shown himself to be cool and courageous whenever the police were in hot pursuit. By offering him a conditional pardon, his services would render the police more efficient, the colony would be rid of a determined but not dangerous highwayman, and his change of status would deter other young Australians from choosing the same despicable bushranging lifestyle.

Just in case the Governor might think that his request was motivated by a personal knowledge of the bushranger, Lethbridge advised that he had never met the man. From reports alone, however, he could not class Ward with the reckless bloodthirsty ruffians whose exploits were regularly described in the press, both because of his general knowledge of Ward and because of the account provided by a lady friend who had received a visit from Ward and his accomplices when her husband was absent. 'Ward's kindness of manner, his politeness of address and extreme consideration lest she should feel the least alarmed was so great that, though she could not bear the look of his accomplices, yet she wished to retain him as her protector and though he told her on her asking him several times that he was also a bushranger, she could hardly believe it.'

Lethbridge explained that he was as much a stickler for justice as any other magistrate in the territory; however, he was induced to offer the suggestion believing that Ward had seen the error of his previous conduct and would gladly change his present mode of life for one more honour-able. Moreover, it would save him from total recklessness and protect the community from the danger this posed. But most importantly, his services would be an invaluable asset to the Crown.

The suggestion of 'putting a thief to catch a thief' had been proposed two years previously by a letter-writer to the *Sydney Morning Herald* after John Dunn murdered Constable Nelson. But nothing had been done then, or would be done in response to Lethbridge's appeal. It would take political courage to make such a decision, to look beyond the man's criminality to the greater good. Indeed, the great and the good would be the ones most likely to smite anyone who made such a decision. And of course, the miscre-ant himself would need to be willing to cross the respectability picket line.

'A pardon could not be granted in this case,' replied the Governor dismissively, 'but it might not be necessary to hang Ward if he voluntarily surrenders himself.'

34

Any existence deprived of freedom is a kind of death.

General Michel Aoun

Mary Ann was as angry as Fred. She had no intention of going silently into her Maitland Gaol cell. The New South Wales Governor had released her from her previous vagrancy sentence; she would appeal again for his assistance.

'The Humble Petition of Mary Ann Ward, a confine in Her Majesty's Gaol at East Maitland' was prepared a short time later. Mary Ann showed no reluctance to admit to her relationship with one of the country's most notorious criminals. 'Your petitioner is the wife of Frederick Ward, commonly called "Thunderbolt",' she proudly advised. She described the circumstances of her apprehension and explained that she was unable to produce any witnesses to confirm the truth of her statement, as no subpoenas had been granted nor any enquiries made on her behalf by the police. She begged His Excellency to enquire into the truth or falsity of her statement and signed her plea with a neat little hand, 'Mary Ann Ward'.

Prisoner petitions were forwarded to the gaol's visiting magistrate, whose job was to veto unnecessary or vexatious petitions, otherwise the state's prisoners would spend every minute of every day thinking up grievances and flooding the Governor with impassioned pleas for their release. Maitland Gaol's visiting magistrate, Edward Denny Day, was a forthright character. He was the man responsible for apprehending the white killers of the Myall Creek Aboriginals thirty years previously, a man with a keen eye for signs of injustice, and he was seeing its ugly stain spread across Mary Ann Ward's petition.

Magistrate Day considered his options. Wolfe and Gorrick's popular store lay in High Street, West Maitland, not far from his own East Maitland home. The proprietor, Jacob Ephraim Wolfe, was a man he knew well—a reliable and trustworthy magistrate who acted as chairman of the Bench when he himself served as police magistrate. Day would visit the store himself and make enquiries into the woman's allegations.

Mary Ann was standing among a group of female prisoners when the warden ushered Magistrate Day and another man into the room. Day waited patiently while his companion glanced from one woman to another. The man's eyes alighted on Mary Ann, then he pointed to her and said something to the magistrate.

Mary Ann recognised the magistrate's companion, although she did not know his name. He was the draper from Wolfe and Gorrick's, the man who had sold her the 'stolen' fabric.

Frederick Edwards had immediately recognised the fabric when Mr Day brought it to Wolfe and Gorrick's store. He had told the magistrate that he could remember both the sale and the purchaser, and he opened his account book and pointed to the purchase details. And now, without a moment's hesitation, he had identified Mrs Ward as the purchaser.

Magistrate Day informed his shopkeeping friends of the result of his investigation. Soon afterwards, Wolfe and Gorrick themselves wrote to the Attorney General urging an enquiry. Meanwhile another concerned Hunter resident berated the authorities through the letter pages of the *Maitland Mercury*. 'This seems to be a case of gross injustice and I trust the attention of the proper authorities may be directed to this matter.' He declared that the woman was as illegally in custody on this occasion as when she was arrested and convicted under the Vagrant Act. 'Seemingly the sins of Thunderbolt are again visited on this unfortunate woman.'

The unexpected community interest turned the previously disinterested reports of the local Paterson correspondent into an impassioned attack. 'Absurd' was his denunciation of the grounds for Mary Ann's conviction. He revealed that she had initially been arraigned for horse-stealing but that this charge fell through for lack of proof, and that the fabric 'possession' charge followed. Seemingly, the authorities were so desperate to convict her that they were latching onto any charge they could think up. A remand had been granted so she could find proof of her legal possession. 'But how was she to get that proof,' he entreated the community, 'being incarcerated in our gaol, without one penny in her pocket—without a friend? Even if she could bring up the very person who served her with the articles, is it likely that after the lapse of a month, they could identify her or the articles she purchased?'

Of course, the correspondent failed to mention that Mary Ann was not just any customer. How many shopkeepers would forget a beautiful part-Aboriginal woman who spoke perfect English?

'Whatever has been her former conduct,' the correspondent continued, 'I must contend that in this matter she has been wrongfully imprisoned.' He reminded the community that on a previous occasion Parliament had decided that she was unjustly imprisoned. In his own opinion, there were more grounds for her imprisonment then than in this instance. Unfortunately, Parliament was not sitting so her case could not be raised in that venue again. 'It is a matter which should be looked into by our Government,' he urged.

Censorious newspaper reports; pleading letters and petitions: Thunderbolt's woman was demanding the government's intercession again. Please advise, was the request from the Attorney General in Sydney to the Police Superintendent of the North Western district.

Superintendent Morisset conducted his own investigation, reporting back on 26 February 1867 that problems had occurred with subpoenaing witnesses because the woman could not provide names and because Paterson's only mounted constable was busy collecting the Electoral Roll. He advised that he had personally questioned Wolfe and Gorrick's draper and shown him the fabric. The man had signed a statement saying that the derry cloth corresponded with the fabric he had sold her, although he did not recognise the calico. Then Morisset sent all the paperwork to the Attorney General and left Mary Ann's case in the government's hand.

The doors of Maitland Gaol opened again three days later.

Why the continued community support for Mary Ann when so many others, men as well as women, were in gaol for vagrancy or questionable 'possession' charges? Edward Denny Day was a powerful and respected man and when he cried injustice, everyone listened. No doubt Day's initial alarm reflected some degree of paternalistic concern because of Mary Ann's Aboriginality, his awareness that the court system would not necessarily work in her favour, and his realisation that she might not understand the system enough to be able to appropriately defend herself. Yet, surprisingly, Mary Ann's Aboriginal heritage was not mentioned in any of the newspaper reports. The broader community concern reflected a different paternalism, that for the little woman unjustly suffering the sins of her nefarious husband.

Yet underneath the vehement cries of 'injustice' was also the community's fear of the abuse of police power—one of the primary reasons why Britain had so stubbornly resisted the establishment of a centralised police force. Memories of a certain guillotine in the hands of the unworthy would take a very long time to fade.

PART 7

RETRIBUTION

In death there is life.

Writings and translations of Myles Coverdale

35

It is anything but creditable to the police that the silly vapouring creature known by the 'sobriquet' of Thunderbolt should still be at large.

Maitland Ensign, 1 May 1867

The Tamworth police looked up at the clear night sky, at the Paschal or 'Passover' full moon shedding its brilliance over the towns and villages and roads in their district. Night after night the moon had hung there, stubbornly lighting up the neighbourhood, drawing out lunatics and ne'er-do-wells and other night-time creatures. Would Captain Thunderbolt be among them? The ruffian might call himself Thunderbolt rather than Moonlight or Starlight, but a bright night enticed him onto the country's highways and byways as surely as it did his other heavenly brethren.

Reportedly he had been seen near Goonoo Goonoo, south of Tamworth, just a few days previously. Significantly, two horses were discovered missing a day later. The police kept on the alert, just in case he ventured out again. He had remained quiet since the robberies at the Denison diggings, and the local press speculated that the difficulty of travelling through the bush at night from his old haunts in the Paterson and Stroud districts had probably kept him out of sight. Whatever the reason, they knew that he was now lurking in their district, where the full moon continued to cast its powerful lures.

Mr Brereton was driving his mail coach south along the Great North Road on Sunday 21 April 1867. Around 9.30 pm, when he was about three miles past Bendemeer, a horseman rode up beside him and called out, 'Is the escort with the coach?'

Unthinkingly, Brereton replied that it wasn't—and realised his mistake a moment later. He screamed at his horses to go faster, flinging his arms up and down as he lashed at their backs with the reins, trying to outrun the now pistol-carrying horseman, but the man kept pace with him, forcing him to pull over.

Not that the bushranger's audacity benefitted him much. As he and his companion tore open the letters and parcels, Brereton saw that the mail contained little of the craved riches, just a bit of cash and a few cheques.

After the Denison robberies, Fred had chosen not to return to his favourite robbery ground near Manilla. Instead, he and Mason crossed the Moonbi Ranges and headed towards Bendemeer, where Fred had the prudence to enquire first about the armed escort before revealing his true vocation. Which partly explained why he was still successfully highway-robbing while his more daring colleagues were pushing up daisies.

From Bendemeer they travelled north to Bonshaw, a village lying 50 miles west of Tenterfield, where on 8 May 1867 Thunderbolt held his gun to the head of innkeeper James Roper and demanded that he open his money drawer. As the innkeeper attempted to turn the key, he noticed that the bushranger's hand was trembling as much as his own.

Thunderbolt scared? The gentleman bushranger suddenly aware of his own mortality? This was his first 'house' robbery since the mighty Scotsman had nearly scuppered his bushranging career. Frightened criminals often became more dangerous, but not Fred; his menace as a bushranger had never been founded upon his own violence. Rather, he had ridden into each robbery clutching the invisible horse-tails of other bushrangers' menace. He preferred carousing with his victims than shooting them.

Emboldened by Thunderbolt's nervousness, and his consideration in handing back the ostler's money and some silver to carry on his own business, Roper began to remonstrate with him. As they sat on the verandah drinking some of the robbers' takings, he advised, 'Give it up before you commit murder. Go where you are not known and take a stockman's situation, and if that won't do, take a pick and shovel on some diggings.'

'Thank you for your advice,' was the polite response, 'but I have tried it once and it does not suit, for I am too well known and a marked man.'

As they talked, Thunderbolt's pistol was always at the ready and his eyes never relaxed, darting towards one road then the other, then back to the verandah—the unceasing vigilance that had helped keep him alive for so long.

With the murderous Clarke brothers of Braidwood in gaol facing trial, the community demanded that the government look to the north again. An increased reward? A few disciplined bushmen acting in the service of the Crown? Would the police and the government do something to relieve them from the terrors of lawless ruffianism, from the abominable pests still defiantly pacing the Queen's highway?

The Acting Inspector General put pen to paper immediately after news reached him of another mail robbery in the Manilla vicinity on 22 May 1867, after Thunderbolt had dared once more to call 'halt' to Her Majesty's mail. Three robberies in a month, two targeting the mail. Three hundred miles travelled between the first and the last. What hope had the police of ever capturing him?

Thunderbolt had been at large for four years, he wrote to the Principal Under Secretary, constantly committing mail robberies and other serious crimes, and being supported by friends and paid harbourers. He advised the government to increase the reward to £200 for the capture of Thunderbolt and to £50 for each of his accomplices. He also reported that he was despatching some of his best bush-constables from the southern districts, now that the Clarke brothers were in gaol, so they could be exclusively employed in the efforts to capture Ward.

The ink had barely dried on the government's new reward notice when Thunderbolt and his mate robbed the northern mail again. In the eight days since the Manilla robbery, they had travelled another 90 miles south to Wallabadah, bailing up another mail coach on 30 May. The same day, news of the increased reward was published in the *Maitland Mercury* and other local papers, and police descended on the district. The bushranging pair wisely disappeared.

A letter to the *Maitland Ensign* railed against the policy of offering such rewards, seeing them as a disincentive for police efficiency rather than an incentive for the public. 'The police seldom capture a bushranger till some fabulous price is set upon his head. From this it would seem that they have no proper sense of duty, and that they will only perform it when they have been bribed with a thousand pounds.'

Continuing his vicious attack, the letter-writer observed that most bushrangers had previously been in and out of gaol for various crimes and had been encouraged in their nefarious course by their treatment while in gaol, that 'hard work on the roads' was a mere farce, and that the country's prisoners were far better off than many hard-working men who were honestly struggling to maintain themselves and their families. He declared that nothing was more efficacious than the lash for punishing bold and reckless criminals, and that it should be regularly used in the country's gaols. 'Boys and youths, especially, ought to be punished in this way; while it would do them no permanent injury, the pain would remain long in their memory.'

'Is it the intention of Government to temporarily increase the police force in the Northern districts?' George Ferrers Pickering demanded of Colonial Secretary Henry Parkes in Parliament on 22 August 1867.

Thunderbolt and Mason had struck again, sticking up two more mail coaches, one north of Murrurundi, the other west of Scone. Although Thunderbolt normally hibernated while Jack Frost roamed the countryside, winter had ended early for this bushranging pair. No one had offered up their heads so they had taken to the roads again.

Pickering and Parkes knew each other well from their journalistic endeavours. Pickering, the editor of *Bell's Life in Sydney and Sporting Chronicle*, was a quiet, genial fellow who delighted in the absurd and had long taken a malicious pleasure in tormenting the police for their persistent failures in apprehending the bushrangers. 'Is it the intention of Government to dispatch a special party with a view to the capture of the bushranger "Thunderbolt"?' he continued. 'Has any additional assistance been given to the ordinary police in these districts for the furtherance of this object?'

Henry Parkes, one-time radical who had mellowed into a gentler liberalness, had himself wagged many a journalistic finger at the inept police as editor of *The Empire* newspaper. But now, as Colonial Secretary, he had different allegiances. 'I think the honourable member will see that it would be extremely injudicious to state publicly what steps have been taken to effect Thunderbolt's capture,' he warned, meaningfully. 'Any such statement must necessarily tend to deflect the object of the Government, and the only good that could result would be good for the bushranger.' He added that if the honourable member wanted to have a quiet conversation, he would be willing to oblige him.

The following issue of *Bell's Life* reported that bushranging was almost exterminated in the colony, that the only ruffian still carrying on his nefarious calling was the arrant coward Thunderbolt, whose reckless conduct reflected his belief in the inadequacy of the police. 'The Government has intimated its determination, however, to run the miscreant down without delay or mercy,' the editor advised the community.

36

Thunderbolt seems to be generally regarded as the last of the Mohicans but I fear it will be found that there are still dozens of young rats in the nests. It will take years to purge the country.

Brisbane Courier, 5 June 1867

For seven or eight miles, they pushed through the scrub at the base of the mountain searching for horseshoe tracks. Locals had told them that the only shod horses in the mountains between Narrabri and Barraba belonged to bushrangers. Faces and hands scratched, clothes torn, the colonial-born trooper and his blacktracker companion eventually reached grassy land where they bedded down for the night. The ground was damp and they had to make beds of sticks and stones to lie upon. Tracking bushrangers was not for the faint-hearted.

Eventually they found some horseshoe tracks and followed them for mile after mile, convinced that these were Thunderbolt's tracks, that he took this route when coming down from the Gallathera Plains to visit his wife. They had been told that Mrs Ward was staying at a sheep station with a part-Aboriginal shepherdess, but they were not sure where. Short of rations, the pair cut across to Barraba, to meet up with another two Braidwood troopers who had also been sent north to find Thunderbolt after the Clarke brothers were apprehended. They swapped partners, deciding that each pair would take a different route in the hope of flushing Thunderbolt from the mountains. They agreed to meet again three days hence.

•

'You are after Thunderbolt but you are off the scent,' announced a surly part-Aboriginal woman who came out of a hut on the second day of their search. She started poking fun at the two 'bushmen', who bantered back good-naturedly. The troopers then rode off in a different direction to their meeting place, not wanting to give their game away.

About a mile further on, the men heard loud noises behind them. Looking back they saw the hut-woman and a friend racing after them on stock horses, the two women an intimidating sight as they stood up in the saddle with their petticoats flapping. The hut-woman rode up to them and said she wanted to introduce her cousin Mary, who had been away visiting her father, but was now back and wanted a husband. She gestured towards Mary, who had reined in her horse on a spur about 200 yards away and was watching the two men with unabashed curiosity.

The colonial-born trooper was instantly suspicious. He eyed her and she eyed him back, and he knew they were in the presence of Mrs Thunderbolt. But he didn't want her to know that he knew, nor to discern his true purpose, so he told the hut-woman that he wanted a wife and would be glad of an introduction.

After much persuasion Mary came over and the colonial-born trooper offered the necessary introductions, calling his partner 'Mr Squatter Dixon' and himself 'Mr MacGatterie'. The women invited them to their hut for breakfast, but the men tried to fob them off. The women insisted that they join them. From the look in Mary's intelligent brown eyes, it was clear that she suspected they knew her identity. The men pleaded urgent business and rode off, but they were unable to elude the women until they reached thick scrub.

Believing they were now alone, the troopers headed for their meeting place, but the other troopers failed to turn up. They left word of a new meeting place, then gathered some more rations and headed back to watch the two women, encountering them about two miles from the hut. That's when they discovered that they hadn't lost the women after all. The pair took great delight in describing where the men had camped and where they obtained their dinner, adding that they knew the men had come back to watch them.

'Checkmated,' thought 'Mr MacGatterie' with resignation, wondering how to turn the situation to his advantage. He allowed the women to persuade them to visit their hut. He soon learnt that his suspicions were correct—that Mary was indeed Thunderbolt's woman—but he obtained little other useful information.

The following morning the men headed across the mountains to Narrabri, a 70-mile journey, in an attempt to give the tenacious women the slip. After resting his horse, 'Mr MacGatterie' returned alone to the mountains to search for Thunderbolt, although he had limited time as he had an appointment in Sydney to give evidence in some Braidwood cases. He visited the women's hut, but Mary was not there. Soon afterwards, a friend told him that Thunderbolt had reportedly gone down to Murrurundi to stick up the mail and that his woman had followed him, having arranged a meeting place in the aftermath. He alerted the local police but they dismissed his news, as they had dismissed all his other information and suggestions.

He wasn't surprised. He had already learnt—at the cost of a badly broken wrist—that most of the British-born troopers were more interested in thwarting the colonial-born troopers' endeavours than in capturing Thunderbolt. 'As things are now,' he would write after leaving the force a few months later, 'Thunderbolt can remain in the mountains five years longer, perfectly secure, with police stations all around him, and he may even become the father of a numerous family.'

While the government was at long last making a concerted effort to capture Thunderbolt, the recruitment decisions they had made so many years previously were continuing to haunt them.

Mary Ann was spotted with Fred and his young accomplice in the aftermath of the coach robberies that sparked further Parliamentary concern. The sightings of the trio were like pins on a map marking their trail north from Merriwa back to Manilla. Then news reached the Tamworth police office on 22 August 1867 that Thunderbolt's gang was camped in the Borah Ranges north-west of Manilla. The bush telegraph was working—in the constabulary's favour, for once. The Tamworth Superintendent instructed Senior Constables Charles Dalton and Peverill Cantrell to try to find them.

Dalton knew Thunderbolt. He had attempted to shoot the bushranger at the Millie gun battle in April 1865. He had followed his tracks after the mail robbery in August 1865, and again in May 1867, but frustratingly had failed to catch up with the scoundrel in either instance. It was just a matter of time, surely.

Accompanied by a blacktracker, the two troopers mounted fresh horses and rode the 28 miles from Tamworth to Manilla, and then a further few miles north-west towards the heavily wooded Borah Ranges. Thunderbolt likely had a number of camps in the vicinity, as he did in other areas—caves with openings visible only to those who knew about them, clearings hidden by thick scrub. Hopefully they would find the bushranger and his little band at one of them.

They headed into the ranges, riding along one track after another, looking for drifts of smoke or gaps in the trees, listening for voices muttering, a horse whinnying, horse-tack jangling, or anything else that might warn of Thunderbolt's presence: stumbling into a bushranger's lair was not only foolish, it was dangerous.

Suddenly the tracker spotted something. They quietly retreated and waited about a mile away, eating their provisions as the shadows lengthened, as the sun's reddish haze faded and the grey gloom wrapped itself around them. They shivered in the brisk evening air, knowing that the night would get much colder. They could not risk lighting a fire to warm themselves.

Long after dark they left their horses hobbled and crept towards the clearing, pausing some distance away in case their movements had alerted anyone. They had to be careful. Thunderbolt had an uncanny knack of sensing danger and his woman had the bush sense of her Aboriginal forebears.

After a while, they dropped to the ground and crawled along the track. They tried to ignore the stones that dug into hands and knees, the scratches from sharp twigs, the grazed knuckles as they bumped into rocks and stumps, the sting of branches clawing at their faces. Rustles in the bushes nearby sent shivers up their spines, but they tried to ignore any thoughts of snakes and spiders and other bush creatures affronted at such an intrusion. At times, six shillings a day didn't seem worth the danger. Only the thought of the reward kept the troopers putting one hand in front of another.

The camp was indeed occupied. The acrid hint of smoke wafted towards them, the snort of a contented horse. They paused and whispered to each other, deciding to wait until dawn before ambushing the inhabitants.

The hours passed. The cold seeped into their bones, stiffening their joints, dulling their senses. A £200 reward . . . £250 if they caught Thunderbolt's young accomplice as well: the words echoed silently with each steamy breath. As the temperature dropped towards zero, as each cold breath bit deeply into their lungs, even the reward seemed hardly worth it.

Gradually, their glazed eyes noticed that the shapes of shrubs and trees were becoming clearer, offset against a lighter background. The veil of darkness was mercifully lifting. They staggered to their feet, their stiff joints protesting, and hobbled towards the camp, guns cocked, hoping to catch the camp dwellers as they awoke, before they registered exactly what was happening.

All that greeted them were the snickers of derision from four horses placidly munching at the grass.

A few hours previously, Mary Ann had awoken suddenly. One of the horses had snorted. She lay there quietly, listening to the rustles in the bushes around her, the warbling of the night-birds. Had the horse sensed another presence? Likely, she decided.

She gently shook the others awake and whispered that they needed to leave the camp, that the horse appeared to have sensed someone and snorted a warning. The trio slipped away, leaving the horses behind, not wanting to make any more noise than necessary. They could always steal more.

They crept towards another camp in the same ranges and bedded down again for the remainder of the night.

The troopers decided they were not giving up that easily. The presence of the four horses indicated that the gang was not far away. With dawn's rays lighting the landscape they circled around to a higher part of the mountain, where the tracker spotted another camp.

The gang was there. They could see them. They crept forward, trying to inch as close as possible before anyone noticed their presence: 100 yards . . . 80 . . . 70 . . . 60 . . .

Then Thunderbolt spotted them. He was getting dressed at that moment, with one boot on and the other in his hand along with his bridle. As his eyes met those of the troopers, he shouted a warning and ran, dropping his boot and bridle as he sprinted into the scrub. Mason bounded after him.

The troopers yelled the usual police command but the bushrangers continued to run. So they raised their rifles and pulled the triggers, pausing for a moment to see if any bodies staggered or tumbled into the bushes. The bushrangers never paused. The troopers sped after them, pushing through scrub, scrambling around large rocks and jumping over smaller ones, a frantic race through a mile of bushland with the occasional pause to fire at the bushrangers. They were cold and stiff from their long night's ambush and their rifles were unwieldy, making it difficult to push through the increasingly dense scrub. Gradually the desperate bushrangers outran them, eventually slipping out of sight altogether.

Exhausted, the troopers stopped and conferred, deciding they should return to the first camp and secure the horses before Thunderbolt's woman took them away and hid them. Without horses and missing a boot, Thunderbolt and his companion would not get far so, if they were lucky, they might stumble upon them again.

Mrs Thunderbolt was back at the camp with the horses, disappointed that the troopers had returned to collect them, but delighted to recount how she had foiled their first ambush. The abject troopers left soon afterwards, taking the four horses with them but leaving her alone to fend for herself. No more attempts to take her into custody: orders from above.

Fred desperately needed more horses—a bushranger's lifeblood, essential for his freedom. Bushrangers who relied on their feet generally had short careers. He and Mason slipped out of the Borah Ranges and stole four more horses from settlers in the district. Free selector William Legard on the Kihi (Maules) Creek was one of their victims, robbed of a horse and two saddles—a hefty loss for one who likely had few assets.

Many claimed that free selectors were the bushrangers' primary supporters, that free selection was one of the primary causes of bushranging as failed selectors took to the roads in an effort to put food on the table. It was just another attempt to blame the less fortunate, while the 'better' classes complacently ignored the roots of the bushranging problem. Although selectors were among the many rural dwellers who supported Thunderbolt—willingly or unwillingly—they were not spared his depredations when his survival was at stake. Whatever he needed he took. Whoever was closest suffered.

Back in the Borah Ranges, Constables James and William Rixon were on foot scouring the area for signs of the bushranging pair. The Rixon cousins were among the small number of colonial-born men who had joined Cowper's police force. New recruits with only seven months on the force, they had not needed the inadequate police training offered to most recruits. They were bushmen who had grown up learning the skills needed to outwit the bushrangers. Appointed to the role of special constables, they had been ordered to use their bush wiles to find and capture the miscreants.

As the Rixon cousins walked the narrow tracks through the ranges, they spotted two horsemen riding along a ridge towards them, the taller bearded bushranger and his young fresh-faced apprentice. They slipped behind some trees as the unwitting bushrangers rode towards them. Silently they waited, their eyes warning each other not to move until the bushrangers came within firing range. The dull thuds as the two horses ambled along the bush trail grew louder, but still they waited until the men were only thirty yards away, then twenty.

'Stand! Police!' they cried as they stepped out from behind the trees. They waited for a moment, their pistols raised, their bodies exposed, to see how the felons responded—as the law demanded.

Thunderbolt and his mate spun their horses and fled.

The Rixons fired after them, the blasts from their guns momentarily silencing the echo of racing hooves. But with the usual luck of the devil, the bushrangers managed to escape.

Tamworth's police superintendent decided there was only one reason why Thunderbolt would have returned to the Borah Ranges after his first encounter with the police: he must be planning to rob the Warialda–Tamworth mailman again. The scoundrel had long shown a fondness for the area, bailing up the mailman five times previously, always striking within ten miles either side of Manilla. The Borah Ranges were undoubtedly his usual hiding place when he was planning a raid.

On 28 August 1867, Constable Lynch from the Moree station and Constable McCausland from Tamworth headed out with the mail from Barraba, travelling south towards Tamworth. Their eyes scoured the trees and bushy areas beside the road, their guns at the ready. They crossed Oakey Creek, where Thunderbolt had robbed the mail two years previously . . . nothing. Past the lookout that provided a bird's-eye view of the road and Manilla township . . . nothing. Down the gentle incline, across the Namoi River, through Manilla itself and south along the road towards Tamworth . . . nothing. Eventually, convinced that the danger was past, the two troopers left the mailman and headed north again.

Beyond Manilla, the pair veered west across the Keepit run, taking the road that skirted the foothills of the Borah Ranges before continuing towards Boggabri. Near Wango Creek, they spotted two horsemen talking to a woman. Noticing that one of the horses looked like Senior Constable Dalton's, they headed towards the group. As they neared, they realised that the horse was not Dalton's after all: they had stumbled upon the two bushrangers on the open plain talking to Thunderbolt's woman. And even though Thunderbolt had clearly managed to steal some more horses, he was still missing his boot—his foot was covered in a black cloth.

The sudden flash of movement and the distinctive pounding of racing hooves were signals that Fred's alert senses were always attuned to. He snapped a command, and he and Mason sped off, their horses' strides quickly lengthening into a furious gallop. He glanced back, his eyes calculating the distance and speed of his pursuers. He snapped another command and, a moment later, their two packhorses slowed to a walk. They had dropped the leads to help increase their own pace.

The pair looked over their shoulders again. Fred barked another order. Their two horses separated, peeling off in different directions.

The police had little trouble deciding which miscreant they should follow. Infamous name, dangerous character, large reward. Hooves pounded along the dirt, guns blazed. Eventually the troopers' horses slowed and wheezed to a stop. They had already worked hard that day, travelling a long distance with the mail. They could go no further.

Disappointedly, the troopers turned around and followed their own tracks back to the meeting place. Along the way, they noticed blood on the trail. Who had been wounded: Thunderbolt or his horse? They knew their own horses had received no injury: the bushrangers had not fired a single shot in any of the skirmishes.

Again they gathered the gang's spare horses. Again they left Mrs Thunderbolt alone. Politics.

'The police are making that part of the country pretty hot for these ruffians,' the *Tamworth Examiner* reported excitedly. 'Thunderbolt is evidently unable or afraid to leave the Borah ranges, and as there are several parties of police out, he may drop into their hands ere long.' A week later the disheartened editor reported that the police had not encountered the gang after all, that the bushrangers had probably escaped from the Borah ranges and gone into hiding again.

Unbeknown to the editor, however, the police were on their way back to Tamworth and were not returning empty-handed.

After the encounter near the Borah Ranges, police from all the Tamworth district stations had descended on the area, spreading out in every direction, asking questions at all the pastoral stations and selectors' plots. Before long, they heard that Mason had been seen around Narrabri, 50 miles north-west of the Borah Ranges, on one of the routes to the north-western plains. This wasn't surprising: Thunderbolt often retreated to the north-western plains when he wanted to hide.

Constables Dalton and Cantrell followed the sighting, calling at the Narrabri police office and asking for reinforcements. By then, the Narrabri police had received word that the lad had been seen around Millie. Four troopers rode out towards Millie, then split up so they could cover more territory. Narrabri's Constable Connatty headed west towards Thalaba Creek. On the morning of 4 September he visited William Dangar's Oreel station to ask questions. There he found Thunderbolt's young apprentice, exhausted and scared, just a boy who had desperately needed a wise counsellor, a father figure who would initiate him into responsible adulthood.

Mason meekly submitted to his arrest, admitting that he was indeed Thunderbolt's companion, and that he had not seen his master since they separated during the police chase. The stolen cheques in his pocket confirmed his identity. He would later plead guilty to the two charges laid against him and petition the court for mercy, saying that Ward had induced him onto the criminal path. The court took pity on him, sentencing him to two three-year terms on the roads, although allowing the terms to be served concurrently.

While Fred might indeed have 'induced' Mason onto a criminal path, he had evidently met little resistance. Only a few days after their meeting, young Mason was scouting the territory before their first robbery and telling a female hostage that he would 'blow her bloody brains out'. Any cloak of civilised behaviour he might previously have worn had been shrugged off with alarming rapidity.

37

No one can confidently say that he will still be living tomorrow.

Euripides

Listen loud, cried Chief Justice Alfred Stephen from Wagga Wagga's judicial pulpit as he sentenced three bushrangers to long terms of imprisonment. He had a message for the youths of Australia. Bushrangers take their victims unarmed and at a disadvantage, he sermonised, and if they meet resistance then murder and bloodshed are the result. Courage? Gallantry? Like all bushrangers, these three plundered rich and poor. What was their reward? Merely a hard, laborious, risky life with the constant fear of apprehension. Of all the country's bushrangers, Thunderbolt alone had long evaded the hands of justice. The others, without exception, had been shot, hanged or imprisoned. Thunderbolt had never committed murder and appeared only at occasional intervals, to which, perhaps, could be attributed his long immunity from capture. But have no doubt: Thunderbolt too would fall into the hands of justice. Bushranging was not a profitable trade.

The Chief Justice's message was not only directed at the tempted but as yet unsullied youths of Australia. It was also intended for Thunderbolt's ears—for all that he ranged a long distance from Wagga Wagga. But Fred was not listening.

'This is not fair,' cried mailman Smith as his mail coach rattled south from Muswellbrook in the early hours of Tuesday morning, 8 October 1867. A horseman had ridden past the coach, then returned and kept pace until the coachman reached the same stretch of road where he had been robbed two weeks previously. 'You should not stick me up twice in a fortnight!' the mailman complained when the horseman, by then recognisable in the glare of the coach lamp as the very same Captain Thunderbolt, presented his revolver.

'It is no matter to you,' retorted Fred. 'I'd stop and rob my own brother!'

Fred looked over at the only passenger, the Sheep Inspector of Scone, and asked if he had any money. The inspector said he had none. Fred left him alone, turning back to the mailman and ordering him to turn out the mailbags.

'I'll not, and I'll see you damned first!'

Cocking his revolver, Fred pushed it close to Smith's head. His tone was menacing as he repeated his demand.

'Shoot away,' Smith challenged. 'I'll not give you the bags.'

In the silence that followed, the night-birds' hoots added to the tension. Smith was determined to assert his manliness after the humiliation of the first robbery, all the while desperately hoping that he had not pushed the 'gentleman bushranger' too far. Fred was astonished at such defiance from a mailman of all people, a man whose own finances were not at stake. He was struggling to keep his anger in check while he decided how best to respond to this challenge to his authority. Meanwhile, the sheep inspector was wishing he'd taken any other damned coach than this one.

Fred turned his gun to face the sheep inspector and repeated his demand. The relieved passenger gladly obliged.

While Mason had ridden to the north-west, Fred had headed south across the Liverpool Ranges, back to the Hunter region of his youth. After twice robbing mailman Smith he fled north again, riding at a furious pace while the police flogged their own horses trying to catch up with him. Back at Manilla, he collected Mary Ann and brought her south to the Hunter region.

The milky-brown countenance, the pert nose and bright, intelligent eyes: Mary Ann's features were instantly recognisable, even in the Scone district where Fred deposited her. The locals noticed her. The police noticed her—and had an idea. Since Thunderbolt generally returned to his woman, perhaps they could use her to lead them to the bushranger. They tried following her, again and again, but the annoying woman kept disappearing before they could track her back to her home. They suspected that locals were sheltering her and providing occasional shelter for Thunderbolt as well, but no one was talking.

Through the medium of the local news correspondent, the police rebuked the harbourers and demanded that all 'loyal people' at the Denison diggings discourage those who were trying to defeat the ends of justice. Help us capture this criminal, they pleaded.

Goulburn River resident William Kirk was becoming increasingly frustrated. The authorities regularly demanded—indeed begged—the community to help them catch the bushrangers and rid the country of their evil curse, but when they attempted to do so the police were 'too busy' to do anything about it.

Kirk had called at the local Denman police station on the evening of Friday 15 November 1867 to report that a man, supposed to be Ward, had been hanging around the district for the past three weeks and had that very day visited his mother-in-law, Mrs Bradford, to purchase some provisions.

The constable's wife apologised and explained that her husband was escorting a prisoner to Muswellbrook, sixteen miles away, and that the village had no other policeman to respond to the sighting. She would pass on his message, however.

Two days later, Constable Patrick McMorrow visited Kirk's mother-in-law at her Mount Hope property some twenty miles from Denman. A widow in her early sixties, Maria Bradford told him that the man first visited her property three weeks previously, although her suspicions had not been raised until his return two days ago, when he had purchased a thirteen-pound block of cheese. 'He never let go of his horse, but held the reins in his hand whilst he was paying for the cheese, and then rode away down the Goulburn River.'

Constable McMorrow told her that unfortunately he was too busy to investigate the sighting at that moment. He had to return to Denman to guard the Cassilis mail run.

On Wednesday 20 November, Kirk sent his son to Denman with the news that Ward had again returned to the Goulburn River. Constable McMorrow was about to leave on a mail run, and could not act on the information; however, he asked the boy to tell his father that the police from Muswell-brook should arrive that day to pursue the sighting.

No one arrived then or later, and the local magistrates would eventually complain officially about the police's 'want of zeal and activity' in pursuing the reports. In fact, the overworked constable had sent a report to his superiors about the sighting. 'Constable McMorrow is at a loss to know what Thunderbolt would want with thirteen pounds of cheese,' wrote Constable McMorrow with a trace of humour, 'but if it was him, he must be still planted about the neighbourhood of Mount Dangar.' McMorrow added that the man had reportedly travelled with the postman to Mrs Bradford's and had mentioned crossing the Manilla mountain on his journey to the Goulburn River. Did that tally with Thunderbolt's movements?

As it transpired, the Muswellbrook police had just heard of a sighting at St Heliers, north-east of Muswellbrook, some 40 miles from the Goulburn River, and were out searching when McMorrow's report reached their office. Believing that the bushranger had left the Goulburn River district, they decided not to pursue Mrs Bradford's sighting. They were still out searching when McMorrow reported the second sighting, informing the Merriwa police when his mail coach halted there on its journey to Cassilis, then telegraphing the Muswellbrook police when the coach arrived at its destination. He was not to know that the Muswellbrook police were out chasing a will-o'-the-wisp while the cheese-munching Thunderbolt was indeed hanging around Mrs Bradford's playing with her grandchildren.

Local magistrate Thomas Hungerford had also heard the reports. On Friday 22 November he wrote to Sub-Inspector Thorpe at Singleton, stating that the bushranger had visited Kitton's and Kirk's within the previous few days and had purchased provisions from Mrs Bradford's three times during the week. He demanded that the police take some action.

Hungerford's brief letter made no attempt to account for the bushranger's extended visit to the district, except for his brief conclusion: 'He has a mate somewhere in the neighbourhood, sick.'

A new accomplice? Mary Ann? Someone or something kept drawing Thunderbolt back to the Goulburn River district, and the news of his presence was spreading.

Parliamentarian James White, who lived at Martindale only a few miles south of Denman, heard that Thunderbolt had apparently visited Kirk's again on the Thursday morning, making 'anxious enquiries'. White penned his own letter to Sub-Inspector Thorpe at Singleton advising of the sightings and rebuking the police for their failure to act on the initial reports. 'In giving this information, these people are acting in good faith and with a view to assist the ends of justice and when they thus put themselves out of the way voluntarily to assist the police, they should be treated with every consideration.'

And he enclosed a letter that Mrs Bradford had written to him. 'There is a man near my place these last three weeks, supposed to be the bushranger Thunderbolt,' she reported. 'He just came and reported to me that he has a woman in the bush. She is in a dying state, if not dead.'

Fred had appeared at her cottage door on Saturday morning, 23 November 1867, armed with pistols and a hasty assurance that he had no intention of scaring or injuring anyone, that he was desperate for help. 'My woman is very ill in the bush. Will you bring her to your house and take care of her?' he begged. 'She will not be long alive.'

Thunderbolt described how to find his woman, explaining that he had marked the location so she would not miss it. Mrs Bradford hesitated, seeming reluctant to assist him, perhaps deterred by the woman's scandalous behaviour or her Aboriginal heritage.

'If you will not promise to take charge of her, I will ask the clergyman to report to the police to have her removed and attended to,' he warned. He had seen Reverend William White driving past his bush camp, so he knew the Muswellbrook clergyman was making one of his periodic visits to the district and could be relied upon to take charge of the dying woman. He also thought that such a threat would spur Mrs Bradford into action: she would not want to seem un-Christian.

Mrs Bradford agreed to help and Fred repeated his instructions. Finally he said, 'I am leaving this part of the country as it is getting too hot for me'—apparently unaware that Mrs Bradford was largely responsible for this particular sizzle.

After he rode off, Mrs Bradford scribbled her note to James White, ordering the messenger to bypass the Denman police station and continue directly to the Parliamentarian's Martindale property. There was little point in alerting the police for a third time, considering their lack of response on the previous occasions.

Helped by an employee or grandson, she hitched a horse to her cart and drove into the lonely mountains, lurching for a couple of miles along the rocky dirt trail as her horse pulled them up the steady incline from the river. She looked above the splashes of spring flowers, above the ferns and tangle of shrubs, up into the hoary old branches, seeking the distinctive marker Thunderbolt said he had left. Then she spotted it: a blanket dangling from the top of a tree.

She looked down again and saw her. Thunderbolt's woman was lying on the ground, protected from the sun's burning rays by a latticework of leaves. A horse was tied up nearby, a piteous sign of Thunderbolt's continued hopefulness, as if Mount Hope itself might work a miracle and allow his woman to wake up recovered and ride away.

Mrs Bradford hurried to the woman's side and bent down to check on her, noticing the sallow countenance and the hint of Aboriginality in her features. Laboured breaths, closed eyes: the woman was unconscious.

They carefully lifted her and carried her to the cart's tray, settling her as comfortably as they could. Then they jolted back down the rough track towards Mrs Bradford's homestead.

The news reached the Muswellbrook police around 9 pm that Saturday night: Thunderbolt was at the Goulburn River again. He and his woman were at Mrs Bradford's out near Mount Dangar. His woman was dying. Hurry!

Constable Boon immediately called for Dr Brown's services and the pair rode out for Mrs Bradford's. They had a long distance to travel, 35 miles or so through the dense mantle of darkness. Likely Thunderbolt himself would be long gone by the time they arrived.

The bush telegraph had also passed the news to Reverend William White, who hastened to Mrs Bradford's where he found Thunderbolt's helpmeet lying on a bed. There was little he could do but sit with the woman, praying for her soul, holding her hand if she seemed to stir. As they attended her during the long November night, Mrs Bradford told him of Thunderbolt's visits and the police's failure to respond, mentioning how easily they could have captured the bushranger because he kept hanging around her cottage playing with the children.

Around nine o'clock on Sunday morning, 24 November 1867, their patient emitted a distinctive rattling breath. With Reverend White praying over her, Thunderbolt's woman took her last breath.

'Inflammation of the lungs' was Dr Brown's verdict at the inquest a few days later, the inflammation itself brought on by exposure. Not tuberculosis, as many would later claim—a condition then referred to as consumption or phthisis—but 'pneumonia'.

Dr Brown and the Muswellbrook constable had arrived at Mrs Bradford's just a few minutes after Reverend White closed the eyes of the 'poor misguided woman' and finished his prayers for her soul. Autopsy, inquest, then a hole dug in the hard-baked earth. As her makeshift coffin was lowered, no one was there to mourn her—no family, no friends, not even Thunderbolt himself.

Fred was indeed long gone. He was making the most of the police's distraction, attempting to hold up a mail coach near Merriwa while the police were looking for him down at the Goulburn River.

38

The descriptions of the ravages of the bushrangers are commonly followed by some reference to the police which reads like a sneer, and probably is intended as such. Yet no man who knows the country, and the conditions under which these persons act, has any right to sneer.

Sydney Morning Herald, 7 February 1865

'A bushranger is at Mr Blanch's public house at Church Gully!' The exhausted hawker who burst through the doors of the Uralla police station shortly after 4 pm on Wednesday 25 May 1870 was not simply passing on a message—he was a victim. Giovanni Cappasotti had been driving his cart south along the Great North Road about 3 pm that Wednesday afternoon when a man on a grey horse rode up to him.

'Stand!' the man yelled, pointing a revolver at the hawker. 'Give up your money!'

The frightened hawker pulled out his purse and handed over £3 13s 6d, a small nugget of gold, and a watch and chain. The bushranger looked into his cart and saw a locked jewellery box. He picked it up and demanded the key. After Cappasotti's trembling fingers opened it, the bushranger lifted out some jewellery, including two pairs of gold earrings. 'What is your name and where have you come from?' he asked as he pocketed the hawker's valuable wares.

Cappasotti said he had been to the Uralla races and was now heading to Tamworth.

'Don't go back to Uralla or I'll have your life,' was the blunt advice. Then the bushranger demanded his revolver.

'I don't have one.'

'If I find one in your cart or any more money, I will burn everything in the dray!'

The bushranger began rifling through the wares but found nothing further of interest. He then kindly invited the hawker to join him for a drink. Cappasotti accepted—desperately needing a stiff drink after the frightening encounter—and they stepped into John Blanch's Royal Oak inn, which was immediately to hand. 'A glass of port wine,' Cappasotti begged the publican, while the bushranger informed the other patrons that he was shouting drinks all round.

The wary publican drew the requested drinks. He knew the calling of his latest patron, having himself been robbed earlier that afternoon.

Blanch and his wife had been returning from Uralla around 2 pm when they saw a horseman near their door, a man riding a grey horse and leading a darker one. The man rode towards them, crossing their path around 200 yards from the inn, and calling out 'Bail up!'

Blanch laughed.

'No humbugging,' the bushranger snapped. 'You would not give me the bottle of rum a few nights ago.'

Blanch immediately recognised the disgruntled patron of a few night's previously. The man had asked for a quart of rum, offering in payment a £5 money order on Wyndhams of Dalwood which the innkeeper had refused to accept—wisely, as it would now appear.

'I am a robber,' the bushranger then announced as he pulled out his revolver, demanding that the publican hand over his money. Blanch offered him the only money he was carrying, four shillings and sixpence, but the robber rejected it. 'The missus has the money on her,' he said cunningly. 'I am laid onto you.'

Mrs Blanch pulled out her purse and began picking out the silver— gentlemen bushrangers reportedly did not accept coppers. 'None of your picking,' he said to her. 'Give me the leather bag!' Yet eventually he chose not to take the silver, after all.

The robber, meanwhile, had been scanning the road in both directions, keeping an eye out for trouble. He noticed some men with packhorses coming towards the inn from the south and he asked Blanch who they were. The publican didn't know.

'Remain where you are,' the bushranger commanded, then rode towards the newcomers. Soon afterwards, he allowed Blanch to enter his inn and ordered the other hostages inside as well. His work done, the carousing could begin.

After finishing his own drink, Cappasotti asked if he could leave.

'Yes. As far as you like that way,' said the bushranger pointing south towards Bendemeer, 'but on peril of your life do not go that way.' And he pointed back towards Uralla. The bushranger clearly knew there was a police station at Uralla—a mere four miles away.

The hawker climbed into his cart and drove south as ordered. As his horse clip-clopped along the road, he ruminated on his ordeal, his anger rising and with it his courage. A mile or two beyond the inn, he saw a selector's property and drew up outside the homestead. He recounted his tale and asked to borrow a saddle, saying that he was going for the police. He untied his horse from the cart's shafts and strapped on the saddle. Leaving his cart at the cottage, he galloped through the bush for a few miles until he was well past the inn. From there, he defiantly took the main road back to Uralla. His horse was knocked up by the time he reached the outskirts, and he ran the rest of the way to the police station, barely able to speak on his arrival from exhaustion and stress. Finally, as he puffed and panted through his tale, he said, 'If you go quick, you will catch him!'

Uralla's Senior Constable John Mulhall knew Blanch's inn well. It lay only a few hundred yards from the Big Rock—or the Split Rock, as it was often called—the strange granite outcrop where Captain Thunderbolt had commenced his notorious career six-and-a-half years previously. He himself had been within a hair's breadth of catching Thunderbolt at that time, following him into the rock itself but finding only his discarded shotgun and bridle. Was the bushranger trying his luck again at that same vantage point?

Thunderbolt's robberies had been sporadic in the previous seventeen months, but the year prior to that had been particularly active. Early in 1868, he had taken on another young accomplice, thirteen-year-old William Monckton. They had enjoyed a riotous year, bailing up mail coaches and travellers, stealing horses, robbing stores and Chinamen—mostly marauding in the New England district, although they had steered clear of the Big Rock itself. The pair had parted company in December of that same year, a couple of weeks before the government raised Thunderbolt's reward to £400. Soon afterwards Monckton was apprehended and sent to gaol. Thunderbolt went quiet again, venturing out for only a handful of mail and hawker robberies, as impossible to catch as his heavenly namesake. He still appeared to be roaming the New England district; at least he was a month previously, when he robbed a hawker on the Paradise run between Inverell and Armidale. If he had returned to pillage at the Big Rock, they might be able to catch him, Mulhall realised.

Mulhall's offsider, Constable Alexander Binney Walker, sprinted up to the police stables and saddled their two horses. He was in civilian clothes rather than his usual uniform, but he was not about to waste time changing.

The hawker stood by the stable door watching Walker saddle and mount. As the two troopers galloped south towards the Big Rock, he continued to watch them until they were out of sight, wondering if the robber would still be there, or if his own mad dash through the bush had been an exhausting exercise in futility.

Publican John Blanch had been keeping his eye on the bushranger, who was having a splendid time. The villain had ordered an old chap to pay for the first shout, having left the man with enough coins to do so after he robbed him. The bushranger himself had shouted the second round—although he hadn't worried about actually paying for the drinks. But he did pay for the third, handing over five shillings and magnanimously refusing to accept any change. And he paid for the fourth and the fifth as well, singing and dancing all the while.

Increasingly garrulous, he lolled over the bar and asked the publican, 'Do you know who I am?'

Blanch admitted that he didn't. Their encounter the few days previously was the only time he had seen him.

'I am called Ward, or Thunderbolt,' the bushranger said. He then paused for a moment, as if expecting to hear a drum roll—as if the heavens themselves would confirm his identity—then continued: 'Do you remember an occurrence some seven years ago with Thunderbolt at the Rocks?' When the publican admitted that he had heard about it, the robber announced, 'I am the man. I got shot in the knee.'

Blanch didn't ask why he would return to the scene of his disastrous inaugural bushranging spree, the occasion when he received his first and only gunshot wound. As he watched Thunderbolt return to his carousing he could only wonder at the fellow's recklessness. Someone could have ridden . . . indeed someone could have *walked* the short distance to the Uralla police station and back in the hours since he had bailed them up.

Senior Constable Mulhall pushed his horse hard as he raced the four miles south to Uralla. As senior officer, he had the better horse and he was soon half a mile in front of Walker as he crested the Big Rock hill and sped down towards Blanch's inn, 300 yards to the south. He could see two men on grey horses near the inn's fence. One immediately began riding towards him, while the second followed. Other victims, perhaps, keen to report further robberies to the distinctively dressed trooper? A few strides on, he realised that the first horseman wasn't interested in reporting anything at all—particularly to a policeman.

Young Michael Coughlan was not about to let the bushranger take the horse. It belonged to his master, Mr Huxham, who would be furious if anything happened to it.

Coughlan had been travelling to Armidale with the horse on a lead when the bushranger bailed him up near Blanch's inn and demanded that he hand it over. Then the bushranger took the saddle from his own horse and strapped it to Huxham's, and was testing its speed and agility when they saw the rider's silhouette on the Big Rock hill.

The bushranger immediately rode towards the Big Rock and Coughlan turned his own horse to follow. He was almost close enough to grab the reins of Huxham's horse when the bushranger pulled out his revolver. A blast followed and a bullet whistled towards the newcomer. And the newcomer fired back.

Constable Walker heard the gunshot blasts even before he reached the top of the Big Rock hill. As he pulled out his pistol, Mulhall's horse crested the hill again.

'There they are!' Mulhall shouted, pointing back towards the inn. 'I have exchanged shots with them. Go ahead. Shoot the wretch!'

Walker slammed his heels into his horse's flanks and raced towards the two horsemen. They looked up and saw him, but neither fired a shot. Instead, the older curly-headed man turned his horse towards the inn, towards the escape route to the south provided by the road beyond it. Strangely, the younger horseman blocked him, crossing his horse in front of his companion's as if trying to stop the man from reaching the road.

Thwarted in his attempt to escape south and with a horseman barrelling towards him from the north, the older man wheeled his horse and raced west along Blanch's fence. His companion took off after him, and the pair followed the line of fence until they reached the bush.

As Walker hurtled after them, his horse stumbled in some swampy soil. He pulled on the reins, desperately trying to keep his horse on its feet, by sheer willpower if nothing else, and accidentally knocked his trigger. The sharp report echoed into the distance.

The older man swivelled in his saddle and looked back at him, then fired his own gun. Walker's next shot was deliberate, despatched with a heartfelt prayer towards the fleeing pair. It did little more than pluck at the dust.

The older bushranger turned towards his companion and shouted something, and the younger man instantly peeled off to the right and galloped away. In their wake, Walker looked from one to the other. Should he follow the shooter or the younger fellow?

Suddenly, the shooter stuck out his arm and beckoned to his pursuer. 'Come on!' he yelled.

'All right!' Walker shouted back and the chase was on.

Walker was only six days shy of his twenty-third birthday when the pursuit of his life began. A three-year veteran, he was one of only eighty or so colonial-born policemen in the 800-strong New South Wales police force, the powers-that-be having largely ignored the calls for more bushmen recruits, despite their desperate need for troopers as skilled as the bushrangers themselves. Quiet and unassuming, he was a fearless rider, a man driven by intelligence and determination rather than recklessness. He was short for a trooper, only five feet five inches in his knitted socks, and slender, appearing little more than a stripling, but he was a bushman through and through, the type of man—some would later say—who was responsible for the phrase 'swears like a trooper'. A cool head on wiry bushman shoulders, Walker was a clever choice for a trooper stationed in Thunderbolt country.

The two horses streaked across the countryside, their riders crouched low in the saddle, heels pummelling, reins whipping, like steeplechase jockeys racing towards an invisible spire. A body swivelled and fired. An answering crack echoed across the dales, but still they kept riding. Across dry creek beds and muddy gullies; through a deep waterhole dotted with stumpy grass tussocks where the bushranger floundered and his pursuer gained ground. Up and down shrubby slopes and across grassy knolls, one horseman doubling like a hare with the other dogging his hooves, their wild race unseen except by the astonished birds who twittered their encouragement. On they rode, eventually bounding up another slope. There, at the ridge, the bushranger stopped and turned to face his adversary.

He paused for a moment, stark against the setting sun, Bellerophon mounted on his Pegasus. Then he charged.

Walker had eased his reins slightly as he looked up the slope and saw the bushranger turning his horse around. Why had the fellow stopped? Perhaps there was an obstruction on the other side. Then the bushranger galloped straight towards him.

A thousand pounds of bone and muscle gathered momentum as horse and rider charged down the hillside on a collision course—nary a whoop nor a primeval roar, just a silent determination. Did the bushranger intend to ram him, to send him tumbling down the hill, or was it merely a show of aggression, with the pup expected to turn tail and flee when the wily old fox bared its sharp teeth?

Walker had only a moment to decide what to do, but he didn't need even that moment. He raised his gun and pulled the trigger.

Strangely, the bushranger didn't fire back. Nor did he use his horse as a battle ram. Instead, he slipped past and continued downhill, his momentum gaining him a considerable lead over his pursuer, who had to wheel his own horse and pick up speed again.

On they raced, the intrepid pup now a worthy adversary in the eyes of the old fox. Leaping over fallen timber, bounding across another grassy concourse, with the pursuer gaining ground again. Six or seven circuitous miles they had travelled when they neared the junction of Kentucky Creek and Chilcott Swamp Creek, only a mile away from Blanch's inn.

Walker was beginning to feel desperate. Time was on the bushranger's side. The sun's brilliance had faded as it slipped below the horizon. The grey shadows were creeping across the countryside. Soon darkness would blanket the countryside. Soon the bushranger would be able to ride into the night and disappear.

He followed the bushranger over a spur and saw a large waterhole in front of them, about 350 yards in length. The man rode up to the water's edge and dropped from his saddle, throwing himself into the water, then wading and swimming towards the other side.

Walker could not risk following on his horse, or on foot for that matter. He was inches shorter and only a lightweight, so the bushranger would have the advantage in a physical fight. The man could drown him as easily as shoot him.

But why had the bushranger left his horse and taken to the water? He must be intending to come back for it—he wouldn't get far without it.

Walker watched the bushranger wallowing for a moment before making up his mind. He rode down to the bank and grabbed the reins of the bushranger's horse. He led it about 25 yards away from the water. Then he shot it.

Fred reached the other shore and scrambled up the bank, then turned around to check on his pursuer. That's when he saw his mount lying on the ground. That last shot from his pursuer's gun was the death knell for his chances of easily escaping into the darkness, as the crafty young pup had evidently realised.

He pulled off his heavy coat as he watched his pursuer gallop towards the end of the waterhole, where it was shallow enough to cross without swimming. Then he took to his heels, sprinting along the bank in the same direction until he saw his pursuer riding towards him. Having reached a narrow channel, about eighteen feet wide, he dashed into the water and waded across to the other side, then began running again.

About 20 yards further on, he saw his pursuer reach the creek bank opposite. He slowed, then stopped running and turned to face his nemesis.

'You had better surrender before you do any harm,' Walker calmly advised, pretending he had the upper hand but knowing otherwise. The bushranger could dart away at any moment and race for the large upper waterhole, then swim across and hide among the granite boulders until darkness fell.

'I will not,' the bushranger snapped, lifting his pistol and pointing it at his pursuer. He paused for a moment then asked curiously, 'Who are you?'

'Never mind who I am.'

'What is your name?' the bushranger repeated. Walker decided to tell him.

'Are you a trooper?'

'Yes,' said the man dressed in civilian clothes.

'Are you a married man?'

The wary trooper replied that indeed he was.

The bushranger shook his revolver at the young trooper as if reprimanding a naughty boy. 'Walker, keep back,' he warned. 'You are a married man; remember your family.'

Walker eyed him for a moment. Was there a lingering spark of humanity behind the haggard face, a genuine concern for the well-being of a trooper's young wife and children? Perhaps the question merely reflected the fellow's reluctance to cold-bloodedly kill another. Or maybe it was just a ruse to make him draw back, or at least hesitate, to offer the vital moment of delay that would allow the bushranger to escape. Whatever the reason, the bushranger's concern failed to deter him. 'I thought about all that,' said Walker dismissively. 'Will you surrender?'

'No,' was the emphatic response. 'I will die first.'

'All right,' said the young trooper decisively, 'it's you or I for it.' And he plunged his horse into the water.

In that moment, high drama almost turned into farce. Or tragedy. His horse went head-first under the water, perhaps stumbling onto its knees from exhaustion or the suddenness of the move. Walker remained seated in his saddle, but he was left high and dry—from the waist up at least —a prime target for the revolver pointing towards him.

But no bullet blasted from the felon's pistol. Nor did the bushranger turn around and try to flee. Instead, he threw himself into the water, one hand still clutching the revolver, and began floundering towards the young trooper—perhaps hoping to pull him from his horse and clamber on himself.

Walker aimed his own gun and fired.

With a mighty splash the bushranger fell into the water and sank for a moment. Then he rose again with water pouring off him, as if a monster had surfaced from the depths of the ocean. He flung himself at the trooper, attempting to pull him off his horse and into the water.

Walker had fired his last bullet, so he smashed his revolver down onto the bushranger's forehead. The man sank again. When next he surfaced he had blood oozing from his mouth.

The bushranger's pistol was gone, dropped into the murky depths, no longer a threat even if the bushranger himself might still have been. Walker turned his horse and rode back to the bank, then dismounted and waded into the waist-high water. He grabbed the man under the arms and pulled him out of the water, then laid him on the bank.

For a moment he stood looking at the balding bushranger, a moment of homage to the first man he had killed. Then he rode back to Blanch's inn to seek help in collecting the body. There he learnt what he had already suspected: the bushranger was none other than the notorious Captain Thunderbolt.

St George had just slain the final dragon. With Thunderbolt's death, the New South Wales bushranging epidemic had officially ended, eight years after the Eugowra gold escort robbery and the establishment of the new police force. In the intervening years, the police had gradually overcome most of their teething problems and were catching or killing the bushrangers, while the bushrangers themselves had outlived their community welcome. The bushranging era should have ended several years previously, but Fred's survival against the odds had dragged out the era—the 'gentleman robber' was the longest-roaming bushranger in Australian history.

But now it was all over. Thunderbolt was no more.

39

Excitement was the breath of life to him. Without it, existence lost its savour and its most potent charm.

William Monckton, *Three Years with Thunderbolt*

Frederick Wordsworth Ward had just ticked the second-last item in the noble outlaw script: he had 'died game'. He had also died in a manner that lovers of irony would appreciate: his first and last bushranging sprees near the Big Rock, soon to become known as Thunderbolt's Rock; his first and last gunshot wounds received in the same vicinity. Hubris indeed.

But there was one more act in the Captain Thunderbolt play.

At Blanch's inn at 2.15 the following afternoon, Armidale's police magistrate opened an inquiry into the bushranger's death. Constable Walker described the dramatic events of the previous day. The dauntless trooper would be promoted to Senior Constable a few days later and to Sergeant soon after, eventually retiring at the age of sixty-five, a much-loved and respected Inspector of Police. Senior Constable Mulhall also testified, as did hawker Giovanni Cappasotti and innkeeper John Blanch. 'Killed from a gunshot wound inflicted by a Member of Police while in the execution of his duty,' announced the police magistrate.

Then came the matter of the bushranger's identity. Innkeeper Blanch reported that the bushranger had identified himself as 'Ward or Thunderbolt' and had mentioned the Big Rock shooting some years previously when he received a gunshot wound to his knee. Armidale's Senior Sergeant John

George Balls, who had worked as Task Work Clerk on Cockatoo Island before joining the police force in 1862, testified that he had minutely examined the body and compared it with the *Police Gazette*'s description of Cockatoo Island escapee Frederick Ward and that it tallied in every way, including the distinctive mole and warts. He added that he could also personally identify the body as being that of Fred Ward, having known Ward while on Cockatoo Island.

Bushman George William Pearson advised that he could also identify the body as that of Fred Ward, having bumped into the fellow only two days previously. The pair had recognised each other as one-time workmates at Cooyal. Pearson did not mention that he had also acted as Fred's only defence witness at his Mudgee horse-stealing trial a decade previously—that they were more than mere acquaintances who might have forgotten each other after such a long time.

Finally, Armidale's medical advisor to the government, Samuel Pearce Spasshatt, confirmed that the body matched the *Police Gazette* description. He provided his own list of the body's physical features, a list that included not only the distinctive mole and warts but an old scar visible on the bushranger's left knee: the gunshot wound inflicted at the Big Rock some seven years previously. He also reported that Walker's bullet had hit Ward below the left collarbone towards the armpit and had travelled through both lungs before exiting through the chest three inches below the right shoulderblade. It was a wound he could not have survived.

After hearing the various testimonies, the police magistrate had no doubt whatsoever that the body was indeed that of Cockatoo Island escapee Frederick Ward, the bushranger Captain Thunderbolt.

Two days later, Fred's body was lying in an open coffin on display at the Uralla Courthouse when a fifteen-year-old lad walked in. By an astonishing piece of fortuitous timing, Fred's young apprentice, William Monckton, had arrived the previous night on the mail coach, having been journeying home to Yarrowitch after his release from gaol in Sydney. The lad ventured over to the coffin, then looked at the uncovered face. 'Oh yes that's him, right enough!' he said, without the slightest hesitation. He later pointed out the scar from the gunshot wound Fred had received at the Big Rock seven years previously, and signed a statement declaring that the body was indeed that of Frederick Ward, commonly called Thunderbolt.

The authorities were satisfied. The lid was screwed down the following afternoon, after photographs and a head-cast had been taken, after hundreds of people had lined up to view the body, touching it, attempting to steal a lock of curly hair, trying to add lustre to their own lives by this vicarious contact with fame—or infamy. Not a tear was shed, only a silent prayer muttered as the handful of attendees watched the coffin being lowered into the ground at Uralla cemetery.

'Had his intellect and natural capabilities been turned to good instead of evil,' moralised the *Armidale Telegraph*, 'he might at the present time have been a useful and worthy member of society, instead of leaving a memory covered with disgrace and his body the tenant of a felon's grave.'

With his burial, the curtain should have fallen on Frederick Ward, alias Captain Thunderbolt, but 'dying game' was not the final item on the outlaw script. It was that the outlaw hero 'cannot be allowed to die', that he must survive his own demise through chance or trickery, despite all evidence to the contrary. Accordingly, Fred Ward—who proclaimed that the government forced his return to crime by granting him no peace— has been refused any peace even in death. Even today, 140 years later, the curtain has *still* not fallen.

Yet by a strange twist, those who refuse to accept the evidence of Fred Ward's death at Kentucky Creek in 1870 are likewise refusing to grant him the dignity of 'dying game'. By declaring instead that he slipped away to America—as some have said—they have reduced his dramatic denouement to the ignominy of a cockroach scuttling through a ship's bowels and down a foot-ramp onto alien soil.

Fred Ward—skilled bushman, courageous Cockatoo Island escapee and gentleman robber—was little more than a thug to the broader community, and a coward, for that matter. Most saw flight rather than fight as the refuge of a craven cur. Even worthies wanted evil-doers to at least show some evidence of 'manliness'. Moreover, while memories of Thunderbolt might have lingered among those he robbed or befriended, his deeds were never daring enough to ensure him a distinguished place in the history books: he didn't steal £14,000 of gold or kidnap a gold commissioner; he didn't bail up a large town, or lumber through a hail of bullets dressed in a makeshift suit of armour; he didn't kill. To step into the bushranging hall of infamy, to have his name emblazoned on an outlaw legend plaque, Fred needed to 'die game' or to be betrayed. And on the banks of Kentucky Creek on 25 May 1870, Constable Walker's bullet propelled him through that iniquitous doorway.

No one else saw the events of that late autumn afternoon, so only Walker's evocative account survives. Yet ironically again, it is this policeman's account that grants Fred Ward his ultimate outlaw hero nobility. Between the lines we read of a felon who fired at the police because he knew they were out to capture or kill him, but who fired upon his 'civilian' pursuer only after believing that his pursuer had fired first—self-defence in another language. We read of a supreme bushman who resorted not simply to horsemanship in his endeavours to evade the law, but who showed pluck and cunning in his attempts to escape. We sense a man who chose to engage with other people even at such a critical moment, which would explain why he was generally liked, as Magistrate Lethbridge had attested; the vicissitudes of penal servitude and his years holding guns to people's heads had not deprived him of all human compassion. We hear curiosity in his questions about his pursuer's identity, revealing admiration for the lad's horsemanship and cunning in shooting Fred's horse, a metaphorical tip of his hat to a worthy adversary. We hear concern for the well-being of the young trooper's family and are reminded that Fred himself was a one-time husband and father, whose own foolishness—while altruistic in intention—had resulted in his return to Cockatoo Island and family's abandonment, and his consequent reincarnation as the bushranger Thunderbolt. And finally we are left in no doubt that this wily man, who had previously chosen to flee rather than fight because it was the wisest choice for all concerned, had decided, when faced with the loss of his usual escape route, to fight for his life rather than suffer the ignominy of a bullet to the back.

Of course, Fred was not to know that Walker had only one more bullet left. Yet he knew first-hand of the poor standard of police marksmanship. And he knew that the cloak of darkness would soon hide him, that escape was still possible even though he had no horse to carry him away. Indeed he had escaped on foot after his first Big Rock bush-ranging spree, and after a number of police chases in the years that followed.

A short time later, a bush acquaintance remarked in the *Armidale Telegraph* that Fred's thoughts and actions had previously focused only upon evading capture, yet at Kentucky Creek his recklessness suggested a desire to court death rather than shun it. Seemingly, in that critical moment, Fred decided that if he was going to die, this was as good a time as any and that he would ensure that he 'died game'.

Ward and Walker. In the century-and-a-half since the Uralla shooting, the pair have been bound together in a symbiotic relationship, Siamese twins joined at the hip by a revolver. Thunderbolt aficionados have loved to loathe Walker, not only because he shot their hero, but because the shooting launched Walker's own meritorious career. They have tried, meta-phorically, to shoot down Walker himself by dishonouring his courage and intrepidity. They have failed to understand that Walker was not the only beneficiary of that dramatic shooting—that his actions transformed their outlaw hero into an outlaw legend, whose name will forever resound in the annals of bushranging history.

Frederick Ward was the last of the New South Wales 'noble' bushrangers, those granted outlaw hero status by a rural community desperately in need of a political voice. The rural community was blamed for causing the bushranging epidemic, for rocking the bushrangers' cradles in their own nurseries, for hiding and feeding them, for idolising them. Ironically, this blame had the unexpected effect of empowering the rural community. It was not a giant leap for them to realise, if only implicitly, that if they 'caused' the bushranging epidemic, then they were largely responsible for the downfall of two governments: political power indeed. The birth of rural unions during the next few decades reflected the rural community's willingness to shoulder responsibility for their own future, the realisation that they were not riding a bridle-less horse, that by pulling on their own reins they had some choice as to which path they would follow.

While New South Wales society consequently no longer needed outlaw heroes, the bushrangers were not forgotten. It seems appropriate somehow, definitely ironic—perhaps even poetic justice in a strange way—that a nation founded as a penal settlement should have such criminals as its folk heroes; indeed, that its greatest folk hero should be an armour-plated bushranger—Australian society continuing to thumb its nose at authority, to some extent, as did our convict forebears.

Yet these bushranging criminals were a different breed to the pick-pockets and poachers, the footpads and forgers transported from Britain during the convict era—men, women and children whose world was circumscribed by desperate, soul-destroying poverty. Most of the bush-rangers were not driven to crime through financial desperation. They had a choice. And in the eyes of the rural community—those who also had no need to resort to crime for survival but had limited opportunities for advancement—that choice empowered the bushrangers. These were men who epitomised the ideal bushman, men who embodied the values of the native-born. To those gazing up at their horse-mounted figures, arrogant with skill and bravado, they seemed like warriors, avengers of justice, righters of wrongs—self-interested though their criminality might truly have been.

A life-size horse-mounted statue honours Frederick Ward in Uralla. A small plaque honours his policeman nemesis. The larrikin streak lives on—in the Australian psyche, at least.

EPILOGUE

J oseph Hopkins dipped his fingers into the makeshift font and gently dabbed the forehead of the infant he was cradling, intoning the words that would wash away the newborn's sins and usher him into God's grace. Then the young Methodist preacher handed the boy back to his mother, and began filling in the register he carried as he visited his flock in his extensive Tamworth Circuit, and welcomed others like the infant Frederick Wordsworth Ward into his church's embrace. He wrote the day's date in the first column and added the child's Christian names in the second. Parents' names? He looked up into the milky-brown countenance of the boy's mother.

'Frederick Wordsworth and Mary Ann Ward,' she told him.

Abode?

'Carroll,' she said, the village where the ceremony was taking place.

Birthdate? And he looked up again at the child's mother.

'26 August 1868.'

November 1867. The press had been titillated, treating the matter as if it was a salacious joke. 'The highwayman Thunderbolt, who appears to have a peculiar penchant for the fair sex, lately took unto himself another fair dulcinea who, having proved false to her lawful lord, determined to share the vicissitudes of her gallant admirer and made a *bolt* with him although probably unaccompanied by the noises of *thunder*,' wrote a *Maitland Mercury* correspondent, amused at his own wit. 'But alas! like all earthly pleasures, the bliss of the new couple was only of a very short duration. The honeymoon proved a short and disastrous one.'

The woman who died near Mount Hope in November 1867 was not Mary Ann Bugg—although, even today, many think it was. Fred's roving eye had alighted upon young Louisa Jane Clark, another part-Aboriginal woman, who only two months previously had married Robert Mason of Rouchel near Scone. Apparently Cranky Bob—as her husband was nicknamed— was most unhappy when Thunderbolt swept into the district and tried to whisk away his 'Yellow Long', as Louisa was often called. 'By what authority do you do such a thing?' Mason had demanded of the arrogant bushranger, who answered, simply, by pointing his revolver. Fred stole a horse for Louisa from the nearby Segenhoe station and the pair rode away.

'It is said that the highwayman's lady is in an interesting situation,' reported the *Maitland Ensign*, 'and that he wants this one to wait on her.' But the correspondent doubted the truth of that rumour and predicted jealousy between the two women. 'One of them, like Delilah of old, will deliver him into the hands of the Philistines.'

Had Mary Ann known? The first report of Fred's elopement was published in the *Maitland Ensign* on 18 November 1867, and others soon followed, some referring to Thunderbolt's latest amour, others simply mentioning the death of his woman, Louisa Mason or 'Yellow Long'. Even if Mary Ann had not read the newspapers, she was residing only a short distance from the scene of the elopement. She must have heard the rumours, surely.

Fred returned to the Denison diggings after leaving the dying Louisa Mason, and collected Mary Ann again, taking her north with him to the Manilla district. She fell pregnant late in November or early in December 1867. They separated soon afterwards, never to be seen together again. Perhaps Fred abandoned her for the pleasures of the bushranging lifestyle— which included the freedom to enjoy other women's company—or maybe Mary Ann spurned him through anger at his public betrayal. Whatever the circumstances, she loved him enough not to deliver him up to the colonial Philistines, and she honoured his memory by bestowing his name upon the last of their children.

In the aftermath of their separation, Mary Ann found work at Griffin's inn at Carroll—an odd choice, considering that it was the site of one of Thunderbolt's shoot-outs with the police. When Fred's namesake was born there in August 1868, the innkeeper's wife and the wife of another robbery victim assisted Mary Ann with her delivery. No doubt they wondered if the sins of the father would be visited on this particular infant boy.

Mary Ann chose not to acknowledge Fred's paternity when she registered her son's birth a couple of months later, and referred to herself only by her legal married name, Mary Ann Baker. Her decision to deny Fred this right, to refuse him this honour, reflected a complex web of emotions: a feeling of abandonment, and perhaps a petty spitefulness; a desire to hide her past, and a determination to get on with her life. Yet her son's given names would serve as an ever-present reminder of a past she seemingly wished to forget.

It is possible that Fred never learnt that he had fathered a son, and even that Fred Junior was unaware that Captain Thunderbolt was his father. Apparently Mary Ann decided to keep that information secret after she met up again with John Burrows, after they re-established the relationship that had ended in the mid-1850s. Fred Junior claimed Burrows as his father, yet he inherited his birth father's passion for horses, working as a groom in his youth and as a horse-trainer in later years. Frederick Wordsworth Burrows never married and died in 1937, leaving no known offspring.

Another five children fathered by John Burrows brought Mary Ann's total to fifteen over a thirty-year period, with thirteen living to adult-hood—a magnificent fecundity at a time when the Aboriginal birth-rate was so low that many were claiming the race was 'dying out'. Of course, Aboriginality is not determined by paternity alone, or even maternity for that matter. Today it largely rests on the foundation of cultural self-identification, the principle that we are who we perceive ourselves to be, who we accept ourselves to be. As the colonial-born also discovered, empowerment lies in making a personal choice.

Yet it would be hard to classify the most notorious and arguably the most intriguing Aboriginal woman in nineteenth-century Australia as 'Aboriginal' on the grounds of cultural self-identification alone. Mary Ann disclaimed her Aboriginal heritage, preferring to tell acquaintances that her native roots lay in a foreign soil, among the headstrong Maori of the islands of New Zealand. It was an expedient fiction, one such a proud and strong-willed woman might not have felt impelled to tell if she had been born in a future era. She apparently severed ties with her Bugg relations, as she was not named on her father's death certificate in 1879, and as Bugg family stories suggest that she disappeared and died soon after Thunderbolt's demise. Perhaps their failure to come to her aid after her fabric possession charge caused a family rift. Whether her children knew the truth about her Aboriginal heritage—about their own heritage—is uncertain. The information they provided for Mary Ann's death certificate and obituary indicates that they maintained the fiction, then and probably thereafter.

Mary Ann lived out her years in the Mudgee district, among the frosty winters and baking summers of the western slopes. In 1876 she used the 'selection' regulations to conditionally purchase 40 acres of land at Warrable Flat in Cooyal Parish, calling herself Mary Ann Burrows and claiming to be a widow—only spinsters and widows could select land in their own right—although she gave birth to the last of John Burrows' children a few years later. She resided on the block for the three years required by the regulations and made £52 worth of 'improvements', building a house and hut, erecting fencing, and clearing and cultivating eight acres of land. In 1879 she sold out to a neighbouring squatter, Samuel Alfred Blackman. Likely, she was 'dummying' for Blackman throughout that period, paid to maintain another fiction so he could increase his own landholdings illegally and at minimal cost. Her disdain for the colonial land laws was understandable, considering her Aboriginal heritage—unless it reflected her continued contempt for authority's rules in general.

That Mary Ann must have felt disdain for the law is obvious. Indeed, by most definitions, her own actions during her years as Thunderbolt's accomplice were in breach of the law. She had harboured an escaped convict and helped him evade the police. She had scouted for him in his role as a bushranger, and had lived off the proceeds of his crimes. Yet Mary Ann had not intentionally become a 'criminal'. She was not one who bucked the rules and flouted the conventions simply because she was expected to abide by them. She was not a rebel who found her cause in the criminal world of bushranging. Nor was she a feeble moth drawn towards a vibrant flame by a craving for excitement, the 'groupie' of a future era trying to add meaning to an inconsequential life by living vicariously through the fame or infamy of others—power by proxy. Rather, she fell in love: deeply, passionately, irrevocably. When she, like Oedipus, stood at the crossroads, she made a choice. She could have ignored Fred's overtures after he escaped from Cockatoo Island and began bushranging. Instead she chose to follow him along the criminal-on-the-run bridle path.

Destiny played little part in Mary Ann's choice. Her Aboriginal heritage had not precluded her from a place in colonial society: she was better educated than most and had been married to a 'white' man in a Christian church—evidence that she was considered socially acceptable, at the very least. She was not suffering the exigencies of poverty and in need of a husband to support herself and her children. She was not living in an environment where desperation drove many to a life of crime, and the choice to resist was the more difficult. Yet her decision to become a bushranger's accomplice reflected her own dissatisfaction with the social status quo, with the law.

While the Thunderbolts' actions might have breached the legal boundaries, clearly they did not breach Mary Ann's own moral boundaries. That she did have moral boundaries is shown by Fred's behaviour when in her company—and out of it. His most active bushranging periods occurred when he had male accomplices: his two gangs in 1865, young Mason in 1867 and young Monckton in 1868. When he was alone with Mary Ann, he committed few crimes—mainly just horse and cattle thefts. She seems to have been able to control his excesses until his own need for adventure and excitement drove him to seek fulfilment in the company of other men. Ultimately, the sense of power that bushranging gave him and the adulation of his supporters proved more satisfying to him than Mary Ann's love.

Like Fred and his fellow bushrangers, Mary Ann was no revolutionary trying to overthrow the colonial power structure. She was not seeking retribution for the sufferings of her mother's people, although she was happy to show her contempt for the colonial authorities. No doubt her behaviour was partly driven by the slights she had personally endured and—consciously or unconsciously—the sufferings of her mother's people. That she was also a convict's child, a rural dweller and a woman perhaps contributed as well. But anger at the treatment meted out to Fred and the consequences of that treatment for her own life and family undoubtedly underpinned much of her 'criminality'.

In the aftermath of her Thunderbolt years, Mary Ann became a woman of secrets, living a life of obscurity, mundane and no doubt dreary in comparison, but safe. She hid her complex web of marital relationships, so much so that even her children seemed confused about the paternity of some of their siblings. Colonial society in the late 1800s was a society of secrets: many dwelt in the sunburnt country for reasons they would prefer others not to know. Rural dwellers in particular knew to ask few questions—about anything in the past. Mary Ann's family was evidently among them.

Dressed in mourning's ebony robes, they stood in the Mudgee cemetery on 24 April 1905, listening to a Church of England layman offering up prayers for the soul of their mother who had died two days previously. Mary Ann's health had been declining for the previous year, preventing her from working as a nurse and supporting herself financially, as she had done in the aftermath of John Burrows' death.

They watched the wooden coffin being lowered into her grave, the sods being shovelled back in. Perhaps they tossed in some autumn flowers as they wiped tears from their eyes.

A *Mudgee Guardian* pressman asked them about their mother's life, and they mentioned her birth in the Bay of Islands, New Zealand, and her arrival in the Bathurst district in 1851. Apart from some references to her children, they said little else about her life in the half-century that followed.

As the pressman sat down to write his short piece about the 'very old Mudgee identity', he had no idea that he had just missed the story of a lifetime—that this senile old woman had once been the feared 'right-hand man' of the notorious Captain Thunderbolt, the feisty young woman who had proudly called herself the Captain's Lady.

AUTHOR'S NOTE AND ACKNOWLEDGEMENTS

It began as a whisper: Thunderbolt did not die; the police shot someone else. It grew louder: the police conspired to hide the bushranger's true identity; he fled to America; he died in Canada. Some 140 years later, it had become a shout: Government conspiracy! We demand the police files! We demand the truth! And Parliament was listening. On 18 March 2010, under Standing Order 53, the New South Wales Legislative Council ordered the Governor of New South Wales to release the police records relating to Thunderbolt's death.

On the advice of the Executive Council, the Lieutenant Governor rejected the order, advising that these pre-federation records were available to the public at the government archives, the State Records Authority of New South Wales. The rejection letter also contained a decided rebuke: that while the documents may be of historical interest, they were not reasonably necessary in order for the House to review the conduct of the state's Executive Government—the grounds for Standing Order 53— and that it was arguably inappropriate for the House to seek to use its constitutional powers to ask the Governor to undertake this research.

On public interest grounds, State Records decided to source and photocopy the requested records—which merely provided further evidence that the dead bushranger was indeed Frederick Wordsworth Ward. The voices piped up again: We demand access to the 'secret' police records! Those determined to believe that their hero had 'lived on' were claiming that the cover-up was still being perpetrated by the government—indeed, that it reached as high as the office of the current Governor of New South Wales.

Ironically, they had become a self-perpetuating part of the Thunderbolt mythology, evidence of the potency of the outlaw hero motifs. Their Parliamentary demand is treated in detail in the article 'Exposing an Exposé: Fact versus fiction in the resurrection of Captain Thunderbolt' by David Andrew Roberts and Carol Baxter (*Journal of Australian Studies*, vol. 36, no. 1, 2012).

I discovered the fascinating tale of Captain Thunderbolt and his lady when I googled 'female bushranger', having decided I would like to write about such a person—if she existed. After receiving the contract from Allen & Unwin, I innocently stepped into the Thunderbolt and Mary Ann paddock—and found I had stumbled into a minefield. Warring parties were camped on either side. Tensions ran high. Punches had been thrown and—some said—knives pulled: all over events that had happened (or, some claimed, had not happened) one-and-a-half centuries ago.

Historian Henry Reynolds concluded his article 'Aboriginal–European contact history: Problems and issues' with the quote: 'To be a good judge [of history], we must not care what the truth is we are seeking. We must be concerned only with finding it.' This wise principle guides my research. I try to close my eyes to everything that has previously been published and start from scratch—the null hypothesis approach. And I shut my ears to those who care too deeply what particular 'truths' are found. In redoing all the Thunderbolt research using primary-source records, I discovered something astonishing. Many of the long-accepted beliefs—the Thunderbolt traditions—are not facts but myths repeated ad infinitum for the last 150 years. For example, it has long been claimed that Fred escaped Cockatoo Island through Mary Ann's assistance, that she took a job in Balmain and swam from there to Cockatoo Island to help him flee, and that they then swam back to Balmain where she hid him in a disused boiler; in truth, Mary Ann remained in the Dungog district during Fred's second incarceration, as a letter from the local magistrate and reports from the local press make clear. The facts I discovered—the evidence-based history—provide the foundation for the narrative in *Captain Thunderbolt and His Lady*.

In the northern districts of New South Wales, everyone with deeply planted roots seems to have a Thunderbolt story—which is not surprising since he roamed there for many years and survived partly through community support. However, most stories are unsubstantiated anecdotes that are impossible to verify. Inevitably, given human nature, some are apocryphal—rural myths that have been absorbed into a family's or community's history—while others have been distorted over time. Unsubstantiated history is mythology. Since the aim of this book is to communicate the facts rather than the myths, anecdotal information has been omitted unless it tallies neatly with and expands upon information found in primary-source records.

Naturally, it is essential to substantiate the results of my research. To this end, I have prepared annotated timelines for Fred and Mary Ann and the other important people in their lives, detailing all the primary-source information discovered and the sources for that information. My original intention was to publish these timelines at the end of the book but they proved too large. Instead, they are published on the internet, along with analyses of the evidence regarding the many controversial claims concerning Fred and Mary Ann and their families. The website address is:

www.thunderboltbushranger.com.au

As for pictures: while one of Mary Ann Bugg has survived and is displayed at the start of the book, the only known pictures of Fred Ward are post mortem—grotesque by any description. For that reason, the full view is included here and not alongside Mary Ann's.

History provides the best stories: full of drama and action, mystery and romance. Fiction writers often draw upon true stories for their novels, yet history does not need to be fictionalised to be interesting. Dialogue doesn't need to be made up; it's already there in the records, in the 'he said'/'she said' statements found in newspaper reports, court transcripts and letters. Character similarly; the forces that drive protagonists can be glimpsed between the lines; 'actions speak louder than words'. The scenic backdrop doesn't need to be plucked from the imagination; rather background research provides locational descriptions as well as the relevant

Captain Thunderbolt, photographed
by Mr Cunningham of Armidale at the
morgue (Mitchell Library, State Library
of New South Wales, a837032)

historical and social backdrops. It's all there, for those willing and able to undertake the extensive research necessary to find it. But what brings this research alive for the reader (or, conversely, sends them to sleep!), is how it is transformed into a story.

Most historians telling the tales of history act as an omniscient narrator and use a passive-voice writing style. In effect, it seems as if the narrator is standing at a safe distance and viewing the events of history through a motion-picture lens, as if they are seeing a single stream of events and are merely recounting what they see. But history isn't pre-packaged in this way. Historians make it easy for the reader. They draw their information from reports and letters and journals, from newspaper articles and court records and other documents left by individuals and entities, then transform the results of their research into a seamless narrative. In so doing, however, they can lose the impact of the participants' own accounts, the immediacy of personal experience that novelists have to imagine in order to bring their fiction to life.

In my style of writing history—which falls under the umbrella of narrative or literary or creative non-fiction (it has many names rather than incarnations)—I allow the participants to live their own stories, wherever possible, by having the narrator step into their shoes and experience what they experienced as recounted in their own statements. This offers the immediacy of fiction without fictionalising the narrative. It also allows me to use the active rather than passive voice, so readers feel as if they themselves are participating in the event rather than watching from the sidelines. With the addition of a dash of atmosphere and a pinch of imagination, and the use of structural and literary techniques that novelists also use, history comes alive for the reader. So alive, in fact, that some readers (and reviewers, even) have mistakenly thought I write fictionalised history.

In writing a story like *Captain Thunderbolt and His Lady*, the intention is not simply to exhaustively research the past and communicate social history in a vivid and readable style; it is to open readers' eyes to the past so they can understand the present and ponder the future. What does the story of a bushranging hero tell us? Firstly, that communities need heroes. As evidence, consider the plethora of action-hero movies made in recent years; the fact that more are coming indicates that they are filling a psychological need. And secondly, that the disenfranchised often communicate their dissatisfaction in a manner that the establishment cannot fail to hear, a manner that—however illegal or immoral—can receive broad community support. While history was once largely performed on a parochial stage, it now has a global theatre. Graham Seal argues in *The Outlaw Legend* that the now deceased Osama bin Laden and other religiously motivated terrorists, as well as young computer hackers, are among today's 'outlaw heroes'. It is a thought-provoking observation.

My family complain that I always thank them last, but they can rest assured that to me they always come first: my husband Allan Ashmore and children Camillie and Jaiden, who have long given up asking 'what's for dinner?' and now simply ask if there is anything for dinner—without a question-mark on the end, as if they know the answer and are already thinking about what they can make for themselves; thank you all, and my mother Jill Baxter as well, for your love and forbearance.

To my publisher at Allen & Unwin, Rebecca Kaiser, and my literary agent, Tara Wynne: your continued support and calm confidence mean so much to me (particularly when I am panicking about getting the manuscript finished on time).

Author's note and acknowledgements

To editor Angela Handley, copyeditor Katri Hilden, proofreader Kate Goldsworthy, and readers Michael Flynn (author of *The Second Fleet: Britain's Grim Convict Armada of 1790*), my boss and mentor, Keith Johnson (co-founder of the Biographical Database of Australia), Bruce Kercher, Emeritus Professor of Law and Dr David Andrew Roberts, Senior Lecturer in Australian History at the University of New England (both wonderful historians and writers), friend Mike Elliott, and genealogist Kate Wingrove (who is always right!): my heartfelt thanks for your assistance. My book is so much the better for all your insightful comments and input—and thank goodness you pulled me up on those silly little mistakes!

A big thankyou also to: Jillian Oppenheimer, who paved the way with her articles about Mary Ann Bugg; Lynne Robinson, Honorary Research Officer for the Mudgee Historical Society, who helped determine the truth about Mary Ann Bugg's children and death; Thunderbolt researchers Bob Cummins and Arnold Goode (and special thanks to Arnold and to Bernie Woodward for taking me out to Kentucky Creek, where Thunderbolt died, and to young Patrick Roberts for the pleasure of his company during that trip); Annie Hutchison nee Fletcher of Kentucky Station, Kent Mayo of McCrossins Mill, and Pat Bradley, who holds the Milford memoir; Dr Pennie Pemberton of the Noel Butlin Archives Centre; Dr Ann Curthoys, ARC Professorial Fellow of the University of Sydney; Associate Professor Kirsten Mackenzie and Dr Vicki Grieves, also of the University of Sydney; Dr Lisa Ford, Lecturer in Australian Studies at the University of New South Wales; Associate Professor John Ryan of the University of New England; and Dr Brian Walsh, late of Tocal College. Thanks also to the Ward and Bugg researchers/connections: Lorraine Beckers, Vicki Brown, Berry Cameron, Pam Dewberry, Vicki Dobson, Norma Fisher, Merelynn Miller, Harry Millward, Michael Mina, Neil Robins and Peter Tunchon; Peter Tonkin; and to Gail Davis and the staff of State Records of New South Wales, and everyone else who provided assistance both large and small.

BIBLIOGRAPHY

State Records of New South Wales

Calendar of Persons Tried on Criminal Charges in Sydney Courts (NRS 831 & 1861)

Certificate of Freedom Butts (NRS 12210)

Cockatoo Island: Copies of Letters Sent (NRS 2079)

Cockatoo Island: Daily State of the Establishment, 1856–63 (NRS 2087)

Cockatoo Island: General Regulations and Gaol Orders, 1849–57 (NRS 2088)

Cockatoo Island: Monthly Return (NRS 2091)

Cockatoo Island: Punishment Book (NRS 2090)

Cockatoo Island: Return of Prisoners (NRS 2086)

Cockatoo Island: Transportation Register (Colonial) (NRS 2084)

Cockatoo Island: Visitors Book (NRS 2089)

Colonial Secretary: Copies of Letters Sent re Convicts (NRS 962)

Colonial Secretary: Copies of Letters to Sheriff (NRS 1000)

Colonial Secretary: Registers and Correspondence Files (NRS 922)

Conditional Pardons (NRS 1172)

Convict Death Register (NRS 12213)

Convict Indents (NRS 12188)

Darlinghurst Gaol: Description Book (NRS 2523)

Darlinghurst Gaol: Discharge Book (NRS 2142)

Darlinghurst Gaol: Entrance Book—Indexes and Registers (NRS 2135 & 2134)

Darlinghurst Gaol: Photographic Description Book (NRS 2138)

Maitland Gaol: Description Book (NRS 2320)

Maitland Gaol: Discharge Book (NRS 2329)

Maitland Gaol: Entrance Book (NRS 2317 & 2318)

Maitland Gaol: Record of Prisoner Convictions and Sentences (NRS 2334)

Miscellaneous Correspondence Relating to Aborigines (NRS 13696)

Notebooks of Mr Justice Cheeke: Quarter Sessions (NRS 5777)

Police Service Registers (NRS 10943)

Registers of Baptisms, Marriages and Burials (NRS 12937)

Sheriff: Copies of Letters Sent (NRS 13210)

Supreme Court of New South Wales: Memoranda selected from 24 years of missionary engagements in the S.S. Islands and Australia by L.E. Threlkeld: 5th Report—Annual report of the Aboriginal Mission at Lake Macquarie, NSW, 1835 (NRS 13705)

Supreme Court, Sydney and on Circuit: Papers and Depositions (NRS 880)

Supreme Court, Sydney and on Circuit: Session Returns of Persons Tried and Convicted (NRS 906)

Tickets-of-Leave Butts (NRS 12202)

State and Mitchell Libraries of New South Wales

Historical Records of Australia, Series 1

New South Wales Government Gazette

New South Wales Legislative Council: Votes & Proceedings

Newspapers/magazines (hardcopy and online):

Armidale & District Historical Society: Journal and Proceedings

Armidale Chronicle

Armidale Express

The Australian

Bathurst Free Press

Bathurst Times

Bell's Life in Sydney

The Colonist

The Empire

Hobart Town Courier

Maitland Ensign

Maitland Mercury

Manning River News

The Monitor

Moreton Bay Courier/Brisbane Courier

Mudgee Guardian

Mudgee Liberal

National Indigenous Times
Newcastle Chronicle & Hunter River News
New South Wales Police Gazette
Northern Daily Leader
Northern Times
Singleton Times
Sydney Gazette
Sydney Herald/Sydney Morning Herald
Sydney Mail
Walkabout
Western Post
Newspaper cuttings file: Ward, F.

New South Wales Parliamentary Library

Legislative Assembly Tabled Papers: Statement of John Garbutt Regarding
Ludwig Leichhardt, 1857 (NSWPA LA TP 1857/409)

Noel Butlin Archives Centre, Australian National University, Canberra

Commissioner Colonel Henry Dumaresq's Letter Book, September 1836–January
1838 (117/8/1)
Despatches from NSW to Australian Agricultural Company London Office (78/1)
Draft map of Port Stephens Estate and District, circa 1848, by PG King (1/464
Map A38)

Registry of Births, Deaths and Marriages, NSW

Birth, marriage and death certificates
Online indexes

Other sources

Armstrong, William W., 'Some early recollections of the town and district of
Rylstone, etc.' (Mitchell Library ref: Q981.6/A—typescript)
Atkins, Thomas (Rev.), *Reminiscences of twelve years' residence in Tasmania and
New South Wales, Norfolk Island, and Moreton Bay, Calcutta, Madras, and Cape
Town, the United States of America, and the Canadas*, Malvern, 1869
Attwood, Bain, *The Making of the Aborigines*, Allen & Unwin, Sydney, 1989
Australian Dictionary of Biography Online <http://adbonline.anu.edu.au>
Bailliere's New South Wales Gazetteer & Road Guide, F.F. Bailliere, Sydney, 1870
Bailliere's Queensland Gazetteer & Road Guide, F.F. Bailliere, Sydney, 1876
Bairstow, Damaris, *A Million Pounds, a Million Acres: The pioneer settlement of the
Australian Agricultural Company*, D. Bairstow, Cremorne (NSW), 2003

Balfour, J.O., *A Sketch of New South Wales*, Smith, Elder & Co., London, 1845

Baxter, Carol J. (ed.), *General Muster and Land & Stock Muster of New South Wales 1822*, ABGR in association with SAG, Sydney, 1988

Baxter, Carol J. (ed.), *General Muster List of NSW 1823, 1824, 1825*, ABGR in association with SAG, Sydney, 1999

Bettez, Silvia Cristina, 'Mixed-race women and epistemologies of belonging', *Frontier: A Journal of Women Studies*, vol. 31, no. 1 (2010), pp. 142–65

Bhathal, Ragbir, 'Astronomy in Aboriginal culture', *Astronomy & Geophysics*, vol. 47 (2006), pp. 5:27–5:30

Bierens, Kali, 'The Captain's Lady: Mary Ann Bugg', Honours Thesis, University of Tasmania, 2008 <http://eprints.utas.edu.au/8748/2/02_Bierens_complete. PDF>

Blackton, Charles S., 'Australian nationality and nationalism, 1850–1900', *Journal of Australian Historical Studies*, vol. 9 (1961), no. 36, pp. 351–67

Blainey, Geoffrey, *The Rush That Never Ended*, Melbourne University Press, 2003

Blainey, Geoffrey, *Triumph of the Nomads: A history of ancient Australia*, Macmillan, Melbourne, 1975

Blee, Jill, *Gold: Greed, innovation, daring and wealth*, Exisle, Wollombi (NSW), 2007

Blomfield, Geoffrey, *Baal Belbora: The end of the dancing*, Colonial Research Society, Armidale, 1981

Bowd, D.G., *A Short History of Wilberforce, the Fifth Macquarie Town*, Hawkesbury Consolidated Press, Windsor, 1980

Bradshaw, Jack, *The True History of the Australian Bushrangers*, Workers Trustees, Sydney, c1925

Brennan, Martin, 'Police history of notorious bushrangers of New South Wales and Van Diemen's Land' (Mitchell Library ref: CY 934—typescript)

Breton, Lieutenant, *Excursions in New South Wales, Western Australian and Van Diemen's Land*, Richard Bentley, London, 1833

Broome, Richard, *Aboriginal Australians: A history since 1788*, Allen & Unwin, Sydney, 2010

Broome, Richard, 'Aboriginal victims and voyagers, confronting frontier myths', *Journal of Australian Studies*, vol. 18 (1994), no. 42, pp. 70–7

Brouwer, David, *Captain Thunderbolt: Horsebreaker to bushranger*, CB Alexander Foundation, Tocal (NSW), 2007

Bubacz, Beryl M., 'The Female and Male Orphan Schools in New South Wales, 1801–1850', PhD Doctorate, University of Sydney, 2007 <http://ses.library.usyd. edu.au/handle/2123/2474?mode=full&submit_simple=Show+full+item +record>

Buchanan, D., *Political Portraits of Some Members of Parliament* (Mitchell Library ref: DSM 308/Pa.14), Davies & Co., Sydney, 1863

Butlin, N.G., Cromwell, C.W. & Suthern, K.L. (eds), *General Return of Convicts in NSW 1837*, Australian Biographical & Genealogical Record, Sydney, 1987

Cochrane, Peter, *Colonial Ambition*, Melbourne University Press, 2006

Connelly, C.J., *Mudgee: A history of the town*, C.J. Connelly, St Marys (NSW), c1993

Convicts of the Australian Agricultural Company 1825–1850, Port Stephens Family History Society, Port Stephens (NSW), 2004

Crowley, Frank, *A Documentary History of Australia—Volume 1: Colonial Australia, 1788–1840*, Nelson, Melbourne, 1980

Crowley, Frank, *A Documentary History of Australia—Volume 2: Colonial Australia, 1841–1874*, Nelson, Melbourne, 1980

Crittendon, V., 'Frederick Ward alias Captain Thunderbolt', *Australian Dictionary of Biography*, vol. 6 (1851–90), pp. 353–4

Cunningham, Peter, *Two years in New South Wales; A series of letters comprising sketches of the actual state of society in that colony; of its peculiar advantages to emigrants; of its topography, natural history, &c. &c.*, Henry Colburn, London, 1827

Cummins, Bob, *Thunderbolt: A biography of the last of New South Wales' notorious bushrangers*, R.K. Cummins, Moree (NSW), 1987

Day, David, 'Aliens in a hostile land: A re-appraisal of Australian history', *Journal of Australian Studies*, vol. 12 (1988), no. 23, pp. 3–15

Derrincourt, William, *Old Convict Days*, New Amsterdam Book Company, New York, 1889

Dingle, A.E., '"The Truly Magnificent Thirst": An historical survey of Australian drinking habits', *Journal of Australian Historical Studies*, vol. 19 (1980), no. 75, pp. 227–49

Eburn, Michael, 'Outlawry in colonial Australia: The Felons Apprehension Acts 1865–1899', *Australian & New Zealand Law & History E-journal*, 2005 <www.anzlhsejournal.auckland.ac.nz/pdfs_2005/Eburn.pdf>

Elder, Bruce, *Blood on the Wattle: Massacres and maltreatment of Aboriginal Australians since 1788*, New Holland, Sydney, 2003

Eldershaw, F., *Australia as It Really Is*, Darton & Co., London, 1854

Ellis, Jean A., *Australia's Aboriginal Heritage*, Collins Dove, Melbourne, 1994

Engel, B.A, Winn, J. & Ward, J., *Tea Gardens, Hawks Nest and Northern Port Stephens: A local history of the pioneers of the northern shores of Port Stephens*, privately published, New Lambton (NSW), 2000

Evans, Raymond & Thorpe, Bill, 'Commanding men: Masculinities and the convict system', *Journal of Australian Studies*, vol. 22 (1998), no. 56, pp. 17–34

Ferry, John, *Thematic History of Parry Shire* <www.tamworth.nsw.gov.au/.../2.07.5_Parry_Shire_Community_Based_Heritage_Study_Attachment-small.pdf.aspx>

Fitzpatrick, J.C.L., *The Good Old Days: Being a record of facts and reminiscences concerning the Hawkesbury district*, William Dymock, Sydney, 1900

Frost, Alan, 'New South Wales as terra nullius: The British denial of Aboriginal land rights', *Journal of Australian Historical Studies*, vol. 19 (1981), no. 77, pp. 513–23

Gammage, Bill, 'Historical reconsiderations VIII: Who gained and who was meant to gain from land selection in New South Wales?', *Journal of Australian Historical Studies*, vol. 24 (1990), no. 94, pp. 104–22

Garran, Andrew, *Australia: The first hundred years*, Ure Smith, Sydney, 1974 (a facsimile of *Picturesque Atlas of Australia*, 1886)

Gregson, J., *The Australian Agricultural Company 1824–1875*, Angus & Robertson, Sydney, 1907

Greville's Official Post Office Directory & Gazetteer of New South Wales 1875–1877, Greville & Co., Sydney, c1875

Grieves, Vicki, *Aboriginal Spirituality: Aboriginal philosophy, the basis of Aboriginal social and emotional wellbeing*, Discussion Paper no. 9, Cooperative Research Centre for Aboriginal Health, Darwin, 2009

Hall's Business, Professional & Pastoral Directory of NSW for 1895, Hall's Mercantile Agency, Sydney, 1895

Hanna, Cliff, *Bandits on the Great North Road*, Nimrod Publications, Newcastle, 1993

Hanson, William, *The Pastoral Possessions of New South Wales*, Gibbs, Shallard & Co., Sydney, 1889

Harris, Alexander, *A Guide to Port Stephens in NSW, the colony of the Australian Agricultural Company*, William S. Ore, London, 1849

Harris, Godfrey, *Mudgee Past and Present: An historical guide to the first town of the central tablelands*, Commonwealth Jubilee Committee for the Mudgee Municipal Council, Mudgee, 1951

Hart, Jennifer, 'Religion and social control in the mid-nineteenth century', in A.P. Donajgrodzki (ed.), *Social Control in Nineteenth Century Britain*, Croom Helm, London, 1977

Harwood, Frances, 'Myth, memory and the oral tradition: Cicero in the Trobriands', *American Anthropologist*, vol. 78, no. 4 (Dec 1976), pp. 783–96

Hatheway, Frank, *Bushrangers Bold*, White Lion Publishers, London, 1972

Haygarth, H.W., *Recollections of bush life in Australia, during a residence of eight years in the interior*, John Murray, London, 1864

Henderson, John, *Excursions and adventures in New South Wales: with pictures of squatting and of life in the bush: an account of the climate, productions, and natural history of the colony, and of the manners and customs of the natives, with advice to emigrants, &c*, W. Shobert, London, 1851

Higgins, Matthew, *Gold and Water: A history of Sofala and the Turon Goldfields*, Robstar, Bathurst (NSW), 1990

Hirst, John, *Freedom on the Fatal Shore: Australia's first colony*, Black Inc., Melbourne, 2008

Hood, John, *Australia and the East: Being a journal narrative of a voyage to NSW in an emigrant ship with a residence of some months in Sydney and the Bush, and the route home by way of India and Egypt in the years 1841 and 1842*, John Murray, London, 1843

Joy, W. & Prior, T., *The Bushrangers*, Shakespeare Head Press, Sydney, 1963

Joubert, Jules, *Shavings and Scrapes from Many Parts*, A.S. Gordon, Hobart, 1890

Kerr, James Semple, *Cockatoo Island, Penal and Institutional Remains: An analysis of documentary and physical evidence and an assessment of the cultural significance of the penal and institutional remains above the escarpment*, National Trust of Australia (NSW), 1984

Kirkby, Dianne, 'Frontier violence: Ethnohistory and aboriginal resistance in California and New South Wales, 1770–1840', *Journal of Australian Studies*, vol. 4 (1980), no. 6, pp. 36–48

Lake, Marilyn, 'Historical reconsiderations IV: The politics of respectability: Identifying the masculinist concept', *Journal of Australian Historical Studies*, vol. 22 (1986), no. 86, pp. 116–31

Lang, John Dunmore, *An historical and statistical account of New South Wales: including a visit to the gold regions, and a description of the mines: with an estimate of the probable results of the great discovery*, Longman, Brown, Green, and Longmans, 1852

McCombie, Thomas, *Arabin, or the Adventures of a Colonist in NSW*, Simmonds & Ward, London, 1845

McGrath, Ann, 'The white man's looking glass: Aboriginal-colonial gender relations at Port Jackson', *Journal of Australian Historical Studies*, vol. 24 (1990), no. 95, pp. 189–206

Mackenzie, David (Rev.), *Ten Years in Australia*, William S. Orr & Co., London, 1851

McLaren, Glen & Cooper, William, 'The Saddle-Horse', *Journal of Australian Studies*, vol. 20 (1996), no. 49, pp. 21–32

Maclehose, James, *Maclehose's picture of Sydney and strangers' guide in New South Wales for 1839: embellished with forty four engravings of the public buildings *and picturesque land and water views in and near Sydney*, J. Maclehose, Sydney, c1839

Macleod, A.R., *The Transformation of Manellae: A history of Manilla*, A.R. Macleod, Manilla, 1949

Macnab, Ken & Ward, Russel, 'The nature and nurture of the first generation of native-born Australians', *Journal of Australian Historical Studies*, vol. 10 (1962), no. 39, pp. 289–308

Mantle, Nan, 'Shifting in the saddle', *Journal of Australian Studies*, vol. 20 (1996), no. 49, pp. 33–8

Marjoribanks, Alexander, *Travels in New South Wales*, Smith, Elder & Co., London, 1847

Maxwell, Eileen, *Written in Gold: The story of Gulgong*, E. Maxwell, Gulgong, 1998

Mendham, Roy, *The Dictionary of Australian Bushrangers*, Hawthorn Press, Melbourne, 1975

Milford, Frederick, 'The Diary of Dr Frederick Milford', held by the Bradley family

Moore, Clive, 'Colonial manhood and masculinities', *Journal of Australian Studies*, vol. 22 (1998), no. 56, pp. 35–50

Morris, Barry, 'Frontier colonialism as a culture of terror', *Journal of Australian Studies*, vol. 16 (1992), no. 35, pp. 72–87

Mossman, S. & Banister, T., *Australia visited and revisited: a narrative of recent travels and old experiences in Victoria and New South Wales*, Addey & Co., London, 1853

Muecke, Stephen & Shoemaker, Adam, *Aboriginal Australians: First nations of an ancient continent*, Thames & Hudson, London, 2004

Mundy, Godfrey Charles, *Our antipodes, or, Residence and rambles in the Australasian colonies: with a glimpse of the goldfields*, Richard Bentley, London, 1852

Neal, David, 'Free society, penal colony, slave society, prison?', *Journal of Australian Historical Studies*, vol. 22 (1987), no. 89, pp. 497–518

New South Wales Legislative Council, 'Cockatoo Island: Report from the Board of Enquiry into the management of Cockatoo Island, 1858' (Mitchell Library ref: Q365.99441/2)

O'Malley, Pat, 'Class conflict, land and social banditry: Bushranging in nineteenth century Australia', *Social Problems*, vol. 26, no. 3 (1979), pp. 271–83

Oppenheimer, Jillian, 'Colonel Dumaresq, Captain Thunderbolt and Mary Ann Brigg', *Push from the Bush*, no.16 (1983), pp. 18–23

Oppenheimer, Jillian, 'Mary Ann Brigg (1834–1905?) as Thunderbolt's Lady: Some account of her public life', in J.S. Ryan & Bruce Cady (eds), *New England*

Lives, University of New England with Armidale District Historical Society, Armidale, 1999

Oppenheimer, Jillian, 'Thunderbolt's Mary Ann: An Aboriginal bushranger', *Journal of the Royal Australian Historical Society*, vol. 78, Pts 3&4 (1992), pp. 92–107

O'Toole, Sean, *The History of Australian Corrections*, UNSW Press, Sydney, 2006

Parker, Roger C., *Cockatoo Island: A history*, Nelson, West Melbourne, 1977

Parry, Sir Edward, *In the Service of the Company: Letters of Sir Edward Parry, Commissioner to the Australian Agricultural Company, Volume II: June 1832 to March 1834* <http://epress.anu.edu.au/isc/Intheservice.pdf>

Perkins, John & Thompson, Jack, 'Cattle theft, primitive capital accumulation and pastoral expansion in early New South Wales, 1800–1850', *Journal of Australian Historical Studies*, vol. 29 (1998), no. 111, pp. 289–302

Powell, Alan, *Patrician Democrat: The political life of Charles Cowper, 1843–1870*, Melbourne University Press, 1977

Proceedings of the Old Bailey < www.oldbaileyonline.org>

Ramsland, John, *Custodians of the Soil: A history of Aboriginal–European relationships in the Manning Valley of New South Wales*, Greater Taree City Council, Taree (NSW), 2001

Ramsland, John, *Most Healthily Situated? Maitland Gaol 1844–1998*, Verand, Rose Bay, 2001

Read, C. Rudston, *What I heard, saw and did at the Australian goldfields*, T & W Boone, London, 1853

Reece, R.H.W., *Aborigines and Colonists: Aborigines and colonial society in New South Wales in the 1830s and 1840s*, University of Sydney Press, Sydney, 1974

Reynolds, Henry, 'Aboriginal–European contact history: Problems and issues', *Journal of Australian Studies*, vol. 2 (1978), no. 3, pp. 52–64

Reynolds, Henry, *The Other Side of the Frontier: Aboriginal resistance to the European invasion of Australia*, UNSW Press, Sydney, 2006

Reynolds, Henry, 'The other side of the frontier: Early Aboriginal reactions to pastoral settlement in Queensland and Northern New South Wales', *Journal of Australian Historical Studies*, vol. 17 (1976), no. 66, pp. 50–63

Roberts, David, 'Bells Falls massacre and Bathurst's history of violence: Local tradition and Australian historiography', *Journal of Australian Historical Studies*, vol. 26 (1995), no. 105, pp. 615–33

Rowland, M.J., 'Return of the "noble savage": Misrepresenting the past, present and future', *Journal of Australian Aboriginal Studies*, vol. 2 (2004), pp. 2–14

Rule, John, *Sofala Days and Turonites: With gold-nugget locations and metal detecting maps*, J. Rule, Yagoona (NSW), 1980

Sainty, M.R. & Johnson, K.J. (eds), *Census of New South Wales—November 1828*, Library of Australian History, Sydney, 1985

Saltmarsh, David, 'Celebrating heritage and the Female Orphan School', *International Journal of Heritage Studies*, vol. 12, no. 6 (2006), pp. 536–50

Saltmarsh, David, 'Transforming the Female Orphan School', Presented at AARE 2005 conference <www.aare.edu.au/05pap/sal05288.pdf>

Samson, Walter & Co., *New South Wales National Directory for 1867–68*, Walter Jameson Meyer, Sydney, 1868

Saunders, Kay & Evans, Raymond, *Gender Relations in Australia: Domination and negotiation*, Harcourt, Brace, Jovanovich, Sydney, c1992

Seal, Graham, *Tell 'Em I Died Game: The legend of Ned Kelly*, Hyland House, Flemington, 2002

Seal, Graham, *The Outlaw Legend*, Cambridge University Press, 1996

Seal, Graham, 'The Robin Hood principle: Folklore, history and the social bandit', *Journal of Folklore Research*, vol. 46, no. 1 (2009), pp. 67–89

Shaw, A.G.L., 'British policy towards the Australian Aborigines, 1830–1850', *Journal of Australian Historical Studies*, vol. 25 (1992), no. 99, pp. 265–85

Small, W.G., *Reminiscences of Gaol Life at Berrima*, A.K. Murray & Co., Paddington (NSW), c1923

Staff, Bill, *A History of Rylstone*, William Francis Staff, Rylstone, 1999

The Story of Cockatoo Island, Sydney Harbour Federation Trust, Sydney, 2004

Sturma, Michael, 'Myall Creek and the Psychology of Mass Murder', *Journal of Australian Studies*, vol. 9 (1985), no. 16, pp. 62–70

Sturma, Michael, *Vice in a Vicious Society*, University of Queensland Press, St Lucia, 1983

Summers, Anne, *Damned Whores and God's Police*, Penguin, Melbourne, 2002

Tucker, Maya, 'Building themselves up with Aspros: Pioneer women re-assessed', *Hecate*, vol. 7, no. 2 (1981), pp. 7–19

Tunchon, Peter, *182 Years in Australia: James Bugg & Charlotte Derby of Monkerai, New South Wales; Their early descendants, with some additions*, Peter Tunchon, Pascoe Vale (Vic), 2008

Van Krieken, Robert, 'Towards "good and useful men and women": The state and childhood in Sydney, 1840–1890', *Journal of Australian Historical Studies*, vol. 23 (1989), no. 93, pp. 405–25

Walker, R.B., 'Bushranging in fact and legend', *Journal of Australian Historical Studies*, vol. 11 (1964), no. 42, pp. 206–21

Walker, R.B., 'Captain Thunderbolt, bushranger', *Journal of the Royal Australian Historical Society*, vol. 43 (1957), pp. 223–51

Walker, R.B., 'The New South Wales Police Force, 1862–1900', *Journal of Australian Studies*, vol. 8 (1984), no. 15, pp. 25–38

Walker, William, *Reminiscences (personal, social and political) of a fifty years' residence at Windsor, on the Hawkesbury : A lecture delivered at the Windsor School of Arts, 22nd August, 1890, together with some personal recollections of the late Sir James Martin*, first published 1890, facsimile reprint, Library of Australian History, Sydney, 1977

Waugh, Max, *Forgotten Hero: Richard Bourke, Irish governor of New South Wales 1831–1837*, Australian Scholarly Publishing, Melbourne, 2005

West, Susan, *Bushranging and the Policing of Rural Banditry in New South Wales, 1860–1880*, Australian Scholarly Publishing, Melbourne, 2009

White, C., *History of Australian Bushranging*, Angus & Robertson, Sydney, 1900–1903

Williams, Stephan, *A Ghost Called Thunderbolt: The career and legend of Frederick Ward, bushranger throughout northern New South Wales*, Popinjay, Woden (ACT), 1987

Woollacott, Angela, 'Frontier violence and settler manhood', *History Australia*, vol. 6, no. 1 (2009), pp. 11.1–11.15

Woolmington, Jean, *Aborigines in Colonial Society 1788–1850: From 'Noble Savage' to 'Rural Pest'*, Cassell Australia, Melbourne, 1973

INDEX

This index includes names, crimes and important subjects. More detailed information is available at **www.thunderboltbushranger.com.au**